AF334900

Business of the Heart

Business of the Heart

Religion and Emotion
in the Nineteenth Century

JOHN CORRIGAN

University of California Press

BERKELEY   LOS ANGELES   LONDON

University of California Press
Berkeley and Los Angeles, California

University of California Press, Ltd.
London, England

© 2002 by the Regents of the University of California

A portion of this book appeared in a somewhat different form in
*Emotion and Religion: A Critical Assessment and Annotated
Bibliography,* by John Corrigan, Eric Crump, and John Kloos, published
by Greenwood, an imprint of Greenwood Publishing Group, Inc.,
Westport, Connecticut.

Library of Congress Cataloging-in-Publication Data

Corrigan, John, 1952–
    Business of the heart : religion and emotion in the nineteenth century
/ John Corrigan.
        p.   cm.
    Includes bibliographical references and index.
    ISBN 0-520-22196-6 (alk. paper)
    1. Revivals—Massachusetts—Boston—History—19th century.
2. Emotions—Religious aspects—Christianity—History of
doctrines—19th century.   3. Protestants—Massachusetts—Boston—
History—19th century.   4. Businessmen—Religious life—
Massachusetts—Boston.   I. Title.
BV3775.B7 C65   2002
277.44'61081—dc21   2001004447

Manufactured in the United States of America

09   08   07   06   05   04   03   02

10   9   8   7   6   5   4   3   2   1

The paper used in this publication meets the minimum requirements of
ANSI / NISO Z39 0.48-1992(R 1997) (Permanence of Paper). ∞

For Sheila

The individual . . . appears to construct his own life by a calculated, self-conscious, comprehensive activity; by which he obtains an appearance of consistency, and a consciousness of reality, freedom, and accountability. In this process he appropriates for personal use, from the materials furnished by the manifestations of the mind, such forms as correspond with the present wants of his personal constitution; and makes use of the appropriations, in the relation of cause and effect, as means for the production of ends in securing the greatest amount of good that is possible for him, or what is good for him upon the whole. Thus, instead of a dual and discordant consciousness spontaneously realized, the nature of which is incomprehensible to him, he seems to construct for himself a self-conscious, calculated, comprehensible individuality, which is consistent in character, and the composition and operations of which are thoroughly comprehended, because calculated and constructed by himself. We say that the individual *appears* in this way to construct his own life—that this must so appear to him, in order that any apparent reality or freedom should be communicated to it,—and that it is absolutely necessary that he should believe in his reality, freedom, and accountability; but we do not mean to say that this is the fact.

Ephraim Langdon Frothingham,
Philosophy as Absolute Science (Boston, 1864), 225–26

A commodity appears at first sight, a very trivial thing, and easily understood. Its analysis shows that it is, in reality, a very queer thing, abounding in metaphysical subtleties and theological niceties.

Karl Marx, *Capital*, Part 1 (New York, 1906), 81

Contents

Acknowledgments

It is a pleasure to remember all of those persons who have in some way contributed to this book, and to thank them for their willingness to read, listen, criticize, and suggest. Likewise, I am grateful to the institutions and funders who provided support for this project, and who opened their libraries and archives to me.

A year of research at Harvard courtesy of the Andrew W. Mellon Foundation and a year as Research Associate at the American Antiquarian Society, partly funded by the American Philosophical Society, were crucial to my developing an understanding of religion and culture in antebellum America. I am especially grateful to John Hench and Joanne Chaison at the AAS for their willingness to think with me about what I needed to read, and for their enthusiasm for the project in its early stages. Grants from the National Endowment for the Humanities and Arizona State University made possible numerous visits to collections and provided valuable writing time as my research progressed.

I am grateful to colleagues and their institutions for invitations to present in seminars some of my ideas as they were developing, and for their criticisms of my work, including, at Harvard, Bill Hutchison, David Hall, and Larry Buell; at the University of Chicago, Gary Ebersole and Catherine Brekus; at the University of California Santa Barbara, David White and Cathy Albanese; at Oxford, Eric Rauchway and Daniel Walker Howe; at the School of Advanced Study at the University of London, Gary McDowell and David Cannadine; at the University of Wittenberg-Halle, Axel Schafer; and at the Roosevelt Center in the Netherlands, Cornelis van Minnen. Likewise I thank Peter Stearns, Eric Midelfort, John Demos, and Laurie Maffly-Kipp for valuable comments they made on papers and panel presentations at professional meetings.

Librarians and archivists at several institutions were enormously helpful, including those at the Houghton Library, Congregational Library, Boston Public Library, Boston Athenaeum, Massachusetts Historical Society, Schlesinger Library, and the Library of Congress. Dennis Isbell at my home institution's Fletcher Library proved a genius at finding publications relevant to my research, and arranging for the library to acquire them.

I am lucky enough to have had a series of excellent research assistants during the course of this project. I am grateful to Christy Nabhan, Steve Warren, Julie Walker, Janet Lee, and Becky Brady for their hard work and perceptive queries.

Among the many colleagues who listened thoughtfully to my reports of work-in-progress and suggested leads and linkages, or who offered me access to their own research, I am especially grateful to Tom Cutrer, Emily Cutrer, Richard Wentz, Tod Swanson, Tracy Fessenden, Dottie Broaddus, Becky Nicolaides, Peter Kaufman, David Hackett, Paul Lauter, John Kloos, Carlos Eire, Briane Turley, Rodger Payne, Ben Ray, Jan Shipps, Tracy Leavelle, Eric Crump, Scott Casper, Martin Marty, Ann Braude, Conrad Cherry, Richard D. Brown, Karen Kupperman, Philip Cash, and the late Jerry Brauer.

Peter Williams, Daniel Walker Howe, Marie Griffith, and Susan Gray read the entire manuscript and offered detailed criticisms and suggestions. I thank all of them, knowing what an investment of time and effort they made. I also thank a faculty presenter for the University of California Press, whose excellent suggestions helped me to shape the final manuscript.

I am fortunate to have worked with Reed Malcolm at the University of California Press. In the course of shepherding the manuscript through the publication process, he has managed through his congeniality and directness to keep the author remarkably at ease, a rare feat. Thanks also to my project editor, Jean McAneny, and to Sue Carter for her excellent copy editing. Janet Lee, indexer extraordinaire, worked her usual magic.

Thanks most of all to Sheila, who put her own writing on a back burner and took on an overload of parenting duties so that I could finish the book before the end of the millennium.

Religion, Emotion, and the Double Self

EMOTION AS OBJECT

This is a book about religion and emotion, a history of the Businessmen's Revival in Boston in 1858. It draws eclectically on a broad background of historical, humanistic, and behavioral and social scientific research outlined in the notes and appendices. In some places it explores culturally constructed standards for emotional life as they were articulated in newspapers, magazines, sermons, and literature. Elsewhere, it narrates the emotional lives of people as recoverable from diaries, correspondences, and other sources. Sometimes the focus is on individual emotions such as love, at other times on meta-emotion, and at other times on conceptualizations of emotion itself. Keeping in mind that nineteenth-century writers, like twentieth-century writers, were rarely precise in deploying terminology, I have not attempted to distinguish "emotion," "feeling," and "passion" except in cases where the context clearly warrants it.[1]

The Businessmen's Revival was an affirmation of collective identity, the assertion of white Protestant identity vis-à-vis other groups. The public exercise by which Boston Protestants accomplished this was a performance of emotion in revival. Regulated in certain ways, highly expressive in others, the display of emotion in the revival demonstrated group cohesion and character at the same time that it confirmed boundaries between Protestants of the participating denominations and other, non-participant groups. Emotionality, a certain construction of emotion and its performance, was a primary indicator of membership in the Protestant majority, as much so as language, skin color, dress, diet, and other such factors construed as signs of group belonging.

Boston's Protestants objectified emotion, and made the expression of emotion a matter of transaction. They constructed emotion as a commodity, and conceptualized relations between persons, and between the individual and God, as transactions of emotion, as exchanges governed by contract. Nicknamed the Businessmen's Revival for the unprecedented involvement of young and middle-aged men—the "businessmen"—in its prayer meetings, the revival as an emotional performance represented prayer as commerce. Revivalgoers, who conceived the ritual of the prayer meeting as a forum for exchange, who offered up objectified emotion as a commodity, professed to "give the heart" to God. Meetings were organized around spoken requests from individual participants for peace of mind, assurance, and comfort and joy, as well as for health, the cure of an alcoholic spouse, a job, or firewood. God, under terms of the contract of prayer, responded. Bostonians conducted the "business of the heart" with God as a transaction involving emotion.

Central to this objectification of emotion and its service as commodity in interpersonal exchanges was an understanding of emotional behavior that both encouraged its display and demanded its strict regulation. Just as businessmen were charged with the responsibility for exciting the economy through the investment risks that they took, so individuals were to deploy emotion in such a way as to keep active the great system of exchange, the lively transaction of emotion between persons (and with God). But vigilance was requisite as well, in order to ensure that the system not be overstimulated. The control of emotion, its concealment, its conservation, was fundamental to emotional commerce in the same way that the practice of business required regulation of investment and observation of market fluctuations as safeguards against inflation and collapse. Under this conceptual umbrella, Boston Protestants developed more specific understandings of emotional expression and control that linked emotionality to a host of other factors, and they used such "feeling rules" as conditions for group membership. Persons in out-groups were marked by what was thought a deficient emotionality. Their unfitness for membership was also unfitness for conducting business.

THE DOUBLE SELF

Protestant construction of emotion as object was fostered by medical theorizing that embodied emotion in the heart—a pump—and in blood that coursed through the veins, and elsewhere in an organism increasingly read as a machine, as a complex of operations susceptible to scientific investigation and testing.[2] Indeed, as Otniel E. Dror has shown, late Victorian interest in the emotions was manifest in Boston as clinical studies of heart murmurs and other unusual physiological data. This understanding of the emotional self rendered it mundane, earthly, prosaic, a product of bodily processes constitutive of all humans. It grounded emotion in organic existence.[3]

Even as New Englanders objectified emotion, however, they insisted on its essential subjectivity. That subjectivity was understood as a spiritual essence, and was relentlessly expressed as such in religious and domestic settings, in courtship and child-rearing exercises, in ruminations about the experience of nature, and about national destiny. Peter N. Stearns, pointing out how "Victorian emotional style depended heavily on rapid changes in religious culture and in turn contributed to these changes," has argued that the "emotional intensity" of interpersonal relations in Victorian America became "an equivalent to a religious experience," through "the spiritualizing of key emotions." Victorian thinking about the self accordingly evinced an awareness of emotion as sublime, personal, transcendent, and subjective. In evangelical Protestantism, it was present as love, the love given and received by the autonomous subject, in what Richard Rabinowitz has called the "one-on-one" relationship: "Love was an ever more important aim and standard of religious life as the devotionalists restructured it during the middle decades of the nineteenth century. And the love they spoke of so frequently was increasingly identical in all its manifestations— in the love between spouses, between parent and child, between friends, and between Christ and Christian." Imbedded in antebellum philosophical and theological traditions that represented it as an aspect of the soul, emotion was spiritualized in a way that rendered it extraordinary and private, a core reality of the self. It also was, in the lingo of the revival, "democratic" in that it expressed, for Bostonians, the authentic self. That is, emotionality was a claim for and a demonstration of the legitimacy of the subjective self, of the capacity of the self to freely choose. Rabinowitz's study of the antebellum spiritual self concludes that the Protestant construction of self in New England increasingly emphasized "personal judgments," as part of a process in which "religious feelings . . . became the core of true religion."[4] Profoundly influenced by the Common Sense philosophy, New Englanders conceived a self in which emotion and judgment, by virtue of their being closely allied in the subject, strengthened its legitimacy.[5]

The irresistible logic of each of the two competing views of the self— as spiritual and emotional subject as opposed to embodied, mechanical object—in the end required that the self be both. The nineteenth-century Protestant mythology of the autonomous human feeling and thinking subject in fact rested on an assumption about the complementarity of body and soul, of an inner subjective world and a mechanical, objective outer realm somehow conjoined. That coupling had been addressed at the beginning of the nineteenth century by German Protestant theologian Friedrich Schleiermacher, whose complex notion of the "feeling of absolute dependence" in the "embodied self" was an attempt to locate the self precisely on the border of organic existence and the thinking and feeling "I." As Charles Taylor has suggested, such nineteenth-century projects remarked on a reality in which "a disenchanted world is correlative to a self-defining subject," in this case, with the subject defined especially by emotional experience. But such fence-straddling, such highly tensed constructions of reality on the "border" frustrated theorizing that counted on the discovery of systematic coherence. Instead, thinking about emotion and organic existence, the soul and the body, increasingly veered toward tacit acknowledgment, even embrace, of dichotomy.[6]

As Daniel Walker Howe recently has asserted, in antebellum America a "properly constructed self . . . expressed and developed all aspects of human nature—intellectual, spiritual, emotional, physical . . . " But as mid-century approached, the fully developed self as a complex of emotional subjectivity and organic, mechanical object increasingly was cast as the "double self." In antebellum New England, and especially during the 1850s, it is more appropriate to speak of a *doppelgänger*, of one self alongside another. Charles Rzepka, in *The Self as Mind*, has described the gothic nightmare of such a representation as it emerged in the nineteenth century as obverse subjectivities, as a state of affairs in which "life in general appears 'theatrical,' a 'death-in-life,' and embodied selves become mere actors or caricatures, or in the more severe cases, insensate things altogether, like automata or walking corpses." The construction of the middle-class Protestant self in Boston was not yet the nightmare that Rzepka describes. But as the Victorian era got under way, Bostonians were attempting to come to terms with two views of the self and its emotions.[7]

In the industrializing capitalist urban environments of the 1830s and 1840s, academic and middle-brow publications, including literature, were making specific references to the double self, within a matrix of medical-theological writings. Ralph Waldo Emerson, in a lecture at the Masonic Temple in Boston in 1842 (subsequently published as "The Transcendentalist"), reinforced the notion that subjectivity involved an inescapable but uneasy relation between body and soul. Arguing that people are distinguishable as "Idealists" or "Materialists," Emerson maintained that the materialist "insists on facts, on history, on the force of circumstances, and the animal wants of man; the idealist on the power of Thought and Will, on inspiration, on miracle, on individual culture." In fact, wrote Emerson, each person experienced both sides of this dichotomous life, and each person struggled to reconcile them. "The worst feature of this double consciousness," said Emerson, "is that the two lives, of the understanding and of the soul, which we lead really show very little relation to one another. Never meet and assure each other." Returning to a theme of the materialist as a social self deeply embedded in historical circumstances and the idealist as one oriented to the ethereal, pure, and heavenly, Emerson deployed an image of the marketplace in asserting that "one prevails now, all buzz and din; and the other prevails then, all infinitude and paradise; and, with the progress of life, the two discover no greater disposition to reconcile themselves."[8]

Such a notion of double consciousness had precedents in German Romanticism and in English literature as well, but in New England the notion had coalesced as a by-product of medical discourse, beginning with commentary on the case of Mary Reynolds, which was reported in the New York *Medical Repository* in 1817. The nineteen-year-old Reynolds juggled two selves—neither aware of the other—over the course of fifteen years, a condition that the journal labeled "double consciousness." Hubbard Winslow, in *Elements of Intellectual Philosophy*, which was published in Boston in 1853, discussed that case and similar ones as examples of "a complete state of double consciousness" in which individual persons "manifested all the powers of the mind" but appeared to alternate between different selves. The following year Edward Hitchcock also published in Boston a book on geology and the Bible that managed to deploy the term in a discussion of mental powers, including seemingly telepathic communication, Hitchcock urging his readers to examine "the facts respecting double consciousness." Francis Wayland used the term in *The Elements of Intellectual Philosophy*, which appeared in Boston in 1855. John Abercrombie's *Inquiries concerning the Intellectual Powers* (1859), discussed the "state of double consciousness" at length, drawing on the accounts popularized by phrenologists George Combes and Johann Gaspar Spurzheim, and concluding that the two consciousnesses appeared to alternate rather than overlap. In journalistic writing, the concept appeared under a variety of rubrics, including an instance in the *Ladies Repository* in Cincinnati, which published an article by Lucy Towne asserting: "From the lowly violet up to the monoecious and dioecious tree, and through every order of animated being up to the Self-Existent, a dual nature in all things seems necessary to the perfection of unity." Henry Adams, in a reference to his boyhood, took the same tack in describing at the outset of *The Education of Henry Adams* how "the

Bostonian could not but develop a double nature" in the face of "irreducible opposites" and "antipathies" (including "sensual" summer versus the "separate nature" of winter). For Adams, "Life was a double thing" and "the boy inherited his double nature."[9]

Edgar Allan Poe, as literary critics John Herdman and Karl Miller have pointed out, was a master of the literary depiction of the double self in the 1830s, as in the appearances of Coppelius and his evil correlate Coppola in "The Black Cat," or the "double Dupin" in "The Murders in the Rue Morgue." Boston's Oliver Wendell Holmes, who wrote extensively about medical theory and his practice of it, dramatically illustrated the double in the psychological novel *Elsie Venner* (1861), wherein Elsie's doctor remarks that "she has lived a double being." Elsie's cousin Dick likewise "had two sides in his nature, almost as distinct as those persons who are the subjects of the condition known as *double consciousness*." An additional character, Sophy, likewise manifests the two selves, and as the critic Dorothy Broaddus has observed, the doubleness on the part of each of the three characters is made clear in their biological constitution: Elsie is half human and half snake, Dick is half "Portugee" from Brazil and half Anglo-American, and Sophy has African American grandparents but has embraced New England Protestantism. Double consciousness rooted in an overdrawn "animal" nature and an ethereal, white, spiritual Protestant nature was unmistakable in such a characterization. Holmes's readers themselves would have been aware of the reference to double consciousness not only because the term had been in circulation for two decades but because *Harper's* had run an article in 1860 reminding its readers of the origins of the term: "Mary Reynolds: A Case of Double Consciousness." Such discussions of the complex self were, then, well established by 1865, when Presbyterian theologian William Pratt Breed published *Anthropos*, a concise summary of much of the speculations about mind and self, in which he made clear that "each conception of the self, contains a double self, the self as the object conceived, and the self as the conceiving subject." By the 1880s William James had pronounced that "a man has as many social selves as there are individuals who recognize him and carry an image of him in their mind," and early in the next century W. E. B. DuBois would establish the category of the double self as a key concept in the analysis of African American experience, writing of the "double-consciousness, this sense of always looking at one's self through the eyes of others."[10]

Georg Lukács, in the course of surveying the failure of philosophical claims for the unity of subject and object, and as part of his analysis of a nineteenth-century reification of consciousness, described one of the central antinomies of bourgeois thought as the failure to close the breach between "appearance and essence," the consequence of which was that "the duality is itself introduced into the subject. Even the subject is split into phenomenon and noumenon ... " The constructed emotional self in Boston in the 1850s exhibited such duality. Emotional life was simultaneously a matter of one-on-one engagement between subjects in which sublime, spiritualized emotion was manifest, and a matter of objectified emotion, of emotional life experienced as the transaction of emotional commodities. Late in the decade, these selves would perform together in the Businessmen's Revival, when Bostonians transacted emotion with God, offering the sublime contents of the heart (which was at the same time a merely physiological organ) in exchange for divine favors. The dual selfhood of Bostonians was intimately bound up with the commodification of emotion in what was conceived as a transactional relationship with God. At the same time, as part of the process of revival, certain population groups, such as the "young men," asserted their social identities as they had not previously. Protestants as whole reinforced their sense of group, underscoring boundaries—marked by perceived innate emotional differences—that separated them from other populations. The revival accordingly was a matter not only of the exploitation of the constructed double self in service to the religious exercise of emotional transaction, but a social project that established meaning through the assertion of group belonging.[11]

THE STORY OF THE REVIVAL

In a demonstration of their investment in the notion of a double self, Protestants in Boston conceived emotion as spiritually sublime at the same time that they placed it on the bargaining table before God in the late 1850s.[12] This history of the Businessmen's Revival narrates the events and processes that led to Bostonians transacting business of the heart with God. The story develops over ten chapters and an epilogue, beginning with an outline of the chronology of the revival, its sweep, and its mechanics—known to its detractors as its "machinery."

Chapter 1 locates the revival within a long series of revivals in Boston, of "seasons of refreshment" that had visited the city over the preceding four decades. The centrality of the prayer meeting, the substantially diminished role of the clergy, the participation of young men, and the role of the press in promoting the excitement were characteristic features of the revival in Boston. Participants wept and petitioned God for favors in noon hour prayer meetings (and in other ones, too) where a code of emotional expression, of feeling rules, organized the nature of the assembly. Promoted as a symbol of unity, the revival was at least as much a platform for the assertion of specific group identities, including women, laity, whites, firemen, newsboys, the North, sailors—and the "young men."

Some Bostonians thought their city the Athens of the West, while others experienced it as the pinnacle of Greek tragedy. Chapter 2 describes a city in flux, noting population instability caused by in- and out-migration, disagreements over the nature of civil authority, widespread concerns about vice and violence, and a sense of the corrosive experience of urban life as traditions unraveled in the face of social change. Such an environment was by no means anomic, but its inconsistency and instability invited efforts to order it (rhetorically and practically), and those attempts frequently eventuated in public performances of collective identities.

The Businessmen's Revival followed on the heels of a financial crash. Chapter 3 details the nature of that crash, including its causes, its consequences for the city of Boston—from pervasive business failures, to a spike in the crime rate, to homelessness—and subsequent resolutions about financial reform. Most important among those resolutions was the demand for "regulation" of an "overexcited market," alongside the acknowledgment that excitement was at the same time fundamental to the vitality of the market and ought to be encouraged. The following year a similar notion of the utility of controlled excitement was applied to the revival. Some analysts assigned culpability for the crash to businessmen, casting them as buccaneers without consciences, as dishonest servants of Mammon. At the same time, the idealized picture of the merchant as an industrious, persevering, and punctual social servant re-emerged in force. That dichotomous rendering of businessmen complicated the self-understanding of businessmen themselves (at least those who had not committed suicide or left for the West), and urged upon them the business of publicly defining their group.

Performances of any sort in Boston involved emotion. Public spectacle as parades, celebrations, anniversaries, theatre, or street corner fistfights was thrilling. Chapter 4 outlines some of the ways in which Bostonians collectively displayed emotion in such contexts, and how critics of that enterprise condemned it as the squandering of emotion. Opponents of the theatre saw in audiences' emotional response to dramatic productions a reckless and promiscuous excitation of emotion, and critics of dime novels and penny presses thought that such reading misspent allocations from a seemingly finite personal treasury of emotion. For others, emotional experiences were worth the penny, or dime, or six dollars (for a theatre seat), or other costs to get a good seat at a fireworks display or space in a candlelit procession. All such debate about emotion as something to be spent or saved, invested or squandered, reinforced the conception of emotion as a "thing," as a commodity suitable for commercial transaction.

Like the city, the Protestant churches in Boston in the mid-nineteenth century were troubled by a degree of unsettledness. Pastors came and went, churches opened and closed, houses of worship were moved from one part of town to another, and laity openly criticized clergy for their unemotionalness, their "lack of heart." Chapter 5 details these developments and notices as well the phenomenon of Spiritualism, which, with its trances and highly emotional settings, attracted large numbers of persons, both the curious and the committed, to its ideas and rituals. The temperance crusade offered a similarly alternative context for the pursuit of spiritual improvement, and its emotional campaigns within the city and the nation proved a magnet for persons from various walks of life, including those who drank while they crusaded. The revival emerged directly out discontent about the emotional barrenness in the churches and as a response to perceptions of disorder and corruption in the churches.

Investigation of the "public" expression of emotion, perhaps more so than any other topic in Victorian history, invites the analysis of gender. Chapter 6 addresses the Victorian construction of the emotionality of women and men, and the construction as well of the domestic and public spheres. These categories—masculine/feminine and private/public—were to a certain extent detectable with reference to boundaries that they drew through the social world as a whole. At the same time, they were fluid, highly flexible categories, imbricated at some points, bleeding into each other at others. That fluidity authorized a measure of coincidence of a masculinized public sphere with a feminized private sphere, and the linkage of commercial discourse with domestic language about emotion, leading to the business of the heart. Revival participants incorporated boldness, a decidedly masculine trait, in making their prayer requests in meeting, at the same time that they openly displayed through weeping, body language, and words their feelings, that is, a feminine side.

Against the background of the objectification of emotion, the business of the heart acquired its characteristic shape as the transaction of emotion. Chapter 7 focuses on the manner in which relations between men and women increasingly were conceived as the negotiation of feelings, as transactions involving emotional property, and on child rearing as domestic practice in which emotion was withheld or bestowed as part of a program of nurturance and control. The notion of contract underlying such relations extended as well to the classroom, where teachers acting *in loco parentis* were expected to enforce the same regime of emotional exchange as was undertaken in the home. As Bostonians adapted the language of business to their emotional relations with one another, they advanced the nascent process of the commodification of emotion, ensuring that it would profoundly shape the Businessmen's Revival.

Chapter 8 describes the salient aspects of an emergent boyculture in Boston. As apprentices, clerks, laborers, or other kinds of workers, unmarried young men in their late teens and twenties created for themselves a community, an urban subculture, in the years leading up to the revival. Raised by mothers who indoctrinated them into the principles and aspirations of commercial life—and above all, the importance of boldness, of pluck, to the realization of their manhood—many young men came to the city armed with plans for conquering it by industry, initiative, and drive. Boyculture reinforced such virtues through its focus on sports, and especially on a view of sports as the proving ground for the sort of manly strength and will that was required to succeed in business.

Emotion, the fluidity of gender categories, public/private coincidence, manly pluck, and notions of transaction all converged in the primary ritual of the revival, the prayer meeting. Chapter 9 examines prayer as a platform for "giving the heart to God" in exchange for certain favors which—as was the revival practice—were boldly voiced to the congregation, to the persons assembled for the prayer meeting. Revivalgoers trusted in the efficacy of prayer and came to meetings determined to transact with God through prayer. Emotion, as commentators wrote, was like electricity moving through the telegraph line to God, who would respond to the sender upon receiving the message. The notion of emotion as a publicly traded commodity was central to the success of the revival.

Chapter 10 paints in broader strokes the way in which white Protestant identity was consolidated through a strategy of negatively constructing the emotionality of others. Protestant Bostonians' elaborations on the "Irish temper" marked the Irish more clearly as outsiders at the same time that it reinforced certain notions of white Protestant emotionality and identity. The same is true for white construction of African American emotionality as inferior in several ways. And abolitionists, too close to blacks themselves, were painted with a similar brush. All such projects were a way for the dominant Protestant population to understand and assert itself by creating contrastive relations with other populations in the city. For white Protestants, then, the Irish did not join the revival because they were emotionally unfit for it, African American participation was minimal for the same reasons, and abolitionists, due to their defective emotionality, simply did not understand. All three groups likewise were unfit to conduct any sort of important business, not just the business of the heart.

The historical fallout from the revival was variously durable. Most importantly, the revival inaugurated a period of intense interest in "muscular Christianity." The epilogue addresses the legacy of the revival, detailing the beginnings of muscular Christianity, its early installation as a standard part of the religious landscape of Protestantism, and its distinctive emphases on gender and prayer. Beginning with the period of the Civil War, this last chapter traces the development of muscular Christianity through the revivalism of Billy Sunday and Aimee Semple McPherson up to the Promise Keepers movement of the late twentieth century.

STUDYING RELIGION AND EMOTION

Religion and emotion are historically linked not only in the Protestant past of the United States, but in many religious traditions, in cultures all over the globe. Exploration of this linkage to date has proceeded in fits and starts, without the confidence that comes with the utilization of established methods and goals, and in the absence of a tradition of investigation that maps to a greater or lesser extent the terrain. In order for the historical study of religion and emotion to realize its ample possibilities, it will have to generate classifications of its subject matter while avoiding doctrinaire taxonomies, it must remain sensitive to the differences and similarities between culturally constructed standards for emotion and the varied emotional experiences of people, and, most importantly, it must engage the theories and methods utilized in the study of emotions in the behavioral and social sciences, in literary studies, and in philosophy and theological studies. This book embodies an attempt to demonstrate some of those possibilities and to bring clarity to an aspect of the past that is acknowledged by virtually all observers, but is seen only as through a glass, darkly.

ONE

The Businessmen's Revival

BEGINNINGS

The "religious excitement" of 1858 found its way into the press under various headings, including "The Great Revival," "Great Awakening," "Laymen's Revival," "Holiness Revival," "YMCA Revival," "Union Revival, " "Laymen's Prayer Revival," "Prayer Meeting Revival," "Revival of 1858," and "Businessmen's Revival." The diverse emphases of these headings reflect the multifacetedness and complexity of the revival. Laity, the YMCA, prayer meetings, businessmen, and union, all were fundamental to its coalescence, climax, and denouement. So also were a number of other factors that were only barely visible to the participants in the revival and to its defenders, or subsequently were shrugged off by historians in the following century and half. Those factors include immigration, population instability, abolitionism, temperance, woman's rights, the decay of New England Federalism and domestic patriarchy, the rise of Spiritualism and the theatre in Boston, the gradual objectification of emotion, and other transforming forces.[1]

The Businessmen's Revival was one revival among many nineteenth-century revivals in Boston. In 1859, a committee celebrating the semi-centennial of the Park Street Church surveyed the religious landscape of the nineteenth century and found that the city had experienced revivals in 1823, 1826, 1827, 1830–31, 1840–42, and 1849–50. The religious press in Boston, over the course of the previous fifteen years, had discovered a number of others. The *Christian Parlor Magazine* reported in 1845 on "The Domestic Revival," claiming that it had seen people in the throes of religious excitement "swayed to and fro and bowing to the ground" and heard the "cries for mercy" and "sobs of uncontrollable anguish." The *Christian Observatory* a few years later featured stories on the revival among Unitarians in the city, noting that "the present excitement" was "a good omen, shewing that they are dissatisfied with their condition." The *Boston Recorder* made official the extent of the Unitarian excitement: "It *is* a revival." Bostonians read of the "great and precious results" of the revival at Amherst in 1850, and the following year, Eliphay Arnold Jr., a twenty-four-year-old religious seeker, wept copious tears at prayer meetings in Boston and exulted in the apparent spread of the revival impulse: "There was a large revival down on the Cape and the news made me feel happy." In 1852 the *Youth's Companion* announced a "Revival in Boston" that was several months running, interdenominational, and noteworthy in one particular aspect: "One of the most auspicious features of this revival is, the number of active and influential young men, who have been brought to the knowledge of the truth." Arthur Howard Nichols, eleven years old at the time, noted that "there is an interesting revival going on in our church. The first two seats in the vestry were entirely covered with boys this evening." In 1854, the *Watchman* reported a revival in Cheshire, and in 1855, magazines and newspapers covered revivals in Boston, South Boston, Amherst again, and in Plymouth, where "a large number of the subjects of the work, are from sixteen to twenty years of age." The following year the report of the Massachusetts Home Missionary Society noted a number of revivals, including one "at the colored congregation in Pittsfield," where twenty-five persons were converted. A revival at South Royalston had grown steadily from its first signs in the autumn of 1854, so that by 1856 it "embraced many heads of families, among whom are some of the most active business men in the place." The *Evangelist* and the *Watchman* saw signs suggesting a revival in Boston in the fall of that year. In 1857, well before anyone proposed that there was a national or even a major revival under way, a wave of revivalism swept through the New England colleges (and some further west), involving, by one count, 3,400 students and reaping 414 conversions. And the religious excitement continued in Pittsfield.[2]

In the several decades leading up to the great events of 1858, revivals were a more or less standard feature of Protestant life in Massachusetts, and especially in the Boston area. Sometimes those revivals were localized in a church, and at other times they encompassed a specific group (e.g., college students) or took a regional profile. Whatever form they took, they were welcomed by New Englanders, who prayed constantly for a "season of refreshment," for a revival that would draw sinners back to God and breathe life into congregations that had become comfortable in their religious routines. Church leaders agonized constantly over the condition of their congregations, complaining about the loss of vitality in religion and pointing to the signs that warned of the onset of spiritual corruption. Indeed, at the same time that the press reported revivals in churches and towns, they published letters from ministers, or ran editorials, that entreated readers to pray for divine help in stemming the tide of declension. It may have been the case in some instances that spiritual stirrings in a congregation emboldened a minister to call for revival in what had seemed a declining church, so that evidences of an emergent revival overlapped with the rhetoric of declension. It likewise was probably true that a revival in one town caused neighboring towns to wonder and worry about their own spiritual health. Theodore Parker took a longer historical view, arguing that the churches had in fact institutionalized the machinery of complaint, that ministers since 1636 had preached unceasingly about the decline of piety. In any event the clergy complained even during times of revival. During a lively period of renewal in the churches in 1849, the *Boston Recorder* published a scathing criticism of the state of religious piety, accusing its readers of excessive worldliness and, observing that "times of declension try professors of religion," it urged repentance and prayer so that "every heart know its own bitterness." In early 1857, in the midst of widespread campus revivals, the *Evangelist* pined for "the days of Griffin and Richards and Nettleton" and wondered: "Why is it that the showers are withheld?" The *Independent*, in the very same week that it described a revival in "many of the churches" in Philadelphia in which "crowds are unable to obtain even standing room," ran an article entitled, "The Present Dearth of Revivals." And the *Watchman*, which had covered the numerous revivals of 1850–1855, started off the new year, 1856, with an article entitled "A Great Revival Needed." The great revival did indeed arrive late the next year. But even then, some clergy were dissatisfied with it, and some churchgoers were unmoved, in spite of the fact that "it has saved many churches from virtual extinction."[3]

The Businessmen's Revival took place against a historical backdrop not only of previous revivals, but revivals in which young men and male heads of households played a central role. The geographical context also was expansive. The events of 1858 have been described as "transatlantic revivalism" because of the religious excitement in Ireland and Scotland, and the Boston press regularly passed along "reports from the North of Ireland" which "speak of large and crowded prayer meetings." Moreover, they were influenced by the preaching and example of Phoebe Palmer, who as a layperson contributed substantially to local and regional revivals in Canada, the United States, and the British Isles, and who, together with her sister Mrs. Sarah Lankford, had organized the Tuesday Meeting in New York

City in 1835. She visited Boston and led meetings in various churches in 1850 and 1854, modeling lay leadership in impressive fashion, and bringing with her a holiness theology that eventually claimed Plummer Professor F. D. Huntington of Harvard. Her distinctive view of the prayer meeting also predicted the style of meeting associated with the revival. Her description of it resonated with the ideals of American democracy: "After the opening exercises, any one is at liberty to speak, sing, or propose united prayer. . . . In these meetings the utmost freedom prevails. The ministry does not wait for the laity, neither does the laity wait for the ministry. . . . How small do all merely earthly distinctions appear, when brought under the equalizing influences of pure, perfect love! And it is this equalizing process, that, to our mind, forms one of the most important characteristics of this meeting."[4]

The starting point for the story of the revival in Boston is the founding of the morning prayer meeting at the Park Street Church, "Brimstone Corner," in 1840. Deacon Daniel Stafford had organized the daily meeting (Sunday excepted) during the revival in the spring of that year—in the midst of the "cheering religious intelligence" that the revival was spreading worldwide—and it remained a part of the worship at Park Street until 1850, when it was relocated to the Old South Church. In the late 1840s the meeting had gradually been opened to persons of other denominations, and at Old South it was from the outset a union meeting. During the warm season it commenced at eight o'clock and in colder weather at eight-thirty. At Park Street the meeting drew between thirty and three hundred people during the 1840s. Attendees prayed "for the influences of the Holy Spirit upon the city." The standard for prayers voiced in the meeting was established over the course of the first few years and grounded in appeal to scripture: "Prayers in the Bible are remarkable for brevity, simplicity, directness, and pleading or argument." Briefly, during 1847, the meeting convened at the Mount Vernon Church while its pastor, Edward Kirk, was off in Europe. At Old South, the meeting acquired its distinctive cast, which then-pastor Edward Beecher described as "so great and so uniform solemnity of feeling and expression." A report of the church in 1855 elaborated: "This one prominent feature of the meeting deserves to be dwelt on, and distinctly noticed. The just government of the affections, in a subject of a nature so momentous as that of religion, is all-important." By 1859, the meeting had become near-legendary, and the church celebrated its ninth anniversary with a day of speeches and extra prayers.[5]

The salutary effects of the prayer meeting across denominations inspired a number of other churches eventually to institute their own meetings. And *Zion's Herald and Wesleyan Journal* went so far as to suggest "street prayer meetings" as a supplement to street preaching. The real impetus for the expansion of prayer meetings to other parts of the city came through the activity of Charles Grandison Finney and Mrs. Elizabeth Finney, however, who came to the city in December 1856, and remained until April 1857. Park Street pastor Andrew Leete Stone, one of the most influential, and, with a salary of four thousand dollars a year, one of the best-paid ministers in the city, had tried to arrange for a joint invitation with the Pine Street and Mount Vernon Churches. Neither would cooperate, which was, in the case of Mount Vernon, not surprising, given that its pastor, Kirk, had public disagreements with Finney. Essex Street (where Finney had served as replacement pastor in 1831–32) and Winter Street churches openly opposed the invitation. Stone subsequently made the invitation on behalf of just Park Street and the Finneys moved into the home of Park Street deacon Edwin Lamson. Finney preached every day, usually in the evening, and twice on Sundays, primarily at Park Street, but also at assorted other churches, and began his campaign with sermons about excessive formalism in religion. By early March, the press began to notice the increase in church attendance and surmised that the cause was Finney's preaching. The *Evangelist* reported that "a general interest on the subject of religion is felt throughout the city, among all denominations of Christians. The services of eminent preachers has been procured, and the result of their labor is now being felt." Noting that "all classes of men" were involved, the paper prayed that "the Union feeling, now so prevalent among all Christians, may be abundantly succeeded by a powerful revelation." In subsequent articles, the paper observed that "seldom has such a season of extended revival interest been known, as at the present time," and all of it "under the ordinary means of grace." The *Watchman* stressed the role of Finney's preaching at Park and Somerset Streets churches, and at the Shawmut Avenue Church, and proposed that "there is good reason to believe that a revival influence is extending within, and beyond the city." Finney's preaching had by mid-March begun to draw into the Park Street Church that class of men for whom the revival would be named: "On Friday afternoon, men left their business so generally, that the large church was crowded with solemn listeners to the word of God, quite a number expressing a Christian hope." Wherever he went, Finney's preaching intersected decisively with the city's tradition of prayer meetings. Addressing a very large congregation at the Chestnut Street Church in Chelsea, Finney "was listened to with solemn interest." That week, "a union prayer meeting, three mornings in the week" was established in Chelsea and "nearly filled" the Broadway Church chapel. At the same time, Rev. F. D. Huntington, the Harvard professor, instituted a prayer meeting at the college and counted five converts for his efforts. Such was especially noteworthy considering both the college's reputation as an unpromising ground for revival and Huntington's own reputation as a preacher. Frances Merritt—herself eventually a teacher at the school for girls in Framingham—described his style as sedate, overly philosophical, and lacking in the "<u>spiritual</u> convictions of the reality and power of revivals of religion."[6]

Consistently characterizing the emergent revival as "solemn," the religious press tried during the summer months to fuel interest in it, but, with Finney gone, and the usual preoccupation with business that came with the warm weather, the revival lost momentum. Given the city's experiences with revivals that had come and gone over the course of the previous ten or twenty years, the quieting of the religious excitement was not unusual, and, in fact, it was expected. In July, the *Evangelist* reported the revival in the past tense, noting that between January and June "there were many instances of revivals of religion, most of which occurred under the ordinary means of grace." The paper singled out Finney for his labors in the city, calculating that "the number of hopeful conversions attributed directly or indirectly to these labors was said to have been estimated at more than five hundred." The great and general awakening for which Bostonians had prayed had not yet arrived, however. But the wheels were beginning to turn in that direction. As Frank Beardsley wrote, Finney's preaching in Boston during the winter of 1856–57 was a "forerunner" to the revival. And during the late fall and winter, when the weather turned cold, the nation's financial systems collapsed, and Finney returned to the city, the embers of the previous winter's religious excitement would flare up and give the revival its monumental profile.[7]

Lewis Tappan was impressed by the morning prayer meetings when he visited the city during Finney's work there in the winter of 1856–57. Upon returning to New York, he started a morning prayer meeting in Brooklyn and published a tract entitled "Morning Prayer Meetings" to popularize the practice. The following September (1857), Jeremiah C. Lanphier, a missionary hired by the Dutch Reformed consistory to work in New York City, began a noon-hour prayer meeting at the Fulton Street Church. Within three weeks, more than a hundred men attended daily, and over several months time, numerous other prayer meetings were established to meet the overwhelming response by businessmen. Some noon meetings were dedicated to "workingmen" and "coloreds." Some meetings were convened in stores, such as the one at 69 Broadway, where the second floor "was procured and comfortably fitted up for the purpose of prayer-meetings. The room was 25 by 100 feet, and this, from day to day, was filled, and the exercises were solemn beyond description." The noon meetings were organized on the assumption that "if the exercises were confined strictly to the hour, if they were suitably varied by singing and occasional remarks as the feelings of any brother should prompt him, and if it were understood that no one was compelled or even expected to remain the whole time . . . that a meeting so free, so popular, so spontaneous" would be met with favor. Rules governing the assembly were posted on the walls of the meeting rooms and distributed as flyers outside the building. Placards advised that "brethren are earnestly requested to adhere to the five minute rule" when speaking in the meeting, and persons were limited to not more than two consecutive prayers or exhortations. Frequently the notice "No Controverted Points Discussed" appeared as well. The meeting began at twelve o'clock sharp with the remarks of the leader, and proceeded through a precisely organized agenda of singing, reading of scripture, prayer requests (the central and longest part of the meeting), and a closing hymn. The revival in New York and Brooklyn grew rapidly during the winter, eventually numbering 150 morning, noon, and evening meetings.[8]

Late in 1858, arguments about where the revival had started broke out among different factions in the Northeast. The booklet *God Moves in Mysterious Ways* (1858) claimed that it began in Newburyport, Rhode Island in January 1858. Those who located the beginnings in New York appealed to the role of the city as seedbed by virtue of its commercial status, as explained by a writer in the *Evangelist:* "This great heart of the city now became the fountain of religious life sending out its currents to the extremities. . . . Individuals from the East and West, the North and South, came to this business centre, and, like the men of old who visited Jerusalem, they were filled with the Holy Ghost and returned home to kindle the sacred flame at their altars . . ." The Massachusetts position, set out in an article republished throughout the nation, argued that "the first manifestation of the present general awakening was in New England, particularly in Connecticut and Massachusetts, from which the spirit of revival spread rapidly through the Middle and Western states, or rather broke out simultaneously in them all." The debate proved little other than that the revival had caught on in a number of places about the same time, in connection with prayer meetings, and through the participation of men.[9]

OPPOSITION

The religious atmosphere in Boston remained lively during the summer of 1857 and grew progressively more intense during the fall. Susan Brown was present one day in July when fifty persons were admitted to the Park Street Church. Religious services on the Common in August (during a temporary lifting of the preaching ban) brought a large and attentive assembly. And in November, Jacob Merrill Manning, preaching to three thousand persons at the Tremont Temple, wrote that "hundreds could not get in," and that he "had excellent attention." The arrival of Finney on December 2 added momentum, but it was clear at that time as well that some of the city's ministers looked upon the excitement cautiously, and in some cases skeptically. Some, like Kirk, objected to Finney's reappearance. In his memoirs Finney claimed that he "had to struggle against" the "divisive influence" of Kirk, who had returned to Boston from another trip to Europe. Finney wrote that "when he came home and found that I was expected there the next autumn, he endeavored to 'head it off,' as I have said, by some articles in the newspaper." During Finney's visit, Kirk wrote to him, plainly expressing his opposition to Finney's theology and his Boston campaign: "I did not request you to come to Boston to labor, and am entirely unable to regard myself as responsible for the results of your labors . . . I told you when you were about to embark for Europe, that I would not invite you to labor with me until you or I was changed. I have seen no reason to alter that decision." Manning secured the Old South Chapel for Finney two days after his arrival, and by the following Sunday Finney was preaching "to an overflowing house." Manning and Kirk had words at a wedding ceremony two weeks later that left Manning with a bad impression: "There met Mr. Kirk, who does not like the plan of having Mr. Finney here. This is strange. He is an evangelist formerly. Came here, and drew off his church from the other churches; and now, forsooth, he does not like letting Mr. Finney preach to his people." Kirk nevertheless emerged as an important figure during the revival, preaching to a packed Mount Vernon Church, and visiting the Joy Street Church and others. Whatever reputation he acquired during the winter was not enough, however, to prevent his replacement at the last minute by Manning for Fourth-of-July-week services on the Common in 1859.[10]

Over time there was other opposition to the revival. It began slowly, and peaked at about the time the revival peaked in March and April of 1858. The *Evangelist* claimed that the revival was initially welcomed by everyone, but that in the course of several months, "those in the community, who had generally set themselves against revivals of religion, in the evangelical sense," had begun to "show . . . their repugnance to the whole movement. Hardly a day, and not a Sabbath passes, without some vehement protest . . ."

The paper singled out Rev. T. Starr King, the Universalist Unitarian, who "came out upon the subject. . . . His language is stronger and more objectionable, and in worse taste, than one would have anticipated from the known pleasing character of the man." In fact, other clergy, primarily but not exclusively Unitarian, had expressed doubts as well. The Unitarian minister Orville Dewey wrote that the revival "I am inclined to think differs very little from the thing of Old. Father Taylor [Methodist], I hear, preached vehemently against it last Sunday evening."[11] Ezra Stiles Gannett from the Unitarian Federal Street Church visited the prayer meetings at Old South and Park Street and pronounced himself "disappointed at both places—want of fervor—human not divine element manifest." This was in spite of the fact that he led several meetings at Bedford Street. The *Liberator* saw the matter in another way, as unprincipled overexcitement that distracted persons from the work of reform: "The whole thing, comprehensively speaking, is an emotional contagion without principle, an imposition upon weak and unexcited minds . . . a diversion from the field of reform." At the same time that Gannett was meeting with the city's ministers for "discussion on the present revival and what we ought to do," the *Liberator* was accusing the ministry of deliberately manipulating Bostonians in a scheme to extend their power. "Jealous ministers seek to change the state of things," said the *Liberator*, by bringing on "one of these fanatical awakenings." And, in the midst of this, one disgruntled layperson wrote the *New York Observer* with the surprising intelligence that "there is but one church in Boston that we can attend, and feel sure that the sermon, will not be on some secular subject."[12]

One bone of contention was the issue of means. The *Evangelist* noted that "no feature of a Revival is more often ridiculed than what is called the 'machinery,'" and it took to task clerical critics of the revival who "redouble their ribaldry" and "intermix, in unusual proportions, raillery with religion, low comedy with lessons in virtue." The complaint may have been aimed at Theodore Parker, whose open opposition to the revival had earned him more than the usual share of condemnation by the revival churches. Parker had been under particular scrutiny since the winter of 1856–57, when Finney publicly pronounced that he was seeking Parker's conversion. During the revival, by agreement among the various denominations involved, congregations regularly offered up public prayers in service to that cause.[13] As it became clear that Parker, who was sick with consumption, was not going to convert, the prayers turned sour, as on the occasion of a meeting at the Park Street Church that was reported by the *Liberator:*

> From thirty to forty persons were assembled at this meeting, and nine or ten of them spoke and prayed, all in relation to Mr. Parker, and all in the same strain. They prayed that God would destroy his life; or, if not his life, his reason; that confusion and distraction might be sent into his study, so that he should not be able to finish his sermon for the next Sunday: or, if he were allowed to finish it, that he might be miraculously prevented from delivering it; that he might be confounded and brought to shame before the people; and lastly, if God did not please to grant these petitions, that he would miraculously influence Mr. Parker's audience to "leave that house, and come up to this"! [14]

Parker was not the only person targeted for conversion by prayer meetings, and he was not the only religious leader judged unconverted. In late March, a well-known missionary with liberal leanings had spoken in a meeting, and, at the conclusion of his prayer, another man rose and "announced to the meeting that the last speaker was not a 'Bible Christian,' and proposed prayers for his conversion!" The prayers offered explicitly for Parker's destruction were unusual, however, and in the second of his lectures on revivalism, he addressed the matter directly: "Misguided ministers may believe in the damnation of babies never born, may pray curses on us all; they cannot light a faggot to burn a man. Their spirit is willing but their flesh is weak." The context of his rebuttal was "The Revival of Religion Which We Need," preached to three thousand persons in the Music Hall on April 11. In that sermon, Parker declared: "How much we need a real Revival of Religion! Not a renewal of Ecclesiastical Theology, but a revival of Piety and Morality in men's hearts." For Parker, the religion of the revival was incapable of satisfying public demand for spiritual renewal. Noting the success of Spiritualism in gaining "millions" of followers, he observed that "Spiritualism had something to offer which the churches could not give." The current religious excitement in the churches was a similar case of popular demand, of people who "*feel* this need." The revival, "foolish as is the conduct of it, selfish as are the managers who pull the strings—with the people it indicates a profound discontent in the dull death of our churches." For Parker, the revival was a retreat from confronting the five great evils of 1858, namely war, corruption of the federal government, slavery, a "war of business" that bred "robbers in a peaceful way," and the subjugation of women. Ministers, who "come mainly from that class of people who are most affected by religious emotions," and who "think they can tease God to do what they want done," promoted emotional prayer as the focus of revival, and overlooked the necessity for reform, for unceasing work dedicated to the eradification of the world's evils. Advocating his own brand of revival, Parker argued that "work is the only coin which is current the world over. . . . In that coin we pay for all things." The work of reform, not emotions aroused in service to outdated theologies, would lead to "a world full of noble men and women, all their faculties developed well, they serving God with that love which casts out fear." [15]

Criticism of the revival that focused on its emotionalism and the machinery deployed by the clergy to produce that emotionalism was grounded in a well-established discourse. Through a half-century filled with economic crises caused by reckless speculation in an overexcited market, and religious revivals characterized by many as fanatical (including one associated with Finney), Bostonians had become wary of awakenings. In 1850, the *Puritan Recorder*, looking back over recent revivals, reminded its readers: "When the wild-fire connected with the pernicious labors of evangelists was desolating our churches a few years ago, it was necessary to utter many warnings against a spurious and dangerous excitement. . . . It is not strange that the fears then awakened and the language of warning then made familiar should remain." Those fears were kept alive by press accounts of the ongoing Methodist camp meetings held at nearby Eastham, Massachusetts during fair weather. Sometimes Father Taylor, a critic of the 1858 revival, attended them, along with as many as fifty other clergy. Observers believed that the passion of the Eastham meetings fueled a carnival spirit rather than a religious one, and spilled over into relations between men and women, leading to the downfall of virtue and, inevitably, reputation. The *Transcript* reported in 1831 that the activities at Eastham "render the name and sound of camp meeting odious," and sermonized: "We deeply regret that our Cape Towns are so frequently the receptacles or land of refuge of these followers of the camp. Conducted as the camp meetings usually are, they are sources of folly, and are resorts of immorality and licentiousness." The *Transcript* worried especially for the virtue of "delicate and modest females" at "a distance from home." *Gleason's*, ordinarily in the business of selling a rosy view of the world, ran a large woodcut and story on the gathering at Eastham in 1851 that concluded: "For ourselves, we look upon this class of devotional meetings, to say the least of it, as being of a most questionable character." And the *Evangelist* in 1856 noted that even the sponsors were having second thoughts about it: "It came very near being given up this year, on account of the growing conviction among the Methodist Churches of Boston, that the dissipation and other evils attending it more than counterbalance the good results." The fact remained that Methodism was the fastest growing Protestant denomination in Massachusetts at the time, and the church could not simply discontinue the performances of piety and conversion that had gained it that position.[16]

Most accounts of the Businessmen's Revival hurried to declare it safe from emotional excess. The *Congregationalist,* reporting on the early progress of the revival in Boston in November 1858, noticed "the philosophy of one feature of the revival—its stillness and freedom from fanaticism and extravagance—we imagine is not generally apprehended." In fact, said the paper, "the present religious movement is, in its tone, the gauge of rational progress among the American people." If the *Congregationalist* was guilty of having "protested too much," such protest was understandable, and was by no means isolated. The Leyden Chapel manual had been informing its readers for some time that "there may be a revival when there is not much excitement or noise," and even the *Liberator,* which often criticized the revival, thought that a case might be made for it if it evidenced over time "a silent and steady energy" instead of "spasms." But newspaper and magazine accounts of the revival that assured readers that the excitement was under control sometimes had little to do with the perceptions of the people who viewed it at street level. Participants and observers both understood what was at stake. Typical was the observation of William Gray Brooks: "The religious interest is the great local topic of the times—it is indeed wonderful and will long be remembered as 'the great awakening[']— . . . but although going on very well now, it will require all the worldly wisdom of the conductors to carry it on without excess and excitement and so as to prevent a reaction of which there is a great danger."[17]

Public concern over the deterioration of the revival into emotional fanaticism was linked to perception about the possible presence of the "machinery" of revival. On the same day that Theodore Parker was preaching to a large audience at the Music Hall on the misguided emotionalism of the revival, Harvard preacher F. D. Huntington was defending the revival in a sermon in the chapel at the College. He faced the predominant criticism of religious revival—the inappropriate use of means—and attempted to disarm it. "It is said a social religious interest is made dependent on 'machinery,' is 'manufactured,'" Huntington began. But "in its own place, machinery is very far from being evil." Huntington argued that when "machinery" was used "out of its sphere" in such a way as to illegitimately influence the "affections," it was "mischievous utterly." But the use of means such as the meeting house, the vestry, "the order of exercises in worship," pictures on the church walls, bells, and so forth were fit and familiar, and should not be stigmatized as "machinery." Surveying the nature of the revival across the nation, Huntington then wondered who might have put into gear the machinery about which critics were complaining, and what those persons had to gain from so doing: "It does seem strange that a wide-spread spirit of religious inquiry and resolve, appearing simultaneously in all parts of a vast country, not suggested by a priesthood, but often encountering clerical opposition, proceeding almost wholly by unpremeditated operation, having simple and unlettered prayers for its chief utterance . . . that this should be held up to reprobation as an article of a crafty 'manufacture.'" Rejecting the thesis that the clergy had launched a secret campaign to inflate church membership, Huntington simply concluded that "the entire movement emphasizes the efficiency of means" in producing a "feeling" of the "presence of God."[18]

EMOTIONAL LAITY

Professor Huntington's claim that the revival was not led by the clergy was in fact his best chance at persuading his audience of the viability and desirability of the revival, because it was apparent to almost everyone that the revival was led by laity. The *Congregationalist* reported on this fact at the outset of the revival in November: "In the past the 'machinery' of religion was put in place & ignored & allowed to 'run down.' A beginning has now been made in the operation of an entirely different system. The prayer meetings are conducted by laymen." The pattern continued, so that six months later William Gray Brooks could write that "the religious interest still continues unabated and is still conducted & carried on by laymen." Charles Finney himself admitted that the revival "was carried on to a large extent through lay influence, so much so as to almost throw the ministers into the shade." The *New Englander*, steadfast defender of orthodoxy, was moved to a new vision of the Boston churches by the spectacle of laity so involved: "It is here too, and in this movement, that the churches have emancipated themselves from whatever priestly bonds may till now have confined and impeded their action. They have here realized rather that old and blessed promise . . . His people shall become a nation of priests." Samuel Prime, reporting that the clergy took their seats with the laity, explained pointedly, "They assume no control." In a book dedicated to the converts of the 1858 revival, the Rev. Harvey Newcomb stated that the role even of the lay leader was not actually to lead, but instead to serve as a moderator of sorts: "The leader should feel that his place is not himself to occupy the time, but to call out and direct others." And although Bostonians believed that no one literally controlled the revival's progress, they embraced the role of lay advocates of the revival, in conversations, social gatherings, newspaper reports, and in the meetings themselves. An Old South Church report in January of 1859 accordingly remarked that "another feature of this revival has been, and is, the engagedness of laymen in promoting it zealously."[19]

The laymen who promoted the revival broadcast the heartfelt prayer, the seizures of conscience, the crying out, and the weeping. "Sometimes," said one observer, "the whole audience would be bathed in tears." The Old South meeting "was thronged with business men" so affected that "oftentimes the tears ran down the cheeks like rain." But the lay leaders and participants also brought to the revival what William Gray Brooks and many others called a "solid and serious cast." Regulatory measures such as limitations on individual members' prayers, the amount of time allowed for speaking, and so forth—all of the measures that had been established originally in New York—were refined and enforced in Boston. Refinement in most cases meant stricter limitations. Meetings in New York had allowed for five minutes per person, but leaders at the Old South Church rang the bell after only three minutes and even then the meeting realized it was "obliged to enforce the three minute rule more strictly." Some saw in such measures the hand of businessmen, who, it was thought, brought organizational skills and innovation to the meetings. But it was the fact of the large turnout of male heads of households—whether they were merchants, carpenters, or policemen—that made necessary the concluding of a meeting in an hour so that participants could return to their jobs. As Frances Merritt wrote, "businessmen leave their employments and go to the place of prayer," and they expected to return to that place of employment on time. The *Congregationalist* provided the overview of the national scene: "It is recognized as a notable feature of the awakening that business men are largely engaged in it. In fact, they seem to be the prominent class interested."[20]

The founding of a noon prayer meeting at Old South in March 1858 to accommodate businessmen took place against overlapping backgrounds. The first of these was the tradition of noon prayer. It was not invented by Lanphier in New York. Noon prayer had deep roots in Roman Catholic tradition, and it was familiar to Bostonians through a devotional manual published in Boston in 1842 which not only advocated noon prayer but specified "Intercessory Prayer at Noon," that is, petitionary prayer for friends and neighbors, the destitute and afflicted, backsliders, the nation, and so forth. Second, Bostonians in general took businessmen as a distinct class of persons. For religious leaders, that meant that businessmen "speak in the same dialect," and accordingly could serve effectively as spiritual guides to each other. As the *Watchman* explained: "They are peculiarly fitted to benefit those, in moral and spiritual things, with whom they are associated in the common transactions of life. Their minds have been formed in the same mould . . . and are consequently better suited to enlighten each other's understanding, and move each other's heart." Third, the prayer meeting did draw directly upon the model of Lanphier's Fulton gathering, which was to some extent indebted to Phoebe Palmer's Tuesday Meeting. As in New York, rules were established, but within those rules there was a large amount of freedom for participants. Sometimes the meeting was characterized by prayer, at other times by scripture reading, and at other times by singing, and persons were free to come and go, a message made clear in the notices distributed by the Old South organizers to "come in, stay five, ten, or twenty minutes, or longer if possible." Fourth, the meeting at Old South was less of an experiment than meetings established in other cities. Old South had sponsored morning prayer meetings in its chapel for many years, so that the scheduling of a meeting at noon was largely a matter of accommodating persons who could not attend otherwise, rather than as the first step in an entirely new program of Christian ministry. Finally, early in 1858 some churches already had established meetings for businessmen at four-thirty on Wednesday and Friday afternoons, and these were well attended. The noon prayer accordingly was innovative in a rather limited sense, at Old South and at North Street and other places. Inasmuch as it succeeded, it did so because it blended relatively well-established thinking about businessmen, noon prayer, and prayer meetings.[21]

Unlike businessmen, sailors did not work according to a schedule that suited attendance at noon meetings. But news of sailors' conversions was of particular interest to Bostonians. Boston as a port city not only relied on the sea for its economic vitality, but drew liberally upon images of the seafaring life in its self-understanding. The culture of whaling and sea trade, and the stories of captains and of boys who became men on the high seas were essential aspects of the city's history and imagination. The harbor extended along the waterfront from Harrison Avenue in the South Boston Bay all the way to the Navy Yard in Charlestown, over a hundred wharves in all. Sailors gathered on the docks and around the warehouses, and populated nearby neighborhoods, where the majority lived in boarding houses. Some took shelter in alleys or sheds. Boys came to watch them work, and Bostonians of all sorts kept their eyes on the water, marking, like John

Henry Kenneally, the arrival and departure of ships, the growing or shrinking piles of commodities stacked on the docks, and the appearances of sailors and sea captains in various places in the city. The religious press likewise charted the drift of sailors in and out of prayer meetings, and reported in detail their experiences at those meetings, highlighting certain instances. Typical were cases in which sailors converted at prayer meetings set sail with unconverted shipmates, returning months later to report that many on board now also were converted. The *Dashaway* experienced such a revival on a voyage from Boston to San Francisco. For the *Ohio*, eight conversions took place while the ship was still tied up in the Navy Yard. Sometimes American sailors would gather with their counterparts in England for prayer, on one occasion marking the site by display of the Stars and Stripes alongside the Union Jack outside the meeting place. Such instances were paid notice by the network of newspapers and magazines that reprinted each other's articles up and down the eastern seaboard, almost always adding their own editorial comments. The *Evangelist,* for example, in the course of listing various instances of conversions of seamen, projected a rapid and dramatic reform of religion on the high seas: "I expect ere long that ships will be officered and manned by pious men, for God has promised that the abundance of the sea shall be converted unto Him." Turnouts at sailors' churches for a while seemed to point toward that abundant future. Father Taylor, the "Seamen's Chaplain" down in the "Black Sea" section of the city, preached to overflow crowds of sailors for months during the revival. And many other churches, including some of the oldest and richest, welcomed sailors into their prayer gatherings and lectures. A transcription of a prayer meeting at Old South featured the testimony of several ships' captains and sailors, including that of a Captain Bartlett, who envisioned a holy work of sailors throughout the world: "I know of two sailors who have been [on] a voyage to India and back. One was converted before he left, and the other down in the Roads. . . . We have a letter from one who went to Havana, full of love for Jesus Christ. These are the first fruits from among those who are on the sea. I want you to pray for seamen. . . . God is bringing that class into the fold of Christ, who are to go forth and spread the tidings of a Saviour's love over the earth." Such words encouraged Bostonians' interest in sailors' religious lives. And that interest was all the more profound because, as we shall see, it was bound up with ideas about gender, about the public roles of men and women in an urban society, and about the ways in which emotional life was constructed in those roles. The conversion of sailors spoke eloquently about the boundaries and flexibility of those constructions.[22]

Boys in their teens and early twenties formed a key part of the population of revival participants. The press had been reporting the large numbers of boys in revivals since 1852, during the revival in Boston, and, as we have seen, elsewhere, such as in 1855 in Plymouth. At the college in Cambridge young men pressed into the chapel to hear Huntington and others, and converted in numbers that made the school's Unitarian leadership blush. "New influences seem to have found their way into Harvard College," said the *Evangelist.* "Not many years since, a Unitarian print spoke of a revival there, in a defiant tone, as a thing impossible, " but "the long banished prayer meeting has been brought back to its old home, and there has been earnest, yea, anxious interest in the subject of personal religion." Jacob Merrill Manning met with young converts during the spring of 1858. Almost all were young men. At Old South, young men frequently gave testimony about their conversion and the course of their subsequent religious progress. Patrick Collins, addressing a morning prayer meeting there, clearly identified his membership in a specific group of the converted: "I was converted a year ago last November. I am one of the *young* converts. We have young men's prayer-meetings in our chapel, and I call myself one of the *young men,* and join with them." Most impressive were the meetings organized by the YMCA at the Tremont Temple. At the height of the revival, young men filled the room—one of the largest in the city—for the daily prayer meeting that began at five-thirty in the afternoon. The YMCA vigorously advertised the meeting, both to young men and to their parents: "If the parents or friends of any young man who is in Boston, desire that he should attend these meetings, and will send a note expressing that desire, giving the address of the individual . . . he shall receive a personal invitation from some member of the association."[23]

The revival was not exclusively a male exercise. Women were involved from the very beginning, as participants and as leaders of various sorts.[24] Charles Finney noted in his memoirs that the "energetic efforts of the laity, male and female," carried the revival forward. Elizabeth Finney began leading prayer meetings at the Park Street Church during the winter of 1857, and as the meetings progressed she was aided by several other women. In 1842 the Mount Vernon Church had organized the Maternal Association for "the better qualification of the members for the responsibilities of their stations as mothers and the preparation of their children" for their duties as Christians. This group provided a core of support for Mrs. Finney's prayer meetings and for her lectures, such as the one she delivered at Park Street to thirteen Mount Vernon mothers in 1857. Drawing on her own experience as the mother of nine children, she spoke about the importance of the prompt obedience of children and the necessity of putting a child to bed "awake." Maternal Associations organized before and during the revival at other churches also served as a link with Mrs. Finney's ministry, so that the prayer meetings that winter in the Park Street vestry were widely popular, women lining up in the cold outside the packed room for as far as they could hear the proceedings. Women also remained in some churches for one half-hour after the general morning prayer meeting, and at Park Street for one half-hour following the adjournment of the afternoon meeting at four o'clock. An 1859 study of the revival recognized the exclusively "female prayer-meeting" as a "new feature" of religious life in Boston. Female leadership of prayer meetings, however, was not unusual. Arthur Nichols attended Mrs. Ricker's prayer meetings in 1852, and a woman from east Boston organized a meeting in 1855. Bostonians knew about the revival successes of a young Irish woman, about a society lady who turned her billiard room into a prayer meeting, and about a reformed prostitute in New York, who, "like Mary Magdalene of old," awakened conscience in backsliders: "Many a man kneels upon that floor in prayer, led to Christ by her urgent and tender appeals." Women's ongoing participation in prayer meetings over the years was, moreover, the foundation upon which the overflowing meetings of 1858 were built. Mary Mudge's mother went to Boston prayer meetings every day in the mid-1850s, and the revival in Warren, Maine actually began as a prayer meeting of women. Some women were so thoroughly involved in formal religious life—prayer meetings, church attendance, lectures—that they seem not to have noticed that a revival was in progress in 1857–58. Susan Brown fastidiously recorded her visits to services, meetings, and classes but, unlike almost every other diary writer, churched or unchurched, she made no reference to the revival while it was in progress. Catherine Flint, also a regular churchgoer, failed to mention the revival as well. For other women, such as Susan Heath, the revival inspired her to attend church for the first time in four months.[25]

It is clear that both men and women participated in the revival. Bostonians, and revival-watchers around the country, noticed male participation because an unusually large number of men participated. At a time when the ratio of female to male church members in Boston was two to one, the fact of prayer meetings overflowing with men lent the revival its distinctive profile. Women attended their own prayer meetings, just as men did, but both sexes attended prayer meetings together, and, in fact, such mixed meetings formed the backbone of the revival, the common ground upon which the revival was built. In short, the revival featured three kinds of prayer meetings: male, female, and mixed. The significance of this will become clearer as we examine the issue of gender in detail, but a clue to its importance is found in a sermon preached by George Ellis at the height of the revival in May 1858. Ellis rejected the traditional view of conversion as a process in which a person's experience must conform to certain marks of genuineness at each step along the way so that "each convert is expected to put the same old meaning into the same old phases." Instead, Ellis argued, conversion should be understood as a process of blending involving gendered aspects of religious experience: "We must combine more of the robust and masculine elements of influence with the feminine sentimentality of religion. Considering what august and engaging themes are offered in the higher ranges of religious instruction, we ought not to be satisfied with that feeble dispensation of it [male influence] which perhaps may have as much to do as does sinfulness of heart and life in accounting for the slender hold we have upon the manhood of the age."[26]

Another aspect of religious experience that was fundamental to the revival was emotion. The revival was a prayer revival, and prayer, as the *Christian Observatory* was keen to point out, was a matter of emotion. "All intense emotions burn to impart themselves," said the *Observatory*. "And this is true especially of the religious sentiment, the most powerful of all the passions man can feel. There is a craving for communion with God, and with men who are like God, bearing his image and breathing his spirit." People accordingly believe that they "must assemble themselves together," so that "they may feel themselves in a congenial atmosphere." Church services of a standard sort are not sufficient for the expression of this intense emotion, even though people do "give vent to their pent-up emotions in prayers, and praises, and privileges of the great congregation; but they must impart their sentiments still more freely in the less formal and restrained meeting for Christian conference. This is the origin of prayer-meetings." F. D. Huntington likewise referred to "the free unlocking of those grand, commanding affections and aspirations in us" in a social setting, and *The Harvest and the Reapers* (Boston, 1858) characterized prayer as "pleading" and "weeping" and "unity of feeling" among the members of the church. Such feeling invariably was a mixture of anguish and joy, but this, said the *Puritan Recorder*, was "the business of religion," and "will ensure a satisfying answer to our prayers." Criticism of this aspect of the revival sometimes took a proto-Freudian turn in its emphasis on the recovery of infancy: "Can we not see greatly what is in great part the attraction of these large meetings? . . . It is the revival of early impressions. It is the delight one feels in the indulgence of sensibility, in feeling good, which is a very different thing from being good or doing good." Defenders of the revival stood with Huntington, who predictably stressed the continuity of "'right feeling, right thinking, right acting, right being.'" We shall explore in detail the matter of religion as an emotional business, as a transaction involving emotion, in a subsequent chapter.[27]

UNITY AND SEPARATENESS

The ideal of unity permeated the revival. Rev. Harvey Newcomb looked over the progress of the revival and concluded that "a very important point in social prayer is, that the hearts of all present must be united in their feelings, desires, and petitions." The ideal was evident in the formation of neighborhood meetings throughout the city, where persons could connect more closely to fellow worshippers and prayer requests were more fully comprehended by informed neighbors. Jacob Manning had mixed feelings about the revival in the churches, but the smaller meetings appealed to him: "Have become much interested in neighborhood prayer-meetings of late." The neighborhood meetings were developed in Boston through the practice of visitation, an urban outreach activity pioneered by Phoebe Palmer when she worked for the Methodist Tract Society in New York City in the late 1840s. Boston was unique in developing the practice of visitation as part of the infrastructure of revival by linking it to regular neighborhood meetings, an initiative launched in March 1858. The *Christian Advocate and Journal* reported on its genesis: "At a meeting held in the Park Street Church on the 2nd nite another Boston 'motion' was projected. This was to district the city, and assign a portion to each denomination for systematic visitation." Persons from five denominations subsequently fanned out across the city to visit individually with prospective converts and to promote neighborhood meetings.[28]

The impulse to promote unity in fact served not only to connect individuals and groups, but also to establish or strengthen distinct social identities for each of those groups. The neighborhood meetings served on one level to engender unity, but on another, they helped to draw or redraw boundaries that separated one neighborhood from another. The aim of unity in this case came about by "districting the city," as the Park Street Church proposed it, and assigning to each district a different denomination, a process that recognized and reinforced religious differences among the five participating denominations. On a broader front, the same dichotomous process repeatedly occurred at a number of levels of inclusion/dis-inclusion. Henry Newcomb characterized it as "localizing" activity that went hand-in-hand with a history of revival about people who "have thought and felt alike."[29]

Revival leaders and participants boasted throughout the winter of 1857 and 1858 that the religious excitement was a union (i.e., ecumenical) revival. Bostonians knew from reading the Rev. James Porter's *Revivals of Religion; Their Theory, Means, Obstructions, Uses and Importance* (Boston, 1849) that "God may delay to answer our prayers for sinners, because there is not sufficient <u>union</u> among us." In view of the fact that large parts of prayer meetings were testimonials from persons who had had their prayers answered, it was logical to assume that lack of unity was not obstructing divine action. The Old South report on its prayer meeting in 1859 was quick to note that it was "in name and reality, an 'union'" meeting of persons from various denominations. Newspapers reported aspects of the unity and diarists reiterated them. Everyone who commented on unity stressed like Finney that it included "all classes of people," and that meant economic class as well as other categories of class. The "higher classes" in Boston were engaged, wrote Finney, a judgment seconded by William Gray Brooks, who enthused that "all classes are brought in at all hours of the day." The religious press reported that Jews and Roman Catholics and African Americans attended. (Very few actually did attend, but the fiction fit the publicity frame for the revival.) During a run of several days during which Jews were converted each day, a man stood up and "earnestly addressed the meeting in behalf of his kinsmen." He gave evidence that the Old Testament prophecies were realized in Jesus of Nazareth, and so "he is now preaching the faith that he once destroyed." At Old South, a Catholic priest was converted, and an African American man gave his testimony. Talcott Chambers, writing about the revival in New York City, stressed that it was "free from any fractitious excitement" and that mail brought prayer requests from all over the country, "and also from beyond the sea, from towns in England, Germany, Switzerland." The same was true in Boston, where the practice of reading the written requests for prayers from home and overseas took place alongside live "reports from Christian friends who have come in from abroad." A "union service of the Episcopal churches" emerged as "a new but appropriate service," and the Congregational churches united "for religious services appropriate to the present time."[30]

The revival also brought together persons of similar occupations for special prayer meetings. As one historian has written, "One of the unusual evangelistic techniques developed during the revival was the targeting of professions and classes for special revivalistic appeals." Churches sponsored prayer meetings exclusively for lawyers, policemen, firemen, sailors, carpenters, journeymen printers, newsboys, and other occupational groups. Such meetings, established as a way of drawing a broader spectrum of persons into the revival, nevertheless by their nature served to reinforce identity in each group, to underscore difference at the same time that they suggested inclusiveness. A businessmen's meeting strengthened the notion of businessmen as a specific social group, a fireman's meeting cultivated solidarity among firemen, and gatherings of sailors reinforced the collective identity of that group of persons. This innovation of the revival, while probably effective as a strategy to reach persons who might not otherwise attend the prayer meetings, accordingly accented boundaries between groups at the same time that it enabled promoters to declare that various groups' participation in the revival was evidence of unity among the city's population. The practice especially underscored class differences, as, for example, between "businessmen" and "workingmen."[31]

One current of thinking among revival participants was that the revival, as a national phenomenon, was succeeding in uniting the nation. The mounting crisis over slavery already had resulted in bloodshed west of the Mississippi and soon would lead to the debacle at Harper's Ferry (a scheme hatched with the support of Massachusetts abolitionists). The Boston press, as well as sermons and public lectures, observed North and South on the threshold of the secessionist crisis, and predicted a tragic future. Seth Bliss, Boston secretary for the American Tract Society, wrote movingly about the slavery controversy, deploring the widening gulf between northern and southern "factions," and pleading for "union." Some thought that the revival was a step toward overcoming the divisiveness of those years. According to historian Leonard Sweet, the revival was in fact an effort by Americans to establish a fresh basis for communicating about the issue of slavery that divided the nation. Though overstated, that thesis nevertheless acknowledges the fact of hopefulness on the part of participants that the revival might serve as the ground for national reconciliation. Such hopefulness was grounded in the seeming abatement of group differences, the blurring of boundaries between denominations, men and women, rich and poor, white and black, and the cultures of various regions of the country. And it was manifest for some persons as the dawning of a distinctly American revival and a new era of cooperation for the American people. For the *New Englander,* it was "in all, in short . . . an American revival." To Dwight L. Moody, viewing the revival from Scotland, it was American for its egalitarianism and openness. In words reminiscent of Phoebe Palmer's description of the Tuesday Meeting he declared: "Previous to the revival in

1859 the prayer meetings in America were all of a stereotype, but now the stiffness and formality were broken up and anyone could rise up in the meetings and give his experience." In the eyes of its supporters it was even construed to meet the standard of "democratically organized" religion set by Theodore Parker. And for the *Congregationalist,* it forecasted a bright collective future: "The present religious movement is, in its tone, the gauge of rational progress among the American people."[32]

Alongside claims that the revival was bringing together a nation riven by the issue of slavery, however, were the observations of northerners that the revival was not progressing in the South. Only a handful of references to revival in the South appeared in Boston magazines and papers during 1857–59. The religious press frequently published detailed reports of conversions and additions to the membership of churches for cities and towns in New England, as well as New York, Philadelphia, Baltimore, Louisville, Cincinnati, Cleveland, Chicago, and sometimes the figures for Iowa, Missouri, and the trans-Mississippi. Conspicuously lacking in all such reports were any figures for southern states. The *New York Daily Tribune* reported in 1858 that the revival had made little inroad in the south, confirming Charles Finney's impression, stated forthrightly in his *Memoirs:* "Slavery seemed to shut it out from the South." According to Finney, southerners "were in such a state of irritation, of vexation, and of committal to their peculiar institution, which had come to be assailed on every side, that the spirit of God seemed to be grieved away from them. There seemed to be no place found for him in the hearts of the southern people at that time." In fact, there were significant eruptions of revivalistic fervor in the south at this time, some of it in connection with the effort of the itinerant Rev. Daniel Baker, and some just as localized religious excitement, such as that reported by a Boston woman visiting Charleston: "It is an interesting site [*sic*] to see the large circular church crowded to overflowing, seats in the aisles and hundreds of gentlemen standing. . . . One of the large galleries is always left for the colored people." But such testimonies to religious activity in the South only rarely made news in Boston. In fact, accounts of revivals published in the North had overlooked southern religion for most of the century. Joshua Bradley's *Accounts of Religious Revivals in Many Parts of the United States from 1815 to 1818* dedicated six pages out of a total of three hundred to southern revivals. Bostonians perceived the south as a spiritually barren land, and increasingly so as abolitionism pressed its case. It did not matter that there were instances of revival in the South. Boston and the rest of the Northeast were too deeply invested in a notion of their own moral and religious superiority to consider any evidence of pious awakenings there.[33]

The assertion of group identities—businessmen, women, mothers, young men, firemen, police, Americans (e.g. northern or anti-slavery Americans), etc.—was one aspect of a "muscular Christianity" which came into focus during the revival. It included the affirmation of Anglo-Saxon identity against other ethnic groups, and especially against Irish immigrants and African Americans. This book will explore these aspects of emergent muscular Christianity in later chapters. It is worth noting at this point, however, that all such assertions were carried out in the interest of unity. When businessmen gathered in exclusively male meetings, or mothers attended prayer meetings reserved for members of a Maternal Association, or fireman met with other firemen, or boys joined in prayer at a YMCA site, all of this was interpreted as evidence of the breadth of the revival and declared a confirmation of its unfolding as a grand union of all persons. In conceptualizing the revival, Bostonians exploited a rhetoric about unity. In practice, the revival was as much a matter of boundary-drawing as it was a mingling of classes, sexes, ages, denominations, and regions.

PUBLICIZING THE REVIVAL

The envisioning of the revival as a "prayer union" was significantly abetted by the press, which benefited by the improved efficiency of the telegraph in communicating news of revivals around the country. A report of conversions in Pittsburgh on Sunday could be in the Boston papers by Tuesday, and excerpts from a sermon could be distributed throughout much of the nation in a matter of days. The secular press was better positioned financially and politically to exploit rapid means of communication, and, departing from a *de facto* policy of disinterest in revivals, major city papers allotted substantial space to the events of 1858. In February of that year New York editors Horace Greeley and James Gordon Bennett began running editorials supportive of the revival alongside reports of conversions and anecdotes about specific cases of backsliders who were saved in prayer meetings. Editors at other major newspapers, including the *Boston Evening Transcript* and the *Boston Daily Advertiser,* followed their lead. Such coverage contributed substantially not only to the image of the breadth and "unity" in the revival, but it carried it to places it otherwise might not have reached. The *Puritan Recorder* accordingly exulted:

"Whether it be a change in public sentiment favorable to religion, or of other causes, it deserves notice as a significant and important fact, that intelligence of the progress of the revival, especially in the cities, fills a large space in the daily papers. . . . This is a thing to be rejoiced in . . ." Rejoicing over the coverage took place even in prayer meetings themselves. David Snow told the Old South Chapel meeting one morning that "we want also to diffuse the same spirit abroad over the land. We know that our religious papers do not convey the intelligence to the very class of men we wish to reach; but, if it is published in the secular papers, they will read it, and a great good will result." Noting "how much interest the secular papers took up the revival in New York . . . and how the news went broadcast over the land," Snow proclaimed that publication of actual transcriptions of Old South prayer meetings should be "diffused abroad over the land," reminding a reporter who was transcribing that very meeting that "if any secular paper wants to have a wide circulation, it must report the proceedings of such meetings as these." Even Heman Humphrey, who thought the revival fundamentally the "effect of a supernatural Divine influence," credited the big city newspapers, observing that because the revival took place across denominations the secular press could report it without appearing partisan. The religious press of course made the revival its bread and butter, filling their pages with statistics, inspiring stories, and personal testimonies in the form of letters. The *Evangelist* bluntly proposed a focus on the revival as a marketing strategy. Urging its readers to promote the paper by working to expand its subscription base, it advised: "How easy for a young man in a congregation where there has been a revival of religion, resulting in fifty or one hundred conversions, to go round and in a few hours get at least a dozen or twenty new names." *Zion's Herald and Wesleyan Journal*, which was founded in Boston in 1831 and claimed to be the world's oldest Methodist newspaper, crafted a less mercenary public image: "Our readers may be assured that the publishers of the Herald, deriving not one cent directly or indirectly from it, are actuated by a simple desire to glorify God and to promote the interests of our common Zion."[34]

Newspaper reports of conversion statistics were a key part of the coverage of the revival. So also were announcements of sermons and lectures, published reviews of those sermons after they were published, and books about the revival. In the *Boston Evening Transcript*, readers could find publication announcements of books such as *Revival Gems*, a volume "particularly adapted for seasons of religious revival," reports of "crowds that daily throng Father Mason's Chapel, in North Street," and news of prayer meetings that were "so well attended" that they had to farm out some persons to other sites. The Finneys, Parker, Huntington, Kirk, Norris Day, and other celebrities were constantly in the papers for their lectures, publications, appearances at prayer meetings, or other activities. The words, "filled the house to its utmost capacity—many persons retiring for want of even a standing place within its walls" became almost a stock expression of the revival's popularity. It was almost as common as "unusually large." Weekly editions told of church admissions on the previous Sunday from around the state: 286 in Bedford, 143 in Lowell, 100 in Springfield, 140 in Providence, and an even 500 in Lawrence, where Joanne Harvey agonized about so many people suffering in the cold after the crash. Reports of the business conducted at yearly and quarterly Associational Meetings overflowed with congratulations, hopefulness, exhortations to deeper piety, and numbers—conversions, church memberships, attendance at meetings, and so forth. The marshalling of statistics in support of revival had been a part of the American Protestant landscape since the eighteenth century. During the Businessmen's Revival numbers were placed in the foreground of the story. Ministers, newspaper reporters, and people in the pews all speculated about the size of the revival and, while it lasted, its upward curve. The *Evangelist* promised its readers "the most careful and accurate estimate we are able to make of conversions." Finney estimated that at its height, the revival was producing over fifty thousand conversions a week. He added: "It was estimated that during this revival not less than five hundred thousand souls were converted in the **Northern states.**" A century after Finney, J. Edwin Orr thought the revival had produced a million converts.[35]

THE END OF THE PERFORMANCE

When the revival began to slow in late spring, the press noticed that as well. The *Evangelist* reported in May of 1858 that "the attendance on the meetings in Boston is reported to be decidedly falling off." The following month it observed that "the public generally are less affected by the movement than they were some weeks since." In July, it informed its readers that "the meeting at midday is not as fully attended as it was several months since" at the Old South. And late that month, reading the signs from around the nation, it published an article entitled "Keep the Revival Alive," advising more house-to-house visitation and urging Sabbath School teachers to "do more for the members of their classes." Most Bostonians who followed the progress of revivals already knew that the impulse for revival faded in the late spring and as business picked up. The *Evangelist* already was concerned in April that "the numbers present at the different prayer-meetings held each day, may not be as large as it was before the opening of the Spring and the revival of business." Coming off a very bad six months, the revival of business was especially important, a fact not lost on the religious press, which addressed the matter repeatedly in Boston, and as far away as St. Louis: "We have not been without the apprehension that the revival of business might interfere with the progress of the revival of religion." The *Puritan Recorder* had warned against the distractions of summer in 1850, explaining that "Christians are more apt to become worldly-minded, and lose the spirit of watchfulness and prayer than in the winter. General experience proves this." Commentary on the Businessmen's Revival repeated that warning, at the same time hoping, as did the *Evangelist*, that "the revival will not be brought to an end by the hot season of the year." But the tone of most reports was acquiescent, in the same way that Rev. Heman Humphrey, a seasoned revival watcher, had been when he surveyed the excitement of the previous year: "I believe that at least nine out of ten of the great revivals since I came upon the stage, have taken place between the months of October and May. May not one great reason be, that in the winter months, favored by the long evenings, the people at large have more leisure for attending religious meetings . . . than in the Summer?" The *Independent* concurred, bluntly noting that "revivals rarely take place in the summer." But supporters of the revival refused to accept the historical pattern, urging continued attendance at church, and a renewal of commitment to the movement during the warm season, or, as the *Puritan Recorder* had phrased the matter a number of years earlier: "Go to the summer prayer meeting; and for the winter prayer meeting you need not fear."[36]

By mid-summer the revival had lost its momentum. In the fall and during the winter of 1858–59 there was a mild invigoration of religious life that fell far short of the activity the previous winter, and the press all but stopped publishing conversion statistics. The warm weather and the rapid re-establishment of commerce correlated once again with the end of a revival. It may have been the case as well that the performance was simply over. Samuel Prime, the author of the most popular book on the revival (it had gone through five editions by 1859), had predicted that the revival "will go on, until these meetings are forsaken, or become formal, or vain, or self-righteous, or theatres of display." In fact, as early as March 1858 William Gray Brooks had concluded just that. After hearing a lecture at his Sunday School on the revival, he wrote that "I believe one's religion ought to be between himself and God, and not a mere form, to be paraded before the eyes of his fellow men; and that the first place for religious exercises is one's own closet. . . . But I do sincerely believe that these revivals are productive of no good, in comparison with the harm they accomplish." The *Liberator,* mocking the maudlin quality of the petitions in prayer meetings, called the central feature of the revival a "theatrical prayer meeting," while an insider at the Old South church referred to the "exhibitions of Christian experience . . . by interesting narratives of personal joys, sorrows, and efforts." Either way one viewed the matter, the element of performance was inescapable. And the course of the revival had in various ways underscored performance, none better than the highly publicized meetings in theatres themselves. A leading story in book-length accounts of the revivals and in newspapers everywhere was the transformation of Burton's theatre on Chambers Street in New York into a room for prayer meetings. A *New York Tribune* summary related that "a few years ago there suddenly arose, in one of the thriving cities of western New-York, an imperious popular demand for theatrical entertainments," and "there being no edifice in place a church was hired" and transformed by "carpenters and scene-painters" into a theatre. The transformation of a theatre into a church in New York City was "a fitting retributive compensation." Burton's attracted overflow crowds of twenty-five hundred. The revival in Chicago claimed the Metropolitan Theatre for meetings of three thousand persons. In Boston, the Music Hall and the Museum Theatre hosted the revival, and the Howard Athenaeum, once a Millerite tabernacle, returned to its roots as a house of religion on a number of occasions. And in case the connection between the staging of plays and the performance of revival was not obvious to everyone, Rev. Theodore Cuyler, in opening the first meeting at Burton's, made the linkage explicit: "Today . . . we set apart a disused play-house for a house of worship. Oh! What soul-tragedies may have been enacted in this very building! From yonder 'pit' how many may have gone down to the pit of everlasting despair!" Over time, revival preaching in theatres produced concern on the part of some columnists. One in the *Northern Christian Advocate* warned that "going into theatres on Sunday evening to preach" initiated a scenario in which "the vast difference between theatre and the church is insensibly lessened." Where theatres were not available, revival promoters frequently sought other public venues for prayer meetings. In New York and Boston, stores and counting houses and fire stations were opened to meetings, and the organization of the noon meeting at the Old South in May 1858 came only after the site committee first had been unable to obtain Faneuil Hall, and then failed to secure a room in the heart of the commercial district on State Street. When the meeting was established, however, the church reported that "it was a spectacle like Boston had never seen before." Revival was spectacle and theatre.[37]

BETWEEN PULPIT AND CLOSET

The revival that began during an economic crisis faded as the economy re-bounded and the spring turned to summer. It had brought lay leadership and prayer to the forefront of religious life in Boston, and had afforded the opportunity for specific groups to publicly assert themselves, at the same time that it set into motion a rhetoric that valued equality, freedom, and unity. Its image of controlled devotional fervor, solemnity, and weeping appealed to persons who had come to disapprove of a revival machinery that appeared to manufacture hyperenthusiastic performances of jerky, noisy lamentation. It drew young and middle-aged men into the churches in numbers that surpassed those of previous times of revival. The newspapers communicated it across the nation and the Atlantic, while individual Christians carried it to homes within their neighborhood or district. The revival's detractors accused it of being overly emotional, and theatrical. It was in fact a complex collective emotional performance, a multidimensional ritual enactment of relations between individuals and groups, that dramatically asserted Protestant identity in Boston at the same time that it represented a contractual understanding of relations between individuals and God. The revival accordingly was both a public process and a feat of personal renewal, or, as the *Evangelist* wrote, "the prayer meeting is half-way between the pulpit and the closet—the spot where public instruction and private meditation meet, . . ." an exercise that confirmed social and personal boundaries at the same time that it challenged them, a place "halfway between."[38]

TWO

The Anxiety of Boston at Mid-Century

PRIDE AND DISMAY

The Businessmen's Revival in Boston emerged against a background of rapid social change, economic catastrophe, broad reconceptualizations of family and gender, difficult ecclesiastical politics, and a number of other factors crucial to the historical positioning of the city as a beginning point for the revival. The lavish manifestation of emotion in religious gatherings was a distinguishing feature of the revival, but so were the precautions taken to ensure that emotion was properly channeled, and made subservient to good order in the noon hour and evening prayer meetings. The fact of simultaneous expectations for emotional expression and emotional control in public settings did not originate solely in religion. It represented something of the larger experience of life in Boston, of the mixed motives and impulses of the inhabitants. It betokened, more specifically, the perception of urban life at mid-century as an unstable compound of advantage and liability, as enthusiasm for life in Boston alongside a sense of foreboding that called for the exercise of caution and control.

Bostonians were proud of their city. They also feared that it had passed its prime, that it teetered on the edge of decay and anomie, chaos slowly overtaking order in strings of disasters. The ebullience manifest in Bostonians' observations on city life was tinctured with panic. Boosterish declarations of the glories of the city were liable at any moment to devolve into nervous concern for its very survival. The white Protestant citizenry kept track of the city's truly impressive achievements in the ordering of urban space: the development and improvement of their neighborhoods, the construction of parks and gardens, Tremont and Commonwealth Streets, the ongoing enhancement of the Common, the emergent South End, the impressive buildings associated with banking and trading enterprises. It also fretted openly about immigration, urban blight, the decay of character, and the seeming evanescing of the New England traditions of the public meeting and the authority of the "old families." People worried that public order was collapsing, and their fearfulness led them to enact new ordinances and to more vigorously enforce old ones bearing on the behavior of persons in the streets, on the Common, in public buildings, in private homes, and even in churches. With mixed feelings of pride and trepidation, they reflected on what it meant to be a Bostonian, and how as Bostonians they were related to persons elsewhere, in New York, the West, and the South.

The uneasiness in being a Bostonian was rooted in the facts of change in the city. Demographic change—not only immigration from overseas but the high turnover rate of the city's population—was everywhere evident. The physical layout of the city was in a state of flux as well. Streets were rerouted, buildings were thrown up and torn down, neighborhoods sprouted where birds had nested in watery habitats, dress and other fashions were transformed seemingly overnight, and gardens disappeared under warehouse floors. Civility was said to have all but disappeared at a time when civility was crucial to Bostonians' envisioning of their city's future. The uneasiness was all the more profound because, in fact, there was also so much to crow about. The new neighborhoods were beautiful. The construction of new gardens and public squares, ornamented with benches and statues, were a priority of the city's planners throughout the 1850s. The Common was constantly being improved. The value of personal and real estate rose dramatically. And periodically the city would gather in an exemplary show of geniality to celebrate a civil holiday or to remember and honor a personage from its past in a candlelit procession. Bostonians wanted to believe in the future of the city at the same time that they shied away from investing their hopes in it. They were exuberant, but also hesitant. Like their feelings about the local economy, their feelings about being Bostonians sometimes shot up with pride and expectation, but at other times they wondered whether such feelings were warranted, whether they were an exaggerated and dangerous perception of city life. In observing their society, Bostonians gushed openly about its magnificence while, anxious about crime and corruption, they devised ever more elaborate means to try to control everyday social life.

As we shall see, Protestants active in the Businessmen's Revival constructed emotion in a complex way, stressing the unstable relationship between its beauties and dangers, conceiving emotional life as a highly tensed coalition of emotional expression and emotional control. City life to a certain extent framed this understanding. The dichotomous experience of satisfaction with continuity and prosperity on the one hand, and concern, on the other hand, that change was spinning the city uncontrollably out of its proper orbit, conditioned the display of emotion in the revival.

In 1853, J. T. S. Lidstone published *The Bostoniad: Giving a Full Description of the Principal Establishments, Together with the Most Honorable and Substantial Businessmen in the Athens of America*. Mingling political and commercial themes, and including a poem for each of the mercantile establishments in the city, the *Bostoniad* created an assortment of tableaux celebrating the achievements of the city's residents. Typical was the paean to Alderman Lyman Perry: "Hail! Alderman, by muses crown'd, / Commission MERCHANT far renown'd, / A Provision dealer, much the best, / In Boston, Athens of the West."[1]

The population of the city of Boston in 1850 was 138,788. That was 105,000 more persons than lived in the city in 1810, approximately double the population of 1830, and 25,000 more than the previous census in 1845. Ongoing immigration from overseas, the flow of people, and especially young men, from New England towns to Boston, and the annexation of surrounding areas such as Charlestown in the fall of 1854 assured that the population would continue to grow throughout the decade. There were some defections to the suburbs, but not enough to significantly retard population growth in the city. The valuation of real estate in the city in 1857 was set by the city assessors at $148, 902,100, an increase of five million dollars over the previous year. Personal estate was valued at $108,291,000, an increase of almost three million dollars over the previous year. In the five years leading up to 1857 the total valuation (real estate and personal estate) increased sixty-nine million dollars, or 27 percent. In 1855, thirty-seven Boston banks were large enough to pay semi-annual dividends of three dollars or more per share. The Suffolk Bank, the Freeman's Bank, and the Market Bank paid five dollars a share. One in four persons kept a bank account. By the mid-1850s a large number of Boston manufacturing and railroad stocks had been traded for twenty years or more, successfully weathering periodic national credit and financial crises. In 1857, approximately five thousand persons and corporations were taxed on ten thousand dollars and upward. People who had money spent it on houses, clothes, travel, the theatre, charitable causes, and in the 2,000 dram shops and 230 houses of prostitution (the majority of which were in the Sixth Ward and on Ann Street) and in 1,000 private homes such as the boarding houses in the First Ward where liquor and other entertainments were provided for a charge.[2]

Neighborhoods meant a lot to Bostonians. Those with money lived or operated businesses in the Fourth Ward, which included State Street in the center of the city, or, failing that, parts of the Sixth Ward , which ran along Beacon Street. But other neighborhoods were emerging. Gamaliel Bradford recorded in his diary in 1854 that "the population of the city is fast moving to the South End." Sure enough, two years later, the *Transcript* reported that between Dover and Elliott Streets and from Washington Street west, hundreds of houses had just been built, with many more under way together with commercial buildings around eight squares. Over forty thousand persons inhabited the South End, and city planners expected continued growth because of the horse railroad.[3]

The up-and-coming street of the late 1850s was Tremont Street, from Dover Street to Roxbury, a broad street with wide sidewalks which became an artery from the South End to the old peninsula, and which featured many fine homes. Tremont Street, however, was choked down to a narrow passage, like most of the old streets, as it approached the Common. The Common in 1850 was fifty acres of lawns and trees on the southwestern side of the city, bordered by the bay of the Charles River on one side and by rows of houses on two other sides. On the north side of the Common stood the State House. Not far from the Crescent Pond was the Great Elm, a hundred feet in diameter at the greatest extent of its branches and over two hundred years old in 1855. It had been the site at various times in the city's history for hangings-in-effigy. In the mid-1850s the City Forester, John Galvin, rearranged the gutters, planted trees, regraded the walks, and made other Common improvements. The Public Garden and the Conservatory were likewise improved. Families walked on the Common, children played games there, and crowds of people assembled for cultural events in good weather. On June 21, 1855, six thousand people gathered to hear the Boston Brass Band. The next day the New York City Guards performed, and a week later the circus came to the adjacent Public Garden for a week. On the first of May each year, large crowds filled the Common to picnic, play ball or other games, and to take in entertainments. Just as popular was the Fourth of July, which in 1857 featured bands, processions, the ascent of two balloons, "Old America" and "Young America," and the deaths of three men and a boy from fireworks, though injuries as a whole were less than expected because firecrackers were in short supply due to war in China. Sometimes the Common unexpectedly became the scene of merrymaking and leisure, as on Fast Day in 1851, of which James Blake wrote: "Fast & pray says the Governor, Feast & play says the people."[4]

The dome of the State House adjacent to the Common was visible for miles around, but equally impressive was Commonwealth Avenue, as it was laid out in 1859. Two hundred and fifty feet wide, and running a mile and a half westward from the Common, it was the centerpiece of the Back Bay improvement program, and, in the opinion of one writer, having hardly "an equal among the magnificent capitals of Europe." The 1850s brought other improvements as well. Tens of thousands of dollars of appropriations were approved annually for maintenance and upgrade of public squares and gardens. In the fall of 1858, that project was made less burdensome with the beginning of city water, celebrated by William W. Greenough, president of the Boston Public Library, at a ball at Faneuil Hall "in honor of the Introduction of the Water." The city installed drinking fountains and planned more large decorative fountains like the popular one in Chester Square in the South End. The city recycled some of its old buildings, such as the Masonic Temple, which was refurbished as the new United States Court in late 1858. The Boston Athenaeum flourished after reorganizing itself by selling shares for three hundred dollars to prospective proprietors, and the Mount Auburn Cemetery, a remarkable testament to the imagination of the citizenry, continued to derive more income from its investments than from lots. To reach all of these places, the city at the end of the decade planned municipal railroads.[5]

In spite of the many changes in Boston during the first part of the nineteenth century, the old order was very much alive, and Bostonians of various backgrounds rejoiced that they were living in a place that "has ever taken the lead in what is great, good, useful, and profitable." That leadership was said to be manifest in a string of American firsts, including the first school, academy, college, press, book, newspaper, manufactured cloth, paper, canal, and railroad, as well as having planted the first apple tree, caught the first whale, sent the first ship to discover the South Sea islands, coined the first money, and first hoisted the national flag. And then there was the city's role in the Revolution. Outsiders, proclaimed the newspapers, could not help but be impressed by the glory of the place. The press reported that a southern gentleman thought it was "the greatest city in the world,—the greatest in wealth, industry, intellectual and moral power." Charles Dickens, alongside his criticisms of the city, was taken by its "houses so bright and gay," and the colorful signs on the streets. The Fourth Ward, bragged the *Watchman* in 1854, was the richest locality in the nation and worth as much as the city of Baltimore, and Massachusetts was the wealthiest state in the Union, when property was calculated per capita. Boston was the heart of the "New England character," which if blotted from the map of the nation would cripple "our country's progress in all that is good and great." That character was especially evident in the religious history of the city. Revivals were "more frequent and powerful, and more permanent in their results." Indeed, as the *Christian Observatory* queried in language reminiscent of Jonathan Edwards a century earlier, "Will the Millennium Commence in New England?" Answering in the affirmative, the magazine added that "Providence has put it in the hands of New England to control the whole country."[6]

Boston measured itself against the other rapidly growing east coast port city, its neighbor just to the south. Rarely missing an opportunity to show itself favorably against New York, the city boasted all sorts of achievements and attributes, in columns that were matched by writers for the *New York Times* (which was established in 1851) and other publications. The competition sometimes went to extremes, as city officials and newspaper editors crunched numbers to put the best face on their cities. The *Puritan Recorder* revealed that Boston was 217 miles closer to Liverpool, and thus a better port for trade with England. The *Daily Advertiser,* after a close study of the Directories of Boston and New York, reported with satisfaction that the "permanency of the population of Boston" was 50 percent higher than that of New York. The *Watchman-Examiner* pointed out (somewhat exaggeratedly) during the winter of 1856 that New York harbor had been closed for several weeks while the harbor in Boston had not been closed on account of ice for twelve years. The railroad managers were better equipped to remove snow from the tracks as well. New York punched back with articles such as that which appeared in the Sunday *Times* in 1858. With tongue-in-cheek praise for the "gigantic intellects" of Boston, the paper lamented that New York lacked "a single name supposed to be capable of reflecting in an emergency, appropriate honor upon the character of the Empire State! Verily, we have reason to feel humiliated!"[7]

The city rang all its church bells every year for a half-hour on September 17 to celebrate the anniversary of the settlement of Boston. The people who celebrated such occasions in the street were, according to Orville Dewey, more congenial than could be found anywhere: "The great attraction of Boston, I think, is the number of agreeable and admirable men and women in it—greater than can be found in any equal share or population on this continent." A newspaper writer concurred, recommending the "warm-hearted hospitality" of the people and proclaiming that "in the wide world I have never experienced more generous kindness and true affection."[8]

Alongside claims for the ongoing preeminence of the city and its people, Bostonians brooded about disruptions brought by change. The urban geography, as well as the ways in which the population organized themselves in society, were being remade, and not always for the better. Change endangered cherished traditions, some of them as old as the city itself. Invoking the legacy of John Adams, the *Daily Advertiser* moaned that "in the first place, we have abandoned the town organization," and especially the town meeting, which "affects in a vital part the facility of meetings for the purpose of discussing, of deliberating and of judging public affairs."[9] Surveying change in the North End, George Scandlin, a resident of that neighborhood, calculated in the summer of 1856 that "in a few years there will be but few of the better portions of our better citizens remaining in it—as it is changing more and more into a business locality & to the residences of the laboring portion of our community." Even in the 1850s an adjacent area to Scandlin's street had acquired a reputation for poverty and blight. Centered on the corner of North Street (along a stretch known to locals as Ann Street) and Ferry Streets, it was referred to by the *New York Times*—perhaps with a dig in mind—as "a vile locality of Boston, known to police as the "Black Sea." The name of the neighborhood did, in fact, occur frequently in the notes of urban missionaries as well as in police reports. A mission founded there in 1856 took its inspiration from a mission in New York's notorious Five Points neighborhood.[10]

Other testimony painted a darker picture, following the lead of celebrated critics of east coast urban life, such as the Reverend Albert Barnes of Philadelphia, who warned that "evils pour into our great cities like floods from all quarters of the world," rendering them modern day incarnations of Sodom and Gomorrah." A local paper explained, then, how this lethal concoction of vice in turn spilled back into the surrounding areas. Employing the metaphor of a heart, the *Evangelist* confided: "Underground pipes connect the city, which are channels of corruption. There is a vigorous circulation from the heart outward." Persons who arrived in Boston were soon "swayed into the broad road of destruction, by the immediate and powerful influences of the city." The city was a place where "warfare between virtue and vice is in continual progress." Elizur Wright, Boston Insurance Commissioner and editor of *Anti-Slavery Reports*, wrote his brother after years of service as a journalist in Boston that it was a "nasty" place. *The Young Woman's Friend* condemned the city as a show of "the most unbounded extravagance, and the utmost extremes of fashion and vanity." *Little Mabel,* a book of sentimental fiction produced in 1859 for the children of the city of Boston, blamed the "temptations" of the city for the death of Mabel's mother and brother. Work in the city was "drudgery," deadening labor inside a tomb of bricks and mortar that led to a "listless indifference." The lucky escaped to the countryside, or for a period of rest and moral recuperation to Franconia Notch, New Hampshire, or one of the other physician-approved resorts advertised in the Boston papers. The city, said the *Boston Evening Transcript* in 1858, has "only three or four correctly built private buildings, and not a dozen handsome private houses." The avenues of the city were "almost entirely destitute of architectural beauty, uniform only in ugliness," and marked here and there by "expressionless warehouses of the flimsiest granite, *tabarded* all over with monstrous signs" or "a long dismal line of brick houses, kneaded into every shape save that of beauty." Samuel May, a leader of the anti-slavery movement in the city, wrote his colleague Richard Davis Webb in 1857 about the progress of decay: "When I was a boy Boston had a great many fine gardens in it, which have now (every one I believe) been given over to Goths & Vandals & filled up with brick and stone in various sightly and unsightly shapes." Mary Gardner Davis made the point more dramatically in her commonplace book the following year: "We gravely and wearily walk past each other, along the noisy streets, taking care to express nothing." And in a perverse twist on the favorite analogy to Athens, she confessed: "Like the Athenians, we send every year a ship heavily laden with youths & maidens as a tribute to that monster who rules the labyrinth of our modern society;—what is his name—fashion, Propriety, mammon, Etiquette, or What not?"[11]

Bostonians' consciousness of demographic change fueled their anxieties about the state of the city. The *Boston Directory* (which listed persons with a recognized abode or store) in 1858 contained just over fifty thousand names, about the same as the previous year, but during that year, fourteen thousand entries had been erased (some moved to the suburbs), and fifteen thousand added. The rate of turnover left the impression of an unstable social order. Knyvet Winthrop Sears read a letter from his mother in early 1860 commenting on the fluidity of the upper parts of society. Explaining that she had attended a party with the Cabots and Endicotts, she fussed over the absence of so many persons that she expected to see, concluding, "society seems to change here with the wind." The *Evangelist and Religious Review* summarized the changes in 1858: "There is not, probably, a city in the old thirteen States, that has undergone such marked changes, within the last twenty-five years, in all its relations, social, political, religious, as Boston. . . . There was an aristocracy of birth and wealth . . . into which it was very difficult for a stranger to gain admission. . . . All this prestige has now passed away. . . . The free schools of Boston are fitting the plebians to become patricians . . . The old families are 'obsolete ideas.'"[12]

Change and trouble took various forms. Transients thronged to the city in the winter seeking refuge in church-run homes or flophouses. In the summer, many Bostonians left for long visits to the countryside. Some stayed away the entire summer. Emigrants included merchants and professional people, and the clergy. Style-conscious Bostonians who stayed in the city year-round tried to keep up with the various paradings of hoop skirts and bloomers, and red petticoats, which fashion-watcher Charles French in the winter of 1857 declared "all the rage now." Art lovers complained of the constant thefts; one gallery was burglarized of its entire contents in April of that year. The streets were populated with rabble-rousers such as John Orralias, the "Angel Gabriel," who preached extempore against Roman Catholics on the streets of the city and somehow managed to be in the vicinity whenever a riot broke out. When Francis Bennett and his father stopped to hear him on the Custom House steps one night in 1854 he was vexed to the point of exhaustion. Other speakers opted for more traditional venues. On one occasion, a large, well-dressed middle-aged man, "a maniac," burst into a church in the middle of services, seized the pulpit, and, flapping his arms wildly, proclaimed: "Do you know me? I am God Almighty; I am the Lord God; begone—away with you, or I'll send you to hell!"[13]

Not all the difficulties of city life derived from choices that people made about the ways in which they wished to live. In his profile of life in nineteenth-century Boston, historian Peter Knights stressed "the perils of everyday life," observing that "disaster surrounded the people of mid-nineteenth-century Boston, or so it seemed."[14] Bostonians, as Knights pointed out, discovered almost daily that a man had been killed by a falling block of lumber, a woman by a horse's kick to the head, a child by slipping through the railings of a bridge. Property was destroyed in routine or sometimes extraordinary ways. The Boston weather was sometimes responsible. The winter of 1857 was brutal, with record temperatures between twenty and thirty below zero in January and February, as well as a large snowfall. Charles Low of Charlestown recorded minus thirty-seven on January 20. For merchants and investors facing a full-scale breakdown of the national system of credit, the disruption of commerce caused by the weather could not have come at a worse time. The suffering of Bostonians was intensified by an outbreak of scarlet fever in December 1856, during which month 115 persons died, a rate of death roughly matched in January. Later in the year, an outbreak of cholera would claim many infants and young children. For Edward Savage, who had removed dozens of bodies from homes during the previous epidemic in 1854, the outbreak was horrifying. When epidemics peaked, police stations and watchhouses were used as hospitals.[15]

SOCIAL DISORDER

The well-honed sense of disaster, of imminent crises that characterized the culture of the city, was, at mid-century, fueled especially by the citizenry's reflection upon crime and corrupt politics. Just before mid-century the *Christian Observatory* was warning of "Secret Societies," of men who "band themselves together to carry out schemes of wickedness," who were in concert "for the purposes of crime." Groups such as the emergent Know-Nothings fit the bill to some extent, but the tone of apprehension suggested more sinister gang crime (and especially that thought to involve Irish immigrants). By late 1857, when Susan Brown was busying herself attending Dr. Bellow's lectures on "Crime" and "The Sources of Crime," things had deteriorated as the result of a nationwide financial catastrophe. Charles Henry Harvey observed that "the papers were filled with crime," and indeed they were. *Ballou's Pictorial,* which normally practiced an editorial policy of decidedly upbeat reporting, complained that young men between the ages of seventeen and twenty were guilty of "the most atrocious crimes," and that the evil they wrought was "one of the most discouraging features of the age we live in." When Edward E. Hale preached his election sermon before Governor Banks early in 1859, he railed against "this disease, crime,—which eats into men's hearts, which destroys the very essence of their manliness." When on a Sunday in July several months later only one person (a drunken man from the North End) was arrested on a Sunday night, the *Boston Evening Transcript* exulted: "Only one individual was committed to the Tombs during the 24 hours ending last night."[16]

Crime fascinated even those who deplored it. Israel Lombard, a devoted father and ardent theatregoer, was, like many Bostonians, highly attentive to the trial of John Webster, accused of murdering Doctor George Parkman. He marked his diary entry on the verdict with a scary skull and crossbones. Charles Low was a Cambridge teenager who enjoyed having "a good time gunning and roving around," and especially, "ratting" (hunting rats and skinning them), during the hours he was not in school studying French and

Geometry. He recorded in his diary news of forgeries, murders, and other felonies, sometimes with commentary regarding unusually strong public interest, as in 1857: "A murder case in Hingam is exciting much attention." John Henry Kenneally, a Catholic shipping merchant who joined the Freemasons in 1858, followed cases of murder and adultery. Bostonians found cases with a racial component particularly interesting, a fact not lost on newspaper editors. The *Transcript* story "Hot Revenge" reported on the arrest and trial of a woman of color in Ann Street who poured boiling water over another woman during an altercation. Accounts of criminal women also were granted significant column space, especially in the case of female pickpockets and shoplifters who dressed well—some because they were gentry.[17]

Bostonians sought to control crime through ordinances and their enforcement. Police protection and investigation accordingly changed dramatically during the 1850s. During several months of 1854–55 the Boston Watch was renamed the Boston Police Department and staffed with 246 officers (for a population of 160,000). As pressure "to preserve order" mounted, the Police Department was periodically enlarged and ceremoniously displayed, as on July 4, 1856, when temporary cops recruited to monitor the celebrations swelled the force to triple its size. After the murderer of a policeman in east Boston in the fall of 1857 escaped, the force was uniformed in blue and brass, making their public image more visible and dramatic. (One Irish immigrant, Barney McGinniskin, was appointed a police officer during the 1850s, but his appointment was rescinded after a public outcry.) About the same time, the Know-Nothing legislature created the Massachusetts State Police, who were charged with enforcing the liquor laws passed in 1854, even though the city already had doubled the number of officers on that detail. The liquor legislation arose from temperance agitation and stipulated that liquor sellers were responsible for damage caused by persons who became intoxicated on alcohol the sellers provided to them. The ordinance was reinforced in 1858 when the Massachusetts Supreme Court upheld an 1835 ruling that outlawed drunkenness whether it be in public or not. Not surprisingly, between 1856 and 1860 the number of annual arrests for drunkenness doubled, with impoverished immigrants making up the vast majority of collars. Disorderly conduct and assault placed a distant second and third. Charles French was certain that the liquor law would not work, and commenting on a meeting of liquor sellers attended by his father, he suggested that "much money will be spent (I think) to try to evade the law." The financial investment clearly yielded some results, in view of the testimony of another Bostonian in late 1859 that the "liquor agents rascality" was the leading topic of conversation. Frustration with enforcing the liquor laws fed the fears of that part of the population already anxious about the seeming breakdown of order, and contributed to calls for more efficient administration of justice, such as shortening the time between conviction and execution.[18]

Increasingly, Bostonians who visited the city parks or traveled on the city streets were subject to rules and regulations enacted to control social life. Alone among all large eastern seaboard cities, Boston prohibited smoking in public, except within the Smoker's Circle on the Common. Anyone caught smoking "the bewitching weed" on the street was subject to a fine. Newsboys were required to obtain a license in order to hawk papers on street corners. Dogs were to be licensed. City authorities ordered the marshal to stop all sleighs traveling too fast. The long arm of the law reached even into corners considered by some of the populace sacrosanct. Cases involving the violation of preaching laws appeared with some regularity before the courts, and the authorities did not hesitate to launch preemptive strikes against persons suspected of planning violations. On November 24, 1858, a sheriff and posse burst into the church where Orville Dewey was preaching and loudly informed him "that the judge desired nothing—no allusion in the services sh'd be made to the trial pending," a case of ship mutiny involving deaths. Private organizations, ranging from the Boot and Shoe Makers Association to The Boston Infidel Relief Society to the Home for the Fallen, produced lists of "Rules and Regulations" that prohibited spitting, profanity, tardiness at meals, and similar behaviors. And sometimes Bostonians demanded of the city even more surveillance and control than the police or sheriff provided, as in the case of Sabbath laws. In early 1857 the *Evangelist* connected the "great increase in Sabbath-breaking" with murder convictions, which it claimed had increased fivefold in six years, and demanded more vigorous enforcement of both the Sabbath laws and the anti-smoking ordinance. The next year, the drug stores in Boston, which long had enjoyed an exemption to Sabbath laws, collectively determined to close on Sundays, and by the following year, police were breaking into buildings to arrest persons for "entertaining on the Sabbath." [19]

One of the ways in which lawmakers sought to control crime was by limiting or carefully regulating public gatherings, and especially those that might provoke an emotional response from the crowd. The regulations governing the use of the Boston Common were of such a nature. During the 1850s, a series of controversies broke out over the right of citizens to gather there for events involving the display of emotion. On Wednesdays and Saturdays in the summer of 1853, Bostonians came to the Common to hear music performed, sometimes in large numbers, as on August 10, 1853, when fifteen thousand gathered. The following summer, Francis Bennett heard a late summer performance at which the crowd cheered "Yankee Doodle" and "Hail Columbia," but vigorously hissed "St Patrick's Day in the Morning." That was a sign that things were to change. By 1857, the city had decided not to fund music on the Common, and announced their decision just before the Fourth of July. Reflecting on that decision, young Charles French made the following telling notation in his diary: "Their pretended reason . . . is that many disreputable persons frequent the place. Ha! Ha! What an excuse!" Early the following summer, after debate, the city decided to continue the policy by postponing indefinitely a Common Council request for funds for musical performances. About this time, the city also chose to enforce the prohibition of preaching on the Common. A Methodist preacher had gotten away with it in the summer of 1789, and in subsequent years there were some other cases. But in the heat of the revival of 1858, the city drew the line. The mayor and alderman steadfastly refused the petitions of citizens to use the Common for regular preaching, citing its traditional use for exercise and entertainment. Critics cast the city government not merely as the opponent of preaching but of "public speaking," a right dear to the hearts of Bostonians. The *Evangelist and Religious Review* appealed in vain to the historical example of George Whitefield and his ten thousand auditors.[20]

Bostonians wondered about the extent to which public expression should be controlled, and who exactly ought to oversee the enforcement of regulations. Those who saw Athenian glory in the city naturally believed the police force to be among the finest in the world, "those sensible, vigilant officers, who do so much to make Boston the orderly city it is." Others persons concerned about the quality of public life thought the police brutal. Miriam Sears wrote her son Knyvet in 1859 about the case of a boy caught playing a prank at school. When a policeman, who had staked out the site at the urging of the faculty, grabbed the boy, a struggle ensued. The cop shot his revolver in the air, and then smashed the boy with a billy club. Miriam said that the "silly trick" the boy was playing should not have brought him to "risk losing his life . . . at the discretion of a person in that class of life that seldom control their tempers." The fact that the Hanover Street Chapel in the North End was situated upstairs of Police Station No. 1 apparently was not enough to inspire universal trust in the force. It may have been the case that the police had adopted an assertive stance toward the citizenry as a consequence of the increase in crime and the rumors of crime.[21]

Public perception of politicians, like that of the police, mixed respect with disgust. Bostonians, like the rest of the country, rejoiced on February 22, 1857, the first observance of the legal holiday of George Washington's birthday. Beneath the surface of the celebration, however, was anxiety about politics and suspicion about the character and intentions of politicians. Several years earlier, in 1854, the Know-Nothings had carried the day, causing quite a bit of excitement, according to Francis Bennett. Their sweep of the city and the state was, in essence, "a revolt of laymen against professionals." The state legislature nevertheless included thirteen members of the clergy in early 1857, possibly a sign of the durability of their authority, or merely a reflection of their abundance in the Bay State. In any event, newspapers and magazines nevertheless regularly condemned politicians because they "sneer at religious excitements," because they were "narrow-minded," caring only for "what concerns their own little clique, or coterie, or party." Too many persons "dictate politics to the devil," endangering the cause of religion and overlooking the fact that "the very history of the country forbids the divorce of politics and religion." In a scathing indictment of politicians, the *Evangelist and Religious Review* in 1857 cast politicians as corrupt deceivers bent on self-enrichment, as hypocrites who had traded their backbones for money: "A screw loose in a man's moral principles constitutes an important item in his political 'availability.' He must be morally flexible, and religiously liberal, in order to be a candidate for office. The man of unquestioned piety is not wanted. He is a stiff-backed puritan. There is no *dough* in his composition." The *Liberator* published the text of a prayer for Christians "to remember the legislature of this state to the throne of Divine Grace," and the prayer was not complimentary: "Save their lives until they may return to their homes, and then put it into the hearts of the people to keep them there, and return men . . . who will do some good." The circus atmosphere of politics in the late 1850s only reinforced popular perception that it was tainted. On the local scene, the Angel Gabriel, with his horn and Scottish accent and wild theatrics, regularly delivered incendiary "political lectures" on street corners in Boston and its suburbs. Reflecting on the national front, Theodore Parker made a list of the epithets James Buchanan's camp attempted to stick onto the Republican candidate John Charles Fremont in the 1856 election. Among other things, Fremont was said to be a "Catholic, Know Nothing, Jesuit, swindler, mutineer, gambler, foreigner, mutineer, duelist, renegade, monster, thief, dog eater, bastard, coward, bully, apostate, villain, cheat, millionaire, bankrupt, Frenchman, Canadian, slaveholder, animal, scoundrel, liar."[22]

BOSTON AND THE WEST

Bostonians were especially anxious as they considered the politics of the settlement of the West. And their anxiety was complex, grounded not only in their perception of deals involving western lands as bad-faith ventures, but in their difficulties in coming to terms with the fact that the nation was in fact moving westward, and that the city increasingly would be hard-pressed to defend its claim to Athenian status. Observing the process of settlement, Bostonians were provoked to think harder about who they were, to define themselves in relation to the West (and to the South), to confront one more layer of the problem of their identity.

Thinking about the West was marked both by interest in the advantages it might offer vis-à-vis Boston, and by certainty that it was inferior to Boston in every way. Echoes of the rivalry with New York were audible in the report of the *Transcript* in 1858 that Chicago was "a city of sewers, rats, and Germans," an ugly mudhole devoid of pretty women and children and policed by stupid-looking men who knew nothing about law and order. Sometimes, conversation about the West focused on its curiosities and the character of the men and women who were settling it. Bostonians flocked to lectures on the West when the speaker was reputed as knowledgeable, as was the case for the lecture at the large Tremont Temple, at which William Milburn spoke in 1854. Families whose sons had gone to California with gold fever passed around the journals that their boys sent back home to them. Virtually everyone knew about "the glittering mines of California" and the "boisterous health and animal spirits" of those who had breathed the pure air of the West. A *Trumpet and Universalist* article entitled "A Western Woman" referred to her "feats of industry," which "will doubtless be regarded as fabulous by many of our delicate and do nothing city ladies." By early summer 1851, the Oregon Territory numbered fifteen thousand transplanted easterners, with thousands more expected by the fall, leading the *Independent* to note with satisfaction that the territory was "rapidly filling up with a most desirable population." That "desirable" population included Germans and Irish from Boston, who somehow became "hard-working," "thrifty," "industrious," and "enterprising," once they crossed the Mississippi River. German Catholics—who on one occasion packed up for the West so fast that they left behind an expensive half-built and never-used church they had been constructing on Tremont Street— were subject to belittlement while they inhabited Boston but were transformed in the pages of magazines such as the *Independent* into industrious pioneers who kept holy the Sabbath in St. Louis in family gatherings featuring "beer gardens, music, and dancing." At the "Irish Romanists" convention in Buffalo in 1856, leaders promoted a plan for Irish settlement of the West which "meets with favor among philanthropic Protestants." In the Boston Protestant imagination, Chicago, St. Louis, California, and all points in between were not even remotely the equal of Boston, but were more than good enough for Germans, Irish, and other out-groups, who appeared almost legitimate against the background of such inferior places. One exception was the Mormons, who were excoriated in the press and loathed by loyal Bostonians such as William Gray Brooks, who in 1858 entered into his diary the premature "good news" that "the Mormon settlement has been broken up by the government—it is hoped that this may be the final death of this detestable establishment."[23]

The churching of the West was a matter of some concern to leaders of Boston's Protestant congregations and reflection on it was conflicted. Protestant churches in Boston and other parts of New England sent money and missionaries westward in the hopes that the settlement of the West would be accompanied by grass-roots Protestantization of the immigrant and native populations. Such enterprise included the efforts not only of numerous association organizations and interdenominational groups, but the initiative of private citizens as well. In 1857, a wealthy man from Boston offered to pay half the expenses for establishing the first two new Sabbath Schools west of the Mississippi and north of Louisiana, with the funding adjusted upward to meet the needs of potentially large enrollments. At the same time, however, the Protestant press fretted that the drain of money to western territories ultimately would impoverish the churches of New England. One article asserted in 1857 that "the money which has flowed from East to West to establish churches must come back again," so that the "feebler churches" of New England which had supplied the funding for westward expansion would "be aided by flourishing, wealthy, western churches, who owe their existence under God, to the Christian enterprise and benevolence of New England."[24]

The mixed feelings of Bostonians about the West were complicated further by the Mexican War and the disastrous consequences of the Kansas-Nebraska legislation, both of which inclined Bostonians toward feelings of fear about the future of the nation that they so proudly claimed to have founded. The war fought with Mexico in 1846–47 was seen by northerners as an attempt by the South to expand the cotton culture and lay the foundation for the admission of new states as slave states. The Missouri Compromise of 1820 had admitted Missouri as a slave state and Maine as a free state, and had established that all territory south of a line 36 degrees

30 minutes within the Louisiana Purchase would thenceforth be admitted as slave states. Well before the war ended with the occupation of Mexico City in September of 1847, Representative David Wilmot of Pennsylvania introduced the Wilmot Proviso, which would have banned slavery in any territory that came under United States control through its war with Mexico. The caustic debate of the failed bill opened the old wounds of the 1820 Compromise, and greatly aggravated regional differences. Bostonians— and especially those in abolitionist circles—accordingly viewed with horror the annexation of the vast tracts of land, virtually the entire American Southwest, derived from the victory over Mexico. The 1850 Compromise, which was engineered (like the Missouri Compromise) by Henry Clay and supported by Daniel Webster, resolved the issue of California's admittance as a free state but did nothing to alleviate the rising tensions over slavery in the West. Four years later, the Kansas-Nebraska Act provided that popular sovereignty be the basis for admission of Kansas and Nebraska as states. Consequently pro-slave and anti-slavery groups organized the settlement of the territories, leading to violence that escalated into war during the 1850s as each side attempted to draw up constitutions for statehood.

The violence of "Bleeding Kansas" moreover was enacted on the floor of Congress, in what William Brooks described as a "disgraceful fracas" involving twenty elected officials. The *Liberator* understandably led the doomed fight against the Kansas-Nebraska Act, a month before its passage, printing a prayer that called upon God in covenantal language reminiscent of a Puritan jeremiad: "O Lord, have mercy upon us, an ungrateful, cruel, and backsliding nation; . . . Forbid, O Lord, that we should, as it were, 'fill up the measure of our national delinquency,' by passing that law for laying open the Nebraska territory to the dark and bloody waves of slavery." The *Independent* warned that the "ballot-box . . . *has* been subverted in Kansas. The bloody revolution is there achieved, and Terror reigns. The question of today is . . . shall the reign of terror be established also in the capitol." In 1858 William Brooks sensed the ominous nature of the crisis, confessing that "the proceedings of Congress are now watched with anxiety as the Kansas matters are drawing to a close." And Elizur Wright saw the extent of that anxiety after he entered into a debate with a man about "the Kansas Controversy" on a train from Boston to New York, and within a short time "almost the whole population of the car crowded around" to participate in it. "Much excitement," wrote fifteen-year-old Arthur Nichols, who later served as a corporal in the Civil War. "Great outrages committed by the pro-slavery party in Kansas against the free state settlers there." George Troup, a young man given to drinking with his friends evenings and week-ends, set aside time from his ambitious schedule of theatre-going and bar-hopping to hear a lecture on Kansas in 1858. Lecturers who predicted disaster filled the largest halls in Boston with persons from all ranks of society. Theodore Parker wrote long and moving prayers about the ongoing tragedy of "Kanzas." Abolitionists entered upon complicated schemes to turn the tide against the organized migrations of slavery supporters. But even the church bell in Lawrence, Kansas, sent to the Unitarian congregation there by their Boston coreligionists, could not stop the violence when it first pealed during the summer of 1856. And Bostonians grew ever more anxious about the West as a whole.[25]

Gamaliel Bradford wrote in 1854 that the "repeal of the Missouri Compromise" had given the South the upper hand in instituting slavery in the West, observing that "the public is so irritated by the passage of the Nebraska bill." Southerners as a class were vilified by the Boston press and cast as devils in diary entries. They were "bullies, who having less care for the avoidance of tumult & bloodshed, are bolder & more arrogant in their demands." They could not speak properly, butchering even the simplest of English words, saying "raiding" instead of "reading." The immensely popular *The Mercy-Seat; or, Thoughts on Prayer*, published in Boston after the outbreak of the Civil War, assured readers that southern prayer was corrupt and not a threat to reach the ear of God. The South regularly perpetrated a "cheat in sanded cotton" upon the north, which had been forced to return ten million dollars worth of the stuff to southern ports. And when South Carolina seceded late in 1860, its particular brand of thievery, "man stealing," made it the moral equivalent of an Irish "thafe." Commenting on the Harper's Ferry debacle, the *Liberator* recalled sadly that once upon a time "the religion of the north and the religion of the south were identical," and "we were like a family of children, all in loving harmony." By the late 1850s, few people in Boston thought of persons in the South as family. Neither did Bostonians expect a return to the days of shared religion and sibling-like collaboration.[26]

THE APPROACHING CRISIS

As Bostonians made their way through the 1850s, their lives became increasingly more complicated. The population of the city, swelled by the arrival of Europeans and by hopefuls from the countryside, and by the dispossessed who sought refuge in seasonal migrations to the city, also lost large numbers of persons to westward migration, to the supposedly pure air of the countryside, and to long summer vacations. The population was volatile, rapidly expanding overall, but characterized by a pattern of defections and instabilities that painted city life as impermanent and contingent. Some persons were wealthy, a great many were poor, and ideas about the quality of life in the city varied widely. The city appeared to some as the Athenic pinnacle of Western achievement, and to others as an ongoing Greek tragedy. Some persons demanded order and supported the creation of laws and ordinances and regulations, the enlargement of the police department, rigorous supervision of public gatherings, the control of public speech, and the ongoing verticalization of the city in brick and mortar. Others protested police actions, scoffed at the liquor and tobacco laws, opposed limitations on public preaching, shook their heads at the futile attempts of the city to positivistically shape behavior, and wrung their hands over the city's inhumane design and ugly face. Persons of different social classes worried about the decay of society, while other persons from those same classes questioned the erosion of personal liberties. For a large part of the population, the city was a vision of both the good and the bad.

Contextualizing these worries was a deeper anxiety born of the realization that Boston would not be the commercial center of North America. And wrapped around that was the anticipation and experience of disaster in all of its everyday forms, from arson to rabies. A city like Cincinnati or Louisville could take comfort in its sense of belonging to a great experiment, a daring, imaginative, heroic movement westward, even after the railroads ordained Chicago as the great new center of American life. With the exception of Harvard graduate Francis Parkman and a few other well-supplied adventurers, Bostonians felt little connection with the West, and even less with the South. And the battle with New York was all but lost. With the old Federalist order in ruins about them, the orthodoxies of the Puritan founders under attack, and, as we shall see, family, gender, and ethnic factors all contributing to the unraveling of tradition, Bostonians teetered on the brink of a crisis.

On the eve of the Businessmen's Revival, Protestant Bostonians faced an assortment of difficult issues regarding the nature of public life and the meaning of being an inhabitant of Boston. At times buoyant and proud of their lives as Bostonians, and at other times fearful and dismayed, they experimented with various means to control public life. But they also resisted efforts to limit their freedom of expression, their public spontaneity—whether that was a boy's prank, a day of "feasting and fun" on Fast Day, displays of "kindness" and "hospitality," or a show of fashion in dress. These mixed impulses came to be represented in particularly coherent fashion in the Businessmen's Revival, during which outpourings of emotion were common, but within carefully defined and rigorously enforced limits. Bostonians who joined the revival believed that emotion was a sublime linkage of the soul to God. But they also constructed it as object, as an aspect of life that could be abstracted from the person, that could be considered as a phenomenon apart from the subject. As such, it could be measured and shaped, controlled, and placed within certain parameters. It also could be stimulated, made brighter and more effervescent, displayed openly, when circumstances indicated that such a course was useful. But the pathway to the right combination of excitation and control was a difficult project framed by multiple contexts of life. Not just the urban experience, but economics, church politics, gender, family, boyculture, theological debate, ethnicity, and various other factors all contributed to the shaping of a certain conceptualization of emotion in the revival. One catalyst for that process was the crash of the financial markets.

THREE

Overexcitement, Economic Collapse, and the Regulation of Business

THE EXCITED MARKET

The Businessmen's Revival manifested both emotional excitement and emotional control. The character of the revival as an occasion for carefully regulated public expression of emotion emerged out of Bostonians' experiences in several overlapping spheres of urban life where the issue of excitement and its regulation was conspicuous. Proud of their city, Bostonians worried that their excitement about its beauties and accomplishments might be exaggerated, and so they bridled it, or neutralized it with expressions of concern for the seeming decay of urban life. They organized numerous occasions on the Common and elsewhere for public shows of gaiety and merrymaking, but at the same time became increasingly anxious about social disorder, enforcing statutes that curtailed activities potentially rich in group enactments of emotion, such as preaching on the Common. Such conceptualizations of city life were reinforced by the events that began in late 1857, when the economy, which had been teetering for several years, finally crashed. Reflecting on the crash, Bostonians agreed that the economy had been overexcited and insufficiently regulated.

Bostonians watched the market closely. They were attuned to its ups and downs, were aware of predictors and of unpredictability, and formed theories about the ways in which it flourished and failed. The history of market volatility in the nineteenth century informed their attention to trading and investment. Having experienced several dramatic upward spikings in the economy, and several market debacles, they knew firsthand about the ways in which cycles of business and finance affected their lives. In fact, they spoke specifically of cycles of "excitement" and "dullness" in business, and they speculated about ways in which to lessen the swing between the two.

The market worked best when it was excited just to the point of frenzy. That is, Bostonians believed that businessmen were responsible for developing a highly active market, an "excited" market, as writers described it, in which activity in each of the various areas of investment, trade, speculation, financial transactions, and the production of commodities spurred activity in all of the others. By directing the flow of capital into appropriate enterprises, by managing pricing and distribution, and by foreseeing trends in the valuing of commodities, businessmen were to keep the economy humming along at maximum capacity. Economic downturns were understood to be the product of overexcitement of the market. When speculation became "frenzied," when managers departed from sound standards of regulation of investment, the market in a burst of activity overheated, burning itself out and collapsing. The trick accordingly was in determining just how far to excite the market, how much capital to feed it, so that it attained peak performance without tumbling out of control.

The businessmen charged with overseeing the delicate machinery of the economy were expected to manifest in their own lives the very principles of regulation and excitement that were thought to underlie the activity of the market. That is, businessmen were to embody a combination of boldness and caution, of fidelity to principles of good business (e.g., fairness, honesty, etc.) alongside a willingness to take risks. In good times, businessmen were praised as moral exemplars, but in bad times, they were admonished as dishonest, mean, and selfish. Their immorality was alternately described either as their failure to control their emotions—a shortcoming that made them subject to early death, particularly by overexcitement of the heart, or heart attack—or as their coldly logical, emotionless approach to life. Or, to simplify, too much emotion was as bad as too little emotion in a businessman. In market terms, excitement without regulation was as detrimental to the economy as was over-regulation that prevented excitement.

Bostonians surveyed the consequences of the crash of 1857 and pronounced themselves deeply impressed by the spectacle of suffering and loss, and the instances of the radical disruption of everyday life. They were, in fact, overwhelmed by the sudden disappearance of money, the string of suicides of prominent businessmen, the shortages of food, and the various other catastrophes associated with the crash. To say that the crash focused their thinking more sharply on matters of social order, excitation of the economy, emotional control, and regulation is an understatement. Bostonians were in shock throughout the winter, stuck on trying to understand what had gone wrong, and how to prevent it from happening again. Leaving no stone unturned in theorizing about the causes of the crash, they considered the banking system, the nature of the market, the behavior and character of businessmen, and the moral dimensions of commerce. The conclusions they reached in each of these areas helped them to assemble a view of emotion that would frame the religious revival the following year.

EXCITEMENT AND THE CRASH

The winter of 1857 was brutal. That might have helped the trade in ice—over 150,000 tons had been sent to New Orleans and Mobile a few years earlier—were it not for the nearly impossible harbor navigation. The plunging temperatures and blizzards went on for weeks, inconveniencing some, killing others, making a winter wonderland of skating and sledding for children sent home from drafty schools too cold to remain open. The winter also proved the last important ingredient in a complex of events that were to send Boston, and the rest of the nation, into a catastrophic economic collapse. With the harbor intermittently iced over, and the railroads half-paralyzed because of the snowdrifts, commerce slowed to a snail's pace. And despite the bravado of the newspapers and the exaggerated claims that the state was open for business as usual, the economy had begun a rapid downward spiral. An overview of the city's affairs published in February noted that the temperatures had plummeted below even the records of the "cold Friday" in 1810, and that "such intense cold, with the drifted snow in our streets and the roads in the country, has been a great obstruction to business." The closing of the railroads and harbor created an "embargo" upon the city, which was "severely felt, and has been the occasion of not a little inconvenience and even embarrassment to not a few of our businessmen."[1]

The Boston economy had been flirting with danger for a decade. The initial enthusiasm for California gold and the massive infusions of capital into its pursuit, the "sudden and hurried outfits of the numbers who have rushed upon the gold regions of California, left very little money in circulation." Twelve- and eighteen-month cycles of boom and bust related to the gold rush continued to unsteady the Boston economy throughout the 1850s. The year 1854 had been a period of scandals involving the overissue of railroad stocks. In 1855, as Gamaliel Bradford wrote, the "chief subject of interest in the community seems to be the condition of the banks," as "stocks have fallen heavily." In 1856 the United States Congress was forced to pass the Deficiency Bill, which put three million dollars back into the banks to prop them up while they waited for "another California arrival of gold" and settlement of accounts with "merchants from the West who don't pay *promptly*." Indeed, most of 1855–1856 was a difficult time for Boston, with its fate linked so closely to that of New York, where "millions, and hundreds of millions during that time have been sunk and lost," so that, said the *Independent*, "it is a wonder that a general crash has not long ere swept over the country." Analysis of stock performance in the Boston Stock Market for the period 1835–1855 shows largely downward trends throughout that time, with significant monthly fluctuations on railroad and manufacturing stocks during 1855 and 1856. Land and mining stocks showed enormous monthly fluctuation in 1856, with some stock doubling or tripling in value, and others losing half or more of their value.[2]

The crux of the matter was, as William Gray Brooks noted, that "property has disappeared almost mysteriously." With the collapse of credit, very little money was in circulation, and consequently, very little commerce. Joanne Harvey wrote that "the scarcity of money is all the theme. there has been no such time since 1837. Factories are stopping—all is alarm there is very little confidence in the banks." The panic of 1837, which seriously affected the New York and Philadelphia economies, with manufacturing and banking stocks losing 50 to 75 percent of their value, had less of an effect on the Massachusetts markets, but had left the city with a case of nerves about the volatility of the economy. Bostonians understood that their economic well-being was linked to that of New York, and so, when the Boston banks began to understand the extent of the crash in New York, they closed their doors, "worried as much about the collapse of markets as the nervousness of the population itself." The *Transcript*, reflecting on "the past month of financial excitement," accordingly reported in October 1857: "Under the present excited state of public feeling, and the embarrassment produced by the New York City Banks, the Boston Banks . . . deemed it advisable to suspend specie payment for the present."

Newspapers reported that the crash of 1857 was the outcome of money injudiciously thrown at railroad stocks and the failure of certain key commodities, such as sugar. Israel Lombard constructed memoranda of the decline in consumption of sugar in 1857, calculating that it fell from 378,760 tons in 1856 to 280,765 tons in 1857. Coffee declined from 218 million tons to 172 million tons. Noting that molasses had lost 40 percent of its value in one month, William Gray Brooks wrote that the fall of 1857 was an "excited time and money affairs are disarrayed," but he had no sympathy for the wiped-out sugar and molasses speculators. While Arthur Howard Nichols attended lectures that addressed "the great Financial crisis with which we are now afflicted," Boston lost 253 businesses to bankruptcy, slightly fewer than in Philadelphia and many fewer than the 915 New York failures. As John Robison, missionary to seamen on Richmond Street, preached about "the great pecuniary embarrassment in the business world," Joanne Harvey confided to her diary that "everyone is talking of hard times," and that "money is very scarce I cannot think what poor people will do, never knew such a time." The crash dominated news reporting and conversation for months, and, as the *Atlantic Monthly* suggested, "that great convulsion of finance which has visited us during the last month" engaged just about everyone in one way or another. Playing upon the word "speculation," the magazine declared that in "a season of great public calamity, moreover, everybody feels that he ought to participate in it in some way, if not as a sufferer then as a sympathizer, and, in either capacity, as a speculator on its causes and probable effects."[3]

Those effects, as felt in Boston and the towns of eastern Massachusetts, included numerous factory closings, many of which later were investigated. Five dry goods businesses went down in one day. The firm of Conant and Edwards failed in September, under the weight of forty-five thousand dollars of liabilities. Pemberton Mills lost a million dollars. When Charles H. Mills and Company—a highly regarded commission house—went under in mid-September it brought a word of worry even to the lips of William Brooks, who wrote that it "strikes everyone with wonder, what we are coming to." In nearby Lawrence, the scene was apocalyptic with torchlight processions and "everyone . . . talking of hard times." Joanne Harvey wrote her son Charles that "manufactures have stopped, all the banks suspended payment—and such a sight as Lawrence presents I should never hope to see—5 thousand people, men, women, and children, nothing to do. Winter coming on, nothing to help themselves with . . . daily begging has already commenced." Railroads, desperately in need of cash to overcome the costs of maintenance from the previous winter, remained in dire straits, and as sea trade contracted, sailors were plentiful and lucky to work for fifteen dollars a month, or about one-seventh the price of a share in the Shawmut Bank the previous year. One survey of the condition of manufactures in the state grimly reported that "the machine shops are, for the most part, closed. The workmen who so lately filled them with the hum and clatter of their industry are sent off to find a livelihood in other vocations, and their skill is lost to the general business. Progress is no longer thought of; . . ."[4]

The crash disordered people's lives in numerous ways, and especially in its effect on the availability of food, shelter, and clothing. "Hard Times" headed many columns in the *Transcript*, introducing stories of shortages.

Already in June 1857, food had become very expensive, especially flour. The Harvey family ran a mill and had a sizable store of flour, which, when sold together with their raisin inventory, produced income that kept them solvent throughout the crisis but did little to alleviate their worry. As in previous economic crises, merchants rushed to get their goods out the door, enormously discounting stock, before their debts came due and they were forced to file bankruptcy. Many nevertheless did go bankrupt because no one had the money for clothes. The *Transcript* ran articles with the lead "Bargains in Clothing" that were little more than advertisements for some of the city's oldest and most esteemed clothiers, such as Howles Clothing House, which was selling "at lower prices than at any other store in Boston." The advertising columns of the city's paper were themselves filled with bargains, ranging from 30 percent off on frocks and silk vests for gentlemen, to "winter clothing at auction prices," to mourning dress goods such as "bombazines, paramattas, thibets, cashmeres, coburgs, alpaecas, satin du chine," and "English prints." Such sales made barely a dent in stock. Early in 1858, "immense and unsaleable stacks of merchandise" were piled up in warehouses.[5]

The poor spent the winter jammed into large halls or on the street. Women planned a fair for the poor in February 1858, because "many are anxious to relieve but know not how or where to give." The organizers asked the Boston Provident Society to distribute the money the event raised. The Society's report two months later referred to "the Fair, whose results have been so brilliant and bountiful"; the fair enabled the Society to provide flour and meal, clothes, shoes, sheets, bonnets, and other items to 2,048 families. About the same time, the Boston Society for the Prevention of Pauperism managed to find jobs for "65 Americans or protestants; 296 others," although they were unable to place another nine hundred persons, most of whom were "others." In March, the city made public plans to launch a "Pawner's Bank" as a "great convenience and relief to the poor." But the efforts of organizations and individuals fell far short of caring for everyone hurt by the crash. Joanne Harvey guessed that "our <u>Poorhouses</u> must be filled to overflowing." "Friendless foreigners," especially, "are objects of compassion." But William Gray Brooks took exception to so much of the city's charitable largesse being directed toward the immigrant population. Noting that many fairs and benefits were held during December 1857, he declared that "the greatest difficulty in dispensing charity at such times is when the laboring classes are out of employ and suffering—those who need it most do not get it—they are a class that will not make their sufferings known while the Irish beggars get it all." The *Advertiser* and

Transcript both published articles urging persons not to suspend their charitable giving as the economy improved. There was, as Joanne Harvey wrote, "still much suffering among the <u>poor</u>!"[6]

Impressed by the suffering of the poor, Bostonians also were affected by the stories of suicides of prosperous businessmen who had been wiped out by the crash. Suspecting that big financial losses were instances in which persons had let their emotions get the better of them in speculation on high-risk ventures, Bostonians historically had looked with mixed feelings on cases in which personal fortunes were lost. William Gray Brooks's remark that he had little sympathy for ruined speculators was grounded in a perspective that had developed over the decade of the 1850s as fortunes came and went against the background of California gold. Henry Haynes reflected on the shame of a doctor who had died in 1851 and left his family destitute because he had lost all his money in speculation. Gamaliel Bradford had written in 1854 that "it is the most melancholy sight in the world to see a man who has actually failed." Seeing such a man in the person of his friend Willie, Bradford surmised, "How reckless he must have been." Such failures were frequently reported in the press, as in the case of Samuel Sanford, one of the oldest merchants in Boston, whose debts of six hundred thousand dollars were settled by a commissioner of the state of Massachusetts in 1855. Also reported were the cases of businessmen who were unable to settle, and whose disappearances were presumed suicides. When J. B. Kilbourn of French, Wells & Company disappeared in the late fall of 1855, Gamaliel Bradford wrote that many persons believed he had taken his life. It was simple, wrote William Brooks, observing the panic on the last day of 1857: many of the "wealthy class" had lost their money and were now poor, or dead. George Troup knew a man who committed suicide in a boarding house in January 1858. Henry Larcom Abbot saw a suicide in the canal in April. Sylvester Barnard hanged himself in the cellar of his house that month because of "low spirits, arising from a want of business." The papers reported frequently on "well-dressed" men who were discovered drowned in the waterways around the city. Reports usually referred to "an unknown man." Joseph G. Jameson, a bookkeeper at Chase Brothers & Company, cut a jugular with his razor and died at his parents' house in June. Charles French knew of an official of the Merchant's Bank who hanged himself in the bank's cellar after losing money in speculation a few years earlier.[7]

The papers likewise reported the stories of ruined speculators who went insane. The *Evangelist and Religious Review* claimed in the aftermath of the crash that "a large proportion of the cases of insanity which have arisen from other than physical disorders, have been clearly traced to the commercial crisis." Shortly thereafter, it reported on the case of a man "who became insane as a consequence of a failure in business." The man's explanation, delivered from inside an asylum, was carefully considered: "I am here because of a mere mistake in business. I was engaged during the winter in making mosquitoes wings which I expected to sell in the summer. I had ten thousand of them on hand when the season opened, but unfortunately I had forgotten to make them in pairs. They were all left-handed wings and consequently I lost the sale of them, and was compelled to suspend payment!"[8]

Petty crime was more easily excused than the irresponsible actions of the speculators whose frenzied greed was blamed for the crash. Hard times brought a wave of crime to Boston, from pickpocketing and shoplifting to burglary, called "shopbreaking" or "housebreaking." Churches and their assembled congregations were as likely targets as any other. The Catholic pastor of St. Mary's Church, Father McElroy, warned his congregation in the midst of a service to "beware of the scamps" who were working the church. Even as he spoke eight persons were relieved of their pocketbooks and purses. A women's pickpocketing gang worked the evening shift near Police Station No. 7, the only station without telegraph. Such criminality, though widespread, placed second to the reports of wrongdoing in the financial houses and trading concerns, however. The *Watchman and Reflector* had warned just before the crash that "there exists also an alarming debauchery of public morals in the walks of business and political life. . . . Breaches of trust have become every day occurrences in commercial life. . . ." During the crash, newspapers and magazines throughout the Northeast redoubled the message. The *Independent* condemned check kiting—suspected as a common practice in many firms—as an "abomination" and demanded that "the law should take hold of this class of frauds" and treat its perpetrators as guilty. Speculation was labeled an evil, and condemned everywhere. The *New Englander* declared that a "most powerful evil in our commercial economy is the habit of over-trading and the abuse of credit. Few American merchants think they are doing business enough, so long as there is any chance of doing more." Specifically condemning "stock-gambling" and extreme leveraging of assets, the magazine reviled "the power of ignorant or stupid financiers to work mischief," and, true to the feud with New York, summed up the blameworthy actions of the New York banks in a single phrase: "they recklessly continued.[9]

Analysis of the causes of the crash never deviated from the core observation of lack of control expressed in the ubiquitous terms "the excited market" and "reckless speculation." Typical was the Boston Board of Trade report issued in the spring of 1858, which addressed "the recent monetary difficulties and mercantile embarrassments." The report blamed the tariff of 1846, the short crop of Louisiana sugar, and difficulties arising from the overextension of cotton and woolen manufacturing, all of which, in their own ways, led to excessive importation (and a consequent decrease in consumption because of spiked prices). At the bottom, said the report, abuse of credit and reckless mismanagement in the banking system produced the crises. *Currency Explosions, Their Cause and Cure* (1858) likewise concluded that the root cause of the crisis was the "barbaric system that now prevails in banking." *A Report of the Currency* (1858) was more direct in its consideration of "currency thrown into one of its paroxysms of extreme expansion by the undue enlargement of bank loans . . . [and] overtrading, imprudent credits, reckless speculations, and numerous enterprises of questionable utility and still more questionable morality."[10] All of this news was particularly bitter in view of the claim made by the Boston Board of Trade that speculation had been encouraged by the discovery of gold in California, which had been *"apparently* held in reserve until the advancing civilization of the world had reached a period when . . . events, so sudden and peculiar, placed those resources under the control of the Anglo-Saxon race—a race which seemed eminently qualified to advance the great enterprise of Christian civilization."[11]

Mismanagement had overexcited the market. So much was clear to the young clerks and trainees—the aspiring businessmen—of the Franklin Scientific Association when they met shortly before Christmas, 1857 to debate "the Present Financial Crisis." One disputant "called attention to the blindness which was evinced by many of the mercantile community in conducting the details of their profession," and added that "abuse of the credit system" was to blame as well. His opponent called attention to the "defective system of banking laws" and the regrettable "facility with which credit was obtained." Following discussion, the Association passed a resolution that attributed the crisis to four corrupt practices: (1) "a defective system of banking"; (2) "a ruinous tariff"; (3) "domestic overtrading" that led to "exhaustion of credit"; and (4) "speculation," which "must cause an excited state of the market, prejudicial to the best interests of the public." In short, inadequate rules of exchange, together with failure to abide by those that were accepted as legitimate, led to an "excited" state of the market and financial catastrophe.[12]

The first step in preventing a repeat of the events of 1857, claimed a key report, was to limit the frenzied speculation by enacting strict regulations.

In his address to the American Statistical Association in Boston early in 1858, Samuel Hurd Walley explained the precipitating causes of the crash as "mismanagement of the New York banks" and, especially, their "lending to railroads," which were expanding too rapidly. The "Pandora's Box" of problems that resulted was grounded, however, in a simple truth: "In fine, a spirit of mad and reckless speculation has ruled the hour, and we see and deplore its vile effects." The solution to the problem, argued Walley, was "regulation." The *Independent* previously had proposed that "the time has come when a more rigid credit system must be adopted" because "failures" of businesses "can be directly traced either to recklessness or bad management." It proposed that the issuance of credit be placed under the authority of a set of rules, broaching limits on loan amounts and repayment timetables, and urging ascertainment of sound character in the borrower. That recommendation was taken seriously by E. P. Bigelow, who, in his paper on the crash in Massachusetts, added that regulation should include the provision that no new large corporations be permitted to form in the state. And the Boston Board of Trade published an exceptionally vigorous demand for reform. "The banking system," said the report, "should be regulated by legislation, so as to confine it within the following bounds," and those bounds, as defined by the report, were confining indeed.[13]

The language employed by Bostonians to describe the relationship between the "spirit of mad and reckless speculation" and everyday business was redolent with assumptions about the emotionally driven activities of investors. The *New Englander* referred to such enterprise as "the nervous intentness and restless vigilance which characterize our business community," transformed into a frenzy of wild and highly speculative transactions. That process that led ultimately, through a series of steps, to the depletion of the economic movement or excitement necessary for the everyday functioning of business. Accordingly, at the same time that persons laid the blame for the crash on the mad and reckless spirit of investors and financial institutions, they noted the inactive state of business around town. The *Transcript* reported that "business of all kinds is dull throughout the town." George Troup wrote, "dull as ever in the business way." John Henry Kenneally believed that November 1857 was "dull times for everybody." Charles French gave the term a twist with his observation of "terrible dull times." And William Gray Brooks mourned for the spent energy of the economy, writing that "this has been a dull month for business, and after passing through such a crisis as we have we cannot expect anything better at present." The regulation of banking, which was undertaken as a way to conserve the actual cash assets of large lending institutions, was, then, also the regulation of the excitement that animated the economy. Excitement, like cash, was to be conserved, rather than spent recklessly in a mad spirit.[14]

The recovery of business accordingly rested on new activity in the market. Just as Doctor Benjamin Rush and some of his followers had prescribed wine as a means to rouse a person from dullness—wine, we will see, warmed the emotions and sparked "excitement" or "motion" in the system[15]—so Bostonians expected that the infusion of money into the market would revive business. As William Gray Brooks put the matter, money was "like a drug in the market," exciting it back into operation in 1858. The revival was slow and was retarded in the West, but it encompassed nearly all manufacturing and import firms, including some, such as the Pembroke Forge Company of Boston, which had been shut down for three years. Revenues collected by the port of Boston rose steadily in the late spring and summer of 1858, and the busy wharves in east Boston, where over three hundred vessels had docked the previous summer, began to come alive. Vessels laden with raw materials from Asia, Africa, and the West Indies arrived at the docks in ever-increasing numbers, and the marriage rate, which had plunged during the crash because young men thought themselves too poor to marry, returned to normal levels. The *Transcript* with some confidence accordingly declared in the spring that "<u>trade,</u> in this city, has improved considerably; in some branches of business, the improvement is more apparent than others, but all are experiencing a 'revival.'" At the same time it assured its readers that "there is no danger, however, of our traders extending their businesses beyond safe limits."[16]

The choice of the word "revival" to describe the recovery of business moreover reflected the manner in which thinking about the economy was connected to thinking about the revival of religion, which had developed a critical mass of participants by early spring 1858. Both rested on stimulation or "excitements," and both were carried out with an eye to limits. For some Bostonians, the similarities were made thinkable through articulations of a cause-and-effect linkage. Such a conceptualization overlooked the structural similarities—no one was likely to propose that revivalism and economic recovery were grounded in a common dynamic—but posited kinship nevertheless. Referring to the crash, the *New Englander* proposed to "trace back this movement of the past winter more specially to that which we have made the third of the causes of revival action in the church, and show how the fearful disasters of the autumn, and the general depression and gloom which settled over men's earthly interests and hopes, rather than anything peculiar within the church itself, were the predisposing causes of this present religious interest." The *Transcript* was more blunt, citing an article that claimed "that it is a singular fact that almost all of our great commercial revulsions have been succeeded by a great revival of religion." The *Liberator* exploited the perceived connection in criticizing clergy who stand by "watching the moment when a lull in business, or the cholera, or some other cause, brings on a reaction to seriousness, and then deliberately work up the inflammable material into one of these fanatical awakenings." The *Evangelist and Religious Review*, exploring more difficult terrain, worried that "the revival of business might interfere with the progress of the revival of religion." The message was that an economic recovery would lift the pall of gloom and in so doing rob the revival of the emotion that powered it. All such discourse reinforced ongoing objectification of emotion. Commentators wrote that the revival, coming on the heels of the financial "revulsion," was driven by exploitation of the powerful emotion of gloom. Just as money was a drug to the revival of the market, the "inflammable" stockpile of gloom served the religious revival. Whether gloom, specifically, was the emotion behind the revival is inconsequential. What matters is the perception of revival as a cultural event grounded in the expenditure of a quantity of emotion. How, why, and by what rules that emotion was expended we shall consider later.[17]

BUSINESS AND THE CONTROL OF EMOTION

The nineteenth century gave birth to a wide assortment of theories about economic and historical cycles. The theorizing was ambitious and sometimes included speculations about not only the nuts and bolts of economics, and clearly trackable historical phenomena such as wars, but more subtle aspects of social life as well. One writer in fact suggested in 1855 that collective feeling, the mood of a people, could be predicted according to a theory of cycles. Exploring "the fluctuations of human feeling" as "periods of rise and fall," the author stated: "So through a whole community, the public feelings ebb and flow like those of an individual. It is so in business and in politics, and in all questions of public improvement and reform." Instancing the theory with respect to the national mood, the author proposed that "a whole nation rises to carry some political object, or to honor a favorite son, and throbs like a beating heart with the force of great emotion. Yet a little while, and this excitement subsides, and after the storm there is a great calm." Accordingly, "there are tides in human feelings, as well as in the atmosphere and the ocean."[18]

The notion of cycles of public feeling formed part of the context for perception of the crash as the "dull" counterpart to the highly excited market. Another part of that context was constructed of perceptions of those who acted on the stage of business, the people who made, sold, and delivered goods and services. One writer identified the "MAN OF BUSINESS" as "not the merchant or the trader only," but "all those whose vocation is to organize and direct the industrial forces of the community—the manufacturer, the master mechanic, the contractor, or the superintendent. . . ." Hatting and clothing were major industries in Boston, alongside railroading, importing, and banking. There were 218 shoe houses in Boston in 1858, and every eighth man worked in the shoe business. Because "competition is the life of business," firms large and small frequently risked significant loss in order to survive, sometimes behaving more like buccaneers than brokers. Young male clerks and aspirants to business success were overworked and bored, as Gamaliel Bradford wrote in his diary, with "business too monotonous and uninteresting to appear here." They worked without knowledge of the boss's plans, and, like Francis Bennett, might show up one day to discover "that he was going to sell out and go away. . . . The news came rather unexpected to me." Twenty-year-old Fred Harvey, a typical young clerk, worked at Wilbon's Chemist at the corner of Court and Bullfinch for an annual salary of three hundred dollars. The farm wage at the time was in the neighborhood of twelve to fifteen dollars a month, and a reasonably comfortable boarding house room was two dollars a week. The owners of businesses made much more than that, with thirty to forty thousand dollars a year considered a very handsome income. They socialized in fraternal organizations, such as the Wednesday Evening Century Club, which admitted William Greenough as a member in 1858 under the membership category of "Merchants, Manufacturers, and Gentlemen of Literature and Leisure." Some thought commerce, and those involved in it, to be the glue that joined person to person in goodwill. *Ballou's* suggested that commerce "unites distant branches of the human family, cultivates the relation between them, encourages an interest in each other, and promotes that brotherly feeling which is the strongest guarantee of a permanent friendship."[19]

Literature, ministers, parents, teachers, and art fashioned the ideal businessman as a person whose integrity and determination were the bedrock of his success. Leman Thomas Ride's *The Art of Money-Getting; Showing the Means by Which an Individual May Obtain and Retain Health, Wealth, and Happiness,* published in Boston in 1832, listed ten key characteristics of the "man of business": "1. Education 2. Good Sense 3. Virtue 4. Temperance 5. Regulation of Time 6. Punctuality 7. Ease in doing business 8. Proper expense in living 9. Aversion to the various branches of gaming 10. Firmness of mind to support his character." Subsequent publications developed one or more of Ride's themes. Fifteen years later, *The Man of Business*, which advertised itself as "a volume designed especially for the counsel and instruction of young men entering into business," outlined "the habits which the clerk and the young merchant may form," and especially those of punctuality, industry, honesty, and temperance. By late 1858 the *Evangelist and Religious Review* had boiled it down to industry: "Make up your mind to accomplish whatever you undertake; decide upon some particular employment and persevere in it."[20]

The *Christian Parlor Magazine* invoked Poor Richard to press the case for "honest industry," and the *Trumpet and Universalist* stressed that above all a person had "to be active and industrious, rather than idle and lazy." *The Young Man's Friend* devoted an entire section to "Industry," explaining that "correct business habits" exemplified industry in practice and stressing that "industry is honorable" and that a habit of perseverance was essential to avoid being "deluded by some gold-mine monomania." Like numerous other moral guidebooks it stressed punctuality and honesty as well. Because industry enabled one "to grasp the prizes of society," it was essential that one not be fooled into believing that success, as the *Massachusetts Teacher* warned, arose "from lucky thoughts and out-of-the-way expedients." It was equally true, however, that wealth was "no proof of virtue." Such advice, geared especially to young men in a position to go off to the gold mines or willing to take great risks in a get-rich-quick scheme, was couched largely in the vocabulary of business rather than of religion, and directly challenged the scenario of a gold strike or sudden arrival of a trading vessel laden with coffee. Accordingly, it was not unusual for a magazine such as the *Youth's Companion*, in discussing "truth, honesty, and integrity . . . decision, courage, firmness, and perseverance," to declare: "And it does not take a great while to accumulate a respectable amount of this capital." The *Christian Observatory* was more direct: "The virtuous habits which religion cherishes, naturally lead to the accumulation of property, till the heap becomes too heavy for the floor, and the burdened timbers sink beneath the weight." And there were stories in the religious press about boys who failed to embrace the businessman's virtues. The *Watchman-Examiner* reported on ten boys who had so failed, noting that "one of them is now living in a reputable employment; the other nine became openly vicious. All failed in business and are now dead."[21]

Boys were exposed to this message of success at home, in school, in churches, and lecture-rooms, and in their reading (which included the penny press). Many embraced it. Henry Haynes, a young Latin teacher, gathered with his friends to smoke and talk one evening in the fall of 1858, and, in the course of seven cigars, he "discussed the prospect of young lawyers in Boston. We came to the conclusion that if a young man will be honorable and industrious, he will find business." Alfred Mason Badger, a building contractor, absorbed the message over the course of a lifetime and left an obituary that praised "his enterprise, intelligence, and methodical business habits." Those good habits, understood as the product of a properly engineered boyhood, were the lifeblood of business success at the same time that they subverted other aspects of the businessman's life. When the *New Englander* preached "habits of self-reliance and patient thought," it was not proposing the Emersonian gospel of "sincerity," or any other vision of harmony between a supposed private man of feeling and the activities of public life. Rather, it was emphasizing the importance of duty, of a degree of commitment to industry and perseverance that might hasten success in the business world, and, especially, independence of thought and action in service to commerce.[22]

Business nevertheless was constantly assailed as a world of corruption, duplicity, and meanness. A poem published in the *Boston Anthology and Monthly Review* criticized the city for its devotion to Mammon:

> Boston, thou mart admir'd whose
> prosperous care
> To *Mammon* breathes the vow, and
> pours the prayer,
> Whose throng'd exchange, to christian
> jews a prey,
> Scares the kind hope of liberal trade
> away;
> GOLD is thy GOD, on that thy soul
> relies;
> Beneath whose worship every virtue
> dies,
> Hence, the hush'd banker, scorning to
> relent,
> Till his stor'd coffer teem with cent
> per cent.[23]

A poet from Housatonic, Massachusetts, echoing the theme of "christian jews," usurers who make money unnaturally through the accumulation of interest on their capital, called up the image of a Shakespearean character to make a similar point:

> Will the Wall Street convert spare
> The Shylock knife, and *rest* content?
> Do as he's be done by *there,*
> While interest calls, through cent. per cent.?[24]

Insiders as well as outsiders condemned the Boston business world. Serving a term of fifteen years for forgery, a man in the Charlestown prison bitterly declared in his diary: "Boston—the home of the shrewdest Brokers and Merchants in the Union." Young clerks who observed the mechanics of commerce from their desks and counters inside the firms thought the problem was escalating, turning people into monsters and businesses into the monstrous machinery of greed. Charles French was anxious about a senior trader who was "contemptibly mean, and would cheat a man out of his 'eye teeth' if he could. I like to see a man economical, but can't bear to see a man as mean as he is." For French, the prosperity of the business only aggravated the problem: "The fact is, the firm is getting meaner and meaner, the more money they make." When a member of the board of his company died at the age of eighty-five, Gamaliel Bradford, sixty years younger than the deceased, wrote that the man had practiced good manners, but was "profoundly selfish, though perhaps not more so than all who become rich." The *Massachusetts Teacher* fretted over "the want of honest men" in business, observing that "in trade, assertions are frequently made, which are known to be wrong, or spurious articles are sold for genuine goods." The *Christian Observatory* openly assailed the character of men of business: "In most men of our times, what is termed their consciences seems to be a substitute made, for the most part, of some kind of gum elastic, capable of indefinite expansion, and of being twisted all sorts of ways; so that the owners can sincerely hold that profit is principle, and 'gain is godliness.'" *How to do Business. a pocket manual of practical affairs, and Guide to success in Life* vigorously attacked duplicity in trade, and a writer in the *Evangelist and Religious Review* argued that business practice was so thoroughly infused with trickery that businessmen unknowingly exuded it in an assortment of contexts as an "unconscious influence": "'When you are not thinking' do your clerks, your partner, and those you meet on Change, see you manifesting an unbecoming thirst for gold, stooping to tricks of trade, overreaching the unwary, exacting undue service from those in your employ, and capricious in your temper?" The Leyden Chapel thought the problem was as serious as theatre, identifying as one class of unworthy communicants "All who do not keep their word in business."[25]

Throughout the 1850s ministers and the religious press sustained a stream of criticisms of business and the worship of money. The *Watchman and Reflector* said that "the exposure of men in our community to the perils that lie along the highway of commerce and wealth, is not duly gauged and considered," and, in fact, was "growing with the increased spirit of activity and speculation now abroad." The *Watchman* warned that "Mammon has corrupted and destroyed untold multitudes," because "he has attracted to himself the homage of their hearts." Ezra Stiles Gannett, a man not unaccustomed to comfort, preached a "state of the country" sermon in 1856 in which he railed against American greed and especially American "habits of extravagance." *The Young Man's Friend* urged its readers to avoid the "altar of Mammon." Albert Barnes, in a series of sermons published in the *American National Preacher* and widely reviewed in eastern cities, declared that "the love of gain has become, and still is our besetting sin." James Barnard Blake heard a sermon about the evil of a person going to "prayer meeting in the evening and dealing unfairly with his neighbor the following morning." The *Independent* spelled the matter out in simple terms: "On Sunday, the exemplary merchant hears from the pulpit, 'Look not every man on his own things, but every man also on the things of others,' and he says amen to that. On Monday he hears the genius of Commerce say, 'Every man for himself,' and he says Amen to that. He has one conscience for Sunday and another conscience for Monday." The Rev. James Coolidge, in a sermon to the Boston Young Men's Christian Union in 1853, told that boys that "we have always been, but never more than now, a money-getting and a money-loving people" who have a "passion for gain." Some of the boys listened, and probably spread the message to their friends. Influenced by the campaign of ministers, teachers, and religious magazines that complained that "success is the god that all men worship," they thought twice about their futures. In the case of John Townsend Trowbridge, the picture of corruption in business took hold early, influencing him at the age of twenty-two to "keep my *nom de plume* unspotted from the world of business."[26]

As was clear from *Jimmy, a Christian*, a booklet published by the Massachusetts Sabbath School Society in 1859, the world itself crushed sensitivity out of a person unless valiantly resisted. Little Jimmy, a diseased thirteen-year-old on crutches, peddled pins and trinkets to passersby on a street corner, but fared poorly because people had "no sympathy in their hard faces for the sensitive heart," and Jimmy's own hardened mother, unable to fathom his failure to sell, beat him to death. In the words of Tracy

Patch Cheever, "the busy *world* is heedless, while the great procession of the dead is marching on." Heedless, indeed, of "The True Object in Life," which, as it appeared in the agriculturally inclined pages of the *Massachusetts Ploughman,* was unmistakably dissociated from business. "Commerce," said the magazine, "or any pursuit which is usually called business, is unworthy of being considered the proper occasion of life." Quoting freely from other material, the paper mocked the "mere man of business, a mere slave of men's bodily necessities, a mere idolater of his own purse; . . . his mind like the advertising side of a daily gazette, or the weekly prices current; the sum of his life the balance sheet of his ledger; and who estimates his worth by the dollars and cents that remain to his credit, who would choose for his immortality one eternal Wall street." Such a man had no heart, no feeling, no practice of the economy of the emotions, and at the end of his day's work desperately sought to fill the void, to "dawdle over ephemeral magazines, or newspaper reports of police causes and shocking incidents, . . . exhaust his breath in blowing up every bubble of popular excitement, lisp idle gallantries in ladies' ears, who in their souls despise such emptiness, and but tolerate the fool as they do a pet dog, or a parrot." In language reminiscent of John Trowbridge's anxiety about spoiling his good name, the *Ploughman* declared: "Were I such a man, I would wish my name to die with me, and would ask neither marble not granite . . . to preserve the memory of my sordid selfishness."[27]

"Cold logic," said the *Independent.* "Practical commerce, at best, is as cold as a stone. *Business is business.*" Borrowing language from standard medical warnings about overthinking, the *Massachusetts Teacher* observed that "the close application to business, and incessant intellectual activity which mark the times, have a tendency to check the flow of affection and harden the heart. . . ." Gamaliel Bradford wrote that people replaced their capability to feel with "stern calculations" as "we get into the cold selfish training of the world." Tracy Patch Cheever breathed a sigh of relief as his business took an upward turn in 1854, confessing, "I can truly say that I do not wish my mind to be crusted over with mere business, as to lose either the freshness of feeling, or that higher discipline for the character." Without feeling, the life of the businessman was reduced to mere numbers. *Gleason's* regretted the merchant who would "look upon his children as so many daybooks and ledgers." Obversely, as the *Massachusetts Teacher* pointed out, the "Love of Business" ordinarily "begets in the youthful mind, first, an indifference to the feelings of the parent, and then to the welfare of society." The *Evangelist and Religious Review* suggested that "successful men" were determined, focused, single-minded, and so uncompromising when it came to mastering their passions, that they "know no medium." The magazine asserted that "to be successful and happy costs something." It advised boys who aspired to business: "Away with homesickness and querelous imbecility! Tear up those whining epistles which you have written home. . . . Brace your nerves to meet every engagement." This terrible system, linked to the tyranny of gender roles (as we shall see later), was, said Abby Kelley Foster, the cause of "man . . . reduced to the mere machine for calculating and getting money that he now is." And the toll on everyday life was enormous. Teachers, in their relations with students, "may treat the whole operation as a mere financial, business transaction." A man might not have ruined his relationship with his spouse, and been forced to admit too late that, like the grieving husband of Nellie Brown, he had "been so wickedly absorbed in my business." Even woman, who, with her "keen perception of right and wrong" ordinarily was not employed in "matters of business. . . . in an occupation that would debase her," might suffer through contagion, through her association with men. That issue, which was contextualized by lyceum and newspaper debates over women's rights during the 1850s, was frankly raised in 1853 by *Gleason's*, which invented an "incredulous stranger" who wondered if "Boston women. . . . so business-like, must be a very stern cold set, not at all sociable and gay."[28]

BUSINESSMEN BETWIXT AND BETWEEN

The businessman was idealized in magazines, novels, newspapers, sermons, and the theatre as industrious, persevering, punctual, and methodical, a picture-perfect case of childhood training in virtue brought to fruition in a calling to commerce. At the same time, businessmen were excoriated in print for their duplicity, meanness, trickery, greed, and hardened hearts. Business "crowded devotion out of many so-called religious families." It produced a man who "too much loved the world," and who "devoted the great bulk of his life to business, 'and only a little corner to God.'" Businessmen had "proclivities towards infidelity," were crippled in the conscience, and were well known for heart attacks, the result of their overattention to business and unfeeling relations with their families. The "antagonism between Commerce and Christianity" had led even to the closings of houses of worship in the center of the city due to the expansion of business.[29]

The social role of the businessman, as it was conceived in Boston at midcentury, was, however, a most difficult performance. Businessmen were expected to excite the economy through investment and trade, through speculation on markets futures, through the assumption of risk. The economic system was vitally dependent on such activity, and the businessman, as the agent of such activity, was responsible not only for profits in connection with his own interests, but for the economic health of the nation. "To this class every other community is a debtor," said the *Evangelist*, in ironic language. What could a laborer, clergyman, physician, artisan, scientist, statesman, or any other person accomplish "but for the reliance they are allowed to place on the skill, energy, activity, and faithfulness of the man of business? . . . This class forms the very sinews, ligaments, and conducting arteries of all social organization. He acts as mediator between the individual and the community, and by his agency alone the possessions, talents, and achievements of one acquire a real value for all." Commerce, and the businessman as its agent, "promotes that brotherly feeling."[30]

Businessmen on the other hand were cast as Shylocks who put profit margin ahead of all other concerns. They labored under the burden of four distinct national financial collapses in the nineteenth century, the panic of 1857 being the most severe. They were portrayed—in many cases appropriately—as the cause of those crises, as greedy and reckless business buccaneers whose lust for profits drove speculation sky-high until it collapsed under its own weight.

Businessmen, then, worked in a system that was thought to operate maximally when it was stimulated to the edge of overexcitement. Businessmen were expected to be ambitious, but to control their emotions as well. When the economy failed in 1857, popular sentiment maintained that businessmen had failed to live up to their roles. When Bostonians rethought the nature of the economy—and agreed on the need for regulation—they thought as well about businessmen and pronounced them similarly in need of personal regulation.

The religious excitement that broke out on the heels of the crash developed in conformity with a century of thinking about revival that balanced the wish for a mass stirring of the affections against the hope that such a movement could be disciplined. But during times when there was no revival, when ministers worried about the seemingly low estate of religion and congregations wondered when a season of refreshment would commence, persons were inclined to strategies of renewal that risked overexcitement, to search out ambitiously and unqualifiedly the ways in which the affections might be moved. Like businessmen whose financial risk taking primed the economy, Protestants were inclined to practice their own species of entrepreneurship, to call for the excitation of emotion, in "dull" times. The *Puritan Recorder* in 1850 had enunciated this predilection when it proposed that people ought to pray for an emotionally charged revival of religion and trust God to guide them in how to discipline it: "The question of immediate urgency is, 'How shall we obtain a revival?' rather than, 'How shall it be regulated?'" So strong was this tradition of seeking revival, that even the vision of financial overexcitement that eventuated in the crash of 1857 could not diminish the eagerness with which Boston Protestants anticipated a re-emergence of emotional religion. One consequence of the crash, however, was to lend at atmosphere of control to the revival when it did finally reach a critical mass in Boston in the spring of 1858.[31]

The pursuit of revival, a virtually constant theme in nineteenth-century Protestantism, was part of a larger cultural phenomenon, the pursuit of feeling. As Bostonians by degrees approached revival in 1858, they drew upon a background of familiarity with a wide assortment of public performances of emotion. Bostonians knew what excited them, and how that excitement was to be sought out and structured in various kinds of public display. And even in hard times, even in times when people blamed overexcitement in the market for a host of woes, the lure of feeling was irresistible.

FOUR

Emotion, Collective Performance, and Value

PURSUING FEELING

The Businessmen's Revival in Boston was an exercise in the collective performance of emotion. As it emerged against a complex of overlapping backgrounds that shaped it in various ways, it certainly was not exclusively about emotion. But among the various components that eventually made up the revival, none was more important than the display of emotion by persons gathered in groups large and small, in churches, chapels, theatres, homes, basements, on board ships in the harbor, and in outdoor settings. That display of emotion—in its general contours if not in all of its details—conformed to Protestant expectation for raised affections as part of a revival of religion. It was also in keeping with the pursuit of feeling in everyday life in Boston, in public settings and in private ones, in highly organized public performances that set specific limits for emotional display as well as in off-the-cuff displays of collective feeling. Bostonians were in the habit of constructing occasions for public emotional display, and they were in the habit as well of finding cause for such public display through participation in events that were much less planned, or even entirely unexpected. A fire was as effective in generating a collective performance of emotion as was a parade scheduled to honor the city's founders.

Experienced in the collective expression of their feelings through their participation in various kinds of public events—indeed, repeatedly schooled and reviewed in cultural expectations for that expression as occasions warranted it—Bostonians developed opinions about the nature of emotion: its causes, its uses, and its ends. They debated theories about emotion in newspapers and journals, and from the pulpit, at the lyceum, and in the home. Beneath the surface of this discourse, imbedded in the language about the excitement of emotion, the limits to its display, and the consequences of feeling, was an understanding of emotion as an object, as a "thing" that could be "gotten." This objectification of emotion flowed into an allied understanding, namely, that emotion was a commodity, and as such could be acquired just like any other commodity, that is, for a price.

Fires were free. That is, one was not charged a fee to witness a fire. The same was true with parades and other public celebrations. People learned how and when to hoot and holler, hush and whisper, through participation in such spectacles. Those lessons were reinforced and refined through the experience of various kinds of staged occasions for the exercise of emotion. Bostonians paid to enjoy laughter at comedies and circuses, and paid as well to lament together the unjust fate of a heroine or otherwise to feel melancholy or outrage while attending a dramatic production at one of the many theatres in the city. Men and women paid to attend lyceum poetry readings—where a pulling on the heartstrings was all but guaranteed—and to have their passions roused by music. The efflorescence of a literary culture strengthened the idea of emotion as a commodity, as a broad readership purchased the thrill of reading a sensationalized account in the penny presses, or shelled out more than just pennies for the feelings derived from more richly textured fictions in novels.

Critics of dramatic productions and the booming literary trade operated out of the same general set of assumptions about emotion as did those who bought season tickets to the theatre. They, too, objectified emotion, treating it like a valuable commodity, like gold, in their railings against the "unnatural" expenditure of emotion, in the auditorium or through a person's involvement in a story line. For these critics, the great sin was to "waste" emotion, to squander it crying over a novel, or breathless, on the edge of one's seat, to spill it at a play, as part of an audience that moaned and clapped its collective experience of various feelings. Depending on one's point of view, one might spend money to experience, to obtain, emotion as a member of an audience, or one took care to avoid spending one's own emotion on a play. Either way, the tendency was to objectify emotion as something that could be purchased or something that could be spent. Together, the perspectives from each side filled out the full range of possibilities for emotion as a commodity, as an object to acquire and as capital to spend.

The revival was a public display of emotion, structured in ways that drew upon religious and social traditions, and that was influenced in important ways by the recent history of social change and financial disorder in Boston. The revival was more than simply a display of emotion, however. It was grounded in an understanding of emotion as a valuable commodity that could be exchanged for various other things. So, while Bostonians collectively emoted, they were also participating in an emotional economy. Indeed, the two aspects—the collectivity and the economy of emotion—were closely interwoven, the envaluing of emotion being possible only within a public context that allowed for the assignment of value through social agreement. In a later chapter we will closely examine the nature of the emotional economy, including the structuring of emotional value. For now, we will explore some of the ways in which emotion was objectified and treated as an item desirable enough to justify expensive theatre seats, and valuable enough to warrant precautions against wastefully spending it.

URBAN SPECTACLE

Bostonians, like Americans in other cities, cultivated feeling through their participation in a broad assortment of public performances, from holiday spectacles on the Common to circuses, music recitals, and mob violence. Some of those performances were highly ritualized, others barely so. The social experience in any case mattered because it elicited certain feelings. When a crowd gathered to watch a boat race on the Charles River, no one person's emotional response to the event was likely to be exactly that of another's. But people attended such an event with the anticipation of it proving on some order to be an emotional experience, just as readers bought penny newspapers expecting copy that was sad, frightening, heartwarming, or pathetic.[1]

Spectacles could be large scale or small, intensely emotional or just slightly so. The key element was the shared experience of emotion. Charles French found himself highly excited at the Charles River regatta, where he joined the crowd of spectators on July 10, 1857. The gathering, however, was nowhere near as large as that which drew one hundred thousand people to the Common exactly six years earlier for a fireworks demonstration featuring "the largest and most gorgeous pyrotechnical structure ever produced in this country." *Gleason's* reported that "every one appeared delighted, as was evinced by frequent exclamations of eulogy." Bostonians like the Lombard family went to see balloon ascensions and parades, and although capital punishment was not as public as it once had been, it still provided spectacle to a small number of viewers. Some happenings were unexpected and profoundly public, as when two stores toppled onto Broad Street, killing two children and one man. At other times, they were more organized and circumscribed, as in the case of the baptism of an infant whose mother had died in childbirth. The basin for the infant was placed on top of the coffin of the mother. "An affecting and interesting ceremony," wrote William Brooks. Eleven-year-old Arthur Nichols was moved by the sight of a man beating a horse on Salem Street, and Peter Randolph remembered the scene of excitement at the Long Wharf when he docked with sixty-five other emancipated slaves from Virginia. Men and women responded emotionally to the caged animals they saw in a visiting zoo caravan, and to the wax renderings of murders, pirates, intemperance, and devilry installed in the hallways of the Boston Museum in 1850–51. A female albino Irish preacher caused a stir in 1857, and the merrymaking on Fast Day in 1858 featured hundreds of games of baseball and cricket, streets overflowing with promenaders, and "lager bier free and easies." Perhaps because the celebration took place on a day ostensibly set aside for prayer and fasting, it passed "in an orderly manner, as a whole, and the number of arrests by the police, was small." Anti-slavery demonstrations, as we shall see, proved much more disruptive. Mobs were nothing new to Bostonians, however. Even before the protests against the Fugitive Slave Act broke out, Bostonians had engaged in various sorts of reform-minded social protest. In 1825 a crowd approached a house of prostitution, the Beehive, so-called because of all of the small rooms inside. A policeman recalled the scene:

> About nine o'clock in the evening, there came down from Hanover Street way, about two hundred of the most comical-looking fellows that you ever laid eyes on. They had pitchforks, and poles, and bards, and axes, and conch shells, and gourd shells, and tin horns, and tin pans, and were dressed in all kinds of costume, and their faces were blacker than the bottom of a tar kettle. Well, just as they arrived at the beehive, the band struck up—such music—and the work began, and such work,—why sir, you could not hear yourself think, and in less than ten minutes there was not a piece of door or window or furniture left of the beehive so large as a truck pin.[2]

Fires made for a spectacle on an order that exceeded all else. Diarists filled their books with accounts of burning houses and businesses, some even apologizing for failing to report promptly or thoroughly on them. People left warm beds in the middle of winter nights to follow firefighters to the scene of a fire, some, as Edward Everett Hale wrote, to render assistance, but most to watch and marvel. Charles French got himself out of bed and with "many hundred persons went 3 miles" expecting to see a monumental burn, but it proved to be only swamp grass. George Troup went to fires like he went to a saloon or a card game. Young Arthur Nichols returned to a fire the next day to watch the still-burning ruins crumble. And fires were frequent in the city, even before it grew to over a hundred thousand people. Twenty-eight-year-old machinist Alfred Mason Badger noted that the only reason he was able to do just "a little more scribbling in this book [i.e., diary]," was because of "the almost constant alarms of fire, which has been so numerous of late that it would be altogether out of the question to go back and numerate them." A fire spread fast in a city with old wooden buildings, often destroying a city block before it was controlled. The fifty-eight houses that were destroyed by fire in July of 1852 left a city block blighted, but amounted to only a fraction of the loss from a previous fire in New York in which four thousand houses burned.[3]

For many persons, the large number of fires translated to a cornucopia of excitement. Joanne Harvey wrote her son Charles in the California gold fields of a huge fire in Lawrence in the fall of 1857. "I never saw such a magnificent sight," she exclaimed. Young schoolteacher Henry W. Haynes was out with a group one night when they spotted fire in a stable: "The fire was magnificent—& of course the ladies . . . were delighted." The magnificence of fires proved so powerful a tonic to some persons that they set them at any number of sites around the city, including the Brattle Street Church. Arsonists periodically were caught and hanged, three on one day during one winter. Fires provided a stage for heroics, and diarists sometimes noted the drama of human suffering and heroism at a particular scene: a mother who died after reentering a house to save her child, a young man dragging sleeping Irish from a burning tenement, the bravery and resolute action of a husband in saving the family planing shop. Above all, the loss of property and life to fire was pathetic. And no instance brought more of an emotional shock to the city than the death of a young woman, a Barnard, of the wealthy Beacon Street Barnards, who, having dressed to go to a benefit for the poor, caught fire and burned to death after her dress brushed the coals in the fireplace. A few years later the same fate befell Mary Gardiner Davis, not long after she had cast aspersions upon Boston's Greek pretensions. And where there was no fire, someone made one, said Mary Mudge: "The boys were bound to have a time, so they set the 'Bickford House' on fire, and burnt it to the ground."[4]

Most spectacles were not like fires in that they were planned and they did not prospect loss of life—unless funerals be considered. As in the case of fires, bells were rung for funerals, drawing people to the spectacle of the funeral procession—or "parade" as it was called—and in some cases to the graveside ceremonies, especially if the military was involved. While there, observers formed opinions about the orations. Non-funereal processions, parades of other sorts, were popular with almost everyone. George Troup liked to watch parades, which often were unannounced, and so did seventeen-year-old Francis Bennett, an apprentice recently arrived in the city in 1854, who located the marchers by their band music. Parading as a means of displaying community and group solidarity had become popular in the urban east in the mid-nineteenth century, and many "parades" featured merely a single small body of persons who took to the streets in their distinctive dress, accompanied by a band that sometimes numbered only three or four musicians. Bennett accordingly saw parades composed exclusively of organization members: the Woburn Phalanx, City Guards, North End True Blues, New York Light Guard, various local engine companies, the Guard of Seventy, the "company of K. N.," other political party fife-and-drum bands, the Guard of Liberty, and other such groups. On occasion Bennett would follow the sounds of the music to one parade only to be wooed by the sounds of another band nearby in the neighborhood. Once, just after the Know-Nothing triumphs at the ballot box in November of 1854, he followed a Know-Nothing band through a neighborhood until they unexpectedly bumped into another Know-Nothing group also out marching, eventuating in the formation of one large Know-Nothing parade.[5]

Bostonians arranged public celebrations for all sorts of events, and these often were organized as elaborate and dramatic occasions. A torch light procession and illumination of stores on Cambridge Street marked the opening of the bridge there in 1854. The city put on a "great railroad celebration" for two days in 1851, and the procession and ceremony for the coming of the Cochituate water to Boston—it replaced the antiquated wells and cisterns—was scripted to include the singing of a James Russell Lowell ode by a large choir of schoolchildren on the Common. The author and playwright John Townsend Trowbridge remembered the "wild enthusiasm of the hour," when "the mayor's hand waved, cannon thundered, all the bells of the city clanged," and an eighty-foot plume of water shot out of the fountainhead, "an amazing spectacle." The christening of the Atlantic telegraph cable to England in August 1858, highlighted by the reception of the Queen's message of "friendship" and "reciprocal esteem," included a one-hundred gun salute, wild bell-ringing, the display of flags, and nighttime reverie. Early in the evening "the streets began to fill with people curious to see all that was to take place or to be seen." A crush of people made travel to the Common almost impossible, and several sites—notably the statue of Franklin, the Public Library, and the City Hall—were lit up with gas jets burning brightly. Charles French exulted that *"every one* seemed to take a personal interest in the affair. . . . every individual seemed truly happy."

William Brooks wrote, "I have never seen such enthusiasm." It was no accident that such a remarkable celebration took place in the summer of 1858, in the midst of a sustained religious excitement unparalleled in Boston's history.[6]

The inauguration of the bronze statue of Benjamin Franklin in front of the City Hall two years earlier had similarly excited the citizenry. A four-mile-long procession, "embracing all the trades, professions, societies, & c." made its way to the City Hall, where speeches and ceremonies and garlands of flowers remembered the man better known to the rest of the nation for his residency in the state of Pennsylvania. No man-made spectacle was more awesome, however, than the inauguration of the Boston Public Library, which also took place in the drama-filled year of 1858. Swapping one spectacle for another, Frederic Cunningham and his family gave up the theatre to take part in the festivities. William Brooks came to see the procession and listen to the speeches by Edward Everett Hale and Robert Winthrop. The procession itself was a remarkable gathering of individuals and groups, ranging from the Boston Light Infantry and Flagg's Cornet Band to book-lovers such as the Harvard College faculty, the naval storekeeper, the American Academy of Arts and Sciences, the Boston Statistical Association, the YMCA, and an assortment of scientific, literary, historical, and especially library associations. The fifteen-page booklet printed for the event included information about the ceremonies and its participants, and outlined the route of the procession from City Hall to the Library on Boylston Street.[7]

The planning of celebrations such as that at the Library usually was detailed and explicit, and to some extent balanced the enthusiasm and spontaneity of the crowds who attended. A spectacle after all was an occasion for the performance of emotion, and Bostonians were well aware of the potential for celebrations, inaugurations, and other events to transmogrify into scenes of disorder or outright riot. The burning of the Ursuline convent in Charlestown following Lyman Beecher's incendiary sermon in 1834 was one such instance, and one that recalled the expert looting of the mansion of the British lieutenant governor of Massachusetts after a sermon by Jonathan Mayhew in 1765. The mob activity surrounding the detention of the fugitive slave Anthony Burns in 1854 was a fresher memory, and one that was reinforced on an almost weekly basis through the efforts of abolitionist leaders. And there was the matter of enthusiastic and overly enthusiastic fair-weather crowds on the Common that required overwhelming police supervision on numerous occasions. Accordingly, any large gathering of persons for celebration held the possibility for social breakdown, and Bostonians approached such gatherings with mixed trepidation and exultation. Typical was the perception of Harvard Commencement Day, a state holiday and therefore an opportunity for "feasting and playing" that befitted holidays such as Fast Day. In Cambridge itself, in 1855, a large body of alumni and their families gathered with the graduates and their guests for exercises that reached their peak in a sermon by Henry Ward Beecher on the topic of mirthfulness. Relieved that the boisterousness and chaos of another college celebration, Class Day, did not spill over into the commencement exercises, the *Evangelist and Religious Review* remarked: "We were forcibly struck with the decorum of the audience, and especially the students themselves. . . . There was no frivolity, nor giddiness, nor theatrical display." In fact, marveled the paper, there was "not one bouquet thrown upon the stage the whole day." Like a number of other phenomena connected with the university, the day seems to have served as a standard of sorts for the mingling of celebration with order. The *Monthly Anthology* had observed a half-century earlier that although Commencement Day was "the carnival of the year," for persons of all classes and ages, "reason and feeling combine" in its celebration.[8]

Religious events were organized to structure emotion in certain ways as well, most visibly through elaboration of the "order of service." Printed as broadsides, the programs for anniversaries, ordinations, installations, dedications, cornerstone-layings, and even regular Sunday gatherings carefully detailed the order of services for those in attendance. The lists rarely included fewer than eight items, and usually a dozen, with some running to fourteen distinct exercises. Moreover, there was little change in the length of the lists, or the nature of the exercises, over four decades leading up to the Civil War. The order of services at the installation of Reverend Arthur B. Fuller as the pastor of the New North Religious Society in 1853 followed a standard format: voluntary and anthem (organ and choir), introductory prayer, reading of scripture, hymn, sermon, hymn, prayer of installation, charge, right hand of fellowship, address, concluding prayer, anthem, benediction by the pastor. Such schemes channeled and regulated and likely enhanced as well the feelings of participants. Above all, a wellplanned order of exercises accomplished just that: it lent order to a gathering of persons in a situation likely to arouse deep feelings. As the *Evangelist and Religious Review* pointed out, it served a dual role as a "visible measure to arrest and engage voluntary attention." In the tumult of the late 1850s an explosion of lay prayer meetings altered this tradition in a significant way, but even then, perhaps especially then, ministers and their church committees continued to imbed Sunday gatherings and other church occasions in familiar patterns of decorum.[9]

STAGING EMOTION

Not all spectacles were freely available for public participation. Some were staged, and persons charged admission to them. The rapid growth of the theatre in Boston was grounded in producers' realization that dramatic performances had the potential to stir the emotions at least as effectively as a fire, procession, or installation of a pastor. The "theatrical display" that the *Evangelist and Religious Review* thought inappropriate for Harvard Commencement Day was, in the specially constructed context of the performance hall, a treasure sought after by a broad cross section of the population. Paying six dollars for a private box or twenty-five cents for admission to the family circle, Bostonians supported theatrical performances in such large numbers that between 1856 and 1879 the number of houses mounting productions tripled. Already in 1852 the Boston Music Hall had opened, and was widely regarded as the nation's finest auditorium. That year, reflecting on the extraordinary enthusiasm for the theatre, Arthur Nichols wrote in his diary that "I am somewhat interested in theatricals though I am not yet 'stage struck.'" Among those who were in fact stage struck were seventeen-year-old Charles French, a clerk who need not have recorded in his diary that he followed the theatre "keenly" because of the multitude of entries indicating his attendance. Susan Brown taught at a Jewish school, sometimes attended synagogue services, worshipped in Protestant churches almost daily, and attended performances at night. Twenty-three-year-old Eliphay Arnold, who wrote constantly about weeping tears of religious devotion in his small apartment, spent free evenings taking in musical and dramatic performances. Susan Heath, so sick she thought she would die, attended the theatre and felt much improved. For Charles Low, Israel Lombard, and Henry Wadsworth Longfellow, the theatre occasionally was a family affair. Its attraction was its capability to raise feelings. Francis Bennett, returning with his friends from a play at the Museum Theater in 1854, offered an opinion characteristic of the approach of Boston theatregoers: "The play was a domestic tale of New York entitled 'the dream as truth unveiled.' It was a very affecting piece." Promoters and publicists naturally aimed directly at a market characterized by such appeal to emotion. When "Relief of Lucknow" opened in April of 1858, the notice in the *Transcript* enthused: "The first performance of the thrilling play . . .

will take place this evening. . . . A great sensation was produced in New York by its dramatic power, and similar excitement may be anticipated from its representation in Boston."[10]

In 1856 several good houses were booking theatrical productions. The Boston Museum and Gallery of Fine Arts, established in 1841 at Tremont and Bromfield Streets, established a stock company and opened its first play in 1843. The wax statuary hall, which was added in 1850–51, included "Murder of Miss McCrea," "Scene in the Cabin of a Vessel captured by Pirates," "The Three Stages of Intemperance," and "The Game of Life," which depicted a youth playing chess for his soul with Satan. The entertainments to be had there were commonly described as "vaudeville," but included most of the important dramatic productions of the 1850s, a fact due largely to the foresight and skill of its proprietor, Moses Kimball, and the house producer and actor William Henry Smith. The new Boston Theatre at Mason and Washington Streets was inaugurated in the fall of 1854. Sixty-six feet in height, the building was well designed for dramatic presentations. The Athenaeum on Howard Street, a converted Millerite tabernacle that began productions in 1845, also was a good venue, and the Music Hall, which opened in 1852, was outstanding. The old Federal Street Theatre reopened in 1846 with a production featuring the much-loved actor Charlotte Cushman. The Tremont Temple burned down in March of that year, followed by the National Theatre a month later, likely the work of arsonists. The rebuilt Tremont Temple seated well over a thousand persons, and though better suited to lectures and religious services than to plays, the public supported such productions as were mounted there. But the play remained the thing, and a reasonably good production of a popular story was likely to prove a financial success to producers. A visiting Charles Dickens did not think that the theatres did much of a business in 1842, but by mid-century theatre was hugely popular. The Museum Theatre had a string of such successes in the 1850s, garnering two thousand dollars a week for *Twelfth Night*, three thousand a week for a musical production of *Uncle Tom's Cabin*, and doing well with *The Enchanted Harp*, *The Jewess*, *The Talisman*, and especially with anti-slavery plays such as *Dred* and *Neighbor Jackwood*. Minstrelsy, which continued to feature men in blackface even after African Americans were admitted to the professional stage after the Civil War, filled in between the larger productions.[11]

The surge of interest in the theatre was enough to persuade the legislature to pass a law in 1858 legalizing Saturday evening performances. But even then enthusiasm for theatrical performances spilled over from the auditoriums into more circumscribed circles of association. People met in living rooms and association libraries for readings of plays, especially Shakespeare. Gamaliel Bradford skipped dinner and traveled to Brookline one night to take the part of Prospero. Those who had sufficient room staged small productions in their homes, usually of sentimental favorites such as "Still Water Runs Deep." As Karen Haltunnen has shown, Americans at this time schooled themselves in acting method, consuming manuals or articles such as the one in *Godey's* that taught them to "study the different expressions and suitable actions of the passions," and to learn "a kind of code of expressions, or laws for the better regulation of frowns, smiles, and gestures." Afflicted with a "rage for parlor theatricals," Americans learned how to enact a full range of emotions in their parlors, and, as Haltunnen observes, the audience participated with them in the performance. Sometimes a parlor served as the stage for a play written by a family member for the family actors. New England schoolchildren for generations had composed short plays in connection with their study of literature or morality. But the practice as it was manifest in the 1850s reflected awareness of the rapidly expanding theatre culture, as in the case of Mary Gardiner Davis, who composed a play for Christmas, 1854, entitled "Nathalie or the would-be actress. A vaudeville in two parts."[12]

Bostonians who attended the theatre registered opinions about the acting and staging as well as the story. Some were well equipped to do so because they had attended lectures and read books about the theatre, including books that outlined the ways in which persons could represent emotion in acting. The criticism accordingly ranged from very positive to revulsion. Francis Bennett Jr. saw the *Merchant of Venice* in 1854 and thought Shylock especially good, an interesting judgment given the tarnished reputation of Boston's businessmen at the time. Edward Teulon likewise deemed *Old John and Jacob Gray*, a Museum production, "an excellent comedy." W. H. Hoyt saw a "fine play: splendid scenery." Henry Larcom Abbott, on the other hand, had to sit through "clap trap" one night, and Longfellow thought a production of *Uncle Tom's Cabin* "so badly done!" Gamaliel Bradford, after watching Eliza Logan in "The Lady of Lyons," wrote that her acting was both too emotional and not emotional enough: "Once or twice did she fly into those paroxysms of excitement which are so common & so painful on our stage. But then on the other hand she did not show enough of passion." But there was little argument when a great actor came to the city, regardless of the role or the setting. Fanny Kemble was one such star, capable of enchanting all who witnessed her performances. "We have heard Mrs. Kemble two evi'ings," wrote Mary Dewey to her daughter-in-law Julia, "1rst the 'Tempest' then 'Coriolanus.' Her power must be witnessed to be realized—it is wonderful." Ezra Stiles Gannett, pastor of the Federal Street Church, heard Kemble read *Much Ado about Nothing.* His colleague Orville Dewey exulted in 1860 that he had finally preached "to an audience as large as Mrs. Kemble's." Tracy Patch Cheever, who saw Anna Cora Mowatt at the Athenaeum in 1854, reported the "jam of humans that choked the building nearly to suffocation." [13]

Some persons resisted the theatre, however. Charles Dickens noted in 1842 that the "evangelical ladies" of Boston "have a horror of theatrical entertainment." That horror in fact extended to other parts of the population and was regularly stoked by the conservative press and by ministers looking out for the spiritual good of their flocks. The *New Englander,* in the course of reviewing a passel of books on revivals in 1855, editorialized that in the previous twelve years, "theatres of all sorts have multiplied," carrying off to perdition a population of urban Christians who had fallen into its current. Ministers and lyceum lecturers explored different lines of reasoning in their condemnations of the theatre, but most relied upon the thorough treatment given it by Robert Turnbull in *The Theatre; in Its Influence upon Literature, Morals, and Religion* (1839). Proposing that "<u>young men</u> are especially interested in it," Turnbull argued that persons "are drawn away from religion by it" for two reasons. First, "theatrical amusements, by monopolizing so much of the unoccupied time, especially of young persons, such as merchant's clerks, mechanics, and others, retard the progress of improvement amongst this class." Time spent theatre-going could be more profitably used studying, reading the Bible, or refining virtue. Second, and more importantly, instead of "purging the mind" of those "passions" which subverted right thinking, theatrical performances "unfit the mind by their exciting and dissipating tendencies." By stimulating feelings and failing to direct them to a moral end, the theatre managed only to "dissipate the feelings," to waste them. Underlying this claim was the assumption that emotions were a commodity that could be squandered, that they were a treasure to be husbanded and only judiciously engaged within certain public contexts. The dynamics of exchange featured the "dissipation" of emotion as the price for fun. Feelings were lost, pleasure was gained, and the pleasure was not of equal value to the feelings spent in the process. Such a notion played a role as well in mid-nineteenth-century criticism of young persons' and women's reading, and was present in Turnbull's direct criticisms of Greek and Shakespearean drama as injurious to society. Read or performed, drama led to "moral defects." In fact, as reflected in the title of his book, Turnbull believed that the rise of the theatre had negatively influenced the production of literature. But for Turnbull, the public spectacle of theatre, not reading, was the most ominous of the emergencies threatening the moral core of Boston.[14]

Quoting Francis Wayland, Turnbull affirmed that "the tendencies of all theatres is to licentiousness." For opponents of the theatre, that licentiousness was manifest in various ways. Turnbull was disgusted with the thought that the "youth of our land," in spending money on the theatre, were supporting actors and others, "idle and improvident spendthrifts, many of them licentious foreigners." Reverend Albert Barnes linked the theatre with intoxication. The *Youth's Cabinet* explained that attendance at the theatre led to opium and the grave. And, in fact, even some within the theatre had their suspicions. After interviewing a young woman who wished to be an actress, producer William Henry Smith noted that she "was good looking, but I fear under the influence of opium." *The Young Woman's Friend* warned its readers specifically about licentious theatre passions and folly: "Woman is allowed to appear anywhere, where she can minister to the passions of men. She is admitted to the stage of the theatre; she is allowed to sing, to act, to speak, and perform all the nameless follies of the playhouse." And, in fact, such follies were appreciated by some young males precisely for their "licentious" character. W. H. Hoyt knew full well that his enjoyment of the theatre was multidimensional when he entered in his diary the following coded confession: "In the evening went with Freddie to a friend's (Bill Hinds) & had a very pleasant time with him. [Code begins here.] In imagination. But really went to the opera to see Madame Paroda. . . . hot as sin. . . . altogether have had a grand evening." Other of Hoyt's coded entries recorded his spying of women's cleavage and thighs at the circus, riding academy, theatre, and among the Ann Street prostitutes.[15]

The Leyden Chapel members' manual warned that any persons who attended the theatre, a "place of sinful amusement," would be judged "not worthy Communicants." But many religious persons, including members of the clergy, believed the theatre to be in league with the churches in fighting moral decay. Beginning in 1792, dramas produced at the Boston Theatre were announced as "moral lectures." None other than Doctor Benjamin Rush (whose theories about motion in the body strongly influenced theorizing about emotion) supplied the basis for that claim, drawing out of his pet theory of "excitement" an application to the stage. Because the moral faculty was especially susceptible to the motions of the passions, one could stimulate the moral faculty by moving the passions. The eloquence of the stage was a useful vehicle for moving the passions, Rush averred, specifically and ardently recommending "the language and imagery of

Shakespeare, upon moral and religious subjects, poured upon the passions and the senses, in all the beauty and variety of dramatic representation!" Elizur Wright, responding to a question about the theatre from his sister Harriet, assured her that "our parents" did the best they could, but their view that theatres posed a danger to religion was outmoded and unnecessary. Wright told her that there is "a sort of religion which is always at war with them [theatrical productions], giving no quarter and anything but fair play." Referring to "the Puritan pulpit and the stage," Wright indicted Puritans because they "refused to acknowledge their obligations to the stage for much valuable service to the cause of genuine religion." A person accordingly "may be very familiar with the pious writings of the Puritans but knows very little about cities and the best way to make the best of them, and still less about theatres and what takes place inside them." Indeed, concluded Wright, anyone who lives "in a city must be very blind if he does not see that theatres, on the whole, promote good morals." A great many Bostonians agreed with Wright, and the subject remained a live issue throughout the 1850s. The Park Street Church, among others, addressed it in its lecture series, and the thirty-eight bachelor members of the Franklin Scientific Association (only two of whose members were married) met in 1857 to debate the question, "Is the stage necessarily evil in its influence?"[16]

The opera and musical performances were popular in Boston as well. Charles French wrote in 1858 that "everyone is talking" about opera. Gamaliel Bradford pronounced himself "filled with wonder & delight" by it, and wrote that he had seen one opera twenty times (a doubtful assertion). W. H. Hoyt, always up for a spectacle of costumed women, attended the opera, noting in his diary that he was pleased not only with the performance but with the lovely young women in the audience. William W. Greenough wrote his father asking him for a five-dollar pair of opera glasses in 1858. As interest multiplied, producers brought renowned companies to the city, including the Ronzani Ballet Troupe and the Strakasch Opera Company in the late 1850s. Jenny Lind, the "Swedish Nightingale," proved so strong a draw that a few of the $12\frac{1}{2}$¢ tickets for her performance at the Tremont Temple were auctioned for $625. The music performed in conjunction with such events, as well as in theatre musicals and in recitals around the city, was the subject of much comment. Bostonians embraced musical performances as "charming and sensuous," and "full of delight and entrancement." Gamaliel Bradford was "most passionately fond of music," but believed at the same time that "if an individual especially a man devotes himself to it his mind becomes altogether unstrung for intellectual operation." As in William Collins's early nineteenth-century poem, the passions all played musical instruments. William Buchan and Alexander Anderson, walking a trail blazed by Rush, professed that music could cure disease, and even *The Young Man's Friend* admitted that music had the capability to "make the heart feel." Young men themselves preferred their music, in the parlance of W. H. Hoyt, "hot." Frederic Cunningham noted that at a concert one evening the "music [was] rather too scientific. . . . William Tell Overture and a Strauss march in the last part were quite inspiring."[17]

Whether one condemned theatrical and operatic performances or promoted them as moral lectures, the unmistakable fact was that religion and the theatre had much in common.[18] Boston publications occasionally ran articles about ministers who preached to congregations that had assembled in theatre buildings, the *Transcript* in 1857 referring to a cohort of such men as "our Academy of Music and National Theatre preachers." In another article on the phenomenon it made a more telling reference, arguing that "one class of persons have the same right to hold a religious meeting in the National Theatre on Sunday, as another class have to give an oratorio at the Boston Theatre, or at the Music Hall." Preaching in theatres amounted to a performance closely akin to the "moral lecture" of a play, in terms of both the message of the preaching—it was moral—and its capability to arouse feelings. Preaching, Rush might say, stimulated the passions that moved the moral faculty. Such similarity might prove advantageous, as when a sermon audience, reminded by the stage props behind the minister of the moral message of *Neighbor Jackwood*, experienced a compounding of the process of moral arousal. Precisely because of the closeness of preaching—an event involving performances by both preacher and auditors, and perhaps the choir as well—to theatrical presentations, the practice of preaching in theatres was fraught with danger. An article entitled "Preaching in Theatres" outlined the danger in detail, unwittingly representing preaching and dramatic acting as mutually reinforcing practices:

> We have, for some time, trembled a little at the possible consequences of going into theatres on Sunday evening to preach. . . . it has its perils. Hundreds who would never think of going inside a theatre on a week day, now go on Sunday, and the interior architecture, the snatches of scenery paintings which are partially in view, the sight of the stage the whole arrangement, and above all the irrepressible associations, strike the minds of uninitiated ones, with newness and wonder which naturally excite a desire to see more, and hence to visit the place on another occasion. . . . The vast difference between the theatre and the church is insen-

sibly lessened. It is well, too, if this very practice does not react upon the pulpit and tastes of the people injuriously, so as to create a demand for more histrionic preaching.

Viewed from such a perspective, it was possible to see both dramatic performances and religion as bound up, in Edward Cutbush's words, with "the impulse of the passions and other various occurrences, in this great theatre of the world."[19]

EMOTION IN PRINT

Reading in most cases was not as plainly a collective activity as fire-watching or opera-going. It nevertheless was a means of participation in a shared culture of emotion. And sometimes that sharing was in fact explicit, as in the many cases of social reading, when groups of persons read together from books or magazines or, most commonly, took the parts of characters in parlor readings of plays. Reading out loud taught people about emotion and provided them an opportunity to exercise it. Sometimes the act of speech in such gatherings was itself a stimulus, at least according to the *Massachusetts Teacher*, which, in trying to get its bearings on the matter, argued that "speech is the expression of sentiment and emotion. Often the feeling of the speaker will be understood, when not a word is understood. The expression of emotion is not dependent on words. . . . But all language is the expression of emotion." The words themselves of course were critically important, and as American literary historians have amply demonstrated, the act of reading was profoundly linked to the experience of emotion. (And it is clear that the selling of the emotional experience in performative contexts such as theatre and opera always took place alongside reading). For nineteenth-century commentators, so much was obvious, not least of all to the *New Englander*, which, after a reading of *The Sunny side; or the Country minister's Wife*, accordingly reported: "We confess to have had the fountains of emotion stirred within us by its perusal as they seldom are stirred."[20]

David Reynolds has suggested that the rise of the penny press in the nineteenth century "brought a new hyperbolic emotionalism" to a broad readership, whetting the appetite of the reading public for increasingly sensational stories, shaping the editorial policies of city newspapers and magazines, and profoundly influencing the literature of the American Renaissance. Bostonians, however, did not read detachedly about tragedy and romance, crime and sex, the heroic accumulation of wealth and the corruption of power. To some extent they participated in most of the things that they read about and it was partly through that participation, through shared public experiences of alarm and awe, delight and repulsion, grief and joy, that they cultivated a taste for the conjurings of the printed word. Books and newspapers, and other writings privately executed, were bound together with public experiences by the web of mutually reinforcing connections between the two spheres. Bostonians read, and felt.[21]

Certain kinds of literature, some of which was written by John Townsend Trowbridge for fifty dollars per novelette, were considered so affecting as to overwhelm the sensibilities of persons, especially girls and young women. Sixteen-year-old Sally Ripley had read about the dangers of emotional overstimulation posed by reading romances, but she jumped with both feet into "Blair's Sentimental Beauties" in 1801. Fifty years later, Boston girls were doing the same thing, in spite of repeated warnings from their mothers and ministers. The *Christian Observatory* complained that "this new token of increasing demoralization among the young, is to be ascribed to the reading provided for them. Vile novelettes, garnished with coarse woodcuts, the cheapest trash in all the cheap literature of the day, pamper every romantic sentiment." The heart of the matter had to do with feelings. "The imagination is inflamed," said the magazine, "and the passions are excited to restless cravings." Returning to this theme in a later issue, the magazine took a mocking tone and named names: "The majority of fictitious writings foster sentimentalism; and if there be any valueless member of the family or of society, it is the mere sentimentalist. . . . Such was Laurence Sterne, who could weep over an expiring ass, yet neglect his dying mother." Mothers, indeed, somehow knew their way through the morass of sentimental "trash," knew how to separate it from edifying reading. One of their duties accordingly was to steer their children away from inflammatory literature. The heroine of "My Thimbles," a children's story published in 1852, speechified that she was grateful that her mother "did not suffer me to be tempted much by works of fiction." Conscientious mothers were aided by a host of writings that reinforced the dangers of novel-reading. The *Massachusetts Ploughman* made explicit the connection between a sentimental girl and a potentially bad wife and mother, warning its readers: "When you see a girl with a novel in her hand and a fan in her right, shedding tears, you may be sure she is not fit for a wife." Nothing was worse, said the *Massachusetts Teacher*, than an "over-imaginative, novel-reading, candy-eating creature." But the warnings did not always stick. Consumer demand in Boston supported a lively and varied market in novelettes and romances, as well as other literature that stimulated the emotions. Mary Gardiner Davis copied from an essay on Pope the declaration that "man hardly can believe how many of his own emotions may be traced to books." A broad cross section of Bostonians might not have been stricken with such disbelief.[22]

Boys read, too, and were emotionally affected by their reading, even if they did not describe their experiences as females did. Men rarely confessed, as did Mary Faxon Forbush, that "I have been reading and crying over Copperfield." But Henry Haynes clearly identified with David during his reading of the novel, recording that, "like 'David Copperfield,' I feel 'very young.'" Haynes enjoyed *Reveries of a Bachelor* and Julie Kavanaugh's *Nathalie,* about which he wrote: "It is refreshing once in a while to find a heroine who is not perfect. . . . Here we have for once a perfectly natural woman, with all the excellencies & defects of southern character fully developed." He looked forward to "regular" literature as well, such as Melville's new novel, which he had read about in *Literary World:* "It is a regular novel & Moby Dick, a White Whale, is the hero of it." His reading also included works of criticism. After reading Hazlitt's lectures on the English poets, he wrote that "it is a work of genius & I have learned much from it." Arthur Nichols liked *Uncle Tom's Cabin,* and Tracy Patch Cheever, reading Gibbon's *Decline and Fall of the Roman Empire,* reported that he "loved it." Arthur Nichols filled up the hours in between stretches of picket duty in Kingston, Kentucky during the Civil War with *Abel Drake's Wife, a Romance.*[23]

"Passion, overstatement, ridiculous conceits . . . characterize to a very melancholy degree our recent literature," said the *Massachusetts Teacher* in 1853. That literature included above all the penny press and magazines that both men and women read, passed from hand to hand, and talked about. A generous survey of the city at mid-century identified eighty newspapers in Boston proper. That is a little less than twice the number of publications counted by the statistics-minded Argentinian Domingo Sarmiento during his visit to the city in 1847. Most newspapers and magazines survived by titillating and shocking their readers with stories of catastrophe and corruption. Others, like *Gleason's*—to which Charles French subscribed in 1855 on his small salary of $125 a year— mixed local and national news, and more complex human interest stories, with the fantastic and foreign. *Gleason's* formula enticed even more consumers into the market. *Ballou's,* which had a circulation of 68,000 in 1857, swelled to 116,000 in 1859, and was able to charge one dollar for a year's subscription to twelve 100-page issues. Even publications that presented themselves as high-minded and scholarly regularly published the kind of stories that would cause readers to exclaim or wince. Medical journals and scientific publications reported on startling occurrences in the 1850s in the same way that the *Boston Journal of Philosophy and the Arts* in 1823 related the "extraordinary case" of a man whose feats provided "a most striking illustration of the self-preservation powers of the stomach and the intestines, and their ability to resist the influence of foreign agents." A sailor, it seemed, after excessive drinking would swallow knives, as many as twenty-three at a time, and pass them the next day with apparent ease. After dying from an episode during which he swallowed a horn-handled knife, his insides were examined by a team that found all sorts of foreign objects lodged in his abdominal cavity. The account, which blended medical science with details of the amazing deeds and gory consequences of the case, might just as easily have been published in a sheet that sold for a penny on street corners. In short, as Joanne Harvey noted in 1857, "the papers are full of disasters by sea and murders, and outrages by land."[24]

Sensationalism sometimes was commingled with moral lessons and sometimes it was not. When the normally sober *Christian Register* reported on a boy's prolonged death from rabies, it mentioned that his moral worth made him close friends in life, but the magazine made no attempt to derive a lesson from his "death by hydrophobia." *Gleason's*, one of the best practitioners of the genre, picked up and ran what appears to have been a morally tinctured urban legend about a family whose women were plagued with odd injuries: one ripped skin from cranium because she over-tightened her "French twist" hairstyle, her sister had the cartilage of both ears torn by the weight of her earrings, another sister put her thumb out of joint attempting to don too-tight pigskin gloves, another sister died of overuse of cosmetics, and the youngest female in the family went insane over "the Bloomer dress" and had to be confined as an incurable lunatic. Fortunately, her mother, who previously had gone insane by attempting to lace her dress too tightly, was in the adjacent cell. Such an overdrawn didacticism was laughable, a joke about itself. The real business of the article was the unusual injuries, painful and weird absent a moral. News, commentary, speculation (complete with drawings), and legal instruction about the Forrest divorce case of 1852 sold many issues of newspapers and magazines, including the *Monthly Law Reporter*. Many accounts shied away from framing the case as a lesson in right and wrong. The story was strong enough to rouse a readership without an overlay of lessons. Stories indicating connections between losing one's temper and murder regularly appeared in magazines, but in some cases the perspective was simply that "this sort of thing happens sometimes." And, as always, reports of fires and the deaths they caused made excellent copy, even if, as was usually the case, there was no heroism involved, no daring rescue or last-minute salvation. Fires simply excited people. So did murder, and so did carriage accidents, financial ruin, bigger steam engines, the lives of Sandwich Islanders, and big weddings. In the port city of Boston, however, no theme caught the attention of the reading public more than news of disaster on the high seas. Most spectacular was the loss of five hundred persons in a steamship grounded off Cape Hatteras in the fall of 1857. Joanne Harvey wrote that from one day to another the news of the tragedy "fills the papers." Like much reading, accounts of this catastrophe made little or no appeal to any moral lesson. The story was important simply because it stirred the emotions. Individuals might find the story useful in elaborating their own moral vision, but the emotional punch sold papers.[25]

In the late 1840s the Boston newspapers began dedicating specific column space to fires, sinkings, railroad accidents, and other catastrophes, in the process all but guaranteeing news about those events but also separating them from other kinds of news. In contrast to stories with a transparently moral angle, such columns were presented as "just the facts" reporting. For some of the public, however, the sensationalism of the papers was simply out of control and harmful, especially, to the development of young people. "The disease of the times," said the *Christian Observatory*, is in the "books and newspapers. . . . We say again, <u>the virus takes</u>, and often where it might be least expected." The disease was rooted as well in the art that accompanied such corrupt texts, said another critic. Referring to "that large class of readers captivated by the 'woodcuts,' so conspicuous in many of our weekly papers and magazines," The *Evangelist and Religious Review* condemned the "lavish illustrations" of "horrors" that were printed not to morally instruct but merely to "gratify readers." Not to mention the inaccurate renderings of those horrors by the use of stock engravings. In one case, a drawing of singer Jenny Lind that happened to be on file was printed to illustrate the Sickles murders of 1829. Other critics took authors to task for attempting to pass off "indecent" writing as journalism. The *New Englander* condemned an account of life on the Sandwich Islands: "Disgusting practices, exposures of the person, and open exhibitions of whatever is debasing and loathsome, are described in a style which shows how attractive these things are to the heart of the writer." As always, the religious press was especially sensitive to the power of such narratives to arouse emotion but fail to direct it, thus squandering on the mundane what might have been employed in pursuit of spiritual goals. So much of the sensationalist literature was devoid of a moral lesson that critics took aim at the absence. The *Observatory* declared that "cheap literature" and sensational-

ism in the papers were "decidedly hostile to salutary religious impressions:
and nearly all of it by exciting the passions without giving them any proper
objects to work upon, expand and waste the excitability of the mind. . . . "
Another critic extended the analysis even to some religious works, claiming that descriptions of suffering and pain in religious literature such as
Richard Baxter's *The Saint's Everlasting Rest* (1650) have "been multiplied
and combined, as it were, in an *infernal kaleidoscope,* so as to present images of variegated, picturesque, and transcendent horror." In assailing even
Baxter's moral classic, the opposition to sensational literature made its
point clear: the massage could be bad even when the message was good.[26]

EMOTION, THE THING

Protestant middle-class culture in nineteenth-century Boston constructed
emotion in a complex way. A central element of that construction was the
objectification of emotion, and the corollary assignment of commodity status to it. Traditions of collective performance of emotion—crowds at fires,
gatherings for holidays, audiences at theatres, congregations in churches—
were of fundamental importance in structuring this understanding of emotion. When persons gathered to cheer the opening of a water line, or looked
on in awe as a fire roared through a warehouse, they confirmed and reinforced through their participation cultural codes for expression and concealment of emotion, and shared beliefs about the value of emotion.

Performances of tragedy and romance in mid-nineteenth century Boston ran the gamut from unexpected catastrophes to elaborate public processions and celebrations, theatrical and musical performances, and participation in a reading culture that valued the sensational. Sometimes such
performances included a moral, and sometimes they did not. In all of these
contexts, however, participants expected emotional arousal. In pursuit of
that arousal, they were willing to drag themselves out of bed in the middle
of winter to witness a magnificent fire. They paid hundreds of dollars for
auditorium seats. They supported a very large number of publications, and
especially newspapers, in spite of the frequent warnings of Protestant ministers and other moralists about contracting the virus of promiscuous feeling. In a city laced with crises brought by rapid social change, Bostonians
sought out emotional experience as if it were a commodity. They spent
their money expecting a disturbance of their emotional waters, an experience of tears or delight, of a feeling of puffed-up contentedness or angry
alarm.

Critics of the white, middle-class pursuit of emotional excitement attacked the theatre, penny press, and novels in the same way. They rested their criticisms on the assumption that emotion was a distinct and limited commodity possessed by the individual. They also recognized the high degree of emotional excitement brought on by the performance of a play, or consumption of a novelette. Surveying the broad public engagement in such activities, they complained that emotion that was aroused in connection with those activities was "wasted." The theatre bled a person of feelings that might have been harnessed to a project of spiritual awakening or moral improvement. The emotional excitement that came about through viewing a woodcut in a magazine article about matricide was a terrible loss of a valuable commodity, regardless of whether it was called fear, envy, jealousy, passion, hatred, or any other name. Religious services remained carefully organized in antebellum Boston as a hedge against inadvertent waste of emotion. The order of services channeled and regulated emotion.

When it came to emotion, the consuming public and the critical observers (who themselves might have consumed more than they let on) shaped their behavior and ideas around the belief that emotion was an integral part of a person. We shall see later how there was another side to Bostonians' thinking about emotion, a competing conception that represented the other side of the "double self." We shall see how Bostonians, like all Victorians, spiritualized emotion to a certain extent, and how they arranged that understanding alongside their observation of emotion as something that could be "gotten" in certain ways, and lost in others, and, eventually, as comprehensible under a system of rules of exchange.

The pursuit of feeling evinced in the various forms of collective performance in the 1850s was also visible in the churches. In fact, much of the debate within the churches in the 1850s had to do precisely with the role of emotion in religion, and the responsibilities of the ministers and the laity in cultivating and regulating emotion. The popularity of Spiritualism, and the growth of religiously grounded reform movements in Boston likewise represented the pursuit and performance of emotion. We turn now to a consideration of the problems that complicated congregational life, including the debate about the place of emotion in religion.

FIVE

Emotional Religion and the Ministerial "Balance-Wheel"

MINISTERIAL CONSERVATISM AND EMOTIONAL RELIGION

The emotional tenor of the Businessmen's Revival coalesced in Boston against a background of unsettledness in the Protestant churches, and, especially, within the context of lay dissatisfaction with insufficient ministerial efforts to raise the affections through preaching. The revival developed as one manifestation of the emotional religion to which laity turned during the decade of the 1850s, the others being primarily Spiritualism and reform movements grounded in religious ideals.

Ministers were keenly aware of the rich history of the New England clergy, and particularly the historic incidences that marked the development of Protestantism in Massachusetts Bay, from John Cotton, through the Mathers, Jonathan Edwards, and the various persons associated with the Second Great Awakening. Boston's Protestant clergy at mid-century felt the burden of their responsibility for living up to the past—filiopiety was still an integral component of the ecclesiastical establishment two centuries after its construction as a cornerstone of Bay colony life. They formed congregations, built houses of worship, pondered theological questions as earnestly as their ecclesiastical predecessors, and they steadfastly defended their claim to status based upon traditions of ministerial authority and privilege. Tradition also bequeathed to them anxiety about innovation, not that they were opposed to it, for, in fact, Boston was one of the most theologically innovative cities in the nation. Rather, they agonized over the institutional consequences of change, the potential for institutional failure even in the midst of theological vibrancy and relevance. Boston's Protestant ministers had custody of generations of investment in the religious infrastructure of the city. Accordingly, they were not inclined to take chances with it. Only the seemingly irrefutable precision of theological argumentation, as in the case of the emergence of Unitarianism, or the undeniable hand of God, as represented by the Great Awakenings, could serve as legitimate foundations for the reconstruction of religious life.

Ministers remembered the trouble brought upon them and the institutions that they protected by persons who demanded that religious enthusiasm be recognized as the chief marker of the converted life. Such memory, if not immediate to them, was ingrained in collective memory. A century before the Businessmen's Revival, Charles Chauncy of First Church had excoriated some promoters of revival in Boston for their recklessness in recommending a religious emotionality that seemed to threaten the survival of the most cherished of the city's institutions, i.e., the congregation/ministry nexus that, as far as the clergy were concerned, formed the backbone of the city's social order. In the 1850s a majority of the Boston clergy were as anxious about lay emotionality as Chauncy had been. They worried that it would erode clerical authority, undermine the use of institutional means of grace, and eventuate in social disorder. All of this while at the same time they hoped that God would send the city a "season of refreshment," the ministers reenacting the legendary preaching of New England's best-known eighteenth- and nineteenth-century revivalists. Their anxiety accordingly was complicated by their own conflicted thinking about emotion. They desired it for the good of their congregations, but they feared it for its potential to fracture the traditions that they had been charged with safeguarding.

Frustrated by the ostensibly poor prospect of emotional effervescence within the churches, some Bostonians turned to other kinds of religion, to rituals and para-religious activities that seemed to offer broader possibilities for the emotional thrill. Spiritualism, with its drama and intrigue, became popular in the city at mid-century. So also did the two great causes of nineteenth-century reform, abolitionism and temperance. Men and women found in such movements emotional stimulation that was not available in most churches. Participation in the emotional performances of séances and reform movement activities was an important step toward mass participation in the passionate religiosity of the revival.

The debate about enthusiastic religion, about Spiritualism and the reform movements, took place against the background of unsettledness in the Boston churches. That is, during the 1850s, institutional life was marked by numerous church closings and reopenings (sometimes under the banners of different denominations), high turnover in the ministry, infighting in congregations and across congregations, and the absence of ministers from their pulpits as they traveled to other cities or countries, or retreated to places more pastoral, that is, more rustic, during the summer months. To Bostonians who had been taught for generations that the ministry was the "balance-wheel" of church life, the unfilled pulpits, church financial scandals, an ecclesiastical politics in turmoil, and all of the other commotion in the ministry could not have encouraged confidence in the city's religious leadership. During the revival lay Protestants would set their own agendas, including guidelines for the expression of emotion in religious gatherings.

INVESTMENT IN INSTITUTIONS

The churches in Boston in the late 1850s did not form an unbroken religious and social front. Though not as diverse as it was to become in the late nineteenth century, the landscape of the city was marked here and there by departures from mainstream Protestant emphases. The growing Irish American population staked out its turf with Roman Catholic churches built to simple specifications: bigger, with better stained class, and with an organ with more pipes than the neighborhood Protestant churches. And in conjunction with the leadership in Rome, they increasingly demonstrated their religious faith in public gatherings and well-publicized special occasions. The jubilee month of December 1858, which connected Catholics to a tradition begun by Pope Boniface VIII over five centuries earlier, was respectfully reported by the *Boston Daily Advertiser*. Protestant groups that did not belong to the traditional club of denominations in the city also made their presence known through meetings and various official functions. A conference of Christians believing in the imminent return of Jesus Christ held a "Second Advent Conference" in the city in 1857. Swedenborgians held their General Convention in Boston in 1858, drawing delegates from many states, as well as curious Bostonians such as Catherine Flint. The handful of Presbyterians in the city were served by missionaries from the Montreal Presbytery. Local Millerites attracted attention throughout the city when they advertised that the end of the world would occur in May 1855. The Eastham camp meetings at the Millennial Grove on the sea drew participants and hangers-on during the summers. And for those who stayed in the city, there were lectures (usually mixed with prayer) on all manner of religious topics. William A. Stearns, the president of Amherst College, in an address at the Old South Church in 1857, bragged that "Friday evening in Boston is a season for prayer and godly edification in all our church lecture rooms." The substance of those Friday evening meetings, as we shall see, involved emotional experience on an order not unlike that which was promised in lyceum lectures when speakers such as Mrs. Barrow (who specialized in "sacred readings") were on the program. Her announcement for a lecture in 1858 indicated that she "proposes again delighting her auditors tomorrow evening with an admirable selection of pieces, . . . all appealing to the best emotions of the human heart." Theodore Parker, whose innovative theology and unrelieved stream of criticism of the Protestant clergy made him persona non grata in most churches, took to the lyceum podium and before standing-room-only crowds throughout the 1850s preached "the open infidelity of Parkerism." Had he lived long enough, Parker could have exploited the numerous desirable outdoor venues in the city after the Board of Works suddenly lifted the ban on outdoor regular preaching in 1860. Parker might have been joined by other persons who explored religious standpoints that significantly differed from the norm, such as Henry David Thoreau, who wrote a friend that "to some extent, and at rare intervals, even I am a yogi," or one of the readers of Reverend George Bush's *Life of Mohammed*, which was especially popular in Massachusetts.[1]

Though not all Bostonians were Protestant, congregations in the Protestant denominations formed the majority of the city's religious institutions. Counting steeples in 1850, one writer concluded that there were over two hundred churches in Boston and its suburbs. If enough suburbs were included, such doubtless would have been the case. The 1850 national census counted 99 churches in Boston proper, including 24 Unitarian, 16 Congregational, 13 Baptist, 12 Methodist, 9 Episcopal, 9 Catholic, 6 Universalist, and 1 each Presbyterian, Friends, Jewish, Lutheran, Christian, and Swedenborgian (and several "minor sects"). A reasonably precise statistical analysis conducted in 1857 gathered data on all Protestant churches within a ten-mile radius of the State House. The study counted 154 churches and a total church membership of 27,819: 52 Orthodox (10,701), 42 Baptist (7,914), 33 Methodist (5,616), and 27 Episcopal (3,288). The membership increase over ten years was 5,044, and the growth in the number of churches was 38. Churchgoers poured money into church building projects, maintenance, enlargement, cleaning, and decoration, and paid salaries of ministers and assistants as well. One estimate of the simple upkeep on a "fashionable" church was one hundred dollars per Sunday. Add in salaries (minister, sexton, organist, etc.), depreciation, and other costs and the sum rose to $432 per Sunday, or, in annual terms, roughly the amount earned by forty mechanics in a year. Some denominations in Boston, in keeping with national trends, got by more cheaply. The *Evangelist and Religious Review* concluded that across the United States the annual cost of various denominations maintaining a church was as follows (per person): $3.40 (Baptist / Methodist), $7.00 (Presbyterian), $10.00 (Congregationalist), $14.00 (Roman Catholic), $18.00 (Episcopalian), $23.00 (Unitarian). Though more speculative than calculated, the magazine's numbers nevertheless reflect perception of an important difference between denominations, and one that was frequently exploited when critics of "fashion" set their sights on the churches.[2]

Churches met their expenses in part through pew rents. Fashionable churches charged more than those that counted the poor in their congregations. Pews that became vacant due to dismissals or deaths were advertised for sale (as were pews in a new church). In 1859, a pew at the Park Street Church, unmistakable with its 218-foot spire at the edge of the Common near the big elm, was auctioned for $227.50 as part of the settlement of an estate. Fifteen years earlier, the Mount Vernon Church had valued its pews from $750.00 for one-half of a center row between rows four and ten, to $475 for the sixteenth row center, with the gallery seating much less expensive. Most churches did not rent pews for as much as either of those rates. But pew rents, however scaled, guaranteed admission for some and kept others out: the Warren Street Church posted guards outside its doors on one occasion to turn away non-proprietors. At mid-century, the major churches—which numbered approximately thirty-five—were capable of seating between six hundred and fifteen hundred persons for services. A church with a large congregation, such as Park Street with its eight hundred or so members, could rely on a regular stream of revenue from pews, and was able to collect offerings from visitors on a weekly basis as well. Churches also relied upon anniversary celebrations and fairs to raise the money needed to cover their expenses and to make capital improvements. Young men and women especially attended the fairs, which could feature any number of attractions, from singing and dancing to addresses by celebrities, to musical recitals, all in the service of a particular cause dear to the church. Non-members frequently outnumbered members at such gatherings. Admission usually was charged, and in cases where it was not, items for sale, often at auction, provided the means of profit. Most fairs realized a profit of between two and five thousand dollars. The Pinestreet Society fair, which made thirty-seven hundred dollars in 1860, and an anti-slavery fair, which netted four thousand dollars in 1859, were typical. More than a fourth of the budget for the Warren Street Chapel was derived from fairs in 1857. Anniversaries, on the other hand, generally did not draw much from outside the church membership, and they wore a less appealing face. Tracy Patch Cheever made the point in 1855: "This is 'Anniversary Week' in which all the religious sects assemble to hear speeches upon various topics—of tracts, foreign missions, Sunday schools, anti-slavery—much gas. I can call it by no better word is here annually expended."[3]

In the 1850s Bostonians were constantly engaged in building and rebuilding churches. In the late 1850s, a large number of churches and societies that had been considering erecting or acquiring new structures took the plunge. The Baptist Canton Street Church opened its doors for the first time in 1856. It was followed by Baptist purchase of the four-thousand-seat Tremont Temple, completed in 1858, and the dedication of the building as "a free temple for religious services forever." Other churches followed in 1858. The pew holders of the Federal Street Church voted to sell their building and build a new one on Boylston Street in Back Bay. A new society in South Boston calling itself the Church of the Unity hired a minister from Nantucket and immediately determined to erect a building at a cost of thirty-six thousand dollars, the purchase price of the Tremont Temple a few months earlier. The following year, the Centenary Church in South Boston, a Methodist society and therefore, supposedly, less extravagant than other denominations, decided to build a new twelve-hundred-seat church for twenty thousand dollars. The Zion Methodist Episcopal church, a more extravagant denomination if one accepts the figures published by the *Evangelist and Religious Review,* voted to build that year also, and began sending their "agent" to prospective donors. The Pine Street Church set their sights on a new building that would accommodate as many persons as their own church and the Park Street Church combined, and warrant a reduction of the pew tax by 50 percent by significantly increasing the Sunday attendance. Five thousand seats proved too expensive, so the church planned a forty-five-thousand-dollar building with twenty-five hundred seats. Six hundred persons met for the first time in the basement chapel of the new church in 1860, the church proper being still under construction. The Old South Church was not about to move, but in 1857 it spent ten thousand dollars removing the elevated pulpit, brightening the interior with skylights, replacing the ancient square pews, freshening the stucco, and replacing the organ. The rehabilitation of the building did not cause the inconvenience and disorientation that relocation to a new building would have caused, but it brought with it a troublesome web of problems nevertheless. Contractions, absorptions, and outright colonization characterized the business of some of the larger churches as well. In 1859 the Park Street Church took over a mission school for African Americans, and in the late 1850s the Old South Church opened chapels on Lowell and Chambers Streets. In 1856 the city of Boston opted out of supporting the

New England ministries of the Seamen's Friends Societies except in the city of Boston, and in 1858 a merger—not typical but not unusual—took place, joining the Massachusetts Convention of Universalists, the Massachusetts Sabbath School Association, and the Massachusetts Home Missionary Society.[4]

UNSETTLEDNESS AND DISHARMONY IN THE CHURCHES

When established churches moved, when societies undertook to settle into a neighborhood by building a church, when religious organizations expanded or contracted, or when a renovation brought down to the floor a pulpit that had been raised high up on a column, churchgoers were forced to adjust. Changes were constant in the latter part of the 1850s, seriously disrupting for some Bostonians the patterns of continuity within their religious communities and leaving them uncertain about the future of their institutions. Even George Scandlin, who was awaiting ordination and settlement in a parish, was provoked to pour out his frustration in his diary, ruing "the Din of the city—things around me transient." The problem was intensified by complicated relations between laypersons and ministers. Sometimes, a prominent minister simply left town. The Rev. A. H. Burlingham left the Harvard Street Church for a New York City pastorate in 1856, and Alexander H. Vinton, Rector of St. Paul's Church, fled to Philadelphia. Sometimes a minister was run out of town, as was the case at the Shawmut Church in 1858 when the congregation voted overwhelmingly to dissolve the pastoral relation for "the welfare and stability of the church." Sometimes pastors took leaves of absence, and many took long summer vacations in the country, during which time churches closed, usually in July and August, the "warm season." For those Bostonians who stayed in the city, ministers made arrangements to merge congregations. Three or more congregations would meet at a host church to engage in services led by a Harvard professor or an ambitious young replacement minister brought in from Cincinnati or Hartford or New York. The vacant summer pulpits brought strong criticism from the religious press and from individuals inconvenienced or disoriented. The *Evangelist and Religious Review* scolded absent ministers for leaving their "sheep without a shepherd." Most importantly, the merging of congregations for the summer provided an occasion for differences to flare up, and for problems that ordinarily remained submerged beneath the surface of religious politics to emerge at a time when the clergy was least equipped to respond to them. At times, the problem was intensified by the number of pulpits that were vacant because permanent clergy could not be hired for them. Just after pastors returned from their summer vacations in 1855, the *Watchman-Examiner* took stock and reported that in South Boston, "five churches are destitute of a pastor." Such circumstances probably did not encourage religious persons to invest in the notion that the ministry was the "balance-wheel" of the "whole machinery" of religion, as Rev. Seth Sweetser proclaimed in 1858. For some Bostonians, the "machine" metaphor was becoming more apt than that of the "balance-wheel."[5]

The business of running a church sometimes led to more complicated problems between clergy and their supporters and disenchanted laity. In 1859, Joseph Ballard, a member of the Old South Church, published a forty-six-page booklet entitled "Reasons for the appointment of a committee to investigate the prudential affairs of the Old South Church." Alarmed at the fifty-one-thousand-dollar debt of the church, Ballard claimed that "its business has, in many instances, been transacted in a very irregular manner, (in some cases illegally). . . ." Outvoted in his bid to initiate an investigation, Ballard further claimed that the quorum of fifteen voting members "was made up in such a peculiar, well-organized manner, as almost entirely to forbid any change in the government, or any investigation of its proceedings." The Attorney General of Massachusetts, Steven H. Phillips, filed suit against "the ministers and deacons of the Old South Church," and together with counsel for the prosecution Uriel Crocker, another disgruntled Old South member, forced the leadership of the church, including the lay Standing Committee, to make a full accounting of the money. That accounting eventually disclosed that very large sums of money given to the poor had plunged the church into debt, but not everyone accepted the explanation. Money matters complicated the affairs of several other churches at this time as well, most notably the Pine Street Church, which became involved in legal problems over its handling of a deed, and the Church of the Unity, which gave the appearance of holding secret meetings to plan the erection of a new church building. Such matters were dispatched to the courts. But on occasion, displeased parishioners might as a last resort choose a more informal option, as did a member of the Christ Episcopal Church, when he and a companion engaged the rector and his supporters in fisticuffs during the Sunday service.[6]

Denominational gains and losses were obvious in the 1850s. Methodism expanded with a remarkable ease while the Baptist interest diminished. The second largest denomination in New England by the end of the decade (approximately one hundred thousand members), the Methodists counted ten thriving churches in Boston proper. A letter to the *Baptist Standard* on the other hand voiced a negative opinion about Boston: "I fear that there is a relative decline there." Competition for members was keen, and churches that were unable to compete were drained of members and financial resources, leaving some churches barely standing while others grew large. In 1860 the *Independent* noted the consequences of competition, figuring that "Boston has at least a dozen more Protestant churches than are needed." In the midst of this competition for members, churches recalibrated their covenants. The Federal Street Church opted for a stripped-down statement of the covenant of the church that stressed the mediation of Jesus Christ, obedience to the will of God, and a willingness to deny oneself and take up the cross. The Park Street Church also published a simplified statement of its articles of faith and covenant, which, though not as spare as the Federal Street iteration, listed just five basic points: (1) the authority of the Old Testament and New Testament, (2) Jesus Christ as redeemer, (3) Cambridge Platform polity (i.e., the "congregational form" of church government), (4) examination of all members for admission, and (5) form a whole together as a church. The Old South Church, which was the last church to remove from its building the old, square, Puritanesque pews, retained a long and detailed statement, a "Confession of Faith" that ran to thirty-two chapters. All three churches survived the religious commotion and dislocations of the late 1850s.[7]

Although the First Amendment to the United States Constitution had disallowed establishment on the national level, Massachusetts continued to funnel state money directly into the Congregational churches until the 1830s. Accordingly, the process of competition, which had remade the face of denominationalism in most of the rest of the nation, had been somewhat retarded in Boston. In the decades leading up to the Civil War, as churches came to terms with the consequences of pure voluntarism, intense rivalries took root among the Protestant churches in the city. Differences loomed larger and the religious turf was more openly contested as Bostonians came to appreciate the nature of the new ecclesiastical order. The *Boston Evening Transcript* referred to "that sectarian feeling which lately has become so intense among most of the Protestant sects." The orthodox *New Englander* informed its readers that "holy intelligences must look down on a quarreling church with amazement and sorrow. He who wept over Jerusalem, may well be supposed to weep over a covenanted brotherhood, marred and broken." Surveying the changes in New England life in the fall of 1858, the *Boston Daily Advertiser* delivered the news that John Adam's sacrosanct quaternity of town, church, school, and militia had all but vanished. The most far-reaching of the changes involved the church: "In the church, or the congregations, the change has been still more marked." The old system of a parish, "all the inhabitants of which were obliged by the fundamental law of the state to contribute to the support of public worship, has wholly disappeared." Once called the New England system, the organization of churches "is the New England system no longer. In stead we have half a dozen rival societies in every town, and no compulsory payment."[8]

Ezra Stiles Gannett, having heard a "one-sided" lecture at the Bedford Street Church early in the summer of 1857, spoke the following week at his own Federal Street Church on "1. Unity, but 2. Our difference—dwell—on this point." Differences were sufficient, according to the *Evangelist and Religious Review,* to sabotage good-faith efforts to build unity, so that the churches "derive little advantage from a fraternal exchange of pulpits." The dispute between Congregationalists and Unitarians remained the centerpiece of doctrinal controversy, but the more orthodox of the Congregationalist churches also picked at their differences with Baptists, and especially the Baptist appeal to the emotions. A meeting of the Massachusetts Congregational churches in 1856 was marked by the introduction of a resolution that proposed discontinuing correspondence with all other denominations. A quarrel with the Dutch Reformed Church the following year was sufficient to decide a majority of delegates in favor of the proposal. The *Christian Observatory* thought the religious landscape of the city pocked with "mutual misapprehensions." George Scandlin, the North End minister, recorded in his diary a more forceful opinion, calling the religious debate "a warfare among themselves."[9]

By 1858, the protagonists in the broad public debate about religion indeed had hit their stride, seasoned by a decade's worth of difficult encounters. Ministers feuded with each other in public and in private. Sometimes the issue was doctrine. At other times, the problem grew directly out of the competition between the churches. Fifteen years after the fact, Jacob Merrill Manning still could not forgive Princeton graduate Rev. Edward N. Kirk for coming to Boston and drawing off forty-seven affluent members of the Park Street Church to form the Mount Vernon Church. (Kirk topped the feat in 1857, making bitter enemies in England and vexing Emperor Napoleon III by outrightly purchasing an English church in the Rue d'Aiquessau, Paris, and introducing the American *Common Prayer Book* and extempore prayer.) Manning also was involved in a running disagreement with his partner at Old South Church, Rev. George Blagden, who was, appropriately, a transplanted southerner. And religious leaders at the same time had to field criticisms from persons who found fault with the Protestant churches as a whole. Anti-slavery activist Abby Kelley—among a vocal contingent of other women and men who agitated for civil rights—was regularly cited in the press for her unyielding attacks on the churches, and in the 1850s Theodore Parker was at the height of his powers, vigorously attacking the theological standpoints of virtually all the denominations, and feeling those denominations push back just as hard. Parker outlined the dynamics of the theological debate in a letter to a friend in 1858, observing that "a great change has taken place in the theological opinions of thoughtful men in New England, within ten years. . . . Still the stationary party becomes more intense in its conservatism." Lucy Larcom, once upon a time a mill girl in Lowell and later a teacher at Wheaton Seminary, had seen enough of the squabbling by 1858, explaining in a letter to Esther Humiston that her premeditated break with orthodoxy was grounded in her realization that Christianity did not have to do with "opinions," but rather "with the heart and life." Churches sometimes tried to keep internal dissensions hidden, as was the case for the Shawmut Church during the course of the dismissal of its minister, when it rancorously announced: "Nothing, however, is yet determined on so far as the public know." But enough dirty laundry was hung out in public to negatively impress even occasional churchgoers such as Henry W. Haynes, who in the midst of the debates of the late 1850s surveyed New England's past and surmised that the people of Massachusetts historically had been opposed to religious toleration.[10]

The extent of the friction among the churches and even within churches was reflected in the projects they undertook to cultivate an image of harmony. The installation of Jacob Manning as associate pastor of the Old South Church in 1857 brought out a cast of representatives impressive even by Boston standards. Forty-one pastors and deacons from twenty-three churches showed their colors that day, and in that year before the revival, they listened to an appeal for unity that would have pleased even Lucy Larcom in its emphasis on the communication of religious truth "from heart to heart." The fact was that ministers in Massachusetts had been preaching periodically about the importance of harmony throughout the 1850s. Out in Worcester, for example, James Barnard Blake had heard the clergy repeatedly speak on "accepting other Christian denominations as brothers." And in town, lecturers and ministers had taken up the subject with increasing frequency, clothing it in sobriquets such as "brotherhood," or "neighbors," or in the case of a lecture attended by Susan Brown, under a more ambitious heading, "Unity of the Human Race." Dusting off some traditional strategies for fostering religious unity, ministers also undertook cooperative projects that gave some evidence that they sought to practice what they preached. The series of sermons at the Pitts Street Chapel in the months after Manning's installation—on the topic "What shall I do to be saved?"—seemed to suggest that some of the churches—Baptist, Congregational, Universalist, Episcopal, and Unitarian—could still act together. Such demonstrations, however, could not vanquish the tensions that riddled the churches. George Scandlin, minister to seamen, worried about ever finding a minister whose theological ideas were compatible with his own and who was therefore a possible candidate to share a pulpit with him. He eventually confessed to the flamboyant Methodist Rev. Edward "Father" Taylor, who like Kirk also was a transplanted southerner, his desire simply to be ordained "an independent minister of the gospel to seaman." At the other end of the spectrum was Unitarian pastor Thomas Starr King of Hollis Street, who invited a Trinitarian opponent into his pulpit to preach "The Reasonableness of Endless Punishment." Keenly aware of the shades of theological difference in the thinking of ministers, but encouraged by the example of ministers preaching at each other's churches, churchgoers vigorously pursued a policy of visiting different churches throughout the city for Sunday services as well as for weekday lectures. Bostonians of all sorts participated in the moveable feast of religion, including established residents such as Susan Brown, whose extraordinary record of attendance at church services and lectures included visits to a synagogue; Stephen Salisbury, one of Gannett's flock at the Federal Street Church, who brought the spirit of harmony to his Italian peregrinations, writing his family in 1858 that he had attended mass three times in the Sistine Chapel; Francis Bennett Jr., a recent arrival to the city who recorded his impressions of each of the many churches he visited (e.g., "very good indeed," "a very good sermon"); and the Arthur Nichols family, Old South members who tried out the Catholic, Swedenborgian, Episcopal, and African American churches.[11]

The churches sought to improve harmony in various other ways, both large and small. St. Paul's, an Episcopal church on Tremont Street, in 1858 adopted a plan of admitting to communion all who would come. Exploiting another option, the Boston churches grudgingly agreed in late 1856 to set the time of afternoon Sabbath worship at three o'clock, "instead of half past two, as has been the custom from time to time immemorial" in order to bring uniformity to Sunday services fragmented by renegade churches which had already settled on the later time. In some instances, attempts at harmony were intermingled with efforts to assert difference, as in the winter, 1858 series of sermons, described by William Gray Brooks as "one by a minister of each denomination that is on their distinctive doctrines, the subject for each 'Why am I Episcopalian'—'Why am I Orthodox' or 'Why am I a Unitarian &c—." The denominations seem to have had no problem in meeting together for a conference on Sunday schools held in Montreal in 1857, reported by the religious press with the overstated comment that the event demonstrated how "evangelical Christians of at least seven denominations can cordially co-operate." It may have been that the meeting was dominated by lay teachers rather than clergy. Remarking on a similar gathering in Boston the previous year the press had pointed out, again in a suspiciously straining tone, that "the harmony of the meeting experienced not the slightest jar."[12]

The conciliatory efforts of Sunday school teachers were not enough to solve problems among the churches in Boston, however. Alongside the various disruptions in the churches caused by movings, closings, financial problems, overextension, underservice, absentee pastors, and other shortcomings, the failure of church leaders to hit upon an effective plan for bolstering confidence in the churches was widely noticed. Even the staid *New Englander* in 1856 asked, "Is the Pulpit Losing its Power?" and reckoned that in previous years "a sermon was good that had power on the heart," but that such preaching was currently in short supply. And the *Watchman-Examiner* asserted that "the building of more churches will not meet the difficulty." If there was to be progress, "it must be principally by lay agency. . . . Let them [laity] gather small congregations wherever a few can be collected. . . . The truth is, lay-agency has been too much lost sight of." The concerns of the religious press proved predictive. During the peak months of the 1858 revival, laypersons organized the overflowing morning and noon hour gatherings while ministers sought to come to terms with their expendability in weekly clergy-only prayer meetings.[13]

The clergy made periodic ineffective attempts to shore up its standing. Acting jointly, the ministers defied the governor's injunction against political sermons on Fast Day in 1857, and preached political sermons across the city. Father Taylor of the Bethel Church remained an esteemed figure throughout Boston, nearly a living legend for his ministry to sailors, a calling that earned him notice from Charles Dickens and from Rev. Luther Farnham, who suggested linkage with the Galilean himself. And the clergy continued to take seriously their "contract" with their flocks, articulating it as "a deeper, closer contract" than even that between husband and wife. But Bostonians could not help poking fun at their ministers. Lyceum lecturers who roasted them delivered, as Mary Mudge wrote in her diary one night, "a real feast, we laughed enough for one evening." *Ballou's* sketched a "true to life picture" of the minister replete with waving handkerchief: "I notice in some cases a *handkerchief* habit in the pulpit, which has led me to inquire if that very necessary article is a part of theological training." Playing out the scenario through examples of stuffing, clenching, rolling, and spreading the handkerchief, the writer concluded: "I once went to hear a popular young preacher, and as much as half of his sermon was made up of pocket-handkerchief." On occasion the ministry outdid even the images created by the teasing articles. Rev. Eleazar Williams was widely known in Boston and New York for his claim to be the Dauphin of France. Rev. Thomas Starr King, barely over the trauma of his conversion to Unitarianism, publicly declared that Unitarianism was "the brain of Christianity" (a statement, moreover, intrinsically skeptical with regard to the value of emotion). Loss of confidence was felt even by some ministers. George Scandlin, through no fault of his own, ended up stuck, like the yet-to-be-invented character Joseph K. of Franz Kafka's *The Trial*, expecting each day, month after month, the news from the Committee of the Fraternity that he was to be settled in a church. After a three-and-a-half-years' wait, of regularly confiding his bewilderment to his diary, the news still had not come and he left town.[14]

Complicating all the criticism and rejoinder about ministerial incompetence or unawareness was the ministers' own customary complaint about salary. "My salary, when fully paid, was scarcely sufficient to support a family," wrote one senior minister. *Ballou's* found the city parishes "in favor of holding the pastor to the smallest possible stipend that will keep body and soul together." The religious press complained that "the business men of this city pay our common porters more than many of the poor ministers receive," and offered instructions on "how to discourage a pastor," which began: "Promise him the very smallest salary for which his labors can possibly be obtained, and pay that with the greatest irregularity." Ministers fought back by declaring work-to-rule. "Two sermons in a week cannot be *written*," barked the *New Englander*, as it explored further the question "Is the Pulpit Losing its Power?" But ministers received little sympathy for their sufferings, real and imagined.[15]

MINISTERS AND EMOTION

The most biting complaints of the laity had to do with the failure of ministers to cultivate feeling in their congregations. Ironically, those complaints were fueled in part by a few ministers' own published declarations about the centrality of emotion to religion, and their professions of hope for raised affections in their congregations. Ministers varied in their thinking about emotion, some wanting more controls, more official means by which to channel it, than others. But especially when considering the issue of preaching, they could not escape the hallowed memories of George Whitefield and Jonathan Edwards, as well as the well-known preachers of the early nineteenth century. Two years before the outbreak of the revival, even the conservative *New Englander* waxed eloquently about the role of emotion in Protestantism. Invoking Whitefield, Edwards, John Wesley, Robert Hall, and others, it raved about how a good sermon, "in the rapid and fiery energy of its delivery," enabled a preacher to carry off, "as by a resistless flood, the thoughts and emotions of his hearers." Because "passion is of more value to the preacher than imagination," the sermons of the best preachers "glow with emotion." Drawing upon a metaphor well known to religious Bostonians both through their devotional reading and their participation in the fire-watching culture of the city, the magazine declared, "we must 'ignite our logic' to make eloquence of it," so that a sermon "kindles every sympathy and every emotion of the soul." The following year, still before the final countdown to the revival, George Blagden, pastor of Old South, lectured on "the feelings of a devout man," stressing the importance of emotional expression for both minister and layperson, explaining that God does not hide his feelings, but rather, "he is honest, and chooses to disclose his feelings just as they are. . . ." Such affirmation of disclosure was welcomed by increasingly sophisticated and critical auditors, who, like Susan Brown, could breathily recommend Henry Ward Beecher one day ("I have seldom ever heard his equal") and denounce another minister on another day for even marginal errors ("very eloquent language, but not much of an orator in gestures"). Such criticism was not unusual. Charles French dotted his diary with asides such as "a very thin man, & a very thin sermon." Gamaliel Bradford was tired of sermons that were "flat." W. H. Hoyt was invited by a woman to attend a meeting "to try & get some of the stiffness out of their ministers." *Zion's Herald and Wesleyan Journal,* published by the Boston Wesleyan Association, was dissatisfied with the emotional quality of preaching even at a time when Methodist churches were growing faster than any other denomination. "Our preaching does not move the people to immediate action," it complained. Dull sermons were "one of the greatest defects of our modern, formal, stiffened church exercises" and lacked the emotional staying power to keep people from "cooling off" once they left the church. The *Liberator,* in the course of applauding the uncommon case of a woman who had entered the ministry, suggested that male ministers had buried a feeling, "feminine" side under a "cold and intellectual" Christianity. Gamaliel Bradford criticized a sermon and at the same time acknowledged his conceptualization of the event as a commodity exchange when he wrote: "rather flat, but I put in a quarter." [16]

The discussion of emotion in churches, and specifically of the failure of the ministers to excite it, sometimes was organized with reference to gender. Women were thought more emotional than men and therefore good bets to incite a more robust emotionality in congregations—if, of course, they were allowed to take the pulpit. The unrelenting campaign carried on by the *Liberator* on behalf of woman's rights frequently sized up the clergy as kingpins in a conspiracy to oppress women. Reprinting incendiary articles that declared women unfit for the pulpit, and supplementing those with its own strident demands for equality, the *Liberator* kept the matter before the public throughout the 1850s. Declaring that women had been "shut out from the medical and clerical professions, and transformed to nurses and collectors of alms," the paper added that such a program, like others against women, had been carried out for absurd reasons. Making the point elsewhere, the paper asked: "One of our religious papers (*The Churchman*), expressed itself hostile to the presence of females in the choirs of our churches, on the grounds that their voices are 'sensuous.' We wonder if the writer of that super-pious article entertained a similar opinion of his mother's voice when she sang him to sleep in his infancy on her bosom?" When discussion quieted down, the paper revived it by reprinting conservative screeds, in one case by excerpting from the *Boston Pioneer*, a German paper: "Lord of the heavens and earth . . . withhold women from the pulpit!" It was clear that women's emotionality was suspected by some persons for the very reason that it was promoted by others: it was thought potentially disruptive of congregational order and decorum, and, therefore, the stability of the church and the clergy's reputation and jobs. For as long as the issue of women clergy was before the Boston reading public in the 1850s, so also was the issue of emotion in religion. [17]

The likelihood of reform that would bring emotional revitalization seemed slim for Bostonians, and as a consequence they shopped more determinedly for alternatives. From 1849, when the *Boston Recorder* fretted about a "feeble ministry," to the very middle of the revival, when the *Liberator* referred to "stock" in "ecclesiastical corporations . . . which is badly depreciated just now," laypersons remained anxious about the quality of their religious leadership and the thinness of emotional culture in the churches. Some meetings experimented with the anxious bench. One commentator wrote that there was "a demand for more histrionic preaching." And a magazine article, in considering "stimulating drugs,—opium, tobacco, coffee, and booze," admitted that some of the clergy had become desperate: "We have even heard of ministers of the Gospel, who, when they would produce a highly-wrought, impassioned sermon, resort to similar narcotic aid." The ministry, indeed, was in a state of crisis, and both ministers and laity knew it. Both also knew about supplements or alternatives to religious life within the congregation.[18]

ALTERNATIVE THRILLS:
SPIRITUALISM AND PASSIONATE REFORM

The thrill that at times was lacking in the Protestant churches could be had in the theatre or lyceum, and, increasingly, at a séance. Spiritualism developed rapidly in Boston in the 1850s, attracting a broad base of interest and offering different things to people in the various parts of that base. Some persons embraced Spiritualism's philosophical aspects, others found its emotional components appealing, and still others turned to it in crisis for a sense of stability. Women flourished as leaders within its anti-official organization. Publicists expertly promoted it, exploiting its sensationalist aspects. And many people attended séances simply for entertainment, for a kick.[19] William Gray Brooks wrote during the summer of 1857 that everyone in Boston was excited about it, even as he predicted that it would turn out to be "the greatest humbug of the age." The *New Englander* said that Spiritualism was "marvelous" and full of "wonders," but had long ago been surpassed by the truths of Christianity. Ezra Stiles Gannett, pastor at Federal Street, visited a house where two mediums presided and although the "table tipped. . . . nothing more," he "stay'd an hour." Charlotte Forten, an African American woman fond of the theatre and concerts, attended meetings even as she confessed to her journal, "But I cannot think there is a *spiritual* agency." Analyzing the phenomenon for the Massachusetts Medical Society, Dr. M. S. Perry accused Spiritualism of being contrary to the "accredited truths of philosophy," but noted that it gained converts every day. Mary Mudge attended meetings at which women talked about Spiritualism. George Troup lived in a boardinghouse where a little girl down the hall was a medium. The Melodeon featured trance mediums and Spiritualist lecturers twice a week, and they drew crowds of over a thousand persons. And the *Transcript* reported in 1858 that "a large number of dwellings in all parts of our city have upon them notices of certain 'mediums' to be found inside at specified times, who will tell for a dollar" a patron's future. Taking square aim at the sale of thrills, the paper drew a connection between sensationalist tales in novels and the for-profit enterprises carried out by "mediums of all descriptions." Uncredentialed and unregulated, such persons need only nail upon their door a "seven by nine inch tin plate" advertising their services, and then, "straightway the house will be beset by a pack of inquirers, easily satisfied by a few cunning answers; you exact your fee and the scheme is complete."[20]

One estimate put the number of "secret or open Spiritualists" in Boston in 1857 at twenty-five thousand. That very generous figure, in the unlikely event that it was true, would have been roughly equal to the number of persons who were members of Protestant churches in 1850. The staff of the *Evangelist and Religious Review* perceived an explosion of interest in Spiritualism, and passed that perception along to its readers in various articles mixing curiosity with caution. The Spiritualist *Banner of Light*, which began publication in Boston in 1857, advertised mediums as it disseminated Spiritualist ideas. The *Transcript* also ran advertisements that were not dissimilar to entertainment promotionals: "Spiritual Meetings at the Music Hall every Sunday. Tomorrow, 30th inst:, Thomas Galles Forster will speak under spiritual influence. . . . The singing sisters will take part in the exercises." But if Spiritualism was a matter of "extracting a fee" and "completing the scheme," not everyone welcomed it into the market. A convention of Spiritualists in the city in 1859 were warned by one of their speakers not to be "led away into free love errors," an accusation that the *Advertiser* had made against them the previous year, and one to which Spiritualists everywhere were accustomed. It was a criticism pointed enough to draw public attention but at the same time sufficiently ambiguous, given the parlance of the time, to escape any serious investigation. Spiritualists were also used to being implicated in popular tests of clairvoyance and fortune-telling. Typically, a committee wagered a "spirit-rapper" or other "Spiritualist" that the person could not provide some practical manifestation of spiritual powers. In Boston in 1859, one such arrangement bet a sum of five hundred dollars, seated an investigating committee of "scientists" chaired by Professor Louis Agassiz of Harvard, and proved the Spiritualist claims an "entire failure." The fact that such tests were conducted with money on the table was a key element of their performance. Money was lost and won— or so it appeared at such events—the event itself guaranteeing excitement and strong emotional response regardless of the outcome. George Scandlin, after witnessing an encounter between a clairvoyant and an investigator, reported that "the assembly was outrageous" after the clairvoyant was exposed, and loudly hissed him. Whether spirit-rapping or clairvoyance actually had much to do with Spiritualist ideas as they were articulated by the *Banner of Light* was irrelevant. For many people, rapping, mediumship, séances, religious women, emotion, and public performance were bound together under a makeshift category of "spiritual manifestations." While people filled auditoriums to engage the spectacle of such things, the *Liberator*, caught between its aggressive coverage of women's rights and its skepticism about the "spirit world," fussed that the "spiritual orgies" in the city "encourage Romanism . . . by declaring that a 'medium' is necessary for our reception of truth from the other world." More pointedly, it elsewhere assessed the problem in terms of popular understanding of emotion, explaining that "excitement" in the mind of the "operator" was the key to understanding "the influence of spirits."[21]

Doctor Benjamin Rush, theorist of bodily excitement, would have approved of the excitement that Bostonians experienced at a séance, or in a table-rapping parlor, or at the table of a fortune-teller, inasmuch as such experiences kept the body in motion, and, therefore, healthy. The nature of the emotional stimulus itself was unimportant, and any analysis of "good" emotion or "bad" emotion that might be involved was irrelevant. For persons whose "motion" was retarded because of a shortfall of inspirational preaching—too many "thin" or "flat" sermons—immersion in Spiritualism was a live option. Not all sermons were boring, of course. And, in fact, some of the most intense interest in Spiritualism in antebellum Boston corresponded with the excitement of the revival. But, as Bret Carroll notes, Spiritualists were essentially "comeouters," and they left their denominations when they declared for their new religion. Some persons—Pastor Gannett is an example—sampled spiritualism at a séance or similar occasion, explored what Ann Braude has called "sensational mediumship," and returned to their city congregations. Interest in the various spectacular phenomena lumped together under the category of Spiritualism developed alongside public enchantment with the theatre, concerts, fires, penny press shock journalism, and, ultimately, the evidences of divine providence Bostonians detected in the remarkable events of the prayer revival of 1858.[22]

The two great crusades of the 1850s, abolitionism and temperance, also offered frustrated churchgoers the possibility of emotional engagement. It is worth noting here that the temperance movement, with its carefully choreographed appeals to emotion in stock stories about drunkards' wives, orphan children, lost fortunes, and eternal damnation, offered excitement to Bostonians who actively involved themselves in its cause, as well as to persons who merely observed its public rituals of blame and redemption. The history of the temperance movement is replete with the invention of tactics, subsequently refined over many years, geared to engage the heart, or, in Scottish terms, the faculty of feeling. Emotional meetings, exuberant marches, tear-jerking testimonies, and heartfelt pleas to the electorate characterized the public activity of temperance activism. (Abolitionism, as we shall see in a later chapter, was widely regarded by its critics as the province of the hyper-emotional.) The irony of the movement is that its tactics stood in stark contrast to its message. That message was concisely articulated by the *Boston Medical Intelligencer* in addressing "intemperance, or other habits," that were destructive: "Temperance includes regulation of feeling, due use of the faculties; avoids excess of passion, as excess in food and drink, to preserve entire the intellectual faculties." Excess of drink was associated with excess of feeling, and regulation of drink with regulation of feeling. This theme was developed in many different ways during the course of the temperance movement, and to such an extent that references to intoxication and inebriation came to commonly be associated with overexcitement. Publications of all sorts adopted the discourse linking feeling and drinking. The *Massachusetts Teacher*, for example, wrote about "habits of mental inebriation," that are "systematically formed by our habits of early training. Children learn to live upon excitement and to love it. . . . Common events and common duties become tame and insipid." The *Christian Observatory* found that the excitement of novelty in religion was associated with the same lethal template. "They ask for novelty as the drunkard for intoxicating drink," said the magazine, "that they may forget themselves, the truth, and God, in the dreams of a heated imagination."[23]

In service to eradicating a behavior that overexcited emotion, the temperance movement excited public concern about "drunkard's wives," exhausted women who worked inside and outside the home to support a family, only to have their meager earnings stolen by husbands who were addicted to whiskey. *The Young Women's Friend,* Daniel Eddy's popular manual, devoted an entire chapter to the phenomenon. Theatrical productions mined the rich vein of feeling in the image with ongoing productions of plays such as "The Drunkard," which Susan Brown went to see in 1858. Ministers exploited the image, magazines ran artists' renderings of it, and in case anyone still did not understand, the *Liberator* invoked it constantly in connection with the campaign for women's rights, as in its report on a female temperance lecturer who "established indisputably that woman had an absolute RIGHT to the protection of a stringent prohibitory law, because by law, woman was now entirely at the mercy of any drunken wretch who calls her wife—her earnings, her very clothes are his to pawn for Rum." The correlation of women's rights with temperance proved to be problematic in the long run, however. Christian groups, which in general resisted agitation for a female ministry, came to dominate temperance, intertwining it with an agenda of issues framed in the language of Protestant theology and ethics. Women who had differences with the church-backed movement were not welcomed. Henry Clark Wright explained in his journal in 1853 one incidence of dissociation:

> Met Susan Anthony & her father & had a talk. . . . Susan Anthony has been the principal agent in the Temperance movement among the women of this state this past year. She & Elizabeth Stanton, they started the movement & got it under way. Then the <u>Christian</u> [illeg.] men came in—got control of the society—& turned Susan A & Elizabeth S. out—because they were considered <u>Infidels</u>. <u>Christians</u> cant work with Infidels to rescue a world from Drunkenness. . . . It is a simple fact that these whom the church berates as Infidels are the very men and women who have led the way in every <u>practical</u> reform.[24]

The resort to images of broken homes and shattered childhoods was at least partially successful because it shifted the argument away from the trickier, less productive discursive ground of the relation of alcohol consumption to health. A hundred years earlier, Massachusetts physician John Perkins had written on the beneficial effects of wine, and some subsequent medical opinion had reinforced and enlarged that perspective. Medical theorist Athanasius Fenwick wrote that wine was good for the body, and Dr. Benjamin Rush believed that beer, wine, and hard cider all were advantageous to health. That view, and elaborations of it, were common among Bostonians. Gamaliel Bradford's account of a trip with classmates to Mt. Katahdin in Maine was typical of those who connected alcohol with health. Writing about lumberjacks he encountered, he noted that in the spring they came down the river and gathered "to pass a few months in drinking and frolic there. . . . A finer or more stalwart body of men than these woodsmen I never saw." Magazines such as the *Puritan Recorder* raised the alarm, with panicky stories such as how on "a recent Saturday night," fifteen thousand persons, "mostly young men and boys of fourteen years, and upward," were drinking beer in city saloons. But it did not prevent George Troup from visiting the Pocahontas Saloon for days on end, to play euchre and whist, assemble puzzles, and "to see the boys." And it did not stop liquor vendors from realizing a "rushing trade" when they set up stands out on the harbor ice, during the bitter winter of 1857. It did not stop William Henry Smith from waking up many mornings ashamed at his intoxication the night before ("got dreadfully drunk," "shame! shame!"), nor did it seem to deter Henry Haynes from his overimbibing with friends: "I am ashamed of myself for getting tight. . . . Somehow, I always drink

more than the other fellows & get tighter. . . . a miserable day following, &
it really does not pay."[25]

Temperance advocates sponsored parades, public lectures, protests, and
other public scenes to draw attention to their cause, and were especially ea-
ger to reach young men such as Haynes, who thought temperance "based
upon a logical absurdity." The Young Men's Temperance Society, complete
with a raft of officers and directors, was founded in Boston in 1833. A triumphant Father Mathew led a parade of child pledges through the streets
in 1849. The Grand Division of the Sons of Temperance, presided over by
a Grand Scribe and other officials, launched forty-six new divisions in the
city in 1858. But none of these succeeded in converting the young Arthur
Howard Nichols, who as an eleven-year old attended temperance meetings,
came home, and drank brandy. The real successes of the temperance movement were to come later, but in the 1850s the movement was still something of an entertainment to persons who were not involved in it. A joke
about a drunk who talked back to and belittled a temperance man was published in, of all places, *Young America,* a Boston serial edited by boys. The
1857 inaugural issue of the *Atlantic Monthly* (at that time called *The Atlantic*), featured a story that included a scene in which an audience observed "the temperance missionary and the infuriate liquor-dealer . . .
upon the same platform" at the Melodeon with several other persons. The
narrator described the audience: "A portion had come to be interested, a
portion to be amused. To the former, the object of the meeting was wise
and great; to the latter it was ridiculous enough to be worth an evening's
senseless laughter." Temperance advocates urged prayer (to "God who is so
ready to answer those who ask aright") and took courage that at least their
efforts were stemming the tide of immigration because of "our stringent
laws relative to the sale of liquors." Some Bostonians joined the campaign
and became caught up in its intense emotional performances. Others engaged the movement as an exhibition, as a show of feeling, manifested in
theatrical performances, sensationalist literature, and the public displays of
the passion of temperance men and women.[26]

THE RELUCTANT MINISTRY

Churchgoers in Boston commonly visited different congregations. In some
cases, this was because they were new in town, part of the ongoing, vast migration of people to the city, and they were searching for a home congregation. Some persons went from church to church because over time it had

become customary to do so (a custom reinforced by in-migration). In other cases they were looking for a church better suited to their religious sensibilities, and, especially, for a minister who preached a better sermon. Complaints about ministers focused on their cold, unemotional style, and criticisms about churches centered on their valuing of theological "opinions" over religion of the heart. The context for such criticisms was partly formed by Bostonians' familiarity with emotional preaching from a variety of sources: several in-town ministers, most notably the colorful Father Taylor; visiting preachers, especially those from the West; and their experiences of revivals in the city, including the revival of 1842,[27] and, as it began to unfold in 1858, the Businessmen's Revival.

Relations between Protestants and their ministers were complicated by the unsettledness of the churches, which arose not only as a result of population movements but from relocations of congregations to new church buildings, disagreements over finances and calls, adversarial relations with women's rights advocates, overextension, and competition among the churches themselves. Efforts to promote harmony between churches underscored the fact of competition and sometimes marked boundaries more deeply between them. The environment of uncertainty created by such problems discouraged most of the Protestant ministry from deploying means to cultivate emotion. Services remained carefully arranged in orders of exercises, ministers preached moral lessons, and, while making reference to the importance of heart religion, they reined in their sermons. They were New Englanders who traditionally battened down hatches against Nor-easters and antinomianism, and they were not about to experiment with a program designed to raise the emotions at a time when they might not have the resources of solidarity and influence necessary to control it. The fact that theatrical productions aggressively experimented with more efficient means to rouse the emotions complicated matters.

Alexander Goldenweiser, in his pathbreaking *History, Psychology, and Culture*, holds that the "objectivation" of emotion was fundamental to religion, and he refers to that process simply as the manufacture of the "thrill" of religion.[28] Although it was not yet the case that "the thrill was gone," for some Boston churchgoers it clearly was diminished. Spiritualism and the temperance movement, especially in their spectacular and sensationalistic aspects, offered their own alternative thrills. But most importantly, Spiritualism and the temperance movement, like the theatre, lyceum circuit, or dime novels, served to cultivate an awareness of emotion, of the ways in which emotion was aroused, and the consequences of that arousal for the individual and the group. They enriched discourse about emotion and sustained a view of "objectivation," of emotion as a "thing" that could be possessed in the way that any other thing might be gained, that is, through economic exchange. Bostonians soon would reinvest that emotion in the churches, where it would be intensified and manifested in new ways. During the revival, the element of gender would come to the forefront as well, and in a way that few expected.

SIX

Men, Women, and Emotion

GENDER AND EMOTION

The Businessmen's Revival differed from previous revivals in that it attracted so many males to its prayer meetings, and otherwise garnered male support. Accounts of widespread male weeping and moaning in those meetings, as well as laughing and other displays of emotion, record detail that in some cases includes allegedly verbatim transcription of spiritual testimonies and confessions, invariably of a strikingly emotional nature. Such behavior was atypical for men, who as a group were not thought particularly emotional creatures. Indeed, the nineteenth century had constructed women as the emotional sex, as persons who by nature expressed emotion more freely, who elicited and fostered it in others. These roles for men and women—in simple terms, men as bold, intellectual, geometers, and women as feeling, nurturing, submissives—did not evaporate on the eve of the revival. They remained in force throughout the mid-nineteenth century. Increasingly, however, there was fluidity to gender roles. Some of the boundaries marking cultural expectations for male emotionality and female emotionality became blurred. Attributes and behavioral patterns associated with one sex sometimes leaked into definitions of the other sex, so that by the late 1850s, there was manifest mutability in gender roles. Male emotionality was progressively reconstructed as expressive, and men were encouraged to display their feelings more openly not only in the home but in various public settings as well. Women's intelligence became more visible alongside their emotionality, and public interest in and support for an expansion of the role of women in public life—including recognition of women's capabilities as social leaders—intensified.

A measure of fluidity in gender roles did not mean that previous notions of gender attributes disappeared. On the contrary, in certain cases traditionally male and female characteristics were given greater emphasis. Women remained cast as timid by nature, as dependent and intellectually weak. Their emotionality, which was regarded as the defining feature of their sex, was linked to impulsiveness and recklessness. Accordingly, women were expected to conceal that very aspect of their nature thought most essential to femininity. Those who failed to mask their feelings, to rein them in as it were, ran the risk of being labeled hysterics. Too much concealment, on the other hand, signaled emotional coldness, an offense equally damning. Men were expected to perform boldly and independently in the public arena, in the marketplace, controlling their emotions, but determinedly angling for their interests and speaking out for the good of the polis. At the same time, they had to meet the role requirements of a loving husband and father, through displays of warmth, spontaneity, and sympathy in family settings. Men's emotional lives were complicated as well by their fear of public humiliation and their deep reservations about their feelings, about which they frequently were ashamed.

The reconsideration of various aspects of gender resulted in a certain amount of confusion for both men and women, but it offered opportunities as well. Most importantly for understanding the revival, it helped to create an environment hospitable to the public performance of emotion by men. Such public emotionality was not merely a borrowing of behaviors previously associated with women, however. Men's expression of emotion in the revival was integrated with other traditionally male characteristics, and especially with the view of men's boldness and initiative in the marketplace.

WEAK BODIES, WEAK MINDS

Bostonians, in looking upon men's and women's bodies, drew conclusions about character and emotional makeup based upon the appearance of physical weakness, strength, beauty, and various other features. Women's fragile intellectual constitution was, for example, one component of a view of women derived from the understanding of them as physically weak but attractively packaged creatures. Commentators explored such constructions shamelessly, fashioning linkages between the body and virtually every aspect of female character. "This is an era of light and knowledge," proclaimed the manual *The Art of Kissing.* "Science is gradually illuminating with its divine rays all that was dark, mysterious, and incomprehensible in nature." Among the secrets of nature made visible to the age was the relationship between "amativeness, or the sexual feeling," which was an aspect of character located in the cerebellum, and the physical appearance of a woman. Utilizing the bump-reading science of phrenology to determine the size of the amative area, the book identified, through sketches of various types of women, those who were desirable and those who were not. Women were judged "kissable" on the basis of the shape of the skull, and especially, the size of the amative area. A picture of Eve proved that she "was no prude," while the less comely subject of another sketch was declared a likely member of "a female reform-society." A Rev. Vermyle, addressing a group of girls during the revival, reiterated this wisdom, warning his young subjects not to imitate the women's rights leader Abby Kelley Foster, "a woman with a broad red face, (!) coarse skin, (!!) great veins on her neck, (!!!) and very unkissable." *Ballou's Pictorial* advanced the case in another way, and bolstered it with a reference to the Bible: "We have always found that homely women are the most intelligent. It is according to the rule of St. Paul, 'to the pure all things are pure,' and even so to the plain all things are plain." This left-handed remark was even more sinister given that some Bostonians did not consider intelligence an important or even necessary attribute of womanhood.[1]

Bostonians noticed beauty as well as plainness, and made various judgments about its relation to character. Mary Faxon Forbush, an avid consumer of English-, French-, and German-language works by Voltaire, Hazlitt, Gibbon, Rousseau, Milton, Renan, Tocqueville, Hume, Goethe, and numerous other writers, wrote in her diary after observing an acquaintance during an evening social that the girl "will be brilliant and fascinating" to the "young gentlemen" because "she is so fine-looking and so *naïve*." *Gleason's* explained simply that "there is a spell in woman. . . . Beauty, too, has a natural power over the mind; and it is right that this should be." Mrs. Catherine Flint was less inclined to philosophize, but made frequent notations in her diary of the women she encountered socially. Following a parlor musical recital she thought "the two Mss Duncans very attractive—the eldest very striking," and recorded that two other women in the room "suited my taste." The following week, at a party with the Longfellows, she noticed "a great many pretty young ladies." At a wedding she saw "Miss Susan Shaw," who "was particularly distinguished by her beauty," like the bride herself who was striking because of "her rich dark hair, in its massive folds." Susan Heath likewise noted the beauty of women. She thought it important to mention in her diary that on a walk to her sister Abby's house "I went over the hill in the morn. Saw a pretty lady sitting on the hill drawing the view. . . . lovely and so ladylike." A few days earlier she had noticed Charlotte Hedge, the daughter of her minister: "I saw her lying on the bed—she looked very pretty." Joanne

Harvey saw a "very beautiful girl" singing at a Baptist meeting and knew that in California "Americans choose very large Mexican ladies for beauty."[2]

Young W. H. Hoyt was keenly observant of female beauty as well, literally filling his journal with reports of pretty girls he encountered on his walks through the city. A self-professed admirer of Lord Byron's "noble character," he regularly navigated the streets and alleys of the city in the hopes of glimpsing beauty. "I stroll up and down Washington Street to see the pretty girls. But not seeing any," he wrote, "I stopped to piss in an alley." His reports, which he entered in code in his diary, recount frequent walks on Leverett, Spring, and Poplar Streets, on Washington Street, and especially Hanover Street, which was a short block over from Ann Street, a part of town known for its houses of prostitution. Sometimes Hoyt "did not see a single girl I knew quite provoking," and at other times he found himself in a neighborhood where "few young ladies are better looking," and on Hanover Street was thrilled when he "saw many very pretty girls & and a good large number rather doubtful character." He reported enthusiastically on what was "by far the best occasional sermon I have ever heard Mr. Stone preach," on the topic of the dangers and temptations of the young man in the city, while at the same time prosecuting an agenda of visitations to various locations where he expected to encounter subjects for his gaze. A mid-winter visit to the Howard was typical. The entry began, "In the evening went to the Mercantile Lecture Rooms to hear declamation." Then in code, it continued: "In imagination. My bodily presence being at the Howard. Had a fine time. Very much pleased. Madame Turner a splendid rider. Glorious form so full the curious could see her bubblys quite well." Henry Haynes seems to have looked more closely at women than Hoyt, and sometimes found flaws as a result, as in the case of his encounter with a young woman who he found to be "very smart & witty," but who "would be very pretty, if it were not for eyes, which sometimes are a little crossed."[3]

Hoyt noticed men's bodies, too. His male classmate was "good looking," and he decided that the Rev. Clarke was a handsome man. Henry Haynes kept his eyes open as well, noting a "very fine looking young man" who played piano one night, and underscoring the importance of the "good" sailor as an ideal of masculine attractiveness when he wrote about his visit to Captain Armstrong in Charlestown, reporting that the man was a "noble specimen of a whole-souled, hearty, old sailor; moreover he is a fine looking man, very, [*sic*] tall, & with such a breadth of shoulders. He looks like a fit man for the quarterdeck." Charles French, a nineteen-year-old clerk at George H. Gray and Co. who later opened his own hardware store, fell in love with both young women and young men, and commented regularly on their physical appearances as well as his own. After a meeting with a Miss Moore ("I tho't I used to love her once, but I was mistaken. It was only a temporary affair."), he noted that "she is better looking than ever." Similarly he observed one summer that "Annie is growing quite pretty. Eh bien. Queer world and queerer people." Worried about his future at the firm, he fretted about competition from a new hire: "Just my luck, Young Whitney is a good looking fellow" and therefore likely to advance quickly in the firm. Still smarting from a failed love affair with George Wheelock, he grew his whiskers because a new love, Rayner, liked beards. But at the same time he noted that Rayner "is a very curious boy and think's [*sic*] only of a man's appearance." Women noticed men's bodies, too, and indicated their likes and dislikes in their diaries. Susan Forbes, who habitually commented on the physical appearance of the male lecturers she heard, thought one an "eloquent & a fine looking man & fine speaker," but wrote of another, "Florid looking, light-hair, wears glasses. Not very interesting." Commenting on a fellow teacher, she wrote, "Mr Jacobs in school for the first time. Like his appearance very well." And she found the new chairman at her school, a Mr. Norton, equally attractive: "I like his appearance very much."[4]

Bostonians enhanced their physical appearances, accentuating or downplaying certain aspects of it, through their choices of dress. And they noticed each other doing so. Middle-class observers commented on clothing styles, their appropriateness to the season and occasion, and the meanings of "dressing-up." Charles French knew in February of 1858 that "Red petticoats are all the rage now." A few months earlier William Gray Brooks wrote about the popularity of the hoop skirt in Boston, proposing that this "style of ladies dresses is very costly and extravagant and extends to all classes." He added that he did not like the skirts because they filled up the pews at church and made the procession to communion almost impossible. Catherine Flint made detailed descriptions of clothes that women wore to parties, and, like French and Brooks, looked for trends: "Most of the ladies with low necked dresses." Many men and women who could afford it—Brooks's claim that women of all classes wore hoop skirts was exaggerated—paid close attention to the representation of a self in clothes. When Charles French dressed up in new clothes one day he found his lover attentive: "Rayner took particular notice of me. It shows how he worships dress." Waldo Flint was as concerned about fashion as was his wife, Catherine, and especially about his appearance in fine clothes. In writing to her about his failure to attend the Harvard graduation ceremonies of 1856 he enunciated a special sorrow: "I regret not going this morning in as much as I had put on all my best clothes, and, after a careful examination of my person in the glass, and touching up a little here and a little there, I thought to myself, I was looking uncommonly smart. Perhaps it was nothing but vanity & self love, which led me to [illegible] such an opinion, and so I shall be able, I guess to get over the disappointment, of not showing myself, in my very best attire, to the young men and maidens who will be assembled at Cambridge."[5]

At the same time that Bostonians endeavored to show themselves in their "best attire" they voiced their support for limits on public showiness. Magazines of all sorts regularly published sermonettes on the necessity for restraint in dress, frequently recommending a "masculine" style for both men and women. The *Liberator,* as part of a commentary on "the ruin of a young girl of seventeen, by her pastor," had condemned the man's dressing-up: "Let him be ever so fine-looking and elegant in his tastes, it is shocking to see him adorning his person and dressing with fastidious neatness for the public gaze." The *Liberator* extended the criticism to "the silly butterflies that flutter in the sunshine of fashion, or the designing women that seek to ensnare the innocent men whom they encounter." The editors of *Gleason's Pictorial* took a similar view in an article entitled "Dress," which advised "a manly carelessness" in fashion matters, according to the "three good uses we may lawfully make of apparel; to hide shame, to preserve from cold, and to adorn the body." The *Massachusetts Ploughman* proposed a similarly masculinized, geometric model of dress for women, explaining that "a female of good taste will dress so as to have every part of her dress correspond. This while she avoids what is showy and attractive, everything will be adjusted so as to exhibit symmetry and taste." *Ballou's* likewise advised young men to avoid a "dashing creature . . . showy in dress." Said the magazine, "Choose rather one of those retiring, modest sensible girls . . ." Such a girl might have been the Universalist preacher Mrs. Jenkins, who arrived in Boston in 1858. The *Evangelist,* effusive in its praise of her, remarked of her appearance for a sermon in nearby Lawrence that "at the time to commence, she divested herself of her bonnet (not a gay one), and developed her head, with the hair arranged with faultless simplicity. There was an utter absence of all attempt at show." One message in the *Evangelist's* report on Jenkins was obvious: she was able to function in a public role—in man's world as opposed to woman's sphere—because her appearance sufficiently approximated the ideal of "manly carelessness." But her dress could not conceal her physical characteristics. She was still obviously a woman, and therefore susceptible to analyses of woman that took as their starting point perceived weaknesses of the female body vis-à-vis the male. That perception served as the ground for other ideas about the intellectual and emotional aspects of women's lives.[6]

Reviewing a book on the life of Mary Lyon, the founder of Mt. Holyoke Female Seminary, the *New Englander* summarized the drift of most writing about women with reference to a simple catch phrase: "They apply to the sex the term, 'weaker vessel' . . ." Some years earlier the *American Baptist Magazine*, reviewing *The Works of Jane Taylor*, had demonstrated the step from thinking about the body to thinking about the mind. Reminding its readers that "the intentions of Providence are shown in the formation of the intellectual and physical systems of women," it began by asserting that "woman by the peculiarities of her physical constitution, is shown to have been intended for offices which require no great physical strength." Consequently, the magazine deduced analogous "intellectual peculiarities" which made it "clear that she was designed as the guardian and teacher of childhood," which is "her own proper station." *The Young Woman's Friend*, a companion volume to *The Young Man's Friend* that sold one hundred thousand copies in the mid-1850s, asserted that "the constitution of woman, her physical organization, the structure of her material nature, show that she was not designed for hard, out-of-door service." The *Massachusetts Teacher* explained that the difference between little boys and little girls "is, that the boy is not merely, or chiefly, passing through a state of transition." Because girls have no "cricket, no foot-ball," and no childhood avocations to give meaning and direction to their everyday lives, their childhoods, which are nothing more than a waiting period for their social coming-out and marriage, remain a liminoid "dreary blank." A girl's "insipid and artificial experience" thus is "totally different from the independence and unworldly spirit of a boy," who "lives in a world of his own." As *Ballou's* unsympathetically pointed out, dependence rather than independence accordingly marked the lives of woman as they aged: "The dependence of woman in the common affairs of life is, nevertheless, rather the effect of custom than necessity." But, said the magazine, there were certain aspects of a woman's constitution that cooperated in her dependency. "The secret of her weakness is hidden in the depths of her own bosom," said *Ballou's*, telling the secret: "Timidity is the attribute of her sex." A life of waiting, of dependence, of "busy idleness," timidity, and artificiality produced persons predictably blank, said the unsympathetic *New Englander*, which unwittingly reduced the scenario to a cogent irony: "Many a woman spends her days, as if her mission on earth were principally to exist, and as if that were a burden to bear." The *Christian Observer* communicated its perception of the character of women's lives in a more venomous way:

> Take a woman to board, and (if it is perfectly convenient), she would like a drapery, instead of drop curtains. . . . She would like breakfast about ten minutes later than the usual hour; tea ten minutes earlier, and the gong, which shocks her nerves so, altogether dispensed with. . . . She can't digest a roasted or a fried dish. She might possibly peck at an egg, if it were broiled with one eye on the watch. . . . She is often afflicted with interesting little colds and influenzas, requiring the immediate consolation of a dose of hot lemonade or ginger-tea. . . . I'd rather have a whole regimen of men boarders. All you have to do is, to wind them up in the morning with a powerful cup of coffee, give them a *carte blanche* to smoke, and a night key, and your work is done.

This kind of rhetoric about women's timidity and shallowness, a standard part of lectures, sermons, and journalism, seeped into women's own diaries as they tried to understand their lives. Frances Merritt, who grew up in Boston and then went to Framingham to teach girls at the Normal School, at the age of twenty-five worried about facing her classes of children, remarking in her journal: "My greatest trial in teaching is my timidity and distrust in action." Susan Heath, likewise repeating the language of middle-brow literature, repeatedly described her life in 1858 as "languid and uninterested," and resorted to arsenic to try to cure herself.[7]

Nineteenth-century writers translated ideas about women's physical weakness and constitutional feebleness into arguments about their mental shortcomings. The cornerstone of the argument was, as the *Youth's Companion* stated it, that "women reason more by intuition than by logic." While making protestations about the uniqueness of women's capabilities and the way in which those capabilities complemented the strengths of men, many writers nevertheless supplied the details of women's inability to do the things that would have made them fit for public life. The *Massachusetts Teacher* affirmed that women and men complemented each other in the classroom, but asserted that woman "is accustomed to take concrete views of things. Neither her mental constitution nor her habits, have led her to contemplate things chiefly in the abstract. She paints the imagination, where the male teacher defines and reasons." It was only a short step from this language to explicit statements about female inability to reason a straight line, and, especially, to think abstractly. Enunciating standard doctrine, the *Massachusetts Teacher* advised that girls could memorize but had trouble thinking, and illustrated the point with reference to a case of a girl learning grammar: "I know one, who, in three weeks, learned her text-book from beginning to end, and could give promptly, in course, every definition and paradigm, and every rule of syntax. . . . But she knew very little of the principles or use of grammar till some years afterward." From early in the century Bostonians had read that "these pretty favourites of nature must not too curiously peep into the dark and winding recesses of science." That bias, combined with misgivings about women's capability to "define and reason," supported a worldview repeatedly reinforced by published anecdotes. One such anecdote, which like most was inserted as filler at the end of a column or bottom of a page, was entitled "Practical Illustration": "A gentleman, not long since, took up an apple to show a niece, sixteen years of age, who had studied geography for several years, something about the shape and motion of the earth. She looked at him a few minutes, and said with much earnestness, 'Why, uncle, you don't really mean to say the earth turns round-do you?' He replied, 'But did you not learn that several years ago?' 'Yes sir,' she replied, "I *learned* it, but I never *knew* it.'" [8]

Such notions of female weakness were countered by the arguments of some writers, lecturers, and teachers. Sometimes those arguments were unambiguous. At other times they reflected the complex meanings of gender as they were shaped and reshaped during the turmoil of the 1850s. The *New Englander* in one essay condemned lecturers who assumed "an original and wide disparity between the sexes in point of intellect," asserting that "even if we select the faculty of reasoning, which is the highest and foremost of our intellectual faculties, we shall find no ground" for any distinction between men's and women's intellectual powers. At the same time, however, the magazine accepted the possibility that "mental vision does go *pari passu* with stature and bodily strength." Susan Anthony and other lecturers labored to dispel notions of essential differences of reasoning ability through various rhetorical strategies, including one that appealed to pragmatics, as summarized in the *Liberator* following Anthony's lecture in Boston: "Who ever heard of a masculine or feminine way of solving a problem? As long as boys and girls run together and play in the dirt, they are alike." Some magazines indeed published stories where girls ran faster and jumped higher than boys. They also published material that satirized the issue, such as the article that ridiculed adults who "tell her she is a little lady, and must not run. . . ." Other articles pointed out specific intellectual accomplishments, especially in mathematics and science. One magazine argued against "the general opinion of men in regard to the inability of the female sex to pursue the higher, the abstruser sciences with success," pointing out that women in fact "have grasped even the highest reach of pure mathematics in our universities with marked success." The example of mathematics was especially salient, because, as another writer knew, "the study of arithmetic, if rightly pursued, will tend to the culture of self-reliance." And on occasion the issue of woman's intellectual powers was cast as a matter of organization and communication rather than real differences. Elizabeth Palmer Peabody, who attended Margaret Fuller's "conversation classes," recorded in her notebook the usual line about women, noting "the cultivation of the affections as their special province." She added, however, that the purpose of the class was to "turn these impressions into thoughts, & to systematize these thoughts."[9]

The varied styles of asserting women's capabilities as equal to men's generally tended to broaden and complicate the discussion, rather than focus it. The different strategies for making the point of women's equality did not dissolve into a single, coherent viewpoint at mid-century. Traditional notions of domesticity and feminine emotionality, the ongoing argument about physical differences, and preoccupation with the question of who was smarter remained. Joanne Harvey still wrote that "my heart is right if my head is weak," and Mary Walker, a student at the West Newton Normal School, observed in her journal, "Subject of conversation was whether women are inferior to men in intellect. I believe most of the school thought they were not. But I think they are." The collision of notions of woman's "weaker" nature with assertions of women's equality begot an intellectual environment that encouraged the eclectic organization of ideas, and engendered complex metaphors that blurred some of the lines between men and women at the same time that it reinforced others. In instances where individual women attained public visibility, the rules of gender, and especially a set of suppositions about female weakness and timidity, weighed heavily upon them. Women who flouted such rules ran the risk of being portrayed as impostors, while women who sought to work within those rules faced complications arising from the ambiguity of their position and the volatility of public thinking about what women could and could not do. The ambiguities born of such processes surfaced in a number of ways, including the rhetoric of sexual politics. Elizabeth Palmer Peabody, after her eighteenth conversation class with Fuller, wrote, "Men do not ridicule or expose to suffering the woman who aspires—It is her own sex who brand her—the weak and frivolous of her own sex—but the enigma still remains unsolved—why are so many of the sex weak and frivolous?" And the *New Englander*, in observing that "men form their idea of woman by a mathematical process," confirmed the association of men with science, logic, and reason at the very same time that it scoffed at the notion that male mathematical prowess could fully capture the essence of womanhood.[10]

Beneath the language of debate about the strengths and weaknesses of male and female natures was agreement that the behavior of both women and men was influenced by emotion. Bostonians, like other Victorians, frequently correlated femininity with the heart and masculinity with the head. Such formulas conceal a more complex nineteenth-century understanding of men's and women's emotionality, however. Victorians were largely concerned with the appearance of emotion as an aspect of life in conformity with beliefs about human nature. That is, while embracing the idea that both men and women were emotional, they constructed women's emotionality in such a way as to conform it to notions about women's weakness, timidity, and unsuitability for certain kinds of public life. Men's emotionality was understood in connection with what was believed to be the distinguishing features of maleness: boldness, assertiveness, and action. Both sexes were required to control their emotions, but for somewhat different reasons. In either case, the requirement of control of emotion, reiterated constantly for both men and women, discloses that the surface of the discourse about emotion—which seemed to affirm woman's nature as emotional and men's as intellectual—was more rhetoric and less a descriptor. To construct women as fundamentally emotional creatures and then to assert the importance of their controlling that emotion necessarily invokes as standards other ideas about women's nature and their roles in society. The same is true of men, whose profile as thinkers rather than feelers was complicated by demands both that they control their emotions, especially for the sake of business success, and that they relax control of emotion in family life, in church, and even, sometimes, in the marketplace. In any event, for both men and women, the control of emotion was an undertaking founded on the assumption that feeling was a discrete part of human life that could be channeled, manipulated, repressed, or expressed. Much discussion about control of emotion accordingly implicitly questioned what was "natural," reinforced the abstraction of emotion from the person, and fostered a conceptualization of self as an aggregate of assorted components rather than an organic whole.

When *Gleason's* proclaimed that "a woman's whole life is a history of the affections," or the *Liberator* quoted Emerson remarking that "the life of the affections is the natural life of woman," they simplistically represented a broad complex of ideas about woman's nature and her social roles. Those ideas included Cogan's claim, articulated in *A Philosophical Treatise on the*

Passions (1821), that woman has "a stronger affection for everything that she pursues than men." It meant, as Daniel Eddy wrote, that "no one feels the death of a child as a mother feels it," and, as the *Boston Monthly* pointed out, that the "tie between a mother and a son, which is one of the noblest and purest in nature," naturally "lives in every pulsation of the heart." The *Massachusetts Teacher* explained that girls had their feelings hurt more easily than boys and more often "find their natural relief in tears," and, in fact, were "liable to hysteric fits from fright or other emotions." Woman as a feeler was plagued, said the *Christian Observer*, by "a want of well-trained mental powers and well-exercised self-control," that led to "the languor of hysterical affections."[11]

Women were expected to control and conceal their emotional nature. This requirement applied to their affectionate feelings as well as to their anger, depending on the circumstances. For all of the idealization of women in the nineteenth century, they were, like men, considered to be imperfect. The *Youth's Companion* explained that "it is plain that crooked as is woman's temper, forgive her faults. . . . since it is vain to attempt to straighten what is crooked." Women nevertheless were expected to try to straighten that crooked temper, and were taught various means for doing so. *How to Be a Lady*, a book in its fifteenth edition in 1855, offered the most practical of advice for control of emotion: "Discipline the muscles of the face. . . . If you allow every temper of the heart to find a corresponding expression in the muscles of the face, you will be sure to spoil the fairest countenance." The *Well-Spring*, like many other publications, congratulated the ideal girl "who never speaks or looks cross." The *Child's Friend and Youth's Magazine* encouraged its female readers to make friends with the "angel of self-denial," so that "when someone tries to provoke you, and you are determined not to be angry, the angel of good-temper is near you." The magazine likewise counseled "the quiet look of resigned patience." The appearance, the look, of being in control, whether one was on the verge of anger or in the midst of a romantic attraction, was essential to woman's reputation. So when Georgy Bartlett gave Henry Haynes a "very cool nod" at a dance, he interpreted it as a challenge, and determined to respond with his own performance of control "if that's her play."[12]

Women, like men, of course were criticized for the very things that they were expected to do in the interest of appearing a certain way. In certain instances female control of emotion might be thought of as haughtiness, their cheerfulness interpreted as dumbness, and their appearance of emotional evenness as coldness. In its worst form, such criticism put women in an impossible double-bind, painting them not as expert practitioners of facial-muscle control or accomplished self-deniers, but as charlatans. The *Christian Register* reduced the issue to a simple assertion: "falsehood or a habit of deception is said to be a feminine vice." (Deceptions could be discovered because women betrayed themselves with a blush, "that great index of the feelings."[13]) On the other hand, the pathway to emotional forthrightness brought the risk of appearing assertive, forward, capricious. At the beginning of the century, young Sally Ripley, who had vowed to "govern my passions with absolute sway," adapted Hannah Foster's *The Coquette* for a home production. Set as a dialogue between two sisters, Marcella and Daphne, it was grounded in the former's observation that women had the power "of affecting the hearts of men" through their expressions of interest and feeling. In response to Daphne's point that women must use that power for good, Marcella replied that she took pleasure in capturing men's hearts and then rejecting them, adding that "when they are rejected, it makes me proud as a queen." The moral of the story was enunciated by Daphne: "The caprice of Coquettes is well-known, which is the only reason men do not become infamous by deserting a woman." As *Ballou's* later pointed out, women were subject to the same sort of behaviors from men, so that "women of a little experience," were able to "learn that it is not quite safe to trust boys with the secrets of their hearts."[14]

In 1856, the *Massachusetts Teacher* announced that "the training of the feelings is the most important point in the management of girls." It observed that "most teachers are content to repress by discipline the external signs of temper and other passions, and then think they have done enough." In the case of Susan Heath, the training in repression seems not to have been sufficient: "I know how unbearable I am at times—but I cannot control my feelings." For Lucy Larcom, on the other hand, the training seems to have been all too effective. Writing to Esther Huniston in 1857, she lamented: "My problem is one I have spoken to you of before;—I can't <u>love</u> people; . . . My strongest hold upon human affection is for the hereafter; life would be *nothing* to me without it." For other women, the contradictions inherent in a construction of womanhood variously understood as crooked, affectionate, capricious, self-denying, deceptive, and redemptive frequently begot contradictory thoughts and behaviors in Victorian women. They also scrambled the standards for interpreting a woman's behavior, so that her own perceptions of her behavior frequently did not conform to other persons' opinions of her. So, Gamaliel Bradford, reporting on a discussion with his cousin Sarah, wrote of "her desire to warn me of feeling too deeply" for a certain young woman he had met. But in his next sentence Bradford characterized his cousin in a way that might have surprised her, given the nature of her advice to him: "If her passions were a little better regulated she would be a most superior person."[15]

Female expression of emotion was to some extent curtailed by the cultural commandment that women not appear assertive and, especially, that they bridle their speech. The shared concern of mothers on this count was summarized by Joanne Harvey in reflecting on her daughter's behavior: "Catie is very forward and needs more restraint." Lord Collingwood had given similar advice to his daughter, which was reprinted in Boston as follows: "I cannot forbear pointing out to you, my dearest child, the great advantage that will result from a temperate conduct and sweetness of manner to all people on all occasions. Never forget you are a gentlewoman; and all your words and actions should mark you gentle." Boston commentators boiled down this sort of advice into terms easily accessible to the middle class. *Gleason's* cast it as simple rule: "Tell her not to speak loud, it is so masculine; and that loud laughing is quite ungenteel," while the *Massachusetts Teacher* simply made reference to "the soft and winning voice of woman, in conversation and social intercourse." And in a tribute to the preternatural capabilities of women to communicate without speaking loudly, The *Boston Weekly Magazine* flat-footedly observed: "There is something irresistibly pleasing in the conversation of a fine woman; even though her tongue be silent, the eloquence of her eyes teaches wisdom." Trained to restrain themselves in their speech, women reaped a harvest of undesirable side effects for their trouble, including such an uncomfortableness with testifying in courts of law that they "suffer wrongs and insults rather than go into court and make a complaint." Their investment in the notion of the "silent tongue" also complicated their diary writing. In the case of Susan E. P. Brown, the thought of someone reading her diary terrified her: "What will be herein written? Dread future! None can read thee!"[16]

A woman whose reputation was linked to her ability to restrain her speech was also enjoined to avoid being the subject of the speech of others. The *Boston Monthly*, representing its trust in the timelessness of gender-related wisdom, quoted Pericles in a piece of filler entitled "Advice to the Female Sex": ". . . follow your natural modesty, and think it your greatest commendation, not to be talked of, one way or another." The surest way in which to avoid being talked about was, of course, to give no occasion for it. Such was accomplished by staying at home, which had the added benefit of keeping woman free of "contaminating contact" with the world, and facilitated the cultivation of woman's nature as wife, mother, and feeler. A poem of the time, "The Wife," declared ". . . in that name a world is sphered," and a seemingly endless assortment of other writings referred to that sphere of spousal devotion, affectionate mothering, and industrious house-keeping[17] as "woman's sphere," a space ordained by God as the place of woman. "No sensible person wishes the sphere of either sex changed," said the *New Englander*. "It is the greatest imaginable absurdity to think of it. God has cast the web and woof of society just right. . . ." The image of a woman with her needlework[18] in her lap before the fire, surrounded by children and flanked by a contented, pipe-smoking husband captured the imagination of New Englanders and modeled the role of woman as both emotional and practical. Twentieth-century scholarship that has explored the nineteenth-century "woman's sphere" has developed progressively more complex paradigms of interpretation of this aspect of American life. It is clear from that scholarship, as well as from nineteenth-century ac-counts, that the term "woman's sphere" denotes a rather broad field of ex-pectations of women, and a predicament of conflicting models and ideals, as much as it figures wholeness, coherency, and distinctiveness. Recent schol-arship to an increasing extent has been attentive to the complex social re-alities that framed women's lives, and accordingly has been careful in its use of the term. Mary Ryan's depiction of the multifacetedness of nineteenth-century "public" life, especially with regard to women, and Nancy Fraser's delineation of the notion of "subaltern counterpublics" together raise the question not only of how we locate the boundaries of a "public" space, but how we determine what is "private." The *Christian Observer* might de-clare that "woman's true field is her HOME," but because of the porosity of the categories of public and private, that might not always mean that the home was her true field. Simultaneous leakage across the conceptual line that divided men from women in terms of their capabilities and natures—we shall see more of this—further challenged notions of public and private by calling into question the masculinist underpinnings of the bourgeois ideology that insisted upon separation of private from public in the first place.[19]

The maze of nineteenth-century thinking about the home was further complicated by the fact that domestic life frequently was referred to as a condition of self-denial and sacrifice. At the very same time that the home was identified as the place where the nature of woman would flower most gloriously in the various domestic activities involving children, spouse, cooking, needlework, and moral education, it was presented as the proving ground for what one magazine poet called "the bleeding heart . . . the vir-tuous grief." Joanne Harvey, exasperated with the troubles of her son, tried valiantly to make her home a place of cheerfulness and moral vision, but even when she "retired quite late, feeling I had done all I could to make others happy," she would be beset by anxieties about her own self-denial: "Oh the many bitter thoughts, may he never know how I have suffered for him, and may he be forgiven when I can entreat no more." The *Child's Friend* magazine, under the heading, "Taking up the Cross," gave the following advice to women: "When Christ bore his cross up the steep ascent of Calvary he was not thinking of its weight. . . . You must not think how hard it is for you to bear cross words and looks. You must pity the defects of temper in others which cause them. You must give the soft answer because it turns away the wrath of others. As well as it is because it is right for yourself." Another story commented on the nature of day-to-day activities of a Christian female: "Her Christian education taught her those little acts of self-denial, that quiet, unobtrusive attention to little things, which contribute so much to the happiness of home." The role of designated sufferer extended beyond the walls of the home, shaping the daily activities of women as they moved about the city on errands, visiting, or at work. At least one man saw a tendency to excess in feminine self-denial. Gamaliel Bradford, reporting on the kindness his cousin Sarah had shown in bringing some of his books from Cambridge, remarked: "I believe she would have her head taken off if I asked it."[20]

While some women took up the cross of soft speech and self-denial, and other women created subaltern counterpublics—sewing circles, maternal societies, reform groups, health societies, fund-raising events, and so forth—another section of the female population of Boston sought inroads to the world of business and the professions, to the public world as seen through a masculinist lens. The best rhetoricians of the movement squarely addressed the matter of "woman's sphere." Lucy Stone spoke frequently in Boston, and Boston papers such as the *Liberator* provided detailed accounts of her lectures for those who were not able to attend: "She combated the idea of the distinctive sphere of men and women. . . . Each should be free to do that which he or she prefers and can do best." The *Boston Daily Advertiser* likewise reprinted large sections of woman's rights speeches, including one by Rev. E. H. Chapin of New York, who in 1858 told the boys at the Young Men's South End Benevolent Association that "we have no right to determine what is woman's sphere by any arbitrary prejudices. . . . Woman's orbit is the orbit of her humanity." Alongside of such reporting, the press provided accounts of women who had succeeded in occupations outside the home, in areas normally reserved for men. A woman who ran a coal barge appeared in print as "a perfect master of her craft, lifts coal with Herculean strength, and orders her laboring men about like the sergeant of dragoons. . . . and wo be unto him who disobeys orders or crosses her path." Other models of women's initiatives were the lecturers and preachers, the heads of households, the thirteen female physicians, and women such as Harriet C. Ladd, a member of the faculty of Chauncy Hall, which prepared students for science and engineering at MIT. Letters to editors mixed anger with humor. A seventeen-year-old farmer's daughter wrote the *Massachusetts Ploughman* to protest against "Bettyism," which transformed intelligent and industrious girls into women who "faint or go into spasms at the sight of an insect" and "never touch a pen save to edify some hair-brained popinjay, with soft lovesick nonsense." Stephen Salisbury Jr. might have thought that his sister "Georgia's head runs on plum pudding and mince pie," but Mary Faxon Forbush, like some other women, spilt her anger into diary entries that made clear her unwillingness to embrace "Bettyism." Recounting her visit to a factory in Lowell, she wrote:

> I do not feel particularly amicable or journalistic this morning, I confess. We were accompanied some of the time by Mr. Avery and part of the time by a Mr. Melcher. We were looking at a steam engine and, as I said something about liking to understand it. He said that he did not know that young ladies were taught such things and that he thought it would strengthen our minds quite as much to learn to make <u>puddings and pies</u>! I was quite disgusted and think it quite possible that I expressed myself in a somewhat contemptuous manner. How can men be so blind as to imagine that they will be happier with a wife who knows about nothing but <u>puddings and pies</u>—Bulwer says "Give me the woman who can echo all thoughts that are noblest in man!" <u>Puddings and pies</u>! bah![21]

The woman's rights movement established a strong presence in the Boston area after the National Woman's Rights Conventions of 1850 and 1851, which were held in Worcester. Abby Kelley Foster, who had grown up in Worcester and lived nearby, helped to organize the events, which, in addition to a strong Massachusetts delegation, attracted a large and luminous national participation, and featured stirring speeches by Lucretia Mott, Sojourner Truth, Angelina Grimke, and Frederic Douglass, among others. Kelley was a regular speaker in Boston, as was Lucy Stone, Elizabeth Oakes Smith, who was known for her "extraordinary dress," and Caroline Dall, who was reputed for taking "the extreme ground of women's rights, insisting that the female sex should share in all political, civil, and social privileges with the male, and that both sexes would be gainers by a practical recognition of their equality." Elizabeth Cady Stanton, Susan Anthony, and other leaders of the movement made periodic visits to Boston, and locals such as Ralph Waldo Emerson, Bronson Alcott, Thomas Wentworth Higginson, Theodore Parker, and William Lloyd Garrison spoke, wrote, and edited for equal rights. Like the woman's rights cause nationally, the Boston movement was not univocal by any means, and at times fragmented over issues of abolitionism, marriage, temperance, religion, the Fifteenth Amendment enfranchising black men, and fashion. (At the third Women's Rights Convention in Syracuse in 1852, Susan B. Anthony rejected Elizabeth Oakes Smith for president because she objected to the low-necked dresses worn by Smith and her nominator, Paulina Wright Davis.) The movement nevertheless filled lecture halls and newspaper columns for the entire decade of the 1850s, and was vigorously promoted in Garrison's *Liberator*. The Massachusetts "Act for the more effective protection of the property of married women" was passed in 1848, and the *Liberator* and the *Monthly Law Reporter* commented regularly on cases brought to trial under that statute, including *Westereth v. Gregg* (1852), which seriously limited its scope.[22]

Opposition to the movement took a variety of forms, all of which made for good press. Many writers held fast to the principle enunciated by the shoestring-budget *Budget* in its first edition in 1849: "A woman in politics is like a monkey in a china shop she can do no good and may do great deal of hurt." *The Young Woman's Friend* was equally blunt in 1858: "God has not granted to woman those natural faculties which will render her fitted for a public office in the debates of men," and noted especially that woman had no "gift" for "public speaking." The *Liberator* ran numerous articles in 1851–52 and periodically thereafter accusing the churches of conspiracy to stop the movement. The *Christian Observer* thought the Woman's Rights Conventions "monstrosities," and the *Christian Observatory* cited a "wise Arabian proverb: 'When a hen crows like a cock it is time to cut her head off.'" Another inflammatory article cited a chapter from the "Chronicles of England" suggesting that the hens might in fact do the cutting: "The young queens became rebellious and unmanageable, and their husbands complained to their father, upon that, by advice of Albine, the eldest, who complained that she would never be obedient to her husband while she lived, they all cut their husbands' throats in one night." Writers and lecturers lined up to register their opinions on "masculine women" and the *Youth's Companion* complained about "horrible, gorgonized, strong-minded girls." But such opposition seems to have had less and less effect on young males, some of whom favored the movement for various reasons. Sometimes a general principle was involved. *Young America*, a Boston serial edited by boys, reported in 1858 that "the great and General Court is now in session in this city, some strong minded women on the outskirts (all women of that class now are petitioning for redress of certain grievances, we think redressing would improve them, by diminishing their burthens.)" At other times the reasons were more practical. Young schoolteacher Henry Haynes preferred strong-minded women to Cambridge girls who had "no piquancy," and Tracy Patch Cheever didn't mind being "seized by the ladies and dragged to the dancing hall" during a party.[23]

By the mid-nineteenth century, rhetoric about "woman's sphere" represented a host of contradictions and ambiguities. If the home once was thought a proving ground for uninhibited performances of female emotionality, by the 1850s competing notions of womanhood had so undermined the construct "woman's sphere" that its effectiveness as a conceptual framework for women's emotional lives was greatly diminished. The notion of domestic life as the ideal cultural site for the expression of woman's most profound instincts rubbed hard against the construction of women as sufferers, as persons who constantly denied themselves in order to bring peace, order, cheerfulness, and happiness to the hearth. Women were thought to speak well without opening their mouths, to deceive when they followed the rules for emotional restraint, and to have abandoned the home in responding to invitations to become "factory girls." As Susan Porter has written regarding the last of these points, they were caught "between hegemonic cultural values and the strictly economic values of the marketplace." All such contradictions challenged the adequacy of the ideal of "woman's sphere" to order people's lives, and subsequently promoted leakage across the boundary dividing "woman's sphere" from the masculinist public sphere of the marketplace. The process was advanced by the woman's rights movement. As this happened, the values of the marketplace increasing intruded upon the domestic world, and the emotional transactions thought to occur there.[24]

MEN BEING MEN

A man was a male older than a boy. Beyond that, much was up for grabs in the Victorian conceptualization of manhood. "I like men really to be men," said a contributor to the *Massachusetts Teacher* in 1850, "and in order that it should come to pass, I think it necessary that children should really be children." The line between the two was sometimes clear and sometimes not so clear. Shortly after his twenty-first birthday, Charles French exulted, "So! I am a man" who was "a shade wiser, and more ambitious to do something to my credit" than the "boy I was five years ago." Henry Haynes at the same age had some doubts, however: "It is a short time since I was a boy myself. I am certainly a strange compound; the knowledge of the world & the experience of a man, the youthful feelings of a boy. . . . I feel too somewhat hackneyed." Gamaliel Bradford, who had started Harvard at the age of fifteen, believed that without the guidance and support of his mother he would have had "need of all the manliness which more advanced years can give." For Edward Everett Hale, a male's "boyhood may be said to end and his manhood begin" upon graduation from college. Manhood was clearly something that one developed, or, as a convict knew, one did not develop: "I remember all my boyish longings how I laid awake at night and prayed that I might be a good man, if not a great one, that I might have some way opened to me for the development of the highest manhood." That development was fraught with difficulties, and perhaps most importantly, the challenge of overcoming what the *Child's Friend and Family Magazine* called "the manliness peculiar to boyhood," an exaggerated, roughhouse, brash carelessness that ran the gamut from walking in the rain without an umbrella to death-defying stunts.[25]

One good sign of manhood was evidence of virtue. *The Young Man's Friend*, complaining that so many males "are destitute of the chief elements of a manly character," asked the question: "What, then, are the elements of true manliness?" Rejecting wealth, birth and blood, and intellect ("I admit the power of intellect . . . but a mere intellectualist is not a man"), the magazine concluded that a person showed himself a man "by a manly effort for the promotion of virtue," "by manly interest in the elevation of the race" (including all persons regardless of color), and "by a manly submission to the government of God." William Winter's *The Emotion of Sympathy: A Metrical Essay*, read in Cambridge High School in July 1856, identified an oft-mentioned attribute of manhood in juxtaposing it to womanhood: "Stern manhood's power and noble woman's charm,/ All pain to sooth and every care disarm." A flustered Samuel May, writing to Richard Davis Webb in 1857, underscored the importance of boldness in the adult male character when he fumed that his spineless publishers had not actively promoted his anti-slavery book. He placed a barb about northern waffling on the slavery issue into the complaint: "I don't think that Dix and Edwards have taken the least pains to sell the book. I presume it is a case of the miserable flunkeyism of New York publishers, of which we have had so many,—too contemptible and mean to think of with patience,—but a fair sample of the manliness of most of our Northern Men!" Achievement defined manhood as well. Tracy Patch Cheever, on his thirtieth birthday and seven years after he had been admitted to the Massachusetts bar, wondered whether his achievements were sufficient to define his manhood:

> But apart from my profession—when I consider myself as a <u>man</u>, either intellectually or morally, I know that I have fallen far short of that manhood which I <u>might</u> have reached. . . . Is this the true life—to wait and slumber and suffer occasion and opportunity to pass, and to find as we glide rapidly toward the natural end of our existence—that we might have <u>done</u> something—<u>might</u> have performed a noble work for ourselves and for mankind.

The *Massachusetts Teacher* agreed that "a true man is a nobler thing than a doctor, or a lawyer, or a merchant," and the *Christian Parlor Magazine* proposed that "a great man, if he touches a common thing, ennobles it." Such pronouncements smelled of the same ambiguity that had caused Cheever his existential nausea. Men were expected to be bold, assertive, brave, and calm in a crisis. They were thought to possess a certain kind of reason, a view represented in the pages of George W. Prescott's school notebook, where "Manhood" was studied alongside "Geometry." Bostonians also thought that men were emotional. And so, Daniel Eddy, author of *The Young Man's Friend*, could easily enough conclude his lecture on the distinguishing characteristics of manliness with the following query: "Have I aroused one manly feeling, have I awakened one generous emotion? . . ."[26]

An article reprinted in the *Massachusetts Ploughman* in 1850 stated that "we sometimes meet with men who seem to think that any indulgence in affectionate feeling is weakness." As the issue was continuously debated through the 1850s, popular thinking about it moved perceptibly to a position of support for the feeling man. The *Ploughman* urged men to "Cherish, then, your heart's best affections. Indulge in the warm and gushing emotions of filial, parental, and fraternal love. Think it not a weakness." The *New Englander* proposed that "the best part of any man" appeared "bathed in his own feelings and associated with his own best and strongest emotions." Tracy Cheever, echoing the Scottish faculty psychology, pronounced his belief in "the power of the will when directed by true love . . . that there is no *will* like the *will* of love." Frances Merritt valued "warm family affection" in a man. In addition, men regularly wrote about feeling depressed and about other men feeling depressed. Charles French was sad ("feel blue today"), Steven Salisbury Jr. less so ("I have been blue only once" on a trip to Europe), James Barnard Blake's friend needing cheering ("has the blues"), and Joanne Harvey could recognize when her son Augustus was feeling down ("Gus has the blues"). Men mourned and other men knew they mourned. A widower less than five months into his marriage, George Scandlin wrote: "I can not think of Fan without crying," and Elizur Wright, Boston editor of the *Antislavery Reporter*, heard from his brother Hanford following the death of Elizur's son Charles: "pain must have pierced your heart such as only a parent alone can feel at the sudden loss of a beloved child." On this theme *Gleason's Pictorial* in 1854 published a short account of tragedy entitled "The First Wife," in which a man who had lost his spouse "plunged at once into the deepest purgatory of woe; and though he groaned, wept, wrung his hands, and tore his hair, he regretted exceedingly that he was still unable to express his grief in a manner more adequate to the occasion." But men wrote about their joys as well. Tracy Cheever loved springtime: "So it is with man, while the beauty of the season fills his emotional nature with delight." And Chelsea resident Eliphay Arnold Jr., during and in between visits to prayer meetings, cried "not tears of sorrow but tears of joy" over his spiritual experiences. Arnold's friend J. D. Pratt knew of that joy, and told his friend so: "I think I know something of your feelings and joy at the present time."[27]

Emotion was manly. Gamaliel Bradford on a visit to Mt. Holyoke reflected on his mother's courtship and marriage there, climbed the mountain nearby, and read through the visitors' log at the top. Observing the emotional component of the remarks—especially the descriptions of feeling elicited by the dramatic view—he concluded that the best entry had been made by a man the previous day, and that "the tender outpouring of a manly & affectionate heart was touching in the extreme." Henry William Tisdale, a soldier in 1863, wrote on his twenty-eighth birthday that he accepted the responsibilities of his "Christian manhood" while he cried over letters from home.[28] Indeed, as a recent study by Reid Mitchell suggests, the diaries of Northern men fighting the Civil War demonstrates that even while, as one man wrote, soldiering "benumbs all the tender feelings of men," at the same time it served as a framework for free expression of emotion. One soldier accordingly told his wife, "I cannot sing yet those songs such as, the vacant chair, the tears come," but he added: "A man that cannot shed a tear when he thinks of those he left at home, is no man."[29] For Mitchell, the military culture, especially during the Civil War, produced for soldiers "a synchrony of public and private life," a judgment seconded by Samuel J. Watson, who has argued that for soldiers even before the Civil War "the line between public and private barely existed." Stephen M. Frank likewise has proposed that the letters of Massachusetts men who served in the war reveal an overlapping of the public masculine identity of soldier with the domestic role of father, a connection that helped to produce the "emotional richness" of men's domestic lives in the latter nineteenth century. As in the case of women, the lines between public and private life were redrawn for men, or in some cases even dispensed with, in the second half of the nineteenth century, especially with regard to emotional life. The essential elements of that redrawing were already in process for Bostonians in the 1850s, as definitions of masculine and feminine, public and private, reason and emotion, the marketplace and the home, child and adult, and fatherhood and motherhood were questioned and altered. But that alteration was by no means thoroughgoing. Male emotional life still unfolded under an umbrella of cultural assumptions that frustrated boundary-crossing adventures. Accordingly, even as change was taking place, the *Boston Recorder* reminded its readers that "every husband must weep apart,' and Ephraim Peabody, Rector of King's Chapel, found it impossible as he lay dying to see his two sons, even as he told his doctor that he loved him.[30]

Men, like women, were expected to become practiced in the art of emotional control, and the sooner the better. In the interest of reinforcing this message, writers invoked personages such as William Wordsworth, a Romantic poet who nevertheless modeled the "self-control of manhood," and George Washington, who "could endure steadfastly to the end the daily trial of patience" that was "characteristic of true greatness." For Gamaliel Bradford, William Henry Seward embodied "the most manly judiciousness," and especially, was "temperate." One magazine mourned the late David R. Page as an exemplar of male emotional training, observing that "his self-possession never left him; cool and collected at all times, he could look calmly on when most would have been unduly agitated or confused." Joanne Harvey knew her husband also to be such a man. When, in the spring of 1856 the family sawmill and planing shop caught fire, total destruction of the stock was averted only because "Father maintained the greatest calmness and decision." Such unfortunately was not the case for William Greenough, a member of the board of the Boston Gas-Light Company, who was taken to task by his business colleague Samuel Eliot for inappropriate emotionality during a fire at one of the company's properties. "Your nervous excitability," wrote Eliot, "is such that I set myself seriously to calm it down." For good measure, Eliot added a note on the reaction of another associate: "I found Mr. Giles in the counting room, as calm as a summer's morning, & every thing going on with the customary regularity." Schoolteacher Henry Haynes also experienced difficulty controlling his emotions in the workplace, but his predicament was less serious: "I want to laugh often, when I ought to be severe." Gamaliel Bradford, on the other hand, was well equipped for the business world because he had learned his lesson early in life, albeit through trying circumstances. Remembering the summer after his sophomore year in college, Bradford observed, "It was in this vacation that I had the most tremendous fit of passion that I ever remember in myself." After some girls stole his billiard balls in retaliation for a trick he had played on them, "my rage knew no bounds. I swore at & threatened to kill them, went up to my room & writhed & screamed with passion" until his mother came to his room and straightened him out. "This was just my character then," he wrote, "& the traces of it, though I hope more under control, are still in existence." William Plumer Jr.'s *Manhood, or Scenes from the Past,* one volume in a series of books on the life cycle, included a poem, "One and Twenty," that underscored the change from boy to man in terms of control: "Rouse then to nobler aims thy mind,/ And wake from sloth thy struggling soul;/ call into life each thought refined,/ And every meaner wish control." The *Boston Masonic Mirror* likewise pictured the transition from youth to manhood as a sobering of emotion, and, invoking "passion" as a code word for lack of emotional control, employed the common metaphor of warfare and survival in observing that "when the passions are aroused, and take the field against reason, clamoring imperiously for indulging, the contest is for life. The stake is not a mere transient external advantage, but *manhood itself* . . ."[31]

Reasoning about the need for emotional control in males was predicated on the assumption of men as players in the marketplace, as professionals, as persons whose work and social activities by definition brought them outside the home. This public life of men was described in an assortment of ways in mid-nineteenth-century Boston, but in almost all cases it was cast as a place where "cool and collected" thought and action brought rewards to both the individual and society. The connection of masculinity with a certain kind of life outside the home was well represented in an exhibit at the fair for the Boston Young Men's Christian Association in late 1858. The exhibit, labeled "Birthplace of Franklin, in Milk St. Jan 6, 1706," consisted of a drawing of a man standing in front of a house. The front of the house was a flap, which, when opened, showed the inside, including a mother knitting by the fire, a baby in a cradle beside her, a boy at his desk, and a girl spinning thread. Closing the flap, one exits the house and returns to the very different world of the man outside. A boy's departure from his home, his first step into the world, similarly was a dramatic event. Francis Bennett Jr. took that step at the age of seventeen, when he left home to work in a dry goods store. His account of the moment of leaving underscored the dramatic importance of crossing the threshold of the house on his way out into the world. After breakfast, a man came to get his trunk and valise and then "I left home. I found it pretty hard to keep from crying on leaving the home of my childhood. But I have resolved to be as manly as possible about it. Mother would not say goodbye. . . . I felt pretty pale once starting off." Bennett soon adjusted to the life of a clerk in Boston, but other boys had real difficulty. Henry Hoyt reflected on how his friend Bill had experienced troubles adjusting to his life in the city, writing that Bill "is a good natured fellow but to [*sic*] sensitive to get through the world easy & imagining things very different from the reality & putting a many construction on the commonest expressions." As if in defense of Bill, *The Young Man's Friend* warned boys that "in the crowded city," certain feelings, and especially "sympathy and compassion, those heaven-born virtues [are] ridiculed as effeminate by some." But the *Christian Observatory* was downright praiseworthy in describing the hypercontrolled demeanor of Richard Blackerby: "Though a man whose affections were naturally ardent, yet his passions were so subdued . . . that the loss of the objects of his tenderest attachment could not perturb his mind."[32]

The root problem for those boys who did not adjust to city life was less their sensitivity, their sympathy or compassion, than their inability to embrace a model of behavior that valued bold action. The thoughtful imagination of a Bill, and the display of compassion by any young man, were not in themselves stigmas or real impediments to career advancement. Only if they hindered the forceful exercise of the will were they problematic. "Men," a poem republished in various periodicals in 1855, began "God give us men!" and from there outlined some of the features of manliness, including "men who possess opinion and a will: / . . . In public duty and in private thinking!" An emphasis on force of will was likewise at the center of a short essay titled "True Manliness," which averred: "To be manly is to 'dare to do,'. . ." Men could reason, and men could feel, too, but unless a man acted, his masculinity remained unlegitimated. Accordingly, when James Barnard Blake—who, like Henry Haynes and many other Bostonians, saw in sailors the paradigm for manliness—described Captain Copp, he hinged his assessment of the sailor's manliness on the expression of conscience and heart in actions: "I love to see a man like Capt, altho' I seldom met such an one; he is a true man and I believe a true, sincere Christian; governed by a high moral character; checked by a wakeful conscience; and activated by the impulses of a noble heart, teeming with all that is good, and just, and godlike; his life is an example worthy to follow; and why every act bespeaks the *Man*." The *Liberator*, claiming to summarize the remarks of Ralph Waldo Emerson to a Women's Rights Convention in 1855, wrote that "man is the will, and woman the sentiment," while *Gleason's* published a more dynamic blurb: "His nature leads him forth into the struggle and bustle of the world." Manly action was decisive and bold, and proceeded from deeply held beliefs no matter how out-of-step they might be with popular opinion. One poem from the *Liberator* made this point with reference to the powerful flow of water: "He shall climb and never crawl,- / Two things fashion their own channel- / The strong man and the waterfall." This notion of course was deeply rooted in Protestant ideas about righteousness, conscience, and the fruit of a regenerate soul, and had been kept in play by the churches throughout the nineteenth century as they explained the nature of a call to preach (a principle that women eventually exploited) and sought to promote male commitment to the ministry. "If you are called to preach," said the Evangelist in 1858, "the people will soon find it out." But church leaders at the same time had to be careful not to overplay their hand, because, as the *Watchman* observed, "Christian men pray, of course; but their very interest in action is liable to tempt away the heart."[33]

It is clear that Bostonians considered speech an act. The injunction against women's speech was equivalent to their restriction from participation in certain spheres of action outside the home. The emphasis on free and open speech among men reinforced their role as active agents. Weaving together notions of manliness, fidelity to standards, boldness, and the willingness to stand apart from others, Bostonians came to an understanding about male speech as a marker for the masculine character. The *New Englander* asserted that "the people appreciate manliness, honesty and noble principle. . . . they hail, like the rising sun, a true man who speaks strong, masculine truth, and propounds eternal, sublime principle." James Barnard Blake concurred, adding the important qualification that bold speech not shade into emotionally uncontrolled speech: "I am always gratified to hear a man speak freely and boldly, without any fear whatsoever, when it emanates from a pure heart, and is not tainted with fanaticism." Such speech was detectable in males at an early age, and especially in their instinct to tell the truth even though it might lead to their punishment. The most popular and important example of this was, again, George Washington, who was recognized as a paragon of male virtue, boldness, self-control, and fidelity to principles. The *Child's Friend and Family Magazine* asked its young readers, "What made Washington a patriot?" The answer was his manly character that "had been ripening from his boyhood. It showed itself when he cut the tree, and scorned to tell a lie; . . ." The *Christian Observer* added that boys differed from girls in their capacity to face problems head-on and to persist in a course of action despite criticism from others. In an article entitled "To Boys and Girls," the *Observer* instructed its readers: "Now see how the spirited, manly, true-hearted, clear-tongued boy will do, after an error: He resolutely determines to acknowledge it, without being afraid of anybody's anger—to tell it just the way it was." Mythology such as this was parlayed into all kinds of advice for boys who grew up into businessmen. Assertive action and straightforward speech repeatedly were recommended as the building blocks of business success and frequently were linked with specific pieces of advice in the management of day-to-day affairs at the office. "Be frank at all times with your customers," said the *Independent*, "and let them understand distinctly that you expect *promptness* in the fulfillment of their engagements." Some writers added that frank and open male speech emanated from inner purity. In "What Makes a Man," one poet described manliness as "a truthful soul" and a "spirit firm, erect and free,/ . . . that truly speaks from God within." In the complex and at times contradictory thinking about gender roles at mid-century, the idea of bold, manly speech emanating from a pure male soul was not easily squared with the notion of woman whose soul, cultivated in the refuge of the home, was less corrupted by the world than the soul of man, but who still was expected to speak softly and defer. Such confounds disrupted the integrity of the categories of masculine and feminine, public and private.[34]

A man was expected to "stand alone," and that meant, especially, to fight alone, against overwhelming odds, when his cause was just. The *Monthly Religious Magazine* defined "Christian Manliness" as the courage to stand up and fight for beliefs and convictions. That might translate to the courage of a writer such as James A. Millhouse, who was remembered for his "disdain of adaptation to the popular taste" in "his manly discourse." It could mean something more to middle-class Boston Protestants, or, as the *Evangelist* wrote, something "worthy [of] our Protestant Christianity! We have not stood up in our appropriate places and work, and contended manfully for the field with the Romish Bishop." By far the most important context for the display of manly courage, however, was the debate over slavery. The *Liberator* not surprisingly pointed the way for the linkage of manhood to support for abolitionism. In many articles the *Liberator* insisted upon forthright action on behalf of the cause, and condemned those who failed to act: "He commits moral treason against his own soul. He stultifies and degrades his own manhood, and renders it imbecile and contemptible in his own eyes. His self-respect is gone, his manly dignity and glory are departed." The *New Englander* made a similar case during the pivotal year of 1850, pledging that "we will pray that the representatives of our own and of every other free state may, in this time of their peculiar temptation, have manliness enough, have conscience enough, to resist a demand so monstrous and stand true- . . ." And the *Independent* foreswore publishing profits if such depended upon retreat from its opposition to slavery, pointing out that "during the ten years of its existence, it has found that an honest, frank, and manly course has achieved for it a success unparalleled in the history of journalism . . ." But "if this journal cannot prosper except by holding its peace in presence of the greatest wrong of the age, it does not any longer wish prosperity." [35]

The world of commerce, of business and professional activity, was a key context for the elaboration of the connections between masculinity and speech. Bostonians had mixed perspectives on business, but frequently observed that commercial transactions proceeded most efficiently when the parties involved plainly voiced their interests and objectives. That is, when people bargained forthrightly, business was better. William Henry Smith, producer and actor at the Museum Theatre, represented this point of view in his reflections about contract negotiations with the theatre's owner, Moses Kimball. Over the course of several days of negotiations, Smith and Kimball came to terms. Smith summarized the process as follows: "<u>Had an interview and understanding with *Moses Kimball,* he *behaved man fashion & so did I.*</u> I shall remain with him." The image of the merchant as a frank and forthright negotiator consistently emerged in obituaries in the Boston newspapers, where it was linked with the masculinity of the deceased. Typical was the paragraph remembering Joseph B. Whall, who died in his home on Harrison Avenue at the age of thirty-nine. The *Transcript* wrote that he was distinguished by his "frankness- noble and generous impulses, combined with rare qualities of manliness." As much as they associated manliness with business skill, Bostonians did not equate the two, however. Some ambiguity in the relation of business success to masculinity remained, and it allowed for statements that qualified the relation between manhood and professional attainment. In such statements, business nevertheless loomed large in the background. Theodore Parker, in an open letter to a young man embarking on his first sea voyage, used language that unlinked business and manhood even as it brought them together. "Money," wrote Parker, "will make you acceptable to man: manhood—I mean wisdom justice, affectionateness, and religion—will make you welcome to God, and blessed by him forever. Your business is one help to obtain that manhood, but business alone will not give it to you. You must work for your manhood as much as for your money, and take as much pains to get it, and to keep it, too." Parker's language suggested that money and manhood were in some ways alike and in other ways different, that they were related, but not *necessarily* related. The same perspective is evidenced in lawyer Tracy Patch Cheever's reflections on an upturn in his business. Noting the improvement, he reflected nevertheless that "I can truly say that I do not wish my mind to be crusted over with mere business, as to lose either that freshness of feeling, or that higher discipline for the character, which a proper meditation and perception of my duties and responsibilities as a <u>man</u> should impart. I desire business and money, but neither at the expense of the nobler ends of being." Cheever's remark reveals as well his thinking about the potentially stultifying effects of business on feeling.[36]

One reason for people's mixed thoughts about the connection between masculinity and business success—their linkage of manhood with business at the same time that they demurred from fully identifying one with the other—was their uneasiness about public life. David Leverenz has argued that a key theme of literature of the time was male "fear of humiliation." Such fear was grounded in the enormous male investment in reputation, and awareness of the ever-present possibility of ridicule of one's ideas or actions in public life. "Learn from the earliest days to inure your principles against the peril of ridicule," advised the *Christian Observer* in "A Short Sermon on Manliness." "You can no more exercise your reason if you live in constant dread of laughter, than you can enjoy your life, if you were in constant terror of death." The *Child's Friend and Family Magazine* identified the public context for ridicule, and male fear of humiliation, in a cogent reference to the Victorian world of appearances: "The most reckless of men and boys have by daylight some regard to appearances; . . . when they are under an eye they fear, the public eye." The *Monthly Anthology and Boston Review* grieved that "among other evils, of the first class, is the undeserved loss of reputation. . . . No anguish is equal to his; no tongue can speak his sorrow; no treasures can compensate his loss." Lecturers, writers, clergy, and teachers nevertheless urged men to face their fear of ridicule, to act in a manly way by speaking out their beliefs in public, regardless of the consequences. Alongside such emphases, the focus on the high stakes of male action functioned as a means of further enhancing the heroic nature of male participation in the public life defined by commerce and politics. Urging men forward, The *Massachusetts Teacher* paraphrased Matthew Arnold's remarks on fear as weakness, admonishing its readers that "to be then afraid of other boys is, in a boy, the same sort of weakness as it is in a man to be afraid of other men." With regard to public life, no fear was greater than the ridicule of one's feelings. Men had worried for years about making known their feelings—by emotional expression such as crying or by verbally describing their feelings—and over the course of the nineteenth century had conceptualized, had projected, their own fears of humiliation as a national anxiety. In 1807, Jacob Porter, at a meeting where people talked about their religious life, witnessed a man confessing that he had been determined "to let no one living know my feelings, lest I should be ridiculed, lest I should be laughed at." By 1851, Henry Haynes had come to the conclusion that fear of expressing feeling was a widespread American sickness. Provoked by a comment from his friend Schubert one evening that "'The reason that we Americans & English think a sentimental person a fool is because we are ashamed of our feelings,'" Haynes conceded: "I believe that it comes to this after all. A sentimental person is one who makes an undue display of his feelings—this we consider very absurd. Why? Can it be for any other reason than because we are ashamed of our feelings? And is not such false shame disrespectful to the creator? Does not Shakespeare when he talks of 'the man who wears his heart upon his sleeve for daws to peck at' take the proper view of us?" Charlotte Foster learned grammar and spelling that same year by practicing sentences such as the following, which she wrote in her composition book: "The <u>people</u> and their <u>companions</u> lost their <u>reputation</u> by <u>refusing</u> to <u>regain</u> their composure."[37]

Ashamed of their feelings, fearful of ridicule, anxious about reputation and cognizant always of the possibility of public humiliation, men experienced their predicament as the conflict between expectations for the performance of emotion—especially in the home—and the cultural requirement that they conceal their feelings. The same middle-class culture that enforced such an order also provided therapy for male sickness, however. In Boston, the mid-nineteenth-century construction of emotionality and gender cast women as emotional midwives who elicited male expression of feeling by utilizing their special gifts of patience, affection, and spousal, sisterly, or daughterly devotion. The religious press crackled with reports about women who rescued the man who "tried to hide his feelings" about religion. And because children usually were gendered as feminine when it came to emotion, they, too, were influential in keeping men from hardening their hearts. *Ballou's* 1855 article "Little Children" accordingly explained that "Every infant comes into the world like a delegated prophet and herald of good tidings, whose office it is 'to turn the hearts of their fathers to the children.'" A novelette, "Berenger," elaborated on the manner in which emotional display and bold manliness were brought together in a man's encounter with a child upon returning home from work: "The father looked with hope and pleasure at the handsome, spirited face of his boy, when the fire of his bold, black eyes became softened by these happy domestic intimacies; his ear took in all with a father's delight, the tones of his voice, no longer purposely roughened, under a false idea of manliness and independence, but in harmony with the prevailing tone of the household." Such influence upon males began when they were boys, through the agency both of their mothers and sisters. Mary J. Walker wrote in her diary about "the influence that sisters exert upon brothers," and especially the role played by a sister in refining brothers who were "rough and coarse in their manners." As wives, women wielded "the influence of their declared approbation; of their open, willing, visible, example, enforced by that soft, persuasive, colloquial elegance, which, in some hollowed retirement, exerts such controlled influence over the hard heart of men." A *Gleason's* article entitled "The Influence of Women" declared that "the cultivation of the sentiments and of the social virtues is solely dependent upon women," who by their efforts both soften men and keep them strong. *The Young Woman's Friend* said likewise, and so did William Plumer Jr., in his poem "The Manly Mind." Without womanly guidance and prompting, without the softening influences of the home, the emotional life of men would lose its capacity for affectionate feeling, become hardened, and ultimately transmogrify into the indulgence of cruelty. So said the *Christian Parlor Magazine* in the course of explaining the inhumanity of the celibate "Romish Clergy":

> The cruelties of Nero were tender mercies compared with theirs. . . . How shall we account for the unbounded and atrocious ferocity of these men—for they *were men*, and once drew life from maternal bosoms. The answer which chiefly explains it is—they have ejected themselves as a body from the humanizing influence of the domestic organization— its soft and gracious sway reached not to them, waked not, nurtured not the natural affections in them.[38]

Like ministers who worried ever more loudly about declension when the signs of a revival were present in a neighboring town or congregation, some Bostonians more vigorously defended certain notions of the differences between male and female as rhetoric about the cultivation of male emotionality grew stronger. George William Curtis reminded readers of the *Liberator* that "there is no such contemptuous nickname for a man as to call him 'Miss Nancy.'" Readers could also ponder a reprinted story from the *New York Times* condemning the tactics of women temperance advocates as "the power of these she-males . . . injuring every cause they espouse." Henry W. Haynes complained after a night at the National Theatre that "it always spoils a male character to have it taken by a woman." The newly formed Boston Fencing Club warned in its bylaws that "No female shall be admitted to the club-rooms, under any pretext whatsoever, except by permission of a member of the government of the club." And *Ballou's*, signaling the particular evil of men acting like women, snickered that "the most contemptible animal breathing is a male gossip. . . . A female gossip is disgusting enough—but a male gossip—Faugh!"[39]

"SOME INDEFINABLE PARTIALLY CORRESPONDENT REALITY"

Henry Haynes probably would not have been happy with the fact of Charlotte Cushman playing Romeo at the Boston Theatre during the summer of 1858. But, in fact, the theatre, and many other aspects of Boston life, embodied the crossing of gender lines at mid-century. There were the Bateman sisters, Ellen and Kate, just children, who not only played male roles at the Howard Athenaeum but, because "the genius was innate with these young girls," they were able to expertly portray grown men, men's men such as Richard the Third. While the Batemans were performing, men dressed up as women outside on the streets of Boston. One such "female impostor" appeared as a "rather under-size, well-dressed female, of thin visage, pale face, and sharp nose, with a fashionable hat and a white feather in it," and attempted to beg change from "businessmen." Another man operated a fraudulent mail operation that collected earnest money from would-be husbands who answered a deceptive newspaper advertisement and did not know that "the nice young lady wears bifurcated garments, drinks lager, and shaves every morning." The female bifurcated garment and beard (and the lager, too) were in fact not unknown in Boston, however. "The new female costume," bloomers—called "trousers"—already were in evidence on the streets of the city, and Madame Josephine Fortune Clofullia, a.k.a. "the Bearded Lady of Geneva," was attracting large crowds to Amory Hall, where she exhibited her hirsute development. There were the frequent newspaper accounts of male impersonation by Antoinette Brown, Lucy Stone, and Susan B. Anthony, "who sits with her legs crossed, man-fashion." Teenaged boys and girls engaged in parlor games that carried them across gender lines in various ways, and none more dramatically than by exchanging their clothes before a night of playfulness. Francis Bennett went to a party at a girl's house in late spring, 1852. After a walk, "we went back to her house, to tea. In the evening the boys put on the girls' bonnets & shawls and the girls put on the boys coats and hats and went to ride on John Williams' trucks." They repeated the game on other occasions: "Matilda dressed up in John's clothes this evening. Sarah dressed up as her wife. We had a first rate time." Charles F. Low didn't need the structure of a game to enjoy wearing his friend Carrie's clothes. He wrote: "Went to bed about 10. & having no night dress I used one belonging to Carrie. Of course it was delightful." And even Henry Haynes admitted one night that he aspired to the cleverness and daring of anti-heroine Becky Sharp in William Thackeray's *Vanity Fair.* "I mean to be a man of the world," he wrote, while praising Becky's pluck. Charles French, who experimented with gender roles in various other ways, gushed after sharing his umbrella with his friend Rayner on a walk home, "I love him with a woman's love." [40]

Alongside the rhetoric about separate spheres, and different male and female natures, was, in fact, a substantial outpouring of ideas not only about the ways in which men and women complemented each other, but about the importance of men being feminized and women being masculinized.[41] "The soul of a man, as well as his body, is incomplete without his wife," declared *Ballou's.* The *Massachusetts Teacher* cited Coleridge to make the point more emphatically with regard to men: "There has never been a really great man without a considerable admixture of the feminine—not the effeminate—element in his character." Bringing such wisdom to its reflection on the death of twenty-two-year-old George Williams, the *Monthly Law Reporter* remarked that "his native manliness and vigor were not softened by any effeminating influences but rather were adorned with new graces by them." Having established a discourse about the distinct roles of male and female, Bostonians came to the conclusion that such distinctiveness could only be maintained through frequent and meaningful contact between men and women. That is, gender categories remained powerful only through a process of encounter, as one polished the other in an ongoing process of frictive positioning and repositioning vis-à-vis each other. Or as one writer explained, "the man separated from female society becomes effeminate, less manly and less noble. All history sustains this position. The woman separated from male society, on the other hand, becomes more masculine and less refined." The danger, of course, was that one might overimbibe of the culture of the other sex, leading to the same undesirable consequence as too little encounter. Charles E. French likely had such a problem in mind when he wrote about Samuel Hodges, a clerk at another store: "I think Saml is rather effeminate and rather a ladies man." The *Liberator* said that teachers understood that by educating the sexes together, they would obtain the benefit "of incessant reciprocal action" of boys and girls upon each other. And the *New Englander,* in language that captures something of the fluidity and ambiguity of gender categories at the time, offered the following lesson in logic:

. . . we may apply the feminine pronoun *she* to a ship, using a grammatic term of gender for a descriptive and representative purpose. And then, to represent or connect another impression, we may give the ship a masculine name, such as Hercules or Agamemnon. Whereupon the man of logic, scandalized by so great an absurdity, may begin to argue that since the ship is feminine as to gender, it cannot be masculine: or if it is masculine then it cannot be feminine. But it will be sufficient, for any one but him, to answer that we use these terms of gender only to represent some indefinable partially corespondent reality which we can signify by this short method better than by any other.[42]

In the specific area of religion, there was also some commentary that granted wiggle room to notions of masculinity and femininity, especially when it came to what the *New York Times*, reporting on the Businessmen's Revival, termed "spiritual manliness." Theodore Parker predictably complained that "The popular theology [i.e. elite theology] leaves us nothing feminine in the character of God." The *New Englander* cited with satisfaction the remarks of a well-known minister on the character of great poets and preachers. A great preacher was a "double-natured man" who exhibited "the feminine and manly powers in harmonious union; having the tact, and the sympathy, and the intuition, and the tenderness of a woman, with the breadth and massiveness of the manly intellect, besides the calm justice which is almost exclusively masculine." *The Young Man's Friend* protested that "there is a notion widely spread, that religion is an unmanly thing, that embracing it betrays a womanly weakness . . . But how mistaken are such!" The *New Englander* found in an Old Testament commentary just the right term for religious faith, however: "the perfect womanhood of the soul."[43]

EMOTION AND THE FLUIDITY OF GENDER ROLES

"A fully drawn history of Victorian sex roles," writes Karen Lystra, "demands paradoxical recognition of both the rigidity and fluidity, the division and overlap, of gender lines."[44] To a certain extent Bostonians in 1850 continued to think in terms of separate male and female spheres, and they often distinguished domestic life from public life. Below the surface of the casual rhetoric about such categories, however, lay complex and dynamic sets of ideas that subverted those categories as much as they confirmed them. Bostonians understood the home as the ideal context for the blossoming and application of women's special emotionality. Domestic life nevertheless was constructed as an ongoing process of self-denial for women, as a place of suffering in service to others, and a context for the concealment of emotion as much as for its expression. Women who succeeded in hiding their feelings might be cast as deceivers, while women who did not evidence an appropriate measure of control were demonized as she-males, bold pretenders, or throat-cutters. Men were expected to be bold and active, and to speak forthrightly from the heart, but yet were conformed, like women, to an ideal of emotional control. Men were constructed as creatures of the public sphere, as persons whose natural habitat was the marketplace, where the faculty of speech came naturally, but they were warned repeatedly about the way in which a slip of the tongue or an indiscretion might ruin a reputation. They worried about becoming a "Miss Nancy" even as their ministers and social commentators urged them to try on the feminine. They had to negotiate passage between the Scylla of so hardening their heart through career-related activities that they became hollow men at home, and the Charybdis of letting the emotional life that they were supposed to actively cultivate at home spill into and disrupt the geometry of their business and professional lives. Men feared the public eye as much as they exulted in their role as leaders.

The bleeding across social and gender lines was especially important for the ongoing construction of emotionality in Boston. As familiar patterns of expression and concealment of emotion were challenged or disrupted, as the rules blurred, Bostonians explored new ways of understanding feeling, and, especially, of describing the emotional aspect of interpersonal relations. In the midst of such practice, they experimented with the ethos of the marketplace—commodity, exchange, contract, reciprocation—as a guideline for emotional life. In the areas of courtship, marriage, and child rearing, they began to fashion an understanding of human relationships as emotional exchanges. In so doing, they borrowed phrasings from discourse about commercial transactions, from the speech of the businessman, from language about that most exquisitely abstract of cultural artifacts, money. All of these developments were manifest in the revival.

SEVEN

Domestic Contracts

The noon hour and evening gatherings that formed the core of the Businessmen's Revival were for the most part carefully structured affairs involving testimonies of conversion, petitioning of God, exhortations, and formal and informal prayer. Woven into the fabric of revival on all of these fronts was a notion of the relationship of the individual to God as a matter of contract, of mutual obligation and patterns of exchange. The immediate informing context for this conception was domestic life, and to a certain extent the process of socialization that took place in schools.

The growth of business brought with it a surge in the invention of legal means to conduct it. Essayists formulated theories about the nature of economic exchange, philosophers published books analyzing its relevance to truth, beauty, and not least of all emotion, and handbooks organized the practical side of business by providing boilerplate language for contracts and other official agreements. The idea of contract—that is, the conception of relations between parties as a matter governable by responsibilities and obligations articulated in legal phrasings—to an increasing extent also organized relations between individuals as the businesses of courtship, marriage, child rearing, and education. The term "marriage contract" became widespread in Massachusetts, and so did the idea of companionate marriage as an agreement between equals, and of divorce as breach of contract.

Contracts between individuals in the family—as husband and wife, or as parent and child—involved an exchange, a transaction. Emotion was one of the items involved in such transactions. As an object, as a commodity that had value and that could be traded for other commodities (including an expression of emotion from others), emotion was always in play, being given and taken in a host of domestic situations. Spouses reckoned emotional accounts with each other, and parents with their children—and especially mothers with their sons. Rarely did persons enunciate their interest in gaining an even exchange. Indeed, much of the time persons observed that exchanges involving emotion had been unequal. But in diaries and newspaper columns, sermons and correspondences, the idea of interpersonal relations as a vast field of economic exchange involving feelings organized a great deal of reflection about the nature of domestic life, schooling, and friendship. Emotion to an increasing extent was considered as property, and as such was subjected to exchange schema that persons and groups constructed for transacting it in various situations.

THE MARRIAGE OF EQUALS

In the late 1850s or early 1860s, Emily Dickinson, of Amherst, Massachusetts, wrote "The Contract." Part of her "Master" cycle of poems, it employed "mercantile language" in articulating "desire as economic exchange."[1]

> I gave myself to him,
> And took himself for pay.
> The solemn contract of a life
> Was ratified this way.
>
> The wealth might disappoint,
> Myself a poorer prove
> Than this great purchaser suspect,
> The daily own of Love
>
> Depreciate the vision;
> But, till the merchant buy,
> Still fable, in the isles of spice,
> The subtle cargoes lie.
>
> At least, 't is mutual risk,—
> Some found it mutual gain;
> Sweet debt of Life,—each night to owe,
> Insolvent, every noon.[2]

Dickinson's representation of an emotional relationship as a contractual relationship squared with an important strand of the discourse about marriage and family relations in the mid-nineteenth century. It was connected, in this rapid period of manufacturing growth and trade, to the efflorescence of a business legal culture and the proliferation and refinement of the legal contract as both the conceptual umbrella and the practical instrument for economic exchange. The *Businessmen's Companion*, published in Boston in 1858, explained the details of contract law as gathered from English and American sources and provided many pages of forms for agreements between parties, including for selling, buying, manufacturing, and bartering commodities ranging from real estate to insurance. It defined a contract as "an agreement between two contracting parties, entered into on sufficient consideration, either verbally or in writing." The terms could be express, that is, enunciated at the time of the making of the contract, or implied "as reason and justice dictate." Contractual relationships were the norm for business transactions, and they governed the details of the operation of the city government, where even the widening of a street required prolonged negotiations between the city and "residents in the neighborhood, who pay large taxes" before a contract could be finalized. Apropos Dickinson's poem, relations between individuals increasingly were cast as contractual matters after mid-century. The Massachusetts *Monthly Law Reporter* regularly employed the term "marriage contract" after 1858, reported on legal issues involving prenuptial contracts in Massachusetts, and provided commentary as well on "Parent and Child—Implied Contract" that underscored awareness of legal obligations (and absence of them) between persons living together. Brown University president Francis Wayland, in his influential *Elements of Moral Science* (1835), had blended religious and commercial language in describing marriage as "a most solemn contract." Bostonians construed the relationship between parent and teacher specifically as a contract involving the doctrine of *in loco parentis*, and saw the relationship between teacher and student in a similar light. The increase in the incidence of divorce—previously referred to in New England as "annulling the marriage contract"—reinforced the trend to see some measure of legal transaction in relations between men and women. Occasionally, cases involving contract law in these various areas intersected, creating complicated scenarios for the resolution of complaints, as in the instance of *Farnsworth v. Wakefield*, heard before the Massachusetts Supreme Court in 1858, in which marriage, divorce, and education all converged in a single legal action. We shall see as well that some Protestant Bostonians conceived an emotional relationship with God as a contractual, transactional matter. But first we shall explore the ways in which relationships of marriage, child rearing, and schooling were constructed.[3]

The increasing popularity of the notion of marriage as a contract between two individuals can be gauged from the increase in declarations of resistance to such a conceptualization as mid-century approached. The *Christian Parlor Magazine* set the tone for the opposition by posing a question in 1845: "And is it not the prevalent error of these times, and, perhaps

I may add, of this country, to treat this solemn ordinance as an affair of very trifling moment; as a contract of even less importance and solemnity than some merely secular and civil engagement, in which money, or houses and lands, are the objects of acquisition or transfer?" According to the magazine, the proof for the prevalence of such an attitude lay in the rise in applications for divorce and in "the ease and levity with which they are granted." The transfer of items of value took place within a context defined by understandings of what men and women had to offer. A wife was, first of all, a keeper of the home, a job description encoded in the very name of her job, as *Ballou's* explained in an article on the origins of the word "wife," observing that "the word belongs to the same family as weave, woof, web, and the German *weben:* It is the title given to a person who is engaged at the web and woof, those having been the most ordinary branches of female industry and wifely employment." But the magazine pointed out elsewhere that the appearance of accomplishment in needlework or any other area of domestic life might not always square with the reality of a wife's performance after the honeymoon was over. Accordingly, "we must marry to know what they are worth." To see a woman as a commodity for sale in a transaction completed through a marriage ceremony was, however, repulsive to the *Liberator,* which lamented how girls "are early taught to consider what are their chances and attractions for the market!" Moreover, the buyers sometimes had little to offer, said the *Liberator,* angered by the cases of "young, bright, promising school-girls, dwarfed into young ladies, and the flag hoisted that they are to be sold to the highest bidder! The matter is made still worse by the conditions of the sale, for sobriety, chastity, principle, character, are not required in the purchaser—he only need have wealth, show, or bravado." *Ballou's* took a more pragmatic approach in "A Hint to Wives," which suggested that the bidding continue even after the marriage: "Cultivate your nerves. You can't pet them too much. Something will always be happening in the house, and unless your husband be worse than a stone, every new fright will be as good as a new gown or a new trinket, to you. There are some domestic wounds only to be cured by the jeweller."[4]

The *Youth's Companion* in 1854 proposed a list of ten ways of "How to Avoid a Bad Husband," and topping the list was: "Never marry for wealth." Such advice appeared in press alongside the frequent stories of women who in fact did marry for money, and whose lives consequently took a course that left them bereft of satisfying emotional experiences of love and affection. So common was this perception that newspapers and magazines could work the humor they might find in such situations with confidence that their readership would get it. Such was the case with the coverage of a divorce in *Ballou's*, "in which the plaintiff, who is the wife, sets up the claim that her husband, whom she supposed to be worth $60,000, is not worth more than $5,000. For this, among other sufficient reasons, she prays a court to come over into Macedon and help her." Young men without financial wherewithal found themselves wondering whether they should broach an offer of marriage or wait until they had grown a larger bank account. During the time that Gamaliel Bradford was in love with his "Miss Otis" in 1855 he had a "curious dream, viz, that after some theatricals Robt Ware turned jest to earnest by proposing to Miss Otis & being accepted by her at her father's instigation, on the ground, it seemed, of R's being richer than I." After his cousin Sarah assured him that the young woman had no requirement of fortune in a suitor and would marry purely for love, Bradford's outlook improved, and especially so after Otis refused an offer from another man, paving the way for Bradford's own proposal ("the coast is clear"). But only three weeks later, in view of the fact that the refused suitor was so badly shaken[5] that he left for Europe, and because Otis "has refused more offers than almost any lady in Boston," the twenty-five-year-old Bradford "came to the conclusion that my penchant for Miss Otis has vanished." Boston pundits considered the prolonged bachelorhood of men such as Bradford a terrible situation, and complained frequently of it in articles wrapped up in marriage rate statistics. This was particularly true in the aftermath of the crash of 1857. *Ballou's* wrote in 1858 that "the records of the city registrar of Boston begin to show the effects of hard times in the decrease of applications for the certificates of intentions of marriage," which fell by as much as two hundred per month in 1857. It elsewhere declared that "one of the greatest social evils of this age is admitted to be the reluctance of our young men to early marriages," and outlined the matter in terms of its problematic consequences for both men and women: "But it has become a prevalent sentiment, that a man must acquire his fortune before he marries. . . . This is very unhappy. It fills the community with bachelors . . . it destroys the true economy and design of the domestic institution, and it promotes idleness and inefficiency among females, who are expecting to be taken up by a fortune."[6]

Men could marry for money as well. An old handbook on letter writing presented as an example of a proper letter from a son to his parents a fictional narrative in which the young man informs his parents that her "parents are to pay me five hundred pounds on the day of the marriage," with the promise of the remaining estate when they die. *Young America* connected wealthy women with bought lovers in a more vulgar way, claiming that at Saratoga Springs, the well-known retreat for the rich, women with $100,000 had 1,000 lovers, women with $200,000 had 2,000 lovers, and so forth, with the bottom of the order comprised of pretty girls who had a lover here and there. And *Gleason's*, which like *Ballou's* sold magazines by playing to both sides of the aisle on the issue, ran the sad testimonial of Mrs. E. B. Hall, who confessed that "I was married for my money. That was ten years ago and they have been ten years of purgatory." Detailing the differences with her husband on almost every point of home life and child rearing, Hall, in referring to her two sons, wrote that "I wish I had called them both Cain," and described the deterioration of her physical person as a "cadaverous, long, doleful visage" in the mirror. "Yet half my sex marry as I did," said Hall, "not for love, but for fear."[7]

Condemnations of marriage for money were grounded in a romantic ideal of marriage as the union of two hearts, and in the course of sorrowing over a bad marriage, writers often referred to what could have been if only the parties involved had listened to their hearts. *Gleason's* worried that "even in modern times, there have been perpetrated, in the sacred name of marriage, those cold, formal and selfish alliances, politely termed marriages of convenience, marriages made by parents or friends between cold, indifferent and merely consenting parties, hands united without hearts." It added that such a deplorable sham of the matrimonial order would never take place "if matrimony were generally regarded in its true light as the union of souls, of minds, as well as of persons and estates." The *Youth's Companion* also complained about superficial marriages in which the heart was not involved: "In how many instances of the present day, is marriage merely a union of hands—the affections not ever being taken into consideration. The question on the one side, 'Is she handsome?—has she money?' On the other, "Can he support me in style? Shall I be able to make an appearance?' How much better would it be to ask—'Has the woman a heart capable of true affection?'" To this the *New Englander* added a word against "calculated and heartless husband-hunting." *Ballou's*, seemingly departing momentarily from its reporting on wasted American marriages, set up the straw dog of the capricious and unfaithful French in order to make its point about money and love: "Let us thank heavens that we are not as those benighted Gauls are on the banks of the Seine— that we marry always for love, and yet our love is always sustained by prudence and judgment—that the almighty dollar is never thought of in a matrimonial connection." In another article, "The Game of Life," however, *Ballou's* cogently expressed the complicated and sometimes contradictory thinking of Bostonians when it came to marriage, money, and women. As much as Bostonians might wish to separate marriage as an economic initiative from marriage for love, the two remained mingled in certain ways, so that "in the game of life you always find that the cards ladies are most anxious to play with are diamonds and hearts." The conservative voice of *The Young Woman's Friend* would continue to influence some to think that an arranged marriage was the best marriage, but for women who were becoming more articulate about their rights, only marriage as a union of equal individuals made sense, and only that kind of marriage could provide truly free exchange of affection between husband and wife. "The time is coming," wrote a woman to the *Liberator*, "when virtuous woman will have an equal right with man to give her heart to the object of her choice, instead of being compelled (by female wages and the customs of society) to stoop to legal prostitution."[8]

Equal rights meant a marriage of equal companions, and companionate marriage meant equal rights. In her broad study of romantic love in nineteenth-century America, Karen Lystra has shown that "middle-class men in romantic love most often expressed a companionate ideal." Although that ideal might suffer when they were no longer in love, and in many cases men might not have practiced their relationship according to that ideal, it seems that middle-class men at some times in the course of their relationships with women voiced support for the notion of marriage as a union of equals. Jacqueline S. Reinier has tracked the emergence of companionate marriage to the early eighteenth-century articulation of the "the new concept of the affectionate anti-patriarchal family" and especially to Joseph Addison's linkage of companionate marriage with domestic happiness, popularized in *The Spectator*. Chris Dixon, in a close study of eight mid-nineteenth-century marriages, takes another view of the chronology, proposing that the antebellum example of marriage among anti-slavery couples "foreshadowed the emergent emphasis on companionate marital relations throughout the nation," adding that "an essential aspect of companionate marriage was the increased emphasis on intimacy." Robert H. Chused notes that very few arranged marriages actually took place in the nineteenth century as "romance emerged as the basis for mate selection." These and other studies indicate that by mid-century, companionate marriage as ideal, and to some extent as practice as well, was becoming established in America, and this was especially so in Boston, where agitation for women's rights gave it particular importance and encouragement.[9]

Less than a month after her wedding in late 1858, Mary Faxon Forbush wrote: "My own individuality seems in some way to have parted from me and I have been struggling hard to regain it. . . . There is something melancholy to me." Women at mid-century complained frequently about the loss of individuality in marriage, and by that they meant not only a disorienting sense of intimate connectedness to another person, but frequently, as well, a dissatisfaction with the legal basis for marriage. As the idea of companionate marriage began to catch on, its advocates spoke more boldly. The basis of companionate marriage as far as contract was concerned was grounded in the recognition of each party as an individual, and in the provision in marriage that each party retain its individuality. This agenda of individual rights in marriage was significantly advanced by the women's rights movement, which took square air: at marriage as an arrangement that undermined a woman's legal authority to own property. The linkage of "individuality" with rights in marriage was articulated in a variety of ways, including through reference to the Bible. Elizabeth Wilson drew upon scriptural evidence in arguing in 1850 that "as far as husband and wife are concerned they are pronounced one, and where there is no divisibility, there can be no superiority or inferiority; but they both retain their individuality." The Woman's Rights Convention in Massilon, Ohio two years later employed the same language in its resolution regarding marriage: "Resolved, that to perfect the marriage union, and provide for the inevitable vicissitudes of life, the individuality of both parties should be equally and distinctly recognized by the parties themselves, and by the laws of the land; . . ." Ernestine Rose, speaking before the Assembly in 1855, cited Blackstone's dictum that "the husband and wife are one, and that one is the husband," and then translated it into simpler terms: "When woman marries, in almost every sense, she dies legally." An article in the *Liberator,* "Marriage Contract," outlined in 1860 the legal background for woman's position in marriage, explaining that "the legal existence of the woman is suspended during marriage,—and henceforth she is known but in and through the husband" so that "her moral responsibility, even, is merged in the husband. . . . An unmarried woman can make contracts. . . . but, in marriage, she is robbed by law of all and every natural and civil right." Like abolitionists who campaigned against slavery at the same time that they campaigned against half-way measures for eliminating it, women's rights activists saw no possibility of compromise on the issue of woman's legal status in marriage. "Woman must be a subject or an equal," said one writer, "there is no middle ground." [10]

In 1851, an English observer asserted that "marriage is regarded in the United States, in my opinion, in the rational light of a civil contract, instead of being treated, as in the Established Church of England, as an indefinite religious ceremony." Women's rights advocates in America were not so sure of that, and they agitated throughout the decade for reform of marriage laws. In statehouses and at the national level, in cases here and there, and through legislation constantly revised to spell out more directly the marriage contract, the legal foundation of marriage began to change. On the national level, cases such as *Mahoney v. Porter* (1851), which protected a woman's annuity from access by her husband's debtors, and, that same year, a Massachusetts decision giving a married woman sole control of inherited trust shares chipped away at previous views about women's legal status in marriage. A bill came before the New Jersey Senate in 1853 broadly expanding married women's rights, including giving them "the power of devising and conveying their property without the consent of their husbands," and allowing them "to prosecute in their own names." That same year Elizabeth Stanton, Ernestine Rose, Samuel May, and other advocates for reform published an open letter to New Yorkers urging them "to bring the existing wrongs of Women, in the state of New York, before the Legislature at its next session," including a list of eight complaints that encompassed work, suffrage, and the marital relationship. In 1855, Lucy Stone and Henry B. Blackwell published their own letter of protest on the occasion of their marriage in West Brookfield, Massachusetts. "While we acknowledge our mutual affection, by publicly assuming the sacred relationship of husband and wife," they wrote, "in justice to ourselves and a great principle, we . . . declare that this act on our part implies not sanction of . . . the present laws of marriage." The document included six specific complaints about marriage, all having to do with "the whole system by which 'the legal existence of the wife is suspended during marriage.'"[11]

The Massachusetts Legislature had been limping toward reform of marriage laws since 1845, when it made several small changes. In 1857, the case of *Commonwealth v. Williams* established that property brought by a woman to a marriage could remain her own "and that the earnings of any married woman from her trade or business should be her own." Later that year, the state enlarged women's rights in marriage, and, finally, in 1859, reiterated the findings of *Commonwealth v. Williams* and the 1857 statute in legislation that proposed as well formal language for authorizing prenuptial contracts and other premarital matters. During 1858, Caroline Dall stood before the Massachusetts Legislative Committee and made demands for suffrage, the right to sit on juries, the right to choose her own vocation, and recognition of her agency in making contracts. The following year, commentary on marriage, divorce, and family issues in the *Monthly Law Reporter* rose to an average of two per issue, more than double the coverage in 1858. Protest continued at the Woman's Rights Convention of 1860 and in various state legislatures, including Ohio, where a bill was entered in 1860 that "enables married women to make contracts . . . as if they were single." These events, a sample of the broad activism of those years, added up over time to a substantial reworking of the legal status of women in marriage. And each step toward establishing the rights of married women to contract their own business was also a step toward establishing the viability of the ideal of companionate marriage, which rested on the notion of a union of individuals.[12]

As the notion of companionate marriage, of marriage as a contract between equals, became common in the antebellum Northeast, the emotional aspect of the union found fresh expression in popular literatures. Jacqueline Reinier has stressed the link between consent and marital affect that developed from the time of the Republic up to the mid-nineteenth century: "In a general revolt against tyranny and patriarchy, philosophers, physicians, journalists, and printers championed and publicized the affectionate nuclear family, based on warmly tender, voluntary ties" and "marriage founded on loving consent." Marriage, Steven Mintz has argued, became "a focus for emotions," and the home in which a husband and wife lived their married life was, as *Ballou's* explained, "a temple consecrated to the affections." The mood is apparent in the notes of Henry Clark Wright, who lived in the countryside west of Boston and authored the best-selling *Marriage and Parentage* in 1854. Wright was profoundly affected by a trip to Niagara Falls in 1853. Standing on the overlook, he followed the activity of a married couple nearby as they took turns pulling each other away from the ledge, when "each would see that whatever danger touched one must touch the other." Wright saw in their expressions of concern a world of marital affection. "Five & twenty years have witnessed the growing power & tenderness & depth of their love," he wrote in his diary. "Arm in arm they stand on the 'bridge-' but far more beautiful, more intense, more imposing are their looks when turned upon each other, than when turned upon the waters. . . . It is beautiful to see them!" Reflecting on the spectacular vision of the falls, Wright admitted nevertheless that "I feel desperation excited by the scene around me. Why do people attach more sanctity—more of God to the feelings inspired by these Falls—than to those that binds ['men & women' scratched out] human beings together—or husbands and wives & parents &children—brothers & sisters. . . . Why are the impressions made by these falls counted more sublime . . . than impressions made by loved ones?" Answering his own question, Wright asserted: "Indeed there is a power or energy—a conscious strength and omnipotence in the love that binds husband & wife—the parent & child" that far surpassed the feelings excited by the falls.[13]

Marriage, said *Ballou's*, was a matter of "unspeakable emotions." But such emotions were in fact spoken, and they were wrapped in a vocabulary drawn in part from evangelical religion, which, as Steven Mintz has argued, served as a "symbolic language" for "Victorian feelings about love and marriage," so that "the love of God serves as an analogue for the love between spouses." For the *New Englander* "the marriage relation is by God's law sacred," a "marriage mystical, sacramental; a covenant between spirits." The *Christian Parlor Magazine* likewise advised that "next to the awful solemnity of our covenant and union with the Father, Son, and Holy Ghost, . . . is that of the marriage union . . ." The feelings of husband and wife for each other accordingly were akin to religious affections, as Theodore Parker, not surprisingly, made clear in a public prayer made in mid-April 1858, at the height of the revival:

> We thank thee for the tender ties, newly knit which join the lover and his beloved, the bridegroom and the bride, and all those sweet felicities wherefor the heart, marrying itself to another, before thee pours out its natural psalm of grateful joy. We thank thee for these dear affections, whereby the earth blossoms like a rose, and far-reaching philanthropies go out to bless the distant world, counting mankind our kith an kin. We bless thee for this deep religious faculty which thou hast given us, which through the darkness of earth looks upward to thy exceeding light . . .[14]

Legislation that protected the rights of married women reflected and significantly reinforced the notion of marriage as a contract between equals. That contract was understood to govern a union of hearts, a relationship characterized, as virtually every writer claimed, by "mutuality" and "reciprocity." Marriage, in religious terms, was an emotional relationship resembling a person's relationship to God through the religious affections. Overall, the marital relationship was an emotional contract, an agreement for the exchange of hearts between two persons. And sometimes, such an exchange was explained in terms that underscored the abstraction of emotion, especially in the image of the heart, as in an article simply entitled "A Heart": "What a curious thing a heart is—is it not, young lady? There is as much difference in hearts as faces. A woman's heart is a sacred thing, and full of purity. How proud a man ought to be, to have it placed in his keeping—to have a pretty girl love him so well that she will give it to him, and tell him that it loves him more than any other!"[15]

Reciprocation of feeling of course was not limited to marriage. Historian

Anne C. Rose has written that to an increasing extent, all of Victorian family life was "based on reciprocal sentiments." And in many cases that expectation spilled into the structuring of friendships as well. James Barnard Blake made clear his understanding of the nature of emotional exchange in relationships in an excited diary entry describing how the new year, 1851, "caused my heart to throb with new impulses of affection: I have found a friend! One upon whom I can repose every trust, and when in trouble and affliction can seek relief. . . . Long have I desired a friend, one whom I could trust myself with on this journey of life: one have I endeavored to find one from this cold, self-interested world, and now after an acquaintance of three years I have chosen him as my friend, and he has <u>reciprocated</u>." Sometimes such relationships ran aground. Reflecting on his friend Rayner's attention to another man, Charles French wrote angrily in his diary that "Rayner is false. I am sure of it," and the following day, "He has broken his part of the contract." In a subsequent note to Rayner, French employed the common vocabulary of commercial transaction, informing Rayner that, "as he had broken his promise to me, my promises to him were necessarily null & void." Ruminating elsewhere on his love life, French compared love to a commercial transaction even as he rejected the analogy: "'Tis a very disagreeable thing this being in love. Well 'tis a foolish thing at all events, and not near as substantial as dollars and cents." Joanne Harvey, who was married but not always as happily as she would have liked, complained about married love frequently, and about her relationship with her sons. All of her complaints revolved around her belief that she was not receiving proper affection from her husband (". . . not forgetting his harshness and indifference to me. . . . Is there hope to keep the heart whole") or her children ("George appeared cold as iceland [*sic*])."[16]

Failure to deliver affection, to keep one's contractual obligations to engage in a feeling relationship with a spouse was grounds for divorce. As Glenda Riley has pointed out, divorce was "firmly entrenched in the laws of most states and territories" by 1850, and divorce novels such as *The Deserted Wife* began to appear that same year. The divorce rate grew, especially after the Civil War, as persons came to believe that "a marriage vow was a dissolvable contract." And as Americans thought of marriage as an exchange of hearts between equals, they conceived grounds for divorce to be the failure to participate in the exchange, to deliver the emotional goods. These expectations of marriage were dramatically represented in Theodore Tilton's legal action against Henry Ward Beecher in 1874, for Beecher's causing "alienation of affection" in Tilton's wife Elizabeth.[17]

As the boundaries between masculine/feminine and public/private became more porous, and the categories of gender and "spheres" more fluid, concepts largely associated with the marketplace—contract, individuality, exchange—leaked into thinking about family life and increasingly came to schematize conceptions about the relationship between men and women in marriage. Marriage remained a union of hearts as well as a contract between free and separate individuals, and as such could be dissolved if either party failed to keep the terms of the contract, which included emotional mutuality, or, the exchange of affections. (Recent scholarship has looked closely of the dynamics of such emotional transactions between married persons).[18] The extent to which this understanding came to characterize middle-class thinking about marriage in the mid-nineteenth century sometimes was represented in dramatic fashion in the popular press. So, in an 1857 article entitled "Property," a writer for *Ballou's* proposed that "our legislatures discuss nothing else; our civil tribunals are ordained for no other purposes but the regulation of our system of private property; . . ." Then, turning to the business of the heart, the article pointed out that "even the ecclesiastical courts have references to this also, and to this alone—for what are marriage rights but private property? Or what is defamation of character but a moral attack on private property? Property is generally not understood in this spiritual sense; but the law puts a price upon a wife and a husband's rights—puts a price on a man's feelings, which are all regarded as property."[19]

PARENTS, CHILDREN, AND THE
EMOTIONAL ECONOMY OF THE HOME

Relations between parents and children were not organized as contractual relationships between equal individuals. Mutual responsibility and exchange within a culture of emotion nevertheless was a key aspect of the parent-child relationship. The family itself was variously understood as "a shelter sacred to peace and affection," as "that little empire," and, like much else, Washingtonian, because "a well regulated family leaves each individual; at liberty to do well, but not to do ill,—the liberty of asserting his own rights, without encroaching upon the same rights in his brother." The *New Englander* rejected the idea of "democratic philanthropy" in the family in favor of "the gracious covenant of God" as the "rule of domestic life," and elsewhere obedience, not negotiated differences, was established as the basis for relations between parents and children. The *Christian Parlor Magazine* stressed that "the family is by its constitution and ends essentially a religious organization. Its origin is from God." Its purpose was to foster the "beautiful growth of those sentiments and principles, which prepare us for the service of God and mankind." Children's literature frequently made peace the primary characteristic of home life, and commonly pictured boys and girls recognizing the value of peace in the aftermath of a tragic occurrence, invariably through their "tears—bitter, scalding tears."[20]

As Boston approached the mid-nineteenth century, relations between parents and children increasingly were characterized by an emphasis on parental affection as the means for shaping a child's character. This "new philosophy of human development," Harvey J. Graff has written, "appeared in the manipulation of affection, the difficult relations between emotions and family bonds, and preparation for independence and autonomy in extended dependence." As Victorians increased the emphasis on emotional bonds between parents and children, the details of family relationships came under greater scrutiny and were more finely elaborated. Child rearing became less a matter of breaking children's wills and more a project of persuading them by a show of affection or hurt feelings, or simply through emotional blackmail, to behave nobly. By mid-century, the white, middle-class mother ruled the home by controlling the exchange of affection, and especially by limiting her own display of affection toward her children. As Mary Ryan has written: "Eschewing corporal punishment or material reward, she greeted misbehavior with emotional withdrawal." A primary referent for such policy was Horace Bushnell's theology of childhood, *Views of Christian Nurture* (1847), which redescribed children as capable of good—they were not born depraved—in the course of criticizing the revivalist emphasis on conversion. It provided a theological basis for the full development of a theory of child rearing grounded in the notion of "the malleable child shaped by affectionate parents."[21]

In "Home" (1856), Tamar Ann Kermode versified an analogy between the emotional aspect of domestic life and spiritual reward: " 'Tis the place round which our fondest feelings linger, the very name brings thoughts of joy and love;/ the happiness found round the fireside circle,/ must be the nearest to the joys above." For *Gleason's*, the home was "a central sun, around which revolves a happy and united band of warm, loving hearts," and the *Christian Parlor Magazine* sang of the "primeval sanctity, simplicity and beauty, belonging to the family institution and relations: a naturalness and spontaneity of mutual affection that is like the gushing of springs, the swelling and bursting of flower beds. . . ." In such an environment, it was no wonder that, as Theodore Parker wrote, love worked better than force in raising children. There was simply no other way, argued *Ballou's*:

"Yes, yes—to govern by love is far better than to rule by fear," because when "obedience is only forced, it can't be natural; it doesn't come from the heart. A smile, a loving look, a kind word, does more good with a child than all your angry words." The *Massachusetts Teacher*, stressing like other magazines the importance of raising children "naturally" (a term that became more acceptable in the aftermath of Bushnell's *Views of Christian Nurture*), explained that "strong natural love must be the basis of all beneficial discipline," and added that a parent's role as disciplinarian was not completed, regardless of the child's behavior, until the child "does the right from love, and not through fear of punishment." One writer summarized child rearing as a process in which parents taught by loving their children, and children became obedient inasmuch as they behaved through love. The dynamic of mutuality was understood to extend well beyond the matter of teaching/learning obedience: "Above all things, make them loving; then will they be gentle and obedient; and then also, parents, if you become old and poor, these will be better than friends that will never neglect you. Children brought up lovingly at your knees, will never shut their doors upon you, and point where they would have you go."[22]

Children by their charm advanced the process of building a family government on a foundation of emotion. Children made a house a home, gave off joy as they stood before the hearth, and softened the hearts of fathers who had spent a long day in the treacherous world of business. The *Liberator*, in "Henry C. Wright: Psychometrically Examined," a probing piece on the man who, as we have seen, found inspiration at Niagara Falls, remarked that "he has a sincere and passionate love for children; more particularly of <u>childhood</u>—its simplicity, its spontaneity, its responsiveness, its out-spoken sincerity. In the society of children, this large man himself becomes a child. A child inspires his soul. He loves to breathe in the spirit of children, so that he may be renewed in his love for God and Humanity." The *Christian Observatory* cogently stated this view in remarking: "How great is the power of childhood on home. It tinges all the house. It touches every heart." Parents, of course, were expected to touch the hearts of their children in order to shape their character, and among all the means at the disposal of conscientious parents, one of the most popular was through a show of affection in tears. Literature of the antebellum period overflows with the stock phrase describing a mother's efforts: "She taught and exhorted them with many tears." Mothers made a display of their suffering and concern over children as a way to shame them for misdeeds and bring them back into line. The role of the father was not to suffer in the home, but to correct a child firmly but lovingly. Although corporal punishment had given way to affectionate encouragement by mid-century, children's stories occasionally related a whipping, but with the clear message that such a course was done in love and not in anger. The *Well-Spring* accordingly told the story of "Johnny" who was caught one too many times chasing a neighbor's chickens and took a whipping from his father. "Afterwards," continued the story, "the father and the mother wept. When John saw them weep, he dried his own tears, climbed onto his father's knee," and understood that his parents had suffered, too, so that "he loved them better than before." In the integrated emotional economy of the home, moreover, a show of love or affection in a child could soften the heart of even the meanest father. In one short story, "Peter Peevish," one of the most cross, ill-tempered men who ever lived, who had only "angry words and bitter speeches" for his wife and children, was transformed by the sight of a daughter who refused to hit back when assaulted by a brother. Just as the brother subsequently "burst into tears" and begged forgiveness of his sister, there was "such a happy effect on the feelings and temper of Peter Peevish," who immediately reformed his ways.[23]

The boys and many of the businessmen who flocked to the revival in 1858 had grown up in a family atmosphere that placed particular importance on the mother-son relationship. A depiction of family relations that ran continuously in antebellum Boston publications held that "as fathers love their daughters better than their sons, and mothers love their sons better than their daughters, so do sisters feel towards brothers a more constant sentiment of attachment than towards each other." The mother-son relationship received far more attention than the father-daughter relationship in the 1850s,[24] and was thought important enough to warrant special mention in women's obituaries, from early in the nineteenth century. One such account declared, "There is a tie between a mother and a son, which is one of the noblest and purest in nature; it reaches every fold of the mind, and lives in every pulsation of the heart; it is generally kept more perfect than other bonds of unity . . ." The intensely emotional nature of the mother-son bond was pictured as a combination maternal love and suffering, with barely a boundary between the two. Because there are "no barriers between her soul and her son," a mother will do anything for him. "Her affections know no ebbing tide. They flow on from a pure fountain," said the *Youth's Companion*, "and speak happiness through this vale of tears . . ." Gamaliel Bradford looked back upon his youth and concluded that "if anything of good has appeared in my nature or if I am destined to any success in this world (or the next) I owe it under Divine Providence to my mother." Recalling his rambunctious childhood, he noted that "the pain & grief which my mother's affection caused me were much," and an important step toward his learning to live as a man. Unwittingly prophesying the sadness that would soon engulf the country, *Ballou's* described the way in which "the first thing that rushes to the recollection of a soldier or a sailor, in his heart's difficulty, is his mother," and "his last whisper breathes her name." A mother's job was to form in a boy the habits that made up his character and that would carry him successfully through his life. She did so not only by teaching obedience through manipulation of the emotional exchange— tears of sorrow, emotional withdrawal, joyful encouragement—but by cultivating in her son some measure of the emotional competencies that she exhibited, from the most general "kind feelings towards everyone," to the most intense of religious affections. Joanne Harvey pleaded, begged, offered a bribe of a bag of silver coins, gave voice to her deep despair, and attempted blackmail ("if you have any love for us . . . you would come") in the course of trying to lure her son Charles back to Massachusetts from the California gold fields. Both mother and son knew the routine, as Charles made clear in a letter to her: "all you write seems and reads so Motherly." Charles's devotion to Joanne likewise was deep, at least as measured by the sixty-two letters and four diaries he sent to her over four years (1849– 1853). Those letters reveal that, like George Washington, Charles "revered" his mother.[25]

"Oh! There is an enduring tenderness in the love of a mother to a son, that transcends all other affections of the heart," wrote A. B. Muzzey. Home, said the *Christian Parlor Magazine*, was a place saturated with the "social affections," and the "countless other little kindnesses of genial feelings, . . ." at the same time that it was the means to "develope the treasures of the heart's deep affections." The complex and profound quality of that affection allowed for a special means of expression, for a communication between mother and son that transcended words. The rule of silence for women, the commandment that they keep their tongues and avoid making any sort of a show, even, to some extent, in home life, necessitated extraordinary measures for the expression of emotion. The role of a woman as a spouse, and especially as a mother, accordingly was tricked out with special provisions for "the woman's countenance." Henry Hoyt experienced it one evening when a woman with whom he was acquainted threw him a look "which must be seen to be felt." Magazine writers constantly described the manner in which woman ruled the home with glances and various expressive looks. "A kind word, or even a look of affectionate interest, from the wife to the husband" was sufficient to soothe and heal the wounds suffered in the course of a day spent transacting business. In time, if other members of the family became sufficiently adept at making faces—fathers were emotional too,—the entire household hummed with the busy and joyful activity of persons expressing their deepest feelings in looks and glances. So, the "world has few lovelier sights than a household moving spontaneously, harmoniously, to the impulses of a love which speaks in every glance of the eye, in every expression of the countenance, in every utterance of the tongue." Whether or not the practice of emotional expression in family life lived up to this ideal, Bostonians believed that communication of emotion could take place in such a manner. The emotional economy of the household accordingly unfolded somewhat ambiguously, somewhat tentatively and equivocally. Borrowing terms from sociologist Linda D. Molm, we could say that family life, like all social exchanges framed by dependencies, took shape as a performance in which "actors initiate exchanges without formal negotiations and without explicit agreements of whether, when, or to what degree others will reciprocate. As a consequence, . . . exchange relations develop as extended sequences of interactions in which the 'returns' for one's investment are uncertain, and the distribution of exchange outcomes is determined over time rather than on discrete transactions."[26]

In spite of ambiguities in the domestic emotional economy, Bostonians viewed the exchange of feelings as a key part of their home life, whether orchestrated by a mother, father, sister, or brother. Young James Barnard Blake surveyed his life on the first day of 1851 and found that "nothing has so occurred to mar the beautiful symphony of feeling, or to ruffle the finer affections of the familial circle; everything has moved quietly on under the direction of my highly respected and much beloved father." Blake noted that such a splendid emotional experience was framed within a system of debits and credits, so that it was important that his father live long enough so James could "reciprocate the blessings and cancel the debt which he so kindly imposed upon me." The context for this connection of emotional dividends with a debt to be repaid was articulated in various ways through the utilization of language drawn from business that cast both parents, man and woman alike, as businessmen within the home. The *Massachusetts Teacher* explained, "Every parent who has a child to educate, is not only a stockholder, but a director of an investment of greater value than can be estimated in gold and silver." Elsewhere it declared that "children are advanced payments of heaven. . . . The feeling with which we see them—speak to them—watch their play—listen to and pray for them—is one that may be fully at the lift of spirit-converse hereafter. . . ." The *Christian Observatory* wrote about the diligent parents "who have taken up the business of the mental and moral culture of children and youth, for the purpose of getting just what their wares will bring in the market." A writer for *Gleason's*, sensing a danger in such an objectification of family members and especially children, scorned "certain merchants" who "look upon [their] children as so many daybooks and ledgers." The *Youth's Cabinet* had another kind of complaint, namely the child's rational exploitation of the domestic emotional economy for his or her own purposes. It warned its readers: "The child who withholds his affections from his father or mother, commits a crime against nature." The magazine took no notice, however, of the parental practice of emotional withdrawal as a means of controlling and molding children.[27]

IN LOCO PARENTIS

The relation between teacher and student was similar to that between parent and child. Bostonians turned their children over to teachers who served as parents at school, and who exercised complete power over the child's moral development in a relationship characterized by its emotional quality. The *Massachusetts Teacher* explained all of this in 1858:

> The terms of the contract, as expressed in the law of the land and understood by the generality of mankind, are by no means equivocal. The teacher is an agent for the parent, acting under the supervision of the authorities of the town and state as trustees. So far as he is able, from the nature of the case, he stands in the place of the parent, — in loco parentis. His powers for the time being are plenal. While the pupil is under his charge, those powers are not subject to the will of the parent. They can neither be revoked nor modified by him.

Such an arrangement practically widened the domestic sphere, stretching the roof of the home out over the school classroom. The relationship between student and teacher, then, like that between parent and child, was thought to be grounded in feeling. Just as the parent taught and corrected the child at home through affection, so also was the teacher expected to marshall feelings for students. A Boston lawyer wrote that "the law says the teacher is in loco parentis. As he should feel the emotions of a father, unless he can bring into the school-room something of that kind, he lacks an important element of that character which is necessary to make him useful as a teacher." A teacher's job was to establish a relationship with a student on the ground of emotions, especially because "children and youth are governed more by sympathy and feeling." A story in the *Well-Spring*, "Georgie and His Teacher," illustrated the nature of the bond between teacher and student with typical sentimentality. Learning Georgie was an orphan, Miss Baker "pressed the dear weeping boy to her heart. . . . Ever since this incident, the teacher and Georgie have shown great mutual affection." The *Massachusetts Teacher* warned not only that "a frigid, formal, heartless style of teaching is comparatively worthless," but that a student who was not emotionally bonded to the teacher was in jeopardy, so that parents should "inspire in their children sentiments of love and esteem for" teachers.[28]

In Boston in the 1850s, the purpose of primary education was first of all to form character, and for boys, to specifically shape the character in ways that would maximize the possibility for success in business. One education writer revealed in 1852 that "our aim has been to set forth this idea: that what the student needs to qualify him for the business of future life, he may well be encouraged to acquire in the school-room." Business in this sense meant, specifically, commerce, in addition to its more general meaning of adult responsibilities and duties. Another article that year reiterated the message, opining that the teacher should regularly point out to the student the benefits of an education, "informing him that it will strengthen and invigorate his mind, augment his capacity for business, and mature and qualify him for greater usefulness." The connection was made more explicit in articles published later in the decade, which included forthright assertions such as "It seems to me that the object of education is to produce men practised in business, with enlarged minds and correct judgments, and men of learning not unversed in the world." The question of a separate track for girls aside, educationists already in the 1850s were concerned about the decay of learning as reform forces pressed schools to train students in skills relevant to business success, at the cost of abandoning some of the traditional curriculum. The *Massachusetts Teacher* in the 1850s began to fight what eventually became a rear-guard action against the clamor for "practical" education. It complained: "The sentiment has obtained especially among self-made men, . . . that education, such as the common people want, is only that degree of mental training necessary to conduct respectably the actual business operations of life."[29]

Bostonians need not have worried about the future of the city school system in at least one respect, however. Schools embraced their mission to teach character for the rest of the century. Character was understood in several ways, all of which overlapped. For generations, the discussion of character had been linked to ideas about temperament, about the distinguishing emotional aspects of a person or a group of people or the population of a nation. "National character," as everyone knew, meant emotional temper. In 1720, Massachusetts resident Robert Hale copied into his student notebook the typical doctrine about national character, identifying the French as rash and unsteady; Germans as phlegmatic, good-natured, martial, and passionate about food and drink; the Spaniards as grave, wise, constant, proud, lazy and lustful; the Italians as "of a middle Temp. between the starch't gravity of a Spaniard and the levity of a Fr.," courteous, affable, lustful, jealous, and addicted to war; and the English as "melancholick." A century later, Peter S. Townsend made the connection explicit, writing that "it is most common to depict national character by a representation of their predominating passions." Accordingly, the English were characterized by cold-blooded ferocity, the French by irresistible fury, and the Spanish by inexorable hatred.[30]

At the same time that character was linked with emotion, it was also, as Frances Merritt wrote in her diary, the sum of all "mental and moral habits." Hon. Emory Washburn, speaking before the Young Men's Christian Union in 1855, said that "few measure as they ought the power of what we call habit," and he defined habit as a "second nature." More to the point, Rev. James Coolidge, speaking before the same group two years earlier, had stressed that habit was grounded in emotion, and that good habits, specifically, arose from "those Divine affections, from which all Christian values and all holy worship proceed." The notion of character as the sum of habits which were forged in emotion was embraced by many writers, religious and secular, in the decades before the Civil War, and especially in the Northeast. Catherine Beecher, the founder of Hartford Female Seminary, proposed an understanding of the interrelationship of character, habit, and emotion that influenced a generation of educational and domestic theorists. In *The Elements of Mental and Moral Philosophy* (1831), which drew directly upon Scottish realism, she wrote: "All the phenomena and operations of the mind, are under the influences of these two general principles, habit and emotion." She defined habit as "a facility in performing physical or mental operations, gained by a repetition of such acts," and stressed that emotion was the operative force in the dynamics of association (in the Scottish sense), which produced the habit. Emotion and habit accordingly were interwoven as the warp and woof of character. Beecher, the educator who above all sought to devise ways to inculcate good habits in children and young adults, accordingly argued for programs that would promote emotional growth. Her thinking was adopted by a wide range of persons, including the author of *The Young Man's Friend,* who cogently stated the formula with reference to a model boy: "Reflection led to fixed principles. These have dictated pure and generous affections. Hence have arisen correct habits." For some persons, emotion was the key to the improvement of character, as the *Evangelist* pointed out in discussing one man's reflection upon eternity: "No one can deny that a man may direct his mind to these subjects, so as to become concerned for himself, and that, under the influence of these excited feelings, there may be in him a sudden change of character. This we often see to be the fact. He alters at once his habits—his whole course of life." The formation of character was a process more complex than merely altering one's behavior. As the *New Englander* explained, feeling was fundamental to the process of character development: "A man's character is different from his acts; it is consolidated by his acts. What he continually does, he forms a habit of doing; the feelings habitually indulged become a second nature to him." By the same token, every act and feeling contributed to the formation of character in a certain way, for good or for bad. Accordingly, said the *New Englander,* persons were wise to consider their acts and feelings carefully before indulging them: "The law of habit is familiar; yet in this view of the subject it reveals one of the most fearful facts in the constitution of the human soul; the fact that a man cannot act without affecting his character; that every act he performs, every feeling he indulges, is strengthening invisible chains that bind him, and making it more and more necessary to continue to act in a similar manner and to indulge similar feelings."[31]

Bostonians expected that the relationship between teacher and student, like that between parent and child, would lead to the formation of moral character. In both cases the cultivation of emotion was essential to the formation of good habits, the essence of character. Emotional experience through this process was translated into capabilities that prepared young men for success in business, and prepared girls for their responsibilities in the home, and especially that of shaping the character of their male children. Employing the vocabulary of business, then, writers translated the connection between habit, emotion, and character into terms that commodified it. The *Independent* accordingly wrote that "character is a good, sound, interest-paying stock," and the *Christian Parlor Magazine* praised "the formation of habits and the cultivation of principles which ever secure the confidence of all men. These very habits are to him a passport of credit and a capital." So, as one writer explained, "being a fair-dealer is worth a snug fortune to a merchant, and it is a fortune that accumulates faster than money at compound interest."[32]

CONTRACT EMOTIONOLOGY

Peter N. Stearns and Carol Z. Stearns have coined the term "emotionology" to refer to the cultural expectations for the display and concealment of emotion, and especially, "the social factors that determine and delimit, either implicitly or explicitly, the manner in which emotions are expressed." Among middle-class Bostonians, the emotionology of domestic relations—between spouses, parents and children, and teacher and students—was characterized by an expectation of the cultivation of emotion and emotional exchange. Between husband and wife that exchange was shaped by the conceptualization of marriage as companionate marriage, as a contract between equals. Marriage increasingly was viewed as a framework for emotional transactions between partners, and divorce as a remedy for the failure of one party to live up to its contract to transact. The trend was toward a view of emotion as "property," as a commodity exchanged under contract between equal parties. Emotion was, as sociologist Niklas Luhman has suggested in a history of love, a "token," like money, "a generalized symbolic communicative medium" which, as exchanged between parties, sustained the "system of intimacy." Parents increasingly endeavored to shape and train their children through the manipulation of emotion. Replacing the rod with a program of affectionate encouragement and correction, parents manipulated the emotional life of children in various ways—including through withdrawal of affection—in the interest of building character and inculcating moral principles. Whether a boy concluded that he owed an emotional debt to a parent or a girl responded to her parents' efforts by withdrawing her emotions, the consequence of the new child rearing was the same: parents and children both moved closer to a view of emotion as commodity. In the classroom, where teachers and students were expected to interact according to the doctrine of *in loco parentis,* the cultivation of emotion was essential to the production of character, to the manufacture of habits that would prove to be the "passport of credit and the capital" for investment in business success. And as we shall see, emotion, the "heart," proved to be a commodity essential to the functioning of the revival, where it was given to God in exchange for favor.[33]

EIGHT

Clerks, Apprentices, and Boyculture

THE "YOUNG MEN"

Observers of the revival frequently mentioned the unusually broad participation of adolescent and young adult males in prayer meetings and other religious gatherings during the spring and summer of 1858. Referring to this cohort of clerks, apprentices, students, schoolteachers, and aspiring businessmen, commentators repeatedly cast them as a distinct group—the "young men"—in newspaper reports, journal articles, and in sermons and public addresses. The young men, for their part, likewise sensed their belonging to a social class, that is, to a specific part of the population, one that was rapidly establishing an identity vis-à-vis other social groups, a "boyculture" that embodied notions of masculinity in connection with physical prowess, sports, enterprise, and boldness. Older men recognized them, too, and worried about the challenges that the young men posed to their own established status, authority, and comfort.

Young men from small towns and rural areas migrated to the city in large numbers in the decades before the Civil War. The came for jobs, and often made use of family connections in finding work and arranging for living accommodations. Many stayed at boardinghouses. They formed their own societies at work and in drinking establishments, at church and on the Common, and they organized various literary and business and self-improvement associations, for which they collected dues, sponsored speakers, and mounted debates. They threw parties and attended the theatre together, exchanged books, clothes, and guns. The revival was, in one sense, their coming-out party as a social unit with which other groups thereafter would have to reckon more seriously.

Fundamental to boyculture was athletic endeavor. Boys worked out in gymnasiums, and in their rooms before going to bed, kept track of their exertions in weight lifting and calisthenics, and measured and weighed themselves constantly. Rugged, hearty sailors, brave soldiers, and boxers were their heroes and role models. They associated physical strength with strength of character, and at the YMCA—home away from home for many of them—they learned from books and lectures the myriad ways in which Christianity, muscularity, good character, and business success were interwoven. English and American writers wrote enthusiastically about "athletic spiritualism" and true manhood, and their union in what eventually came to be known as Muscular Christianity.

A leading component of the emergent "muscular" boyculture of the mid-nineteenth century was its emphasis on initiative. In the competitive environment of the workplace, evidence of initiative clearly enhanced one's chances for advancement, and so was thought a necessary male character trait. But the young men considered it as more than merely a useful tactic for economic survival. It was an essential building block of masculinity. Known as "pluck," males relied upon it in leaving their families to seek their fortunes, in courtships, in advancement in their professions, in making contributions to public life and government, and in religion. During the Businessmen's Revival, young men brought pluck to the prayer meeting, and manifested it in their straightforward public requests for divine favor. Accordingly they contributed substantially to the construction of the revival as an extended exercise in negotiation with God, as a transaction involving the exchange of emotion for spiritual and temporal benefits.

WORK, THRILLS, AND GANG CONSCIOUSNESS

The nineteenth-century adage "the country for health, the city for wealth" was deeply ingrained in the consciousness of young males, amply manifested in their large-scale migration to urban areas. Seventeen-year-old Francis Bennett Jr., who came to Boston from Gloucester in the late summer of 1854, reported the event as follows: "I left my beloved home and mother and little sister to seek my fortune in the great city." Other young men like Bennett migrated to Boston in large numbers at mid-century. They came largely from the country, from farms that their parents would work for another thirty years or more before passing them on to whatever family member had been willing to wait them out. Boys who thought about hanging on in the country for a time thought twice because of the prospect of low pay. The influx of Irish had precipitated a downward spiral in farm wages, since, as the *Transcript* said, "a foreigner can live in Massachusetts for about one-third of what it costs a native citizen. . . ." On the other hand, the expanding manufacturing, trade, retailing, and financial businesses in Boston made the city a magnet for disenchanted young men from rural New England, offering them starting salaries of $125 to $300 a year at a time when the ceiling for farm wages was $12 to $15 a month and the net worth of a farmer over forty years of age was $3,000. According to Emory Washburn's calculation in late 1855, as many as ten thousand young men had recently "come up hither, as comparative strangers, from the training of country homes." Entering into the "crowded commercial city," boys inexperienced in urban life faced a plethora of dangers, of moral challenges. The *Observatory* was concerned about "the moral dangers which await the young," who came to Boston "in search of employment; and it especially points out the snares which are set to entrap their purity, and the facilities and temptations which stimulate their baser appetites." William Henry Hoyt, who, as we have seen, had some firsthand knowledge of the temptations of the city, wrote in his journal after hearing a sermon on the subject, that for recent arrivees there was "no father's Admonitions, or Mother's gentle reproof or Sister's persuasive appeals to restrain them" from "worldly objects." The religious press preached constantly on the topic, reporting cases of moral ruin alongside instances in which a boy who "felt yet the power of evil association, and met with many temptations," nevertheless won the battle against sinfulness. "Don't play with bad boys" urged the *Youth's Companion*, summarizing the message of a host of lecturers, newspaper writers, parents, and ministers who constantly warned their sons—whether native Bostonians or not—against bad company, against "street boys," who, as in an instance reported in the *Child's Friend*, would lead a victim "into all their own bad tricks." Rev. W. E. Boardman, in *The Higher Christian Life*, a classic statement of American perfectionist theology published in Boston in 1858, urged interdenominational effort to address the matter. Boardman at the outset of his book stressed that "the invincible strength of an undivided line of battle" was necessary "for the purpose of counteracting the increasing corruptions of our cities in their influence, especially upon the young men drawn from the country, into these great centers of activity and attraction." So dramatic was the migration of young men to the city that males outnumbered females six to five in Boston (with some specific population groups at some times closer to seven to five).[1]

Young men stayed in boardinghouses, or with families with whom they made contracts for an extended period of time, a year or more. Boardinghouse accommodation was spartan, in terms of the room and furnishings, as well as the food. Boardinghouse life differed from family life in that it provided little discipline or guidance for young men, although Elizur

Wright knew of several establishments that enforced "codes, culture, and discipline." Boys who failed in the boardinghouse environment, such as those who were "thrown out of employment for dishonesty," had the option of a mission placement to a farmer's or mechanic's family which ensured that they were "saved by being removed from scenes of temptation in the city." Boys sometimes advertised in Boston papers for a placement. The *Transcript* regularly published ads such as one in 1858 which proposed: "Board Wanted by a young gentleman in a private family, or where there are but few boarders, at the South part of the city, not above Dover Street. Address COZY at this office." A room with a family might reduce the possibility of falling into bad company encountered haphazardly at a boardinghouse. But even those boys who ended up in families had an abundance of opportunities to meet and to socialize with other males their own age, whether at work, church, in saloons, theatres, gymnasiums, on the Common, the docks, or in the streets. And in spite of their elders' encouragements to reticence in forming relationships in the city, boys and young men cultivated friendships with peers and fashioned collective identities in connection with their work, aspirations, religious beliefs, politics, leisure activities, athletic interests, petty criminality, and numerous other interlocking categories of group.[2]

Armed with visions of making their way up through the stages of apprenticeship to acceptance one day into the ranks of mechanics, or possessed of a scheme to clerk just long enough to save money for their own hardware store or to make it to a big desk in a trading firm, almost all boys who came to the city relied upon a family connection as they began their careers. The period of an apprenticeship—seven years was customary—was characterized not only by progressive mastery of a trade, but, because of an apprentice's age, was etched with excitements, dreams, mistakes, and various experiences of youth that rendered it profound. As Joseph Kett has suggested, such a time was a rite of passage rich in emotions of hope, doubt, fear, longing, and joy. Thirty-eight years after his apprenticeship, Arthur Nichols's father still celebrated the day he graduated to tradesman status and adulthood. Clerks advanced on a less certain path, which was measured not so much in terms of their investment of years as in the increase in their pay. Even then, there was no obvious benchmark for clerks' salaries. Eighteen-year-old Charles French earned $125 a year performing work similar to that of Francis Bennett Jr., who, although a year younger and just resettled in Boston, made $250 a year. Some males, such as Fred Harvey, who worked at Wilbon's Chemist making cod liver oil, had trouble separating themselves from their comfortable life at home. Harvey at age twenty made $300 a year, but visited frequently with his parents and siblings in Lawrence, relaxing while his mother waited on him, and prompting her to write of him and his like-minded brother: "Neither Fred nor George will ever work hard for a living." Francis Bennett Jr., on the other hand, after choking back his tears on the occasion of leaving home, threw himself into his work in the housewares department of what he believed was "the largest and handsomest store in the country." He sometimes worked until ten o'clock at night organizing his department for the next morning—the store was illuminated all night—and found time as well for a rich schedule of reading room visits, picnics, exercise, theatre, church, singing, occasional salooning, and periods of reflection. "It was a lovely evening," he wrote in his diary. "The moon was shining brightly. I sat down beside the frog pond and viewed the loveliness of nature." Boys with plans for marriage and a home of their own paid close attention to the advice of the city's elders, who urged punctuality, honesty, industry, and patience upon them. Loyalty, too, was fundamental to success, said James Coolidge, who stressed to his YMCA audience that a boy would advance largely through "an entire devotion to the interests of his employers, a single eye to the main chance, and a determined pursuit of gain." That is, of course, if a boy could find a position from which to launch his career. The course of expansion of the economy was pocked with setbacks, some catastrophic, as in 1857. And as railroads and newspapers spread the news of the boom in Boston, more and more boys came to the city looking for work. After a young man died in a firm in the city, Mary Dewey tried unsuccessfully to obtain the vacant position for her twenty-six-year-old son Charles. "There is such a legion of young men there," she wrote to Charles, that there was little hope of fitting him into a job. She nevertheless urged him on with typical motherly confidence and support: "I feel dear child that there is undeveloped strength in you & god helping I depend upon yr conquering the obstacles that lie in yr path. We have examples enough of good men & boys even who have risen superior to a thousand troubles, to know that the thing <u>can be done</u> . . ."[3]

The workplace served as one setting for the formation of friendships between young men. Sometimes, as we have seen, those friendships were intimate. Bachelors also joined clubs and societies that connected them with persons of similar interests and background. Such clubs might be informal, such as the "Fastastiques," to which Francis Bennett Jr. belonged and which eventually elected him "2nd Lieut." George Troup participated in the activities of the Chicago Mutual Improvement Association, keeping up on the news of his hometown through discussion, and perusing the Chicago papers in the Association reading room while broadening his network of friends in Boston. A few young men were admitted to the Somerset Club, which was itself was divided into sub-clubs, such as the Marshfield Club. Younger boys started clubs at school, such as one in which the members "bound themselves not to steal, lie, or swear." The major nineteenth-century fraternal societies also flourished in Boston. Freemasonry was especially popular and drew membership that pledged that "a brother's welfare I will remember as my own" and embraced the "five points of fellowship" through which "we are linked together in one invisible chain of sincere affection, brotherly love, relief, and truth." Local organizations founded by young middle-class clerks and college graduates, groups like the Mercantile Library Association, flourished as well. Typical of such collectives was the Franklin Scientific Association, which was founded in 1849 and which changed its name to the Franklin Literary Association in 1857 and then to the Franklin Club in 1859. It attracted persons ranging from Charles French, whose father was a city official in charge of the Public Gardens, to George Brooks, son of William Gray Brooks, who had helped to rescue William Lloyd Garrison from a Boston mob in 1835. Thirty-eight of forty members in 1857 were bachelors. The society sponsored debates and lectures attended by as many as 150 persons and attracted 400 persons or more to its anniversaries. Such occasions built bridges to other organizations, and sometimes the society entered into formal relationships with those organizations, as in the case of its union with the Shawmut Association for Young Men. The society also provided an excuse for members to establish acquaintanceships with leading citizens such as Josiah Quincy, Henry Wadsworth Longfellow, and William H. Prescott, from whom they solicited books for the club library. As Marion L. Bell has shown in the case of mid-nineteenth-century Philadelphia, those who migrated to the city formed clubs as a way of establishing community. In Boston, new arrivals joined together with native Bostonians in a broad range of young men's organizations that nurtured bonds of friendship between young men at the same time that they provided a framework for collective identity and a platform for criticism of their elders.[4]

Patricia Cline Cohen, writing about boys in antebellum New York City, has argued that the "social and spatial reorganization of both work and residence made it possible for young people to construct their own youth culture, one greatly at variance with moralistic employers' and parents' expectations. They could construct and adopt multiple identities and put them on and off like masks." Such also was the case in Boston, in that boyculture sometimes served as a display of young males' disagreements with their parents, ministers, and bosses. At the same time, boyculture functioned as a bridge to the world of middle-aged men, and so to a certain extent was conflicted with regard to the issue of generations. Such was clearly the case of the Franklin Scientific Association, which criticized the city's businessmen and other elders, but by and large embraced a staid middle-class agenda of wishes for financial success, nobility born of education, responsible citizenship, and romance. Such was also the case with the Young Men's Christian Association, which was neither founded nor administrated by young men, but was profoundly shaped by their interests and goals.[5]

The Boston YMCA was formed on September 17, 1851. It was the first American branch of the organization founded by George Williams in London seven years earlier. It followed in the footsteps of the Mount Vernon Church Association of Young Men, which had been organized in 1850. The formal announcement of the act of incorporation of the YMCA declared the mission of the Boston chapter to be the rescue of young men who had been thrown into the city, with all its invitations for delinquency and immorality. It was, said one spokesman several years later, "the steady hand of an experienced pilot" that would "guide young men through the crucial years of their coming of age." Sometimes called the Young Men's Christian Union during its early years, the organization declared that its "chief object is to elevate and improve the young men of the city, whom are clerks, mechanics, or apprentices, living, for the most part, in boarding-houses." It proposed a four-point program to attain that object, including "well-lighted and cheerful Rooms" for reading, a library of mostly religious volumes, Sunday evening lectures, and speeches, essays, and declamations of members. By 1855 the library was well stocked with works by A. B. Muzzey and Francis Wayland, Philip's *Manly Piety*, Sprague's *Letters to a Young Man*, and a rich trove of Scottish Common Sense writings, including Brown's *Philosophy of the Human Mind*, Stewart's *Philosophy of the Active and Moral Powers of Man*, and Reid's *Essays on the Intellectual Powers of Man.* In its first eight years, the YMCA managed one lecture series a year, on topics such as "The Christian Fathers," "The Christian History of the Middle Ages," "The Dramatic Element of the New Testament," and the ten-lecture series that corresponded with the revival, "What Must I Do to Be Saved?" In 1859, a series on "The Christian Poets" included lectures on Watts, Wesley, Cowper, Keble, and Milton, among others. The 1860 series, entitled "The Skepticism of Christendom," featured presentations by the city's leading Protestant clergy on "Paine the Deist," "Strauss the Mythist," "Hume the Sceptic," "Holbach the Atheist," and other such figures.[6]

The reading room of the YMCA was a busy place during the 1850s, and especially after its relocation to the Mercantile Building on Summer Street in 1858. Francis Bennett Jr. visited it often, sometimes for eight or ten days in a row, during the mid-1850s. Some days he stayed only ten minutes to read the evening paper or to get a book, while at other times he remained for a good part of the evening. George H. Troup was just as frequent a visitor in 1858, but differed from Bennett in that instead of going home to bed after reading (or for a walk in the city during good weather), he decamped to the Pocahontas Saloon to drink and sing and play darts or cards, or to the theatre. Or, on occasion, after a night with friends in a saloon, Troup would visit the reading room before going home. Bennett and Troup both nevertheless identified closely with the other young men that they met at the YMCA, in the reading room or at YMCA-sponsored lectures that they regularly attended. The company of boys and young men at the YMCA—with all of their differences of family background, hometown, employment, denominational affiliation (if any), leisure-time interests, and education—formed what they perceived to be a little society within the larger society of Boston. Francis Bennett Jr. accordingly rhapsodized about the annual election of officers, which was held in October 1854, "It was the first printed ballot that I ever voted in my life." After "lots of speeches from those elected as well as the members," he and his friends sang the New England standard "Old Hundred" and went out on the town to celebrate having participated in such a group-affirming event.[7]

The second annual report of the YMCA in 1853 counted over eight hundred members, each of whom paid one dollar or more annually for a membership. By 1869 there were 104 YMCAs in Massachusetts, with fourteen thousand members. Local Protestant clergy were by the mid-1850s closely associated with the YMCA, through their informal meetings with YMCA members recently converted, as well as through their participation as lecturers. Some ministers, such as Ezra Stiles Gannett and Jacob Merrill Manning, were deeply involved in the organization's business. Manning, after attracting an overflow crowd to a YMCA lecture at the Tremont Temple in late 1857, was presented with a certificate for life membership. At Park Street, Andrew Stone also built strong ties with the organization through his own YMCA-sponsored lectures, such as the one on "The Young Ruler," from which hundreds were turned away. The YMCA publicized itself effectively to boys in the countryside as well as the city, and served as a model for the organization of church groups for young men. The key in all such cases was the creation of an environment that fostered bonds between young men of strong Christian character, or, as the Waltham branch charter explained, to improve young men by "surrounding them with christian [*sic*] associates." By the time the Young Men's Parochial Association of Christ Church, Boston, was formed in 1858—a clumsy attempt to congregationalize the YMCA mission—the social category of "young men" was well established, even if it was a category "betwixt and between" childhood and adulthood, domestic and public, boy and "man."[8]

The proliferation of boyculture associations—this includes young men—is partly the consequence of the nineteenth-century construction of boys as fish out of water, as persons who did not fit into traditional categories of social role and function. Writing about the nineteenth-century "world of the young," historian Harvey J. Graff has argued: "By the mid-nineteenth century, it was only partially in place, incomplete in its articulation and diffusion, and contradictory to its core." In the rapidly changing environments of family, work, gender, and population in urban Boston, to be young was to be caught between outmoded and decaying notions of adolescence and young adulthood, and new categories that were only partially in place. Henry Ward Beecher outlined the problem for young males in a column in the *Liberator* in 1857. "A boy is a species of existence quite separate from all things else," Beecher began. "The real lives of boys have yet to be written. The lives of pious and good boys, which enrich the catalogues of great publishing societies, resemble a real boy's life about as much as a chicken picked, and larded upon the spit, and ready for a delicious eating, resembles a free fowl in the fields." According to Beecher, boys existed "in an anomalous condition," lived a mysterious predicament of outsiderhood in society, so that it "is an unfathomable mystery that we come to our manhood (as the Israelites reached Canaan) through the wilderness of boyhood." Even Theodore Parker spoke in surprisingly unliberal tones about growing up male, observing with some bewilderment that the pathway from boy to man came about by advance through several stages, from "his <u>animal</u> period," to "his <u>savage</u> period," to "his <u>barbarous</u> period," and then, after learning some measure of tolerance, to a man who "loves his duty." We have seen how Henry W. Haynes understood himself to be "a strange compound" of a man and a boy, and how Emory Washburn identified the predicament of young males as the liminoid experience of "this little space [six years or so] between the free, wild, innocent play of the hopes and dreams, passions and affections, of boyhood, and the sobered feelings, the disciplined judgment, and the subdued fancy of older persons." An article entitled "Young Men" that ran in *Gleason's Pictorial* said that a young man stood in "the world like a self-balanced tower," without the support that society provided women, old persons, and grown men. The *New Englander*, like numerous other magazines, chose not to address the fact of change in family and social life, settling instead for frequent warnings against "the coarsely sensual tastes, and the low and vulgar passions, which are so often the curse and shame of boyhood."[9]

When Patrick Collins said to a group of persons at Old South, "I call myself one of the *young men* and join with them," he was articulating a consciousness shared by clerks, apprentices, and mechanics in the city. And in spite of the underarticulated social grid that made the position of young men ambiguous, the older generation of males understood clearly enough that young men, as a cohort, stood together. Boston clergyman George Scandlin, old before his time after a harrowing naval voyage in which several dozen crew perished from yellow fever off the coast of Brazil, complained of generational friction at a religious conference in 1855: "As a general thing, the discussions were carried on by those who should have gone there to listen = <u>young men</u>." Concerned that "the aged those whose experience is worth much" were slighted, Scandlin concluded, "I think there was a lack of <u>modesty</u> in some young men then present." The pattern continued during the decade, so that by 1860, Orville Dewey, reflecting on the "Cambridge troubles," the factional politics at Harvard, thought that "the question seems fast coming to be, whether boys or men are to rule in College, in New York *salons*, and everywhere else in fact." Edmund Quincy, writing to the editor of the *Boston Post*, argued that the riot that broke out during a speech by Garrison in November 1850 was the deliberate work of a cohort of "organized and disciplined" young men. Distributed throughout the city as a broadside, the letter referred to the "ignorant clamors of Boston shop-boys and apprentices," and proposed that "it behooves the citizens of Boston to look at the remoter issues of this matter, and to consider whether they will permit the class of their inhabitants who committed this outrage to rule over them." When a lady in Lawrence gave a tea party for the young men, she found the affair shockingly rude because, as one observer noted, "the young set will not submit to her rule." On the other side of the aisle, the members of the Franklin Scientific Association, brimming with confidence as their numbers grew, met during the crash in 1857 to debate responsibility for the financial catastrophe. In the course of the debate, Francis A. Brown brought up the matter of "the proneness of the old merchants to remain in business to the exclusion of young men & considered that this was a reason why so many of our young men had gone to the West during the past few years." That kind of attitude earned boys the suspicion of magazine writers, such as one who fussed to the *Massachusetts Teacher* that the young showed "indifference to the feelings of the aged." Another writer referred to "every one of that miserable, premature, nervous, tobacco-cursed class, known as 'Young America' . . ." Against this background of complaint, few who were present on the Common for the balloon launch on the Fourth of July in 1857 could have missed the double meaning, and the illustration of difference, in the naming of the two balloons, "Young America" and "Old America." *Gleason's* urged older persons to tolerance, while the *Christian Observatory* and *Ballou's* thought that the problem was that boys just grew up too fast. The *Evangelist* thought hubris to blame, noting that "young men often begin their career with an extravagant opinion" of themselves, so that "it is often very useful for a young man at the outset to meet with a terrible mortification" on the way to learning his place, and establishing a solid foundation for his career.[10]

The everyday elements of boyculture, the behaviors that marked the personal and collective process of growing up male, included not only activities related to work, association memberships, and church, but a wide range of performances involving guns, girls, mischief, swearing, card-playing, dancing, smoking, fighting, and rioting. In short, a key element of boyculture was the thrill, in whatever form it might take. As Joanne Harvey wrote of her son, "Fred appears all spent [*sic*] lives on excitement." She worried because he was going out five nights a week, and because he "smokes the costliest cigars, rides the fastest horses." For boys who grew up with stories about Davy Crockett and other gun-toting, bear-wrestling heroes, hot lead and encounters with animals were a sure-fire source of thrills. *The Wonderful Adventures of the Little Man and His Little Gun*, published in Boston in 1859, translated the dangerous frontier world of Crockett into an urban environment populated not by bears but by ducks, and by a boy's most dangerous adversary, "his old enemy of the woods, the big black cat." So, versified the book: "There was a little man, and he had a little gun,/ And his bullets were made of lead, lead, lead;/ He went to the brook, and he shot a little duck,/ And he hit her right through the head, head, head." Later, after making a meal of the duck, the hero of the story, "Little Man Christy," shot the archenemy cat because it "provoked" and scratched him. Young Charles F. Low related a similar tale in his diary, although in his case the meal came after the encounter with the cat, which was somewhat cruder in its details: "I killed a large tom-cat this morning: he was walking by one of the cellar windows, and as he disturbed, and greatly annoyed, us during the night: I opened the window and threw the dumb-bell upon him and killed him: dressed the skin: went to dinner." Low otherwise was preoccupied with "ratting," a pastime common among boys in the city. In between playing violin, careful cleanings of his gun, and recuperating from fat lips caused by its recoil, Low "went ratting" on the banks of the Charles River. He often reported success: "Went out after rats: very successful: got 3: came home went to supper: got my quantity: and then skinned them: very good skins: but rather fat." Sometimes he gathered with his friends and simply "had a good time gunning and roving around." On one occasion he successfully pitted his dog against a large wharf rat, and on another he nearly succeeded in a meeting with the archenemy: "In the evening was about to strangle the black cat when the rope broke." The *Massachusetts Teacher*, in a piece entitled "Boys," urged teachers to admonish boys "who take pleasure in tormenting animals and insects." But the practice continued. Francis Minot Weld, a middle-class boy who came to Jamaica Plain as an eleven-year-old (and later graduated from Harvard and established a medical practice), practiced a less gruesome species of hunting that centered largely on partridge and rabbit, but he still displayed his trophy chipmunk skin, and, though expressing some uneasiness with the deed, drowned kittens. Some boys discovered the thrill of hunting relatively late. Charles Dewey, away at school, wrote his father asking for a gun after he had gone hunting with friends a few times and came to "understand the science quite well." In the same letter, he asked his sister Kate, "How's your cat?"[11]

Drinking, smoking, billiards, dancing, and other activities provided excitement and enjoyment for many boys and young men. All were cheap thrills, but were not just cheap thrills. They formed part of a matrix of behaviors that both defined social group and performed it in variously public contexts. In 1858, the *Puritan Recorder* estimated that fifteen thousand persons drank in Boston saloons on a Saturday night, "mostly young men and boys of fourteen years and upward." Many such persons were churchgoing clerks and apprentices, such as George Troup, whose usual evening routine took him to the YMCA reading room or a lecture and then to the Pocahontas Saloon, or Delmonico's in Garrett Square, to drink, dance, and play cards. Gamaliel Bradford, who traced his background to Plymouth Plantation, liked to drink champagne and dance at parties in young women's homes. The schoolteacher Henry Haynes drank bock and smoked cigars at his friend Shubert's. Other young men visited the smoky hotel lounges, "dropping in and out as the humour takes them," as Charles Dickens observed, and imbibing the "Gin-Sling, Cocktail, Sangaree, Mint Julep, Sherry Cobbler, Timber Doodle, and other rare drinks." James Barnard Blake wore himself out at dancing parties ("No party tonight, thank fortune"), and, like Haynes, spent much time in billiard halls, which were, as Steven A. Riess has suggested, a magnet for the "bachelor subculture." Blake, Haynes, Troup, Bradford, Charles French, and Tracy Patch Cheever all played cards often, usually Whist, a precursor to Contract Bridge, which taught principles of contract and exchange. John Townsend Trowbridge also played whist, in a club with James Russell Lowell and other men. Cards were, as Troup wrote, "gaming . . . with the boys." Young women such as Charlotte Foster and Susan Brown played cards, too. But unlike boys, they did not attract the concern of the clergy, perhaps because their card-playing could not be connected to a pattern of thrill-seeking. That pattern included, for Rev. James Coolidge, billiards, drinking, swearing, and the "clubhouse," while the *Youth's Companion* added smoking: "Boys make a sad mistake when they think they appear manly because they chew tobacco, smoke cigars, or use profane language." Other critics of boyculture, including parents, added various offenses to the list, and expressed particular concern about malicious mischief that ranged from window-breaking and teacher-hounding to barn-burning and rioting. When *Ballou's* reported that "the most atrocious crimes are perpetrated by youths of seventeen years or twenty," and recommended "sleepless vigilance" over adolescent boys, it voiced the fears of clergy, teachers, and parents that the thrill of tobacco or dancing might lead to scandal, criminality, or perdition. Boys sought thrills, and that led to trouble, as Mary Mudge reported in her diary: "The boys were bound to have a time, so they set the 'Bickford House' on fire." One instance of thrill-seeking struck especially deep into the religious sensibility of the city: a boy was caught and severely punished at school for surreptitiously "changing the Bible to another edition coming from Yale."[12]

"ATHLETIC SPIRITUALISM AND BOLD INITIATIVE"

After the pursuit of girls,[13] the greatest thrill for boys was sport. Former Cambridge Professor R. S. Calthorp, in a lecture delivered before the American Institute of Instruction in Norwich, Connecticut in 1859, articulated the understanding of sport as joyful play. Later published in Boston, the address asserted: "This then, is what cricket and boating, battledore and archery, shinney and skating, fishing, hunting, shooting, and base-ball mean, namely, that there is a joyous spontaneity in human beings; . . ." For Calthorp and a host of other commentators, sport also was manly, Calthorp insisting that the "sporting world, then, with its manly games and manly sports," and "these manly games at school" and "any manly games whatever" brought forth "true manhood" and "nobleness of character" and reinforced "general belief in the omnipotence of pluck!" Boys, said Calthorp, "learn to drink and swear and debauch, and to spend as fast as possible, in riotous living, the manhood and strength which God has given them. But this I know and publicly declare, that it is the love of manly sports" which keeps "fast young men" from corruption and ruin. The thrill of drinking and smoking was translated onto the playing field as pluck, initiative, boldness, and risk, in appropriate measure: "I think that there is just enough risk in these games to engender a manly contempt for pain, and a bold handling of danger." [14]

Sport was play, but it was serious play. The *Massachusetts Teacher* advised that young persons "will do almost anything . . . to appear manly. Nearly all their sports originate in this feeling, into which they enter as if life and death depended on the result of the game." In an urban environment focused on reputation—and complicated by male fear of giving any sort of appearance of self that might damage a reputation—the serious pursuit of sport was linked to the ongoing project of appearing manly. Magazine readers and writers alike frequently voiced concern about physical unfitness as the decay of manhood. Gamaliel Bradford wrote that a buoyantly healthy and active friend made "me feel as weak and languid as a woman." *Ballou's* complained in 1856 of "a lack of muscle in the men" of Boston, and *Gleason's* fretted that "we are deficient in those manly sports and exercises, which . . . strengthen the physical frame and animate the moral organization . . ." Henry Adams, looking back on the early 1850s, wrote that at that time "sport as a pursuit was unknown." All such rhetoric exaggerated the fitness "problem" (and represents more accurately American attempts to construct an understanding of national character vis-à-vis the English). In fact, young men in the 1850s undertook various regimens of exercise and sports. Charles F. Low found other uses for his dumbbells than felinicide. Gamaliel Bradford exercised with dumbbells before going to bed. Charles French claimed to be able to lift over four hundred pounds on the scales at work. Francis Bennett Jr. took "exercise in some Gymnastic tricks" before going to bed at night, and worked out as well at a local gym with a friend. Mary Dewey wrote her son Charles that "you must mind & exercise enough—a <u>gymnastic course</u> after bathing every morning—[and] before you sleep." Eliphay Arnold Jr., a pious man in his early twenties, went to the gym at 5:30 in the morning, after work, before church, or whenever he could fit a visit into his schedule of prayer meetings, flute playing, and avoiding conversations with girls. George Troup went to the gym evenings after dropping by the YMCA reading room. Arthur Nichols joined Stewart's Gymnasium, "where I frequently spend the evening," on the corner of Washington and Boylston Streets. *Ballou's* praised the place as a "popular establishment . . . liberally patronized, as it deserves to be. . . . It is open day and evening, and furnished with every appliance for muscular exercise, including good teachers." And Francis Weld, eighteen years old, visited Dr. Follen's Gymansium, which was established in 1858 to foster boxing, fencing, cricket, football, boating, and baseball. In Cambridge the students exercised in the Harvard gym that Francis Parkman had established in the early 1840s. All such exercise benefited the soul as well as the body, at least as far as the abolitionist clergyman Thomas Wentworth Higginson was concerned: ". . . his soul is made healthier, larger, freer, stronger, by hours and days of manly exercise."[15]

Male exercisers sought various things in their workouts, but almost all who reported on their visits to the gym or bedtime "tricks" made reference to the manner in which their bodies had become stronger, and therefore more manly.[16] Arthur Nichols was proud to have gone from 83 pounds to 112 pounds in five and a half years. When George Harvey found a moment to scribble a note to his brother (on the back of his mother's letter) he crowed: "I have changed, imagine a 'Young Gent,' six foot high, one hundred and seventy, a 'Perfect Beauty.'" The standard for weight and strength gain, however, was established by G. B. Winship, M.D. in "Physical Culture," an article that appeared in Boston in 1860. Outlining a 46-point plan for physical education, Winship detailed the route by which he accomplished an "astonishing change in my physical condition during the last nine years . . ." At age seventeen, he weighed one hundred pounds and was five feet in height. At age twenty-six he weighed 148 and was five foot, seven inches in height, had strength "more than twice that of an ordinary man," and claimed to be able to lift eleven hundred pounds "with the hands." He recommend lifting, dumbbells, loose dress, exercise every other day, fresh air, a full stomach, and a priority on physical attainment that suggested a renegade mentality: "Conform to the customs of society no further than your health will admit."[17]

There were other reasons for exercise besides weight gain and strength conditioning. Manliness was a matter of character, of morality, as much as it was a matter of physical culture. Thinking about the linkage was grounded in medical theory—a large, fluid field—and especially in Dr. Benjamin Rush's insistence on "the influence of the physical causes on the moral faculty." This understanding was refined and enlarged by a succession of writers—including Dr. Oliver Wendell Holmes, Sr., Thomas Wentworth Higginson, and Edward Everett Hale[18]—and popularized in literature of various sorts, including the *Christian Parlor Magazine*, which, in 1846, declared that "the physical structure, temperament, health and &c., of the individual, exerted often an undefined, mysterious influence upon the feelings and conduct." Noting that "a weak body is often found connected with an infirm will; . . . a timid desponding temperament with an irresolute, faltering, doubting heart," the magazine proposed that "something in the corporeal organization affects the mind," concluding that the "action of strong character seems to demand something to firm it into corporeal basis, as massive engines require for their weight and for their working, to be fixed upon a solid foundation." It thus was entirely understandable that George Scandlin, reflecting on the decay of his character, concluded that it was a consequence of the fact that "I have taken no exercise." It made sense as well that another writer should see in children's athletics on the playground "the arena on which their true character and dispositions are exhibited." And it was natural that Horace Mann should proclaim in 1850: "Should a man love God, he will have ten times the strength for the exercise of it, with a sound body." The connections between physical fitness and character, then, were at least three: A strong body was a necessary foundation for strong character; character naturally was reflected in athletics; and the performance of character—its issuance in acts of Christian virtue—was effective in as much as the body was strong and sound.[19]

The supposed connection between character and the body was the decisive step toward the construction of sports as a fundamentally Christian undertaking. After all, said the *Christian Observer,* Jesus was "a man of stature somewhat tall and comely, with a very ruddy countenance, such as the beholder may both love and fear." Such a description of the man who calmed the Sea of Galilee recalls Henry Haynes's description of another sailor, a "man's man," Captain Armstrong. Thomas Wentworth Higginson explored the relation of sound character to physical development in an article in the *Atlantic Monthly,* and then delivered a series of lectures on "Physical Training for Americans" that elaborated the theme of that article for crowds at the Tremont Temple in October 1858. Andrew Leete Stone, pastor at Park Street, already had established the importance of the matter as a lecture topic in an address to the YMCA the previous spring. Arguing that "it will not do to despise your body," Stone stressed that "our way to the dweller within opens through the flesh," and he encouraged care for the body as essential to a program of Christian moral development. Another writer, arguing that "bodily exercise" and "spiritual exercises" were known to "assist one another very substantially," proposed a term for the person who practiced both: "the athletic spiritualist." The *Christian Observer,* comparing Christianity to the Olympian Games of the Greeks, offered another term, "the Christian racers," to describe the coincidence of spiritual and physical fitness. James Blake attended a lecture by the author of the article and took careful notes on the similarities of "the Olympic games of the Grecians to the life of a Christian." Blake promptly decamped to the billiards parlor, and followed that by wearing himself out dancing at a party. The *Christian Register* frequently reinforced the theory of a connection between physical and spiritual development, and garnished it with occasional militaristic imagery such as: "The Christian is a warrior, and must fight . . ." George Troup and Eliphay Arnold Jr. devised schedules, as we have seen, that followed religious reading or prayer with exercise at the gym, and, as the decade wore on, May Day festivals at other special occasions at the churches increasingly featured sports. The ongoing conjunction of physical strength and endurance with religious character eventually produced two complementary angles of view. One was defined by what the *Christian Parlor Magazine* called "the Christian duty of caring for the bodily health." The other gave sport itself a religious dimension, as in "The Philosophy of Sports," a poem published in the *Liberator:* "All sports that spare the humblest pain,/ That neither maim nor kill-/ That lead us to the quiet field,/ Or to the lonesome hill-/ Are duties which the pure of heart/ Religiously fulfil."[20]

Physical exercise was good for the mind.[21] The *Massachusetts Teacher* published a seemingly endless string of articles during the decade of the 1850s on the importance of children's physical exercise as a prerequisite for learning. Invoking the "Scottish Training System," the magazine declared that "physical exercises . . . are also necessary . . . to arrest and sustain intellectual attention, as well as moral; and, therefore, the most particular care should be given to this department at all times." The goal was "mental action," and the road to that goal was exercise, one mile long, to be exact, to be run every day. *Gleason's* chipped in that "we go for activity—in body in mind, in everything. . . . Keep all things in motion," and the *Christian Register*, like virtually all magazines, reiterated the importance of "air and exercise" to mental acuity. All of this led to the equation of manly sports with manly thinking. In fact, said one writer, as boys came to realize that "'growth by exercise' is the law of their physical system," they would develop a habit of exercise—mental and physical—to sustain the "manhood of the mind." The extension of such a notion to the world of business was natural. The image of the businessman as a dynamic, resolute, mercantile athlete coincided with the image of a cricket player or boxer as a male fiercely determined to leave his mark on the playing field—including the scoreboard. One man made the connection explicit in a provision for two nephews in his will, enjoining them "to prove to the satisfaction of my executors that they have got out of bed in the morning, and either employed themselves in business, or taken exercise in the open air. . . . If they will not do this they shall not receive any of my property."[22]

The gang mentality,[23] the impulse to form associations with other young males, advanced the popularity of team sports such as cricket and baseball. Cricket became widely popular in the 1840s, and by the 1850s all the major eastern seaboard cities had cricket teams. In 1860, by one count, there were four hundred American cricket clubs with ten thousand players. *Ballou's* published a sketch of cricket players on the Common in 1859 and remarked that "the manly game of cricket, we are pleased to see, is enjoying great favor, as it deserves, for it brings into play physical energy and activity, mental calculation, self-control, courage, and activity." By the same token, the *Massachusetts Teacher* connected cricket with "deeds of 'pluck' and hardihood." During the 1850s baseball superseded cricket as the fair-weather sport of choice for men, however. Given relatively precise definition by Abner Doubleday and the New York Knickerbocker Club, baseball had evolved from an assortment of "barn-ball" and "four-old-cat" games to a sport governed by the rules of the National Association of Baseball Players, an organization formed from representatives of twenty-five east coast baseball clubs early in 1858. Oliver Wendell Holmes had played "rounders," a precursor to baseball, at Harvard in 1829. By mid-century, Bostonians such as Arthur Nichols played baseball day after day. Tracy Patch Cheever spent Fast Day, 1854, in baseball, and by 1857, the game was sufficiently popular to inspire Charles French to write that "a great deal of ball playing is lately going on, on our Common." Some literature foresaw the glory of baseball as the national game of the late nineteenth century. In "Song of Myself," Walt Whitman in 1855 looked forward to "picnics or jigs or a good game of base-ball."[24]

Boxing, ice-skating, sledding, and walking were other popular athletic exercises. Steven A. Riess has written that the "spectator sport most admired by the male urban counterculture in the antebellum period was pugilism." By the mid-1850s bare-knuckles bouts in theatres were drawing crowds willing to pay fifty cents a head. New Yorker John Morrisey, whose parents had immigrated from Ireland, was the acknowledged champion, and by virtue of his courage and strength proved a model for Irish and non-Irish boys alike. His reputation was sufficiently well established in Boston in 1858 that a Protestant magazine, the Boston *Christian Register,* thought it necessary to warn its readers that "incredible as it may seem, the Morrisey fever has seized some good men" and to advise Christians to relent from "pounding one another to prove the toughness of their fibre, their wind and power of endurance, &c." Religious commentators viewed ice-skating, on the other hand, as wholesome Christian exercise, and during winter the frozen ponds in and around the city filled with persons of all ages. George H. Troup wrote that two thousand people skated on Jamaica Pond on cold winter days, and *Gleason's* reported that "the whole thing is entered into with a zest and gusto, that makes the participants glow . . ." Skating was not the display of courage or risk that boxing was, but a poem entitled "The Skater's Song" suggested that it nevertheless was for the adventurous, the bold, and not the faint-hearted: "Let others choose more gentle sports / By the side of the winter's hearth, / Or at the ball or, festival / Seek for their share of mirth; / But as for me, away, away / Where the merry skaters be: / Where the fresh wind blows, and the smooth ice glows, / There is the place for me!" Sledding likewise was conceived as a sport requiring all the best qualities of young men. *Ballou's* accompanied a scene entitled "Boys Coasting on the Boston Common" with a commentary that associated pluck, initiative, daring, and forthright speech in the character of sledding boys:

> The spirited picture on this page, drawn expressly for us, represents a locality and a pastime dear to every boy. . . . It was precisely on this spot during the Revolution, that a committee of the boys waited on the British general with a bold complaint of the interference of his troops, then encamped upon the Common, with their winter sports. General Gage admired their Anglo-Saxon pluck, and promised that they should not be disturbed, remarking afterwards to one of his officers, "What are we to expect of one of the fathers, when the sons of rebels exhibit such a spirit."[25]

Female exercise grew in popularity as well in 1850s. However, the arguments for girls' sports or for women's exercise at the gym or on the skating pond focused not on daring and boldness but on exercise as a means to an improved female appearance, to beauty and a healthy look.[26] Catherine Beecher's "Letters to the People on Health and Happiness" complained that the exercise-less upbringing of girls was *destroying female health,*" and she promoted various courses of physical education to remedy that problem. Her views of the importance of exercise were broad, and incorporated theory about the relation of exercise to learning and moral development. But the *Massachusetts Teacher, Ballou's, Gleason's,* and other publications that climbed on the bandwagon were narrow in their views. They encouraged skating, shuttlecock, and archery for American females, while offering the model of the "English girl" who "rides, walks, drives, rows upon the water, runs, dances, sings, jumps the rope, throws the ball, hurls the quoit, draws the bow, keeps up the shuttlecock," and so forth. *Ballou's* even supported ladies' hours at Stewart's Gymnasium. But their reasoning about the importance of female exercise stressed good health, the relationship between mental agility and physical exercise, and, most commonly, the physical appearance of a woman, rather than the elements of character—courage, initiative, leadership, assertiveness, and other "manly" attributes—that were cited in promotions of male exercise. So, in the same paragraph in which *Gleason's* recommended "those manly sports and exercises which . . . animate the moral organization" of a male, it declared that the "evanescent character of American beauty is the result of a want of outdoor exercise. The American girl will tire in a walk of two miles, while an English girl of the same age will walk seven or eight miles before breakfast, and think nothing of the exploit. The consequence of this difference is, that an English lady, at forty, is in the prime of beauty and womanhood, while an American lady, at the same age, subsists on the *souvenir* of what she was in the days of 'auld lang syne.'" Such comparisons of American girls to their English counterparts, rather than to American men, reinforced a gender-specific way of thinking about sports, and ensured that there would be no assignment of manly character attributes to females who ran fast, threw far, skated brilliantly, or rowed as well as a male. American girls, instead, would be judged the equal of English girls, and assigned the most desirable qualities of English girls, namely, their health and beauty. So, said *Ballou's*, "Let them make war on pallor and languor, and beauty will be the result." *Harper's* was more direct, emphasizing above all else, the "perfection of figure," and "the full development of figure" in English women, and the necessity of exercise among American women as the means to "throw color into their cheeks and fulness into their forms."[27]

MASCULINE PLUCK

The urban boyculture of mid-nineteenth-century Boston included adolescents and young men, apprentices and clerks, boys who had recently arrived from the country as well as those who had grown up in the city. The changing conditions of social and family life, work and play in the 1850s allowed for the development of a subculture of bachelors as a distinct social group. Boyculture represented itself in a variety of ways, through associations and clubs as well as in informal matrices of sports, taverngoing, street life, and the YMCA, among others. Boys and young men distinguished themselves as a group from older males, who in turn not only recognized the difference, but worried that the "young men" were too pushy, too assertive, that they no longer knew their place. Seeking various kinds of thrills—not just ratting and dancing, but in a wide range of activities—young males were especially drawn to sports both as play and as a proving ground for their masculinity. For females, sports were constructed differently.

The notion of masculine pluck imbedded in the concept of male sport comported with the Christian notion of character as moral fitness. Sport was conceived as a performance of those aspects of character that New Englanders most valued in males in the years before the Civil War: fidelity to principles, strong-willed devotion to duty, courage to speak one's mind openly, and, especially, initiative, enterprise, drive. These qualities were particularly in evidence during the revival, when the "young men," as Patrick Collins said, brought them to the prayer meeting, and deployed them as part of a negotiation with God. They also brought their hearts—their emotions—and an understanding of emotionality that had been shaped during the turbulent decade of the 1850s. The young men accordingly played a key part in shaping the revival as an extended occasion for petitioning God in prayer, as well as a transactional matter involving the exchange of emotion for various favors.

NINE

Prayerful Transactions

THE CONTRACT WITH GOD

Prayer was the ritual centerpiece of the Businessmen's Revival. A large Protestant readership in Boston for over a decade had spent freely on prayer manuals and handbooks of devotional exercises involving prayer, and, encouraged by the ruminations of various clerical and lay prayer theorists, had reflected on the nature of prayer, its efficacy, its improvement, and its relation to faith.

From their reading about prayer and their practice of it, Bostonians concluded that prayer was a business. It was the means by which humanity negotiated with God. It was a medium for communication with God, a means, as it were, for transactions. Just as the telegraph was the instrument for communication between persons in far distant places, and electricity the substance conveyed, so was prayer the link between God and humanity, and emotion, like electricity, the substance conveyed, at least from the human end. Emotion, a commodity, was offered to God in prayer in exchange for divine favor. The efficacy of prayer—by the late 1850s fully a gospel truth among Protestants—was a sign and measure of faith, and proof of the transactive nature of relations with God. Protestants "gave the heart" and God gave back. Prayer was contract with God.

Petitionary prayer was a mixture of boldness and feeling. Prayer was thought useless, even insulting to God, unless it openly and forthrightly beseeched divine favor in pursuit of specific ends, and not only for comfort and joy, but for health, domestic tranquility, employment, help with alcoholism, food, shelter, and clothing—whatever temporal wants stood at the top of a petitioner's list. It was, accordingly, a mixture of masculine and feminine characteristics: manly in its boldness and womanly in its trust that emotion was fundamental to prayer. In this way, and in several others, it represented the fluidity of gender construction at mid-century. As a public spectacle, as performed in large meetings in churches, theatres, halls, and outdoors, it was grounded in and manifested the culture of collective performance of emotion that was characteristic of Boston public life, that elsewhere was evinced in Spiritualist gatherings, lyceum poetry readings, the theatre, parades and fire-watching. It was as dramatic a response to the perception of clerical inability to raise affections as could be imagined, a message punctuated by the fact of lay leadership of prayer during the revival. Prayer took the form of emotional excitement, but was regulated as well—a legacy of the crash the year before, which had forced Bostonians to reflect upon the fine line between excitement and overexcitement, in the economy as elsewhere. And, not least important, the cohort of "young men" who participated in the revival typified in their unprecedented embrace of prayer-meeting religion the blending of Christian spirituality with notions of muscularity and initiative. Petitionary prayer to God was "plucky," a condensed symbol of boyculture as it was emerging in the 1850s.

THE BUSINESS OF PRAYER

In 1854, the *Christian Observer* asked, "What is the reason that male members of our churches cannot pray?" In fact, males were turning out for prayer meetings in unusually large numbers by the mid-1850s. But perception of male neglect of prayer remained sufficiently imbedded in the urban consciousness that the *Observer* thought the question not only justified, but worthy of a snippy response: "My own view is, after observing such persons attentively for years, that the only reason is this,—*they will not.*" In the spring of 1858, with the revival in full swing, and the extent of male participation apparent, a report in the *Liberator* evidenced the shift in perception: "The very first fruit of revival is an immense multiplication of prayers and prayer-meetings. Under the new excitement of feeling, the voice is unconsciously raised, and the sound of individual and private prayer is heard by those around in the most unaccustomed places. Men pray in their closets, in their bed-chambers, in their counting-rooms, in their solitary walks, morning, noon, evening, and night."[1]

The reasons for male participation in the prayer revival were complex. An important factor, however, was the growing emphasis upon prayer itself, and especially the efficacy of prayer. John Brazer's *The Efficacy of Prayer,* a Unitarian-flavored document published in Boston in 1832, asked simply, "If prayer have no efficacy in procuring God's favor, why do we pray?" The answer, given in a strongly worded advocacy of prayer, was, of course, that prayer indeed was efficacious. This groundwork, partly a product of the Second Great Awakening, was enlarged over the next several decades as clergy hastened to analyze and encourage prayer. The *Christian Observatory*, in the course of an attempt to rescue the reputation of Increase Mather from critical historical revisionists, asserted in 1847 that "there is nothing enthusiastical or unreasonable in believing in the efficacy of prayer." For the *Observatory* "there is such a thing as sensible, intimate, heart-melting communion with God in prayer; such as the venerable Mather sometimes enjoyed, when he prostrated himself in secret before God, and wet his study floor with tears." The *Observatory* generalized that it was proper for persons to undertake prayer with the belief "that the things prayed for will be bestowed." Men like Mather, then, were to be recognized for their steadfast faith, because they "believed not only in the duty, but the *efficacy* of prayer. They *expected* answers to their prayers." By the 1850s, magazines such as the *Child's Friend and Family Magazine* were producing long discussions of the efficacy of prayer, with straightforward, unequivocal assertions of certainty about God's response: "If we ask God to help us in the performance of our duty, we have this assurance,—that he will do so." Moreover, said the magazine in language increasingly common in religious periodicals, "We should not pray to God as to a being who is so far from us that our desires and petitions scarcely reach him; but as to the dearest earthly parent, whose greatest delight is to grant our wishes." The *Christian Observer* added that "there is a God in heaven—that he is both a prayer-hearing and a prayer-answering God" who "compassionates the conditions of men," and the religious press reported with increasing frequency on cases in which prayer brought about a desired end.[2]

Reported examples of the efficacy of prayer were wide ranging. In one case, John the cabin boy opened his Bible to Psalm 55, and "earnestly prayed to God to make the storm cease." So inspiring was his piety that "one by one, the sailors, and even the captain, fell on their knees and prayed with him. It pleased God to hear their prayer; the wind ceased, and the ship went on her way safely." Another account, entitled "The Lost Child," told how a girl stalked by a "bad-looking animal" was rescued by prayer. In one instance, a sailor who had been missing at sea returned home to his mother as a result of her prayers: "What a spectacle: a wild, reckless youth acknowledging the efficacy of prayer." In the midst of a terrible drought in New England a minister led his congregation in prayer for rainfall. In a dramatic display of divine mercy, "plentiful showers fell upon the favored town," while the surrounding towns, which had not prayed for rain, received not even a drop. The minister later reported that "the truth was impressed upon my mind, that the Christian's God was the hearer of prayer." Deliverance of a similar sort took place on another occasion, when storm clouds threatened the meeting of the board of a religious association. Reflecting on the suddenly calm and clear skies, the board concluded that "we cannot explain the happy change on any supposition, except that it was in answer to prayer." Some of the best evidences were ancient. Declaring that the "Bible account of the power of prayer is the best we have, or can have," an article in the *Youth's Companion* listed Old Testament incidences of efficacious prayer, from "Abraham's servant prays—Rebekah appears," to "Asa prays—Israel gains a glorious victory." We already have reviewed the charge that Theodore Parker was "*prayed to death* by 'a praying circle of ladies'" in Boston who were opposed to his liberalism, and who subsequently were condemned by the *New York Tribune* as "a secret society of Destroying Angels." Such devotion was not what the religious press had in mind when they spoke about petitioning God, but careless readers of the myriad published accounts of answered prayer and of commentaries on prayer might be tempted to see such dark possibilities. The tone of the literature was, simply, so clear and final, as in the poem "Temples Not Made with Hands": "Wherever fervent prayer is heard, / He stands recording every word; / in hill, on mountain everywhere, / He never fails to answer prayer. / . . . He loves to hear and answer prayer." Mid-century thinking about prayer, then, was reducible to relatively simple maxims. For the *New Englander*, the heart of the matter was that "we cannot maintain and advance piety, without belief in the efficacy of prayer," while Mary Gardiner Davis explained the matter in more personalized terms: "What thou are so sure thou needest,—pray often for,—in time thy prayer will surely be granted."[3]

Antebellum thinking about prayer drew upon centuries of theorizing about the nature of relations between God and humanity, and the theological roots of New England Congregationalism lacked no commentary on petitionary prayer. John Calvin had written that prayer was undertaken "to make God conscious of our necessities and as it were to pour out our hearts before him," and the Puritan theologian William Perkins had defined prayer as a "request to God according to his word from a contrite heart in the name of Christ with assurance to be heard." Such an understanding of prayer was significantly enlarged in the century after the Great Awakening. The nineteenth-century view of the efficacy of prayer was grounded in a series of arguments that began with rejection of the residual notion that prayer should be dissociated from one's personal happiness. Hannah More, in the early nineteenth-century classic *The Spirit of Prayer* (1825)—a book at the center of Eliphay Arnold Jr.'s devotional life—challenged the view that a person had to renounce any benefit from prayer in order for it to be legitimate. "Yet that prayer cannot be mercenary," she wrote, "which involves God's glory with our own happiness, and makes his will the law of our requests." According to More, God "has graciously permitted, commanded, invited us, to attach our own happiness" to the desire to worship him. Because "the Bible exhibits not only a beautiful, but an inseparable combination" of the pursuit of personal happiness and the worship of God, there was no foundation for the claim that prayer requires "an absolute renunciation of all benefit to ourselves." Indeed, "to disconnect our happiness from his goodness, is at once to detract from his perfections . . ."[4]

Nathaniel Vincent's seventeenth-century treatise, also entitled *The Spirit of Prayer*, was republished in Boston in 1832, with an introductory essay by Enoch Pond. That "Introduction," rather than the book itself, significantly advanced the notion of petitionary prayer articulated in More. Enlarging on the traditional wisdom that "'Prayer moves the hand that moves the world,'" Pond stressed that "acceptable prayer implies a full confidence in all those promises which God has given for our encouragement in this duty, and a strong expectation that, so far as we can on the whole desire it, our prayers will be answered." Without confidence and expectation, prayer was "ineffectual." In the 1850s, explications of prayer were more strongly worded. Gardiner Spring, a Presbyterian pastor in New York City, published *The Mercy Seat; Thoughts Suggested by the Lord's Prayer* (1854), a strongly worded clarification of the process of prayer that edged toward a depiction of it as a transaction involving the acquisition of temporal benefits. Spring argued, first of all, that persons prayed "for the supply of their temporal wants." Approaching his subject as if he were exposing its hidden features to the light of day, he asserted that "the Being prayed to is God himself; nor is the language too strong, to say that the design of praying to him is to influence and induce him to give what we ask for." Again, taking a tone that suggested a revelatory account, he stressed that "there is no mysticism about this plain subject. Prayer itself is just what it purports to be; its object is just what it purports to be. It is to move the Deity, who from eternity determined to be thus moved, to bestow what the suppliant solicits." That same year, the Boston antislavery writer and Unitarian minister James Freeman Clarke took a similar tone in *The Christian Doctrine of Prayer*, which, according to Edward Everett Hale, "was circulated widely among thoughtful people of all communions" because Freeman "understood the language in which the Evangelical churches speak as few Unitarians do." For Clarke, prayer grew directly out of the circumstances of a person's life. The language of prayer was shaped by a person's most recent experiences. "We must have intercourse with God himself," wrote Clarke, "And to commune with him, we must have something to say to him; and that something must be something out of our actual life, something which <u>really</u> interests us." Like More, Clarke directly addressed claims that prayer was compromised by requests for temporal benefits, rejecting "two theories concerning prayer which weaken its spirit;—First, that we ought not to pray for temporal things; second, that the only answer to prayer is its own reaction." On the contrary, argued Clarke, "we may speak to Him of our real wants, and of all of them, and by an earnest petition <u>do something</u> towards realizing those wants." None of this limited God or forced his hand. Following More's tack again, Clarke implied that to not ask for temporal favors was to offend God by denying his rule over all aspects of life.

> Placed as we are, by the necessity of earthly life, in the midst of earthly interests, a large part of our wishes, hopes and efforts necessarily refer to these. If these wishes and hopes are not to be brought before God in prayer, a large part of our life is at once excluded from its domain. In the best of men nine tenths [sic] of his waking hours are occupied with thoughts and hopes bearing on earthly objects. If these may be brought before God, then are they sanctioned and purified in the act of prayer. But if not, and he must only ask for spiritual things, then all of this part of his true life is divorced from God."[5]

By 1863, when Augustus C. Thompson published *The Mercy-Seat; or, Thoughts on Prayer,* ideas about the efficacy of prayer had been tested in the revival. Thompson nevertheless still thought himself engaged in debate with naysayers, and so addressed his audience early in his book: "We only oppose the idea of those who deny all direct efficacy in supplication, and whom affirm that properly there is no such thing as an answer to petitions; that all good is derived by way of action of the worshipper." Such a conception of prayer was, argued Thompson, "subversive of the main office and the chief value of prayer," which was as "a conduit for certain blessings." Reiterating a theme struck by earlier writers, Thompson added, "Belief in this truth is necessary to derive reflex benefits. . . . Complimentary petitions are an insult to God. . . . There is needed a belief that God answers prayers; that suitable requests . . . do certainly bring answers." Christians accordingly were obliged to expect answers to their prayers. Without such expectation, prayer itself was not legitimate: "Suppliants certainly have reason to distrust the integrity of their prayers and their confidence in a prayer-hearing God, if they are not perseveringly on the lookout for returns."[6]

Such thinking about prayer was translated into magazine articles for a wide audience. The *Child's Friend and Family Magazine* explained that "when you kneel to pray, think exactly what you want, and ask God for it, no matter how small it may be. No prayer is beneath his gracious notice, if it be offered in faith and sincerity." That included prayers for temporal benefits: "We may ask for earthly blessing, or release from earthly trial and suffering. . . ." The *Youth's Companion* instructed children: "You may ask God for all sorts of things in prayer; you may ask him to help you do your lessons well; to make your brothers and sisters kind to you; to give you friends to love you . . ." And *Ballou's*, like other non-religious magazines, took up the cause as well, pointing out that "Sir Walter Raleigh one day asking a favor from Queen Elizabeth, the latter said to him—'Raleigh, when will you leave off begging?' To which he answered—'When your majesty leaves off giving.' Ask great things of God. Expect great things of God."[7]

In some rare instances, the *Christian Advocate* argued, individuals offer "mad and fatal petitions" which God in his wisdom fails to grant. Prayer nevertheless ought to be made freely and without reservation. *The Altar at Home*, published in its eighth edition in 1857, consisted of 350 pages of form prayers, and it is clear that individually and in group worship persons relied upon such forms. However, almost all of the Protestant clergy and religious writers at mid-century thought that free prayer was the heart of a Christian's relation to God. Even the conservative *New Englander* was willing to support such a notion, and it drew upon a certain view of New England history to do so: "Accordingly, in proportion as the Puritan party grew in strength, it was generally characterized by a strong preference for free prayer as better any way than any sort of book prayer." Prayer, said the *New Englander*, "should be capable of unlimited variety, adapting itself with a living flexibility to all the varying peculiarities of each occasion." Bostonians thus undertook to offer special prayers for temperance in moments of reform, and prayed fervently for the failure of the Kansas-Nebraska Act in Congress. Requests became even more specific during the revival, when persons asked for wood for the winter, the recovery of a child, the safe return of a husband from sea, jobs, a new roof, or rain, as well as a softened heart and signs of God's love. As we have seen, the revival was manifested largely in the public performance of petitionary prayer, and that prayer might be offered in any number of ways. In New York's large Burton Theatre meetings, Henry Ward Beecher read aloud written requests, a practice not uncommon in many meetings. More common were meetings in which individuals stood up—a moderator limited them to five minutes time—and prayed openly for a specific request, to which the meeting then gave its support. As the *Evangelist* pointed out late in 1858, prayers "should be short, and come to the point at once." Earlier that summer, the *Evangelist* had looked back on the revival and remarked that "the exhortations and prayers are of a different character than they were a year ago. When the brethren rise to speak, they seem to have an idea of what they wish to say, and when they have said it they sit down; consequently, they are brief, pointed, and telling." Such prayer required initiative and boldness. It was the speaking of one's beliefs boldly in public. (During the revival, placards printed with the exhortation "STAND UP FOR JESUS" were placed in shop windows and over church pulpits.) It was, in short, a manly exercise, and as the revival grew in size and influence, this masculinized construction of prayer was recirculated into theological conversation about prayer itself, resulting in a conception of prayer as a matter of bold petitioning. Rev. Norris Day, a leading figure in the Boston revival, made the point in one of his revival sermons: "Having the desire in the heart, and leaving off the <u>asking</u> part, is not prayer. Why? Simply because prayer is asking for things that we need. . . . Why undertake to dodge this plain duty? Why not meet it like a man?"[8]

Activity, not passivity, was one of the defining characteristics of prayer. As Caleb Stetson wrote in *Domestic Worship*, "it is not the design of his government that we should passively receive, but <u>create</u> rather, the good we enjoy." Prayer, said the *Child's Friend*, required "effort." The word most commonly used to describe the petitionary function of prayer, however, was "importunity." So, a minister was said to lead "in prayer with deep religious feeling and earnest importunity." An article entitled "Prayer" in the *Youth's Companion* declared: "Importunity is not necessary to move God; but it is necessary to evince our sincerity, and to prepare us to enjoy his undeserved favors . . ." And Frances Merritt, embracing like many other women at the height of the revival the masculinized notion of prayer, wrote in her journal, "O that this praying revival may teach Christians how to pray, make them value the prayer of faith, the effectual fervent prayer of a righteous man," and prefaced her own prayer with "Let me be importunate in prayer for a blessing here."[9]

"Manly" prayer had a "feminine" side. Emphasis on the courage to ask forthrightly for what one wanted, to speak one's mind, was balanced by trust that emotion was at the heart of prayer. Bostonians' experience of the fluidity of gender categories at mid-century had made such an arrangement possible, had provided context for understanding how one could meet the challenge of prayer "like a man" while at the same time investing in the notion of the "womanhood of the soul." As prayer took on a more masculinized aspect, it did not lose its feminized elements, its emphasis on feeling as a key part of prayer. In fact, as the masculinized elements became more pronounced, clergy and the press reinforced the feminized aspects alongside of them, in some measure effecting a balance—just as we have seen in the case of gender roles overall—between the two. This does not mean that these gendered parts of prayer were simply blended. As in their construction of gender roles at the time, which stressed differences even as it undermined those differences, Bostonians imagined prayer more as a process of give-and-take, a process of dialectic, than a cultural operation in which each side was dissolved in the other. Prayer was simultaneously a masculinized and feminized undertaking, and commentators worked hard to show the vitality of both sides. Each side remained viable only inasmuch as its counterpart remained strong beside it.[10]

"God himself has emotions," wrote S. D. Burchard, Presbyterian pastor of a leading revival church in New York. Therefore, as the Rev. Harvey Newcomb urged, one should "<u>Enter into the feelings of Christ</u>." And God "chooses to disclose his feelings just as they are, and because this openness in disclosing them is essential to the highest good," added Andover Professor Edward A. Park. Thomas W. Jenkyn likewise believed that "even angels look to, and contemplate, the salvation of the world with excited emotion." The revival surely, then, was on the right path because, as the *Boston Journal* reported in March, it was "marked by much earnestness of feeling." The word "earnest" was as important to the revival's view of prayer as was "importunate"; indeed, the two went together. Prayer was the product of "earnest desires from a heart bowed by love," said *Ballou's*. The *Massachusetts Teacher, Youth's Companion,* and a host of other publications, as well as the lectures and sermons of the clergy, resolved likewise, urging "prayer the most earnest, the most urgent." Thomas W. Jenkyn, who thought that "man is a creature of feeling," and that "the success of truth depends very much on its adaptation to man's affections," went so far as to set his analysis in an Enlightenment frame. Citing Dugald Stewart's *Philosophy of Mind*, Jenkyn claimed in 1846 that "God has given laws to the emotions, as well as to the perceptions of the soul. . . . Inattention to the laws of emotion has contributed more than anything else to the short duration . . . of religious revivals." For Hannah More, "prayer is desire," and "an act both of the understanding and of the heart." For Enoch Pond, emotion legitimized prayer, so that for "prayer to be acceptable, it is necessary that it should express our *real feelings,* and that our thoughts and affections should be *interested and engaged in it.*" He also believed that "<u>fervent, effectual</u> prayer not only expresses the real feelings of the worshipper, but is the result of <u>strong</u> feeling. . . . it is the desire, the wish, and the longing, and, so to speak, the opening of the soul." Caleb Stetson offered a concise definition, claiming that "prayer is the natural expression of religious sentiment." Another rendering of the emotional component in prayer was offered by Augustus C. Thompson, who, having had several years time to reflect on the revival, thought that "prayer is a devout movement of the soul God-ward; Not an endeavor of recollection, but an impulse of action; not language so much as desire."[11]

The notion of desire that Thompson and some other theologians had in mind was not merely desire as an emotional longing, however. Desire as emotion was understood in conjunction with the imperative to voice that desire, to translate it, in prayer, into requests, to express it. So when the *Evangelist* spoke of prayer as a combination of *"desire* and *will,"* it was clarifying an understanding of prayer as a process constituted both by simple, unreflective emotional closeness to God and a calculated determination to gain something, to effect change, in the circumstances of one's life. Austin Phelps's *The Still Hour; or Communion with God,* published in Boston in 1867, specifically addressed this matter in a section on "effeminate prayer." Concerned that Christians mistake a "lazy" emotionality for true, heartfelt prayer, Phelps endeavored to reinforce awareness of the intellectual side of prayer, and in so doing made clear the manner in which he conceived prayer as a balancing of gendered elements. Considering religion as "'the homestead of common feelings'" and the profound emotionality of prayer as "'the motion of a hidden fire / that *trembles* in the breast,'" Phelps assured his readers that "all of this is true, and no idea of the intellectuality of prayer should be entertained that conflicts with this." However, unless a person structured prayer purposefully, that is, approached it as a deliberate attempt to obtain benefits by voicing thoughtful requests, that prayer would not be efficacious. An exclusive focus on "the grand thoughts and the grander feeling which the language [of prayer] portrays," produced "effeminate prayer," a mode that luxuriated in emotion at the expense of the male element of bold, resolute pursuit of specific ends. "Effeminate prayer" was for Phelps "an offence of feeling." James Freeman Clarke sought to address the issue in another way, but could not avoid the gendered meanings of his terms. Arguing that prayer was a blending of reason and faith, of "law and love," he invoked matrimonial imagery in asserting that such a combination maximized the potential of prayer: "Science and faith shall then walk hand in hand, and the result of this will be a deeper strain of piety and a higher power of prayer than any yet known."[12]

The essence of prayer remained an "opening of the heart to God," and writers constantly cited examples of prayer as an exercise in which individuals "lift up their hearts to God." For many New Englanders, the relationship to God was, as historian Richard Rabinowitz has written, a "one-on-one" relationship with a God viewed more as a companion than judge.[13] Churches advised persons to state precisely what they wished to gain in prayer, to voice their desire, whatever it might be. But the religious construction of desire meant that the act of speaking boldly one's request was simultaneously an offering of the heart to God. Desire, as both importunity and earnestness, was as much a matter of giving the heart to God as it was an entreaty. One gave the heart to God in prayer and expected God, in turn, to grant a request. Spring's dictum that prayer was to "induce Him to give what we want" and Thompson's insistence that persons continually be "on the lookout for returns" were complemented by the ubiquitous phrase "give my heart to God." Just as a woman gave her heart to a man, a brother to his sister, and so forth,[14] so persons gave the heart to God as part of a transaction in which they received divine favor in exchange. Heman Humphrey's *Revival Sketches and Manual,* which included transcripts of conversations with persons converted in the prayer meetings, made frequent reference to the phrase. One man worried that "it seems as if I ought to repent and give my heart to God in less than a *week,*" another reported that "I did *intend* to repent and give my heart to God, and fixed the time," while another said that "I have fully resolved to give my heart to God." A YMCA volume of hymns collected from the revival included lyrics about giving the heart to God. Rev. James Caughey, writing about his experiences in Boston a few years before the revival, told how one "young man once said, 'After I have been to the ball, I will give my heart to God.' The Spirit was making the last effort with him. He went to the ball and died on the floor." In *The Revivals of the Century,* Lyman A. Atwater commented on the case of a difficult conversion in which a man declared that "'I found I could not give my heart to God.'" A decade after the revival, Joshua Huntington, describing the course of his defection from New England Congregationalism to Roman Catholicism, referred to a telling moment with his minister: "But when I anxiously asked what more was required, I was answered with the usual cant phrases, that I must 'give my heart to God' . . . and other such expressions.'" Twenty years after the revival Edward A. Lawrence wrote in the *Princeton Review* that "as I go to the Old Testament, I find just such phrases as these: 'Look unto Me, and be saved, all ye ends of the earth'; 'Son, give Me thine heart—trust it to me' . . . and as I look and seek and come, and give my heart and trust, I am saved—. . ."[15]

In the words of Caleb Stetson, "the heart breathes out its irrepressible emotions to the Father in filial trust," and the Father responds with favors. In the complex dynamics of the Christian spiritual economy, the commodity of the heart was at the same time the vehicle by which an importunate request for favor was brought to God's ear. That is, the heart was not merely a gift. It was understood to be a spiritual artifact upon which was inscribed a person's deepest desires. In the concise code of nineteenth-century Christianity—a code rooted in centuries of theological reflection and literary and artistic representation of desire—the heart represented the nature of exchange itself, both the giving and the getting.[16] And if this arrangement was sometimes depicted as businesslike, it was because writers intended to convey precisely that impression. *The Still Hour* straightforwardly addressed the matter, explaining that "the prospect of gaining an object, will always affect this the expression of intense desire. The feeling which will become spontaneous with a Christian, under the influence of such a trust, is this: 'I come to my devotions this morning, on an errand of real life. This is no romance and no farce. I do not come here to go through a form of words. I have no hopeless desires to express. I have an object to gain. I have an end to accomplish. This is a *business* in which I am about to engage." Stressing the importance of the heart in prayer, the book continued: "Such a habit of feeling as this will give to prayer that quality which Dr. Chalmers observed as being the characteristic of the prayers of Doddridge,—that they had an intensely 'business-like' spirit."[17]

George S. Hilliard already in 1850 had provided a boiled-down picture of the broader context of transaction. In an address before the "young men" of the Mercantile Library Association, he summarized the circulation and relations of commodities in the market, including the spiritual market.

> The idea of exchange lies at the foundation of the vast aggregation of energy and activity which we call by the comprehensive name of business. One man wants what another man has. On this simple foundation rests the colossal fabric of trade. Indeed, all movement, whether in things spiritual or things material, may be traced back to inequality. . . . One side of a range produces corn, and another wine; the fig is in the valley, the pine on the mountain; the North has furs, the South jewels and spices. Each wants what the other has not.

Of course, Christians did not presume that God actually needed their hearts—even though some theology veered close to such a notion. That did not stop them, however, from construing prayer as an exchange of emotion, of the heart, for a blessing from God. As one would bring a gift to a king who has everything, in exchange for his favor, so Christians gave their hearts to God.[18]

Other writers repeated Hilliard's ideas, and commentary on spiritual life appropriated the vocabulary of economic exchange in making its points.[19] Readers of the *New Englander* learned that "indeed the whole economy of the universe is but one sublime mechanism for the supply of demand." The *Evangelist,* in an article entitled "Profit and Loss in Religion," deployed other commercial terms in declaring that "it is not the highest view of religion which regards it as a matter of profit and loss. Still that is one view, which as our Lord himself presents it, we are not to overlook." Tracy Patch Cheever likewise drew upon the language of business in reviewing the course of his spiritual development. He wrote:

> In the book of my life, these experiences are unerringly debited by the great Accountant, and the thought that the balance may be against one, must needs arise. Yet I am cheered by the hope that so much of providential good has been vouchsafed to me, as to prevent the entire bankruptcy of that treasure which was confided to me to keep and increase. Happy is the man, and happy the world through him, of whom it can be said that he added even a farthing worth to the capital of his soul.[20]

The *Puritan Recorder* presented the transaction with God as a most pleasant exchange, urging its readers to "'Delight thyself in the Lord, and he shall give thee the desires of thy heart.' It will make all the business of religion easy and pleasant to us. . . ." And in churches everywhere, revivalgoers prayed for "every unprofitable heart." Sometimes, business language slipped accidentally into discourse about religion, as in the case reported by the *Youth's Companion* in which a small girl finally unwittingly conveyed to her worldly uncle the meaning of religion when "she folded her little hands and said 'Pay,' meaning pray." And, in April 1858, there was the unusual step taken by persons who wished to promote the revival in Philadelphia: they issued stock certificates entitling the holders to "mansions in the skies" and citizenship in the "celestial city" if they acted "from love to Christ." Said the *Liberator:* "It bears a close resemblance to the old Papal expedient of selling indulgences."[21]

There indeed were certain aspects of the revival that seemed to recall "old expedients." Some of the rhetoric about the heart, petitionary prayer, treasure in heaven, and so forth had been a part of Christian discourse for years, in some cases centuries. What was new was the manner in which older ideas were combined, refined, given specific emphases, and deployed under an articulated understanding of the nature of exchange. Old ideas became new ideas when they were arranged, altered, polished, and re-represented in an urban context defined by rapid demographic and ecclesiastical change, the simultaneous deterioration and reinforcement of gender categories, the permeation of social relations—including domestic relationships—by notions of contract and exchange, post-crash thoughtfulness about the economy, and the progressive abstraction of emotion from the "whole" person. The notion of a contractual relationship with a supernatural being, for example, was not new in the 1850s. Bostonians had read about contracts with the Devil in Washington Irving's *The Devil and Tom Walker* (1824), Thackeray's "The Painter's Bargain" (1834), and other tales. The *Atlantic Monthly* even published the following tidbit in 1857: "We are told that, in selling yourself to the Devil, it is the proper traditionary practice to write the contract in your blood." But an exchange involving emotion as a commodity—prayer as a business of giving the heart and getting favor—was an idea that decisively emerged in American Protestantism only against the background of the social and intellectual changes of midcentury. The *Liberator*, reflecting on petitionary prayer, the heart, businessmen, and prayer meetings, offered an unflattering summary of this business of the heart at the height of the revival: "The business men's *prayer-meetings* are simply prayer meetings, on *business principles*, neither more nor less. Is it anything but natural that those who have run the pecuniary speculation into the ground with their competitive rage, should run salvation into the ground in the same headlong way? They would do up this business of saving souls in the same prompt and expeditious style as they have been trying to do up the business of making money." Competition was clearly evidenced in the rush to make public prayer, argued the *Liberator*, pointing out that at a prayer meetings one saw "men who shaved notes and gambled in stocks last year, in hottest competition of what they term prayer, three minutes each by the hammer, on a plan of mutual accommodation, which gives each his chance to make what he can out of the Lord, in that space of time." The businessmen who turned out in such large numbers for the prayer meetings approached the matter as one would approach a commercial transaction, said the *Liberator*, driving home the point with reference to the gift of the heart:

You hear a great deal said in the Revivalist meetings about stocks in the Bank of Heaven. Do you think men would so glibly employ these analogies with their business life if the *motive* were not essentially the same with their business motives? It is the same, on the whole. They are, on the whole, after precisely what they say—*spiritual "Bank stock."* It is a private speculation to secure them an "interest in the kingdom of heaven"—to secure them against punishment at death. . . . Doubtless it is easy to "give the heart to Christ at just six o'clock last evening." But what was the consideration for this so generous a gift, a gift so important as to be a sign of inward regeneration, so important as to be worthy of a public announcement? Why, bank stock in the kingdom of heaven.[22]

PERFORMING THE TRANSACTION

Bostonians linked masculinity to the public announcement of one's beliefs. Public prayer, and especially the petitionary prayer associated with revival, was a badge of such masculinity, a mark of a man's courage. As the *Youth's Companion* argued, a "Christian man" was not a man unless he had "sufficient courage or piety to kneel down in a steamboat's cabin, and before strangers, acknowledge the goodness of God, or ask his protecting love." For prayer manual authors Reverends Harvey Newcomb, Nathaniel Vincent, and Augustus C. Thompson, public prayer was essential to the Christian life, and "a force of untold value." But the performance of religious belief in prayer meetings was not only through the voicing of words that identified one's transaction with God. It was through shedding tears, as well. Prayer was "pleading" and "weeping," wrote Newcomb during the revival, and Thompson concurred, invoking an ancient rendering of the idea: "Prayers and tears are the Christian's all-prevalent armor." Tears announced religious faith and spiritual striving. They were an expression of religious feeling. Dr. Henry Rose had explained in his medical dissertation a half-century earlier how tears, and especially tears of joy, relieved strains upon the body and made it "more agile and lively." The notion of tears as the release of feeling was a key part of thinking about weeping in the 1850s. "Careless Annie," a character in a children's story, cried "tears of relief." Gamaliel Bradford, after a quarrel with another young man at work, wrote about his tears in a similar way: "I could not even speak for anger. I could not stand it any longer & I really believe should have burst a blood vessel if a flood of tears had not come to my relief." Eliphay Arnold Jr. frequently expressed his feelings in "tears of joy" both at home and in church, and reported sometimes that he wept because his "heart was so full." Children's and adolescent literature overflowed with references to tears, as in H. G. At-well's *Jimmy, a Christian* (1859), wherein the crippled, becrutched boy expressed his "sensitive heart" continuously in tears, and his remorseful mother, after beating him to death, "could not restrain her feelings . . . she sobbed aloud." A book about *Little Mabel* explained that "her heart was full of tears." *Gleason's* versified: "O! rather say each tear's a gem, / For Je-sus wept, and sanctioned them," adding that "it is dangerous to 'dam [*sic*] the eyes'—and should not be attempted." Weeping, said *Gleason's*, was a therapeutic, an "ancient form of hydropathy." Religious literature such as John Eliot's *Tears of Repentance* (1853) freely appropriated the imagery of public spirituality, as did reflections on Puritan ancestors who consecrated the land with their "prayers and tears." Public prayer and public tears were crucial to a revival, said the *Boston Recorder*, incorporating the traditional reference to Christian feeling, "each wept apart, and all wept together." Like the model Christian Cotton Mather, revivalgoers were to perform their piety not only through bold requests, but through public tears, the of-fering of "a heart full of feeling" to God. The *Christian Observatory* drew together the themes of emotion, release, public expression of the heart, and the fundamentally collective nature of revival: "All intense emotions burn to impart themselves. To be in sympathy with such as are like-minded, is necessary to human happiness. No man can keep all to himself that which occupies his whole soul. Be it a secret of love or murder, it must come out. All of this is true especially of the religious sentiment, the most powerful of all the passions man can feel. There is a craving for communion with God, and with men who are like God. . . . They must assemble themselves together. . . . This is the origin of prayer-meetings."[23]

Bostonians sometimes discussed the spectacle of revival prayer through references to technology. In the industrializing Northeast, technology was rapidly transforming manufacturing and communications. Bostonians, like other Americans, recognized it as a challenge to prior ways of life, and en-deavored to understand its effects upon society and the person. Accord-ingly, during the summer of 1858, the city made plans for an "Industrial Museum" which would be an "Exhibition of New Inventions, Domestic Manufactures, and American Fine Arts." The *Boston Recorder* enthused that "this is a day of excitement. The world seems unwilling to advance in the beaten track of former ages. Almost every enterprise must go as if driven by the power of steam." It added that the new age that was dawning required a manliness and boldness, a determination to advance in the face of risk: "It is of course to be expected that occasionally a car will run off the track or that a boiler will explode. But there is one class of men, so fearful of accidents, that they will not even kindle up the fire, lest some disaster befall them." Charles French was taken with the competition between the new steam engine and three conventional fire engines, held in front of the Park Street Church before an audience of six thousand persons. A few years later, in 1858, George Troup reported that "lots of men went down . . . to see the steam engine work." Papers regularly reported on the deeds of Robert Fulton, whose "name is prominently identified with that practical science to which we are indebted for those new applications of principles, which, from time to time, change the social and business relations of the world." The more important application of steam was to railroading. At mid-century, the *Puritan Recorder* proudly pointed out that Boston had over twenty-five hundred miles of railroad "completed at the cost of more than $100,000,000, connecting this city, by railroad and steam navigation, with thirteen states of the Union . . ." But, again, riding the rails was thought to require courage, and Henry Clark Wright, on a trip to northern Ohio, knew that there was such "great fear in this region of accidents on railways," that few people traveled on them. Traveling on a steamboat also required courage, said the *Independent* in commenting on the departure of the steamship *Baltic* to Europe. And that courage was not only in the traveling but simply in approaching "the Machinery": "One trembles to think of the prodigious power of the great pillars of iron, the mighty levers and arms, the ponderous beams, and the broad, massive iron foundations, amid, beneath, and over which he stands, when in the midst of this machinery. There is something colossal, primeval in it; that awes and impresses the manliest courage." Historian Carl Siragusa, quoting Horace Mann, summarized the interest in technology in this way: "The people of Massachusetts, to a greater extent than any other State in the Union, are a mechanical people."[24]

Technology was gendered as masculine and constructed as a representation of life as "public" life. Boel Berner has written that "technology is culturally defined as masculine, despite it being in many instances something which both men and women use and understand." Other scholars have defined it simply as "masculine culture," noting variously that "the culture of masculinity . . . is largely coterminous with the culture of technology," or observing the "strongly gendered notions of the relations a human being should have with a machine." Some writers, such as Margaret Lowe Benston, have extended this analysis to the claim that "the ideal businessman, operating according to objective logic and the latest scientific principles, represents the technical world view in action." The linkage between masculinity and technology in the mid-nineteenth century was profound, ranging from declarations of the necessity for "manly courage" in the experience of technology, to understandings of the "geometrical" male origins of technology, to the exclusion of women such as Mary Faxon Forbush from education in the operation of steam engines. Alongside such explicit notions of technology as "male culture" was the understanding of technology as fundamentally a public phenomenon. Machines represented a masculinized public world growing ever larger and more powerful. Certain expressions commonly in use at the time caught the essential features of such an understanding. Ira Mayhew, author of *Popular Education* (1850), wrote about "the whole machinery of human society," and numerous other writers added their own understanding of aspects of public life best captured in the trope "machinery." Charles Sumner not surprisingly emphasized the "Governors, Secretaries, Legislative Councils, Legislators, Judges, Marshals, and the whole machinery of civil society." Maurice Richter likewise saw in the legislature "the machinery by which the public business is performed." Freeman Hunt, in analyzing the operations of merchants in *Worth and Wealth* (1856), took a more nuts-and-bolts approach, but with a similarly strong emphasis on public life, in emphasizing that "this class owns the machinery of society, in great measure,—the Ships, Factories, Houses, Shops, Water-Privileges, and the like." Rev. Orville Dewey went the other direction, asserting that "the machinery of the public order will not roll on smoothly and safely without intervention; nay, we *are* the machinery. The government cannot go on prosperously without us, we stand aloof and looking on; nay, we *are* the government!" Mark Hopkins, lecturing at the Lowell Institute in Boston, said that "excitement, guidance, restraint" were the key elements of society, and that we "should harmonize these jarring elements, and cause every wheel in the vast machinery of human society to move freely and without interference." For Sylvester Judd, whose *Philo: An Evangeliad* was published in 1850, the machinery included "The Clergy, Statesmen, Poets, every guild, / Estate, profession, calling." There was, however, an exception: "The Reformer / Is inorganic in society, / No wheel in the machinery of life; . . ."[25]

If Judd implied that machines could be "organic," then Daniel Webster came close to anthropomorphizing them. Reflecting on the mechanically operated looms and spinning machines and other mechanical devices he observed during a tour of Lowell, he wrote: "When we look upon one of these, we behold a mute fellow-laborer, of immense power, of mathematical exactness, and of ever-during and unwearied effort. And while he is thus a most skilful and productive laborer, he is a non-consumer, at least beyond the wants of his mechanical being. . . . As if Providence had created a race of giants." And if machines could be seen as men—for Webster, a providence—then men could be seen as machines—but that was problematic. Indeed, the image of a man as a machine, an unfeeling, dehumanized male, laboring in one capacity or another as part of a vast complex of public systems, was common in the 1850s. Stephen Colwell wrote that "this idea of considering men as mere machines for the purpose of creating and distributing wealth, may do very well to round off the periods, the syllogisms, and the statements of political economists; but the whole notion is totally and irreconcilably at variance with Christianity." Francis Wharton's *A Treatise on Theism* likewise objected to "reducing men to mere machines." The metaphor was extended to the family, as when the *New Englander* advised parents "to govern without governing too much, without destroying all voluntariness, without turning the household into a machine."[26]

Thinking about public life was, as we have seen, complex, and it called for a willingness to interweave a substantial amount of contradictory or near-contradictory material, ideas about men, women, emotion, intellect, power, character, and strength. The imagery of technology presented citizenship and work as activities requiring membership in "the machinery of civil society." But to be a machine was bad—even though it was good that machines could mimic human workers. To be a machine was to be without feeling, an automaton, and a family life that was mechanical represented the worst of the bloodless world of machinery. Nevertheless—and here we encounter more evidence of mid-century fluidity of the interlocking categories of male/female, intellect/feeling, public/private—Bostonians thought that religious emotion both required public expression and was developed through it. To make public one's deepest religious feelings was not to expose the soul to a public machinery that would compromise those feelings, that would flatten and ultimately eviscerate them. Rather, as the *Observatory* explained, religious feeling "must come out," and people "must assemble themselves together" in prayer meetings for that purpose. A speaker in a prayer meeting or other religious gathering was joined in emotion to others who were present, with the result that everyone experienced emotional enrichment. Adopting a tone that signaled his sense of emotion as a discrete component of human experience, as an object, Francis Wayland outlined one of the reasons that emotion belonged in public gatherings: "But emotion, though it commence in the bosom of the speaker, is sustained and deepened and rendered more intense by the reciprocal action of the speaker and the audience upon each other. The earnestness of the speaker, shown in the eyes, the gesture, the tones of the voice, arouses the audience to sympathy. Their eyes answer to his eyes; their breathless attention shows that every tone of his voice thrills them with emotion; their whole expression reacts upon him, and a mutual sympathy binds them together."[27]

Representation of the communication of emotion between a person and God in technological imagery focused primarily on electricity and the telegraph. Emotion had been linked with electricity in both medical writing and in poetry for much of the nineteenth century. Theophilus Gale, a self-described "medico-electrician," spoke for many of his colleagues when he claimed that "the electric effluvia is the only active agent in the natural or physical world." He sought to cure hysteria by passing electrical shocks from the bottoms of the feet to the sides of the neck. John Vaughan took the same approach, and so did Edward Cutbush, author of *An Inaugural Dissertation on Insanity*, when he proposed "a violent shock of artificial electricity" to cure mania. For Athanasius Fenwick, "the passions of love, fear, anger, horror" and other feelings moved through the body like "electric fluid . . . in its passage along a wire." Such was the concept of electricity upon which poets drew in representing emotion. It is evidenced in the work of a wide range of poets, from Walt Whitman, who sang the "body electric" and who declared, ". . . little you know the subtle electric fire that for your sake is playing within me," to James Gates Percival, who wrote in "Prometheus": "This is the electric spark sent down from heaven / That woke to second life the man of clay." Julia Ward Howe in 1854 sang "th' electric soul," and "th' electric chain of truth," and figured prayer electric: "As I prayed thus, I wrestled with myself / And wrenched my hands, by loving friends held back / Till they were free and stretched on high to God / Who took them. / As by an electric chain, / The mystical conjunction showed to me / . . ." Augustus Thompson took a similar view in discussing ". . . these little momentary prayers . . . 'the links of an electric chain . . . '" And magazine writers commonly described the emotional engagement between speaker and audience as an electric phenomenon, as in one man's experience of Daniel Webster ("A thrilling sensation, much like the effect of a highly electrified atmosphere upon me . . .") and another's of the revivalist Asahel Nettleton, who "startled and electrified me." Bostonian Edward Hitchcock attempted to frame the matter as a scientific phenomenon in 1854, explaining: "Now, if we admit that mind does operate upon other minds while we are in the body, independent of the body, can we tell how far the influence extends? If electricity, or some other subtle agent, be essential to this action, it would indeed transfer this example to electric reaction, but it would still be real." Perhaps searching for a connection of his own, Eliphay Arnold Jr., who was deeply acquainted with religious emotion, studied a book on electricity and practiced with a galvanic battery in between visits to prayer meetings.[28]

The religious thrill was, to use the now-shopworn term, electric. An article entitled "Religious Excitements" in the *Evangelist* remarked directly on the nature of feeling: "A thrill of emotion sometimes darts through society like electricity, so that for a time thousands are swayed by a single feeling. No matter what the cause." And revivals, said the magazine, were a prime instance of such an electric thrill. The *New Englander,* in language reminiscent of Francis Wayland's writing, filled in some of the details in referring to the development of "the electric circuit of religious emotion through an assembly." Such terminology was grounded in perceptions about the telegraph as the preeminent means of communication. And almost all of what was communicated by telegraph in the years before the Civil War was news about government, catastrophe, financial markets, religious developments, and wars/treaties—in short, news about public life. Frances Bennett Jr. joined a large Boston crowd at the telegraph office on November 14, 1854, to wait for the results of the national polls the previous day. Five years later, the telegraph brought the news of John Brown's execution, along with reports of organized mourning and prayers for him in cities throughout the north. The *Book of the Telegraph,* published in Boston in 1858, played up a masculinist angle, observing that "the electric telegraph is the most wonderful application of the SCIENCE by which man is gradually extending his control over nature," while *Young America* uncovered more male agency in its genesis, a certain Andrew Crosse, who had predicted telegraphic communication in 1816. The most dramatic example of the manner in which the telegraph helped to define a public sphere, however, was the laying of the Atlantic cable, an event that was marked, as we have seen, with rejoicings from Charles French, William Gray Brooks, Jacob Merrill Manning, and a host of other Bostonians. It was a religious event constructed as a prayer in the form of the first official transatlantic telegraph message: "Europe and America are united by telegraphic communication 'Glory to God in the highest—peace on earth and good will to men.'" The Americans answered: "'And let the people say Amen.'" (Anne Ellsworth had sent the first official American telegraph message, "What God hath wrought," between Baltimore and Washington, in 1843.) William B. Sprague welcomed the event with a sermon on the manner in which it showed both the divine glory and the greatness of the human intellect, and Ezra S. Gannett urged a Boston congregation, "let us hail the event . . . as a harbinger of a closer sympathy and more effective cooperation by which not only England and the United States, but the nations of Christendom, and soon all the people of the earth, shall be bound together in an interchange, not of friendly messages alone, but of kind offices and fraternal regards." The telegraph, for Gannett, was a means of speeding feelings around the globe.[29]

Bostonians envisioned "fraternal regards" and other feelings communicated through a public, masculinist technology because they were willing to exploit the ambiguity in categories of male/female, emotion/intellect, and public/private (domestic). Telegraph, powered by electricity—a representation of emotion itself—communicated feeling between two parties. In elaborating on how feminized emotion found expression in the masculinized public sphere, Bostonians increasingly theorized symbiosis at the root of the matter. Arguing that "the man separated from female society becomes effeminate, less manly, and less noble," and that "the woman separated from male society . . . becomes more masculine and less refined," the *New Englander* made the appropriate analogy: "The telegraph may as well operate without the two poles of magnetism. . . ." Manipulating gender, emotional, and social categories, Rev. A. L. Stone similarly told a Park Street congregation that the Atlantic telegraph was "the bridal of the hemispheres," and that the metal "cord" that united England and America was like "the silken one uniting two hearts in wedlock." Such conceptualizations formed the context for the most straightforward discussion of the telegraph and religion during this period, a chapter in Thompson's *The Mercy-Seat* that was entitled, "Prayer a Telegraph." In an exceptionally rich text, Thompson outlined the operation of the telegraph, made analogies to religion, and defined both prayer and the prayer meeting in telegraphic terms. "If now from this world," he wrote,

> . . . there were carried a cable across the vast ocean of space, touching at the moon; then at the nearest planet of our system; thence to the farthest one; thence to some fixed star; and so onward, from constellation to constellation, till that distant place were reached, where we may suppose is the more immediate presence of God—the Trinity Bay of the universe,— and thus between the remote abode and our world, this mere islet of the great sea, instantaneous communications could take place, what a sensation ought it to create![30]

According to Thompson, "Such a spiritual telegraph exists; it was laid centuries ago, and has held two worlds in unbroken connection." Identifying prayer as that spiritual telegraph, Thompson went on to affirm that "this spiritual telegraph is no private enterprise; nor is it designed for the few, but for the many, and is open gratuitously to all." Moreover, it was a perfect mode of communication, because "there are no mistakes in transmission. Much as it may be crowded, various as messages may be in length, topic, and character, they are sent forward without loss of a word. Be the language what it may, grammatical imperfections what they may, there is no confusion and no inaccuracy when despatches reach their destination." And then, focusing precisely on the emotional content of the transmission, on the quality of prayer that made it a spiritual telegraph, Thompson exulted: "Here is the ladder Jacob saw, reaching to heaven, and on which angels ascend and descend. Who need ever be lonely? Here is a nerve going direct to the central heart of the unseen world, and along which every feeling, every desire, may pulsate immediately and sensibly to Him who is head of the church; . . ." In conclusion, Thompson pointed out that as "a direct agency, as a means of obtaining that which comes from above, prayer is a necessity; and it is the appointed exercise in which to expect great favors." The key to religious life, consequently, was the "prayer-meeting."[31]

BUSINESS OF THE HEART

During the Businessmen's Revival, young men, together with women and older men, transacted the business of the heart. In giving the heart to God, they also delivered to him their desires for blessings, and they believed that God responded to their initiative because he was bound by a cosmic law to do so. Embracing a notion of petitionary prayer as a matter of boldness, as the exercise of a manly voice, persons contracted for various favors, including stronger faith, assurance of salvation, recuperation from illness, improved family relations, and other such things. The context for these transactions was public—the prayer meeting—and the character of the prayer was emotional. Revivalgoers performed prayer with words and tears, guided by conceptualizations of their praying as telegraphic communication with God, as the transmission of feelings and desires like electricity into the heavens.

The revival was grounded in a feminized Christianity that valued emotional religion. That style would prevail throughout the rest of the century, and, in various forms, survive the twentieth century. To that feminine element the revival added the emphasis on masculine qualities of initiative, courage, daring, and speaking one's mind. Prayer, the centerpiece of the revival, was conceived as a blending of those masculine and feminine qualities. Men and women gave their hearts to God and expected favors in return. Notions of exchange and contract, of relations with God as contractual relations, as transactions involving emotion, characterized the revival.

All of this took place against a historical background in which emotion had been constructed as part of a self that was paradoxically both subject and object. Emotion accordingly was conceived as both object and spiritualized subjectivity. Also key was the partial unraveling of categories of gender and the social geography, a development that set the stage for a limited blending of male and female elements, of seemingly public and private behaviors, even as the old categories were being propped up.

The performance of prayer in a public meeting was a spectacle into which all persons present were drawn, and it was a spectacle into which they wished to be drawn. When the *Evangelist* reported that the "thrill of emotion sometimes darts through society like electricity," it was representing not only the phenomena of fires, theatre performances, processions, and July Fourth celebrations, but the experience of the prayer-meeting as well. The public aspect of the performance of prayer was a key to its efficacy, for in public the emotions were intensified and focused as in few other contexts. Such was especially the case during a time when the churches were so unsettled, ministers embroiled in debates with their congregations, and laypersons making bids for responsibility and authority. As Bostonians reflected further on religion and emotion, and sought to define their religious and emotional identities more precisely, they contrasted those identities with their constructions of the emotional and religious lives of immigrants and persons of color. Their "public" sphere was, in the end, not so public, and the great prayer-union revival not so much a union as they thought.

TEN

Emotion, Character, and Ethnicity

REVIVAL AND COLLECTIVE IDENTITY

Promoters of the Businessmen's Revival, as well as many of the participants, enthused over the fact that it was a "union revival," that is, a revival that allegedly joined persons of different religious backgrounds in a concerted embrace of God. Few Protestants would have challenged such a conception, for within the Protestant middle-class world of Boston, there was participation from almost every quarter.

Boston in 1858 was not exclusively middle class or Protestant, however. It was African American and Irish as well—which meant a class of Catholics, and, equivalently, poor persons—and it was home to a number of groups, such as abolitionists, whose religious agenda did not correspond with the practice of revival, and who sometimes criticized the revival as a departure from the real business of religion, namely the pursuit of equality and justice in social reform. The Protestant churches, though they did not recognize the eligibility of such groups for inclusion in their scheme of salvation (in its socio-spiritual aspects), nevertheless were aware of blacks and Irish and abolitionist agitators as problems on the periphery of their world. They characterized them in a variety of ways, including through reference to the performance of emotion.

Protestant revivalgoers operated out of a set of assumptions about emotionality that allowed them to characterize out-groups as emotionally defective. That is, they cast African Americans, Irish, and abolitionists as either too emotional, not emotional enough, or both. They painted members of such groups as lacking in regulation of emotion (i.e., the squandering of emotional capital and its disordering consequences), or, in some instances, as overly regulatory (i.e., incapable of initiating/participating in emotional transactions). The Protestant construction of the emotional profile of other groups accordingly functioned as a *primary* means by which to distinguish themselves from such groups. Emotionality, just as importantly as skin color, national origin, language, or social class, served as a marker of difference for the Protestant middle class. In criticizing the emotional performances of other groups, Protestants asserted their collective identity as emotionally healthy persons, which, in the web of culture, implied a host of other things, each confirming the other in a complex network of mutual reinforcements, by category: emotion, capital, class, character, citizenship, authority, power. If a class of persons could not regulate emotion, did not know how to create, conserve, and spend emotional capital, how could they be businessmen? And how, then, could they participate in the Businessmen's Revival?

Protestants asserted collective identity and broadcasted their difference from other groups through their participation in the Businessmen's Revival. The fact of their preoccupation with social difference, and status strata, is visible even in the way in which they sorted themselves into different prayer "ministries" during the revival. Such sorting was by denomination (the division of city into districts and the assignment of each denomination responsibility for home visitations in one of the districts), by occupation (special prayer groups for clerks, carpenters, seamen, railroaders, businessmen, machinists), and, inevitably, by gender (maternal societies, women's prayer groups that met in the vestibules of churches, and so forth). In the complex, seemingly bifurcated world of Boston's Protestants, the revival was indeed a union revival in the sense of its representation of collective identity, but it was also a mass performance of difference, especially with regard to blacks, Irish, and abolitionists.

MIDDLE GROUND FOR THE MIDDLE CLASS

In *Sensational Designs*, Jane Tompkins makes a case for "feeling" as the key to the nineteenth century, at least inasmuch as it was represented in literature. Exactly what that feeling was, or, more appropriately, what those feelings were, is not easy to say, either for us, or for the nineteenth-century persons who experienced them. Peter S. Townsend proposed in 1816 that all emotions were variations of four "primary passions": joy, grief, anger, and fear. Like the four primary colors, they were diluted in various ways into less profound feelings, and there blended and overlapped to produce "mixed feelings." William Cooke, as we shall see, was more liberal in his 1853 taxonomy of emotional life, granting official status to joy, grief, anger, fear, hope, jealousy, envy, desire, humility, pride, pity, hatred, love, and sympathy. That expanded list failed to include what the *Youth's Companion*, among many other religious publications, called "dependence on God," that Schleiermachian standard of nineteenth-century Protestantism. And there were complications with what might at first have seemed relatively simple, everyday emotions. Seemingly harmless emotions such as joy could be constructed in such a way as to lend them an ominous quality, leading to the recommendation that the experience of such an emotion had to be balanced with prayer, which "makes it innocent and safe, and which disarms the future of its portentous aspect." So also the case with love, which was scrutinized by the *Christian Observatory* under the heading "The Heresy of Love." Error came gilded in love, said the magazine, giving examples: "The raving fanatic, the dreamy mystic, the ultra-political reformist, the antinomian perfectionist, the abjurers of penalties and apologists for crime and sin, all profess to be actuated by a spirit of love, and to desire nothing so much as its diffusion." And the time and space of emotional experience was not always what it seemed to be. Some experiences trailed off into an ethereal religious world. Anger might be let off like steam (a common metaphor across cultures), but it was also a long-term problem, leading to misshapen character and spiritual corruption ("Anger is a blot upon your immortal soul"). Other experiences might cross into spiritual realms and at the same time frame a physical hyper-reality. Charlotte Foster's composition class in 1851 accordingly learned that "envy is the rack of the soul, and the torture of the body."[1]

Everyday emotional life was impermanent and ever changing. In both individuals and the community, emotion came and went, like the tides of the sea as they were drawn one way and the other by the moon. "Man is an excitable being," opined the *Evangelist*. "He is a creature of emotion and impulse. His feelings are never stationary. They ebb and flow like the sea. At one instant, he is in a state of exhilaration, the next, of despondence." Community life was marked by the equivalent fluctuation of emotion. One interpretation might be that of "popular feeling as but the inrolling of a tide, which has its regular flow," but, more precisely, "such waves of emotion, rolling over society, are in accordance with the laws of man's nature," so that "public feelings ebb and flow like those of an individual." Revivals, for example, were not outbreaks of fanaticism but events grounded in the emotional cycles of persons and societies. At the same time, as the *Liberator* pointed out, there was constancy in feeling, as in the case of "American feelings," emotion that was connected to "national pride." And Bostonians thought that everyday relations between individuals in families, work circles, and even society as a whole, were influenced by constant feeling between persons, called sympathy. Athanasius Fenwick's *Essay on Volition and Pleasure* had stressed the importance of sympathy as "fellow-feeling," and a rich tradition of English philosophy that included Joseph Butler, Francis Hutcheson, David Hume, John Stuart Mill, and Jeremy Bentham had detailed the nature and function of sympathy as a structural feature of community (and the sentimental novel—such as Samuel Richardson's *Pamela* [1740]—helped to popularize such notions). By 1856, Boston poet William Winter's *The Emotion of Sympathy: A Metrical Essay* was referring to the "Law of Sympathy which God has ordained to govern the human race."[2]

Early in the century, popular understanding of sympathy associated it with the observation of the sufferings of others. As the *Monthly Anthology and Boston Review* explained in 1808, "Sympathy is a motion communicated from the bosom of another. . . . Sympathy in its peculiar sense is used to signify our fellow-feeling with distress." Over the next several decades, fueled by more precise philosophizing in England and America, and against a background of social change and the ongoing abstraction of feeling from the feeler, sympathy came to represent more than a response to others' distress. It took on a more broadly social character. It became an orientation to community, a marker of social belonging. Sympathy was thought to be the feeling of others' feelings, no matter whether others' feelings were engendered by suffering, prosperity, achievement, or any other circumstance. It was, as James Barnard Blake hinted, about living the feelings of other persons. Returning from a party, Blake wrote: "I must confess that had I been influenced by my own feelings altogether, I should have remained at home, but I remember that it is not for myself alone, that I live." One writer in fact proposed that the "power of sympathy" sprang from the fact that everybody was alike, that "human nature is the same in all men," so that "the sympathies which pervade the human breast everywhere are the same." Such self-evident truths, for people at mid-century, led to a further observation, namely that there "is a human magnetism by which feelings spread from mind to mind." The waves of feeling flowing through society accordingly shaped the collective in certain ways. Above all, collective character was a product of the movement of feeling simultaneously in many hearts. "This quick responding of heart to heart is a noble attribute of our nature, and why may it not be turned to the highest of all purposes. . . . Men are not isolated beings—each forming his character apart, by slow and toilsome reflection. They move in masses. The character of each is determined by the character of those around him." Social leaders, then, required a special measure of sympathy, as Old South pastor

George Blagden told an audience that had gathered to formally welcome Rev. Jacob Manning into the Old South community: "This is eminently a social service, requiring, especially, the emotional parts of our nature, and expressive of sympathy and affection." The *New Englander* added that "sympathy is thus a great power in the social world," and the purest, most developed sympathy, was "not only feeling, but regulated feeling—the action of the heart guided by the purest reason."[3]

Sympathy referred to a community of feeling. Those capable of sympathy were members of the community, while the unsympathetic were left out. And although sympathy was said to be "the same in all men," sympathy that was regulated, that was guided by reason, was the purest sympathy. The principle of control was one part of the set of guidelines for emotional expression and concealment for the Protestant middle class, and it functioned together with other rules not only as a means of guiding persons through their socio-emotional lives, but as a means by which to draw boundaries between them and other groups. Bostonians constructed emotional rules as much to represent who they were as to differentiate themselves from other groups. White Protestants constructed, refined, and altered their feeling rules with an eye to the social presence of other groups, and especially to the Irish and African Americans. Accordingly, their guidelines for emotional display and for the control of emotion took shape alongside their construction of other groups' emotionality as different, and therefore inferior.

The expression of emotion could take many forms. Benjamin Rush believed that married persons were healthier than those who were unmarried because they were able to gratify the "domestic affections" through their love of a spouse and children. "Love of liberty," expressed in soldiering, by the same token preserved many men from the cold during the brutal Revolutionary War winters. Expression of emotion in mothers often took place according to a natural process in which "she will *look as she feels.*" And of course language was a prime means for the expression of emotion. But as the *Massachusetts Teacher* explained, sympathy arose easily enough in circumstances in which language proved an insufficient conveyance: "Speech is the expression of sentiment and emotion. Often the feeling of the speaker will be understood, when not a word is understood. The expression of emotion is not dependent upon words. When the curse of the confusion of language came upon man, there still remained the sympathetic expression of feeling." The expression of feelings, like the expression of thoughts, was fundamentally a performance of character. We have seen how habit, the foundation of character, was initiated in feeling. For Henry Clarke

Wright, the concealment of emotion accordingly was the antithesis of character: "Concealment is the death of man's moral nature. Let each one—(1) outwardly Manifest his own inner life—whatever it be—give utterance to his own thought and feeling & then (2) let him call on all to do the same." Such an obligation was examined in particular detail in the case of the teachers—and sometimes models—of character, the clergy. A minister was enjoined "to bring to the presentation of Divine truth the full exercise not only of the gift of expressing thought, but *emotion*." Indeed, said the *New Englander*, "It is evident that this faculty of expressing feeling may be like every other mental endowme..t, improved by practice." A minister was obliged to study voice, gesture, bearing, body language, and other communicative apparatus "so that he may express whatever feeling he may have, with propriety and force." And to ensure the right flow of feeling from person to person, it was important to avoid engaging oneself in work that might inhibit emotional expression. A warning to men stressed that "the close application to business, and incessant intellectual activity which mark the times, have a tendency to check the flow of affection and harden the heart."[4]

Public urgings for the expression of emotion were balanced by concerns about uncontrolled expression. At approximately the same time that Henry Clarke Wright was writing about the importance of expressing feeling, Susan Heath was despairing that "I cannot control my feelings." The rhetoric of emotional control was deeper and richer than that advocating emotional expression, and so could be conveniently mined to make any number of points about the dangers of emotional excess, of the failure to limit the expression of feeling. Older renderings of concern took the form of pronouncements about the destructive force of "passion," understood as intense feeling left unbridled. When the *Baptist Missionary Magazine* in 1824 told its readers that Christians everywhere were obliged to "control our passions," it had in mind the control of potentially criminal impulses, and backed up its admonition with testimony from an incarcerated male on the verge of execution for murder, who pleaded, "Let all *passionate, revengeful tempers*, listen to my dying counsels, and learn to subdue their angry passions!" The connection between criminality and the free exercise of passion was still important at mid-century, when the *Massachusetts Teacher* observed that "many a man of sin has traced his character of crime and infamy to some unwise control. . . ." For a convict incarcerated in Charlestown, the connection proved especially significant, his conviction, he said, coming about as a result of his display of the "anguish in my heart" while the trial was in progress: "Even these uncontrollable emotions were seized upon and portrayed as symbols of guilt." Alongside such depictions of the folly of unguarded emotional display were the pictures of men made less masculine by their failure to reign in their passions. Drawing upon gendered notions of active and passive behavior, the *New Englander* argued that "a passionate man is not an actor, but a receiver of impressions, while the man of real strength is calm and has by his force of will mastery over himself." With such logic, one writer impugned the masculinity of Theodore Parker, asserting that "the strength of his feelings is too much for his judgment to restrain." And alongside criminality and ungendering, one additional consequence of the unreflective expression of feeling was the possibility of simply appearing foolish. One writer made the point in comparing an overly emotional man to an earwig captured in a jar, in the process also depicting the futility of protest against cultural limits imposed upon emotional expression: "Imprisoned him under a tumbler, holding it against the wall. He was in such a fury, or fright, on finding himself hemmed in, that I felt very nervous lest I should not keep the glass walls steady. Finding there was no door of escape, he turned into the tumbler, and immediately his hundred heels flew up and he feel helpless upon the smooth glass. The poor fellow was drowned in spirit, and brought home as a curiosity."[5]

THE "IRISH TEMPER"

Middle-class emotionology, the set of cultural standards for emotional expression and concealment, was not precise. The boundaries that it set—excess of emotion on the one hand and failure to express oneself on the other—were not so much clearly drawn lines of demarcation as a perspective on emotional life itself. In specific contexts, such a scheme could be invoked as a guide to what was appropriate given the circumstances of the occasion. The fact was that feeling rules could be interpreted in any number of ways, as contexts varied from dinner table, to gatherings on the Common, torchlight processions, the prayer meeting, dance parties, or ratting with chums. Middle-class Protestants understood enough of the rules to know, like Susan Heath, when they were not expressing their feelings as they should, or, like Gamaliel Bradford, when they had truly lost control of their feelings in a quarrel with friends. But there was leeway in the application of emotional standards to a given situation, a measure of ambiguity in the fit between cultural expectations and the unfolding of a particular emotional event. It is apparent as well that the ambiguity that allowed for interpretation of a person's emotionality as acceptable, as in conformity with what was expected for membership in the group, could just as easily be exploited in the service of excluding someone. The emotionality of *personae non grata* could easily enough be constructed in such a way as to indicate their breach of middle-class emotionology. That is, perceptions of difference could be reinforced through identification of an unacceptable range of emotionality in a particular group. Such was the case of Protestant middle-class construction of the emotionality of Irish, African Americans, and other social groups. That project helped to define Protestant emotionology by articulating what it was not, to establish its outlines contrastively to other groups. And to say that an Irishman's temper did not fit into the spectrum of what was acceptable was to call into play a host of other characteristics associated with the Irish, thus perversely enriching Protestant middle-class self-understanding through a process of exclusion. In this way, the social function of such comparisons of emotionality was similar to the IQ test of the late twentieth century.[6]

Bostonians did not administer batteries of tests to individuals in order to ascertain their emotional IQ.[7] They nevertheless did seem to believe that some measurement of emotionality was possible, even if it was imprecise. So, for example, *Gleason's*, after examining the autographs of celebrities, found Nicholas Biddle to be nervous and sad, George Law restlessly ambitious, John Hancock proud, and the temperaments of other well-known figures similarly revealed. Most of the time, however, Bostonians limited themselves simply to declaring a member of an out-group to be either too emotional or not emotional enough, or both.[8]

The *Watchman* spoke for most of the press in 1856 when it described the Irish as a "race" characterized by "bitter passions." That idea, which over the decades came to be understood simply as the "Irish temper," remained at the center of Protestant thinking about Irish emotionality. Congregational theologian Laurens P. Hickok's widely adopted *Empirical Psychology: Or, the Human Mind as Given in Consciousness. For the Use of Colleges and Academies* (1855) offered a typical estimation of "the prevalent temperament of the Irish people." The Irish constitution, wrote Hickok, "will readily wake in sudden emotions, and be characterized by ardent feeling, quick passions, impetuous desires, and lively but transient affections. . . . There is a perpetual propensity in all things to excess and exaggeration, to intense feeling and passionate excitement." Other writers made the same point. George Douglas Brewerton's *The War in Kansas*, published in New York in 1856, described a typical member of the proslavery "Border Ruffians" as a man, "who, so far as temperament went, was as Irish a gentleman in his 'suddenness to quarrel' as ever came from that sweet spot for broken necks and dueling—County Galway." Richard Francis Burton took a trip westward to "the city of the saints" in Utah accompanied by "a young second lieutenant of Irish origin, and fiery temper . . ." James W. Redfield made the same point but with a more malicious twist. In *Comparative Physiognomy; or, Resemblances between Men and Animals* (1852), he explained that the "Spaniards resemble cocks as the Irish resemble dogs. . . . The Spaniards and the Irish are as much like each other in their fondness for fighting as the cock is like the dog."[9]

Such aspects of emotionality—impetuosity, quick passions, a love of fighting—were underscored in public discussion of the San Patricio battalion in the Mexican War (1846–1848). Named in honor of the patron saint of Ireland, the two-hundred-strong contingent was recruited largely from Irish deserters from the United States Army, some of whom were furious about American desecration of Roman Catholic churches and convents, and persecution of Mexican clergy and laity. (The majority of deserters from the American force were non-Irish and seven thousand Irish remained under the command of General Winfield Scott.) Led by a Galway man, John Riley, the rogue outfit fought alongside soldiers in the Mexican army before being captured and severely punished (fifty were hanged). Public reaction to the news about the deserters, especially in New England, featured renewed condemnation of the Irish "race" as fickle, reckless, destructively passionate, incapable of emotional control, and, of course, un-American. As if such confirmation of public suspicions of Irish Catholics was necessary, the Protestant press drew connections for years between the crippled, inferior emotionality of the Irish and activities ranging from parochial school construction to house servantry to criminality, all censuring the "Irish temper," by "showing conclusively its un-American character." One Boston woman believed that the only way she could get through to her Irish maid about proper cleaning was by communicating in a way that reached the core of the girl's passionate emotional constitution: "I showed her a table on which I could write 'slut' with my finger in the dust." Other criticism of the Irish temperament blamed it for excessive use of intoxicants. Such criticism hit its mark so regularly, even John Francis Maguire, in his far-reaching history *The Irish in America* (1868), was forced to expend an entire chapter on the subject, beginning with the following admission: "Were I asked to say what I believed the most serious obstacle to the advancement of the Irish in America, I would unhesitatingly answer—Drink." In time, the matter of Irish temperament came to be expressed in explicit comparisons with other groups. Such comparisons showed at once Protestant conceptualizations of the extreme emotionality of the Irish and the careful and measured emotional order of Anglo-Saxons as neither too strong nor too weak. A writer reported in *Appleton's* the following intelligence of his dinner party conversation: "This anecdote was told by the distinguished physician to illustrate the difference among the three kingdoms with respect to temperament—the Irish ardent and impetuous, the Scotch comparatively cool and cautious, while the English are perhaps a fair average between the two." And even when the intent was not deliberately malicious, the construction of the "Irish temper" informed all manner of commentary on Irish lives. Praising the oratory of James T. Brady, New York life chronicler Junius Browne explained, "He has the Irish temperament—a passion for verbal floridity and sensational colorings."[10]

Anti-Catholicism in Boston was well established by mid-century. Anti-Jesuit laws in 1647 and 1700 had set the stage for the nativist reactions to Catholics. Anti-Catholic demonstrations during the Second Great Awakening led to the burning of the Roman Catholic convent in Charlestown in 1834, and to the rise of the Know-Nothing movement in the mid-1850s. Not all Catholics were Irish, but the majority were, and whatever calumny was heaped upon the Irish stuck to some degree to other Catholics as well. And as 28.8 percent of the city's population was Irish in 1855, there was no shortage of targets for Protestant accusations of un-American behavior or corrupt character. Typical of Protestant thinking about Catholics was the diary entry made by James Barnard Blake, who earnestly professed his devotion to the principle of religious freedom in America, and then, as if he were carrying his devotion through to its logical conclusion, added: "The Catholic religion only tends to ignorance, crime, and almost idolatry. . . . I think it is high time that something was done to prevent the expansion of this bigoted religion in this country." Blake's worries about Catholics expressed anxieties about the Irish as well. Indeed, it was perception of the combination of the two—un-American Catholicism and the Irish temper—that underpinned the decidedly negative Protestant characterization of the Irish. The *Evangelist and Religious Review,* like most magazines, implicitly embraced the notion of such an Irish-Catholic complex of threats to the social order when it reported on "Trouble in the Boston Schools" in 1859. After relating that Irish students had refused to participate in reciting the Ten Commandments and singing the "Old Hundred" in the classroom, it explained: "They said *their priest had forbidden them.*" And then, when challenged, the Irish students "engaged in riotous demonstrations." In the Protestant imagination, Irish priests embodied in particular fashion the nefarious mixture of uncontrolled passion and morally bankrupt religion. As Irishmen, they were prone, as the *Youth's Companion* noted, to "a

furious and threatening manner, cursing the heretics and denouncing pur-
gatorial terrors upon" those who disagreed with them. As priests, they
were "patrons of ignorance, vice, filth, and brutish stupidity." So withering
was this criticism that in 1854, as Know-Nothings were learning to exercise their authority in the mayor's office and the statehouse, the *Christian
Watchman* wondered whether Protestants should reconsider their views
about the Irish—but in explaining its position it did not pass up the opportunity to deploy stereotypes. So, "compared with native Americans, of
Puritanic descent, they are in a very low state of civilization," said the magazine, and "there may not be a wild Karen in the jungle who knows less
of the way of salvation than the maid in your kitchen." But it was not fair
that "if any atrocious crime has been committed, an Irishman is at once
suspected as the perpetrator." (Historian Roger Lane has shown that the
vast majority of those arrested for crimes in the 1850s were Irish.) "The
Irishman did not have *the heart of a stranger*," as most people thought,
but rather, had a heart similar to that of the Protestant, except that it was
twisted because of "the power of the priest over the Catholic heart." Theodore Parker also wondered about the control of Catholic priests over their
congregations, but he stated his objections to Catholicism in a typically
maverick fashion, comparing Catholics to Methodists—who, as we have
seen, were known for their rowdy gatherings at Eastham camp meetings,
where emotion, it was said, got the better of the participants and threatened
the virtue of the women in attendance.[11]

CONSTRUCTING AFRICAN AMERICAN EMOTIONALITY

Boston Protestants thought African Americans more emotionally complex than Irish Catholics, which meant, in this case, less emotionally stable.
Constructing the Irish as passionate, and finding them inferior on that
charge, white Bostonians constructed African Americans as deficient on
two fronts: emotionally inactive as well as too passionate. This two-
pronged criticism—its seeming contradictoriness was strategic—guaranteed that African Americans would be found to be inferior to whites, and
was in keeping with a picture of the African temperament as painted in
both Northern and Southern literature.

Whites constructed the Negro "temperament" as impulsive, prone to
extreme and inappropriate emotional performances, and lacking in mechanisms for control of emotion. When Fredrika Bremer visited North America from Stockholm at mid-century, she found what American writers had
been claiming for years, namely the "impulsive negro temperament." It

was an emotional quality that Southern writers, and some Northern ones, too, had assumed was the bedrock of Negro humanity in their reporting on the small and large events of slave and free black communities. Its literary expression took various forms, among which the image of the happy laborer was paramount. Southern journalist E. A. Pollard incorporated it into his perversely romantic picture of slaves bringing in the harvest, of the times "on the old farms, when the golden grain was being cradled by the excited and joyous negroes, singing their rude songs." J. Milton Mackie, arriving in Nassau from Cape Cod, witnessed the return of the fleet to the harbor, an event that entertained the entire populace, but especially blacks, "the negroes' wool hair uncurling from excitement. 'O Lord, massa!' said to me one of the latter, quite dancing with delight, and threatening to spit out all his ivory, as he pointed to the white schooners ploughing into the bright green harbor, 'O Lord, massa! Dere cum de rackers—full of dry-good, silk stocking, eberyting!'" Ephraim Langdon Frothingham's *Philosophy as Absolute Science*, published in Boston in 1864, distilled such ideas into a theory about the emotionality of Negroes as a leading marker of their inferiority to Euro-Americans. Drawing upon Hegel, Frothingham diagnosed blacks as suffering from "Affectionalism, in its immature, primitive, and most concentrated form," in which "the individual, is led to convert the sexual and all the other necessary relationships of life into mere means of sensual gratification and profit, and brutal ferocity and force are introduced as the normal condition of society." Therefore, "by this peculiar construction of the Negro, 'Sociability,' 'Sexuality,' and 'Destruction,' which are the destructive laws of the Affectional Nature, are made to constitute the ruling affectional laws of his constitution." Ruled by the affectional law of destruction, "which is a love of destruction," the Negro was inclined to emotional binges that took the form of destructive acts. Accordingly, "we may see why it is so difficult to restrain the manifestation of this principle in the Negro, when it has become excited. . . ." All of this, concluded Frothingham, proved the degree of difference to be extreme: "How blind, then, are those individuals who would treat such subjects as if they were possessed of the same affections, capacities, sensibilities, and aspirations as themselves!" A Southern writer, in an article entitled "Negro-Mania" (1852), made a similar case, but stated its conclusions more comprehensively, making the important connection between feeling, character, and manliness: "The negroes . . . display . . . an almost entire want of what we comprehend altogether under the expression of elevated sentiments, manly virtues, and moral feeling."[12]

Alongside such pronouncements about the volatility of Negro emotionality were equally forceful and numerous statements about the lack of emotion, or very low degree of feeling, in Negroes. Samuel Stanhope Smith's *An Essay on the Variety of Complexion* (1787) had included the observation that Negroes suffered from "vacancy of mind and want of emotion," and that the lack of emotion had given rise to slack facial features: "The muscles of the face are soft and lax—and the face is dilapidated at the sides—the mouth is large—the lip swelled and protruded—and the nose, in the same proportion, depressed." The most common representation of this belief took the form of complaints about lazy and shiftless slaves, although in the hands of a master apologist for slavery such as Thomas Roderick Dew of the College of William and Mary, it was expressed as if it were transcendent truth about Negroes' "absolute indifference and sloth." William Henry Holcombe's "Characteristics and Capabilities of the Negro Race" (1861) proposed the medico-emotional aspects of Negro sloth, grounding it in "the obtuseness of his nervous system." According to Holcombe, "his nervous system is less impressible, and for that very reason, less capable of reaction . . ." Arguing in exactly the opposite direction from the "passionate Negro" thesis, Holcombe asserted that the "negro is endowed by nature with a will so feeble, passions and impulses so easily mastered, and a disposition so mild and yielding, that he is very easily subjugated by any superior type of man." At the same time, "this is indeed the secret of their obedience and subservience in the South." So passive were such persons emotionally, said Holcombe, that corporal punishment, "instead of leaving them sulky and revengeful, puts them into the best imaginable humor both with themselves and master." All of this made the Negro precisely that thing that Bostonians thought the epitome of an emotionless person, in Holcombe's words, "a strong animal machine." Negroes, said one commentator, were temperamentally suited for slavery because of their feeble emotionality: "the negro race, from their temperament and capacity, are peculiarly suited to the situation which they occupy." That suitability, of course, was a clear indication of their "naturally inferior mind and character." M. Daniel Conway expressed this to his Boston colleagues in 1862 in simple terms: "There is one lesson that the Negro temperament easily learns, and one which a long training has confirmed: that is, *obedience*."[13]

The construction of African American emotionality as outside the range of acceptable or even human emotionality was periodically addressed in Boston commentary about the lives of the city's black residents, who numbered 2,216 (1.3 percent of the city's population) in 1855. Sixty percent of Boston blacks had been born in Massachusetts. Slavery had been abolished in Massachusetts since the Walker case of 1783, and in the decades leading up to the Civil War, free blacks had organized themselves as a community within the city, largely in the First, Fifth, and Eleventh Wards, and especially in the Sixth, on the north slope of Beacon Hill, nicknamed "Nigger Hill." The increasing concentration of blacks in these four wards—87 percent by 1855—reflects the degree to which the city was segregated. By mid-century, black Bostonians had built Baptist churches on Smith Court, off Belknap Street (First African Baptist Church, 1805, later known as the First Independent Baptist Church of People of Color) and on Phillips Street (Twelfth Baptist, or Church of the Fugitive Slaves, 1848), the African Methodist Church on May Street (1818), and the Revere Street Church (1836). These churches, as George A. Levesque has pointed out, developed as a response to the lack of openness to Negroes in the white churches, and over the years they served as a focus for the coalescence of a community identity as well as a retreat: "Thus as an asylum from white prejudice, as a retreat from the repression of resentment, the black church retained in the 1840's and 1850's its powerful *raison d'être*." A separate system of black schools was in place early in the nineteenth century[14] but in 1855 separate schooling was abolished, and a period of uneasy educational integration began. The official report of the Committee of Education stated its "conclusion that colored children make less progress in a separate school and that no practical inconvenience need follow the abolition of such schools." But there would be inconvenience of at least one sort. Alongside the abolitionist movement in Boston, and the real problems brought on by the Fugitive Slave Act, the integration of the schools forced white Bostonians to think hard about the "temperament" and capabilities of blacks. Accordingly, the late 1850s was a time during which some white Bostonians looked for any sort of evidence for their theories about the emotional inferiority of Negroes.[15]

White Bostonians collected evidence about the emotional inferiority of Negroes and made it public in various ways. Accenting the uncontrollable emotional impulses of blacks, the *Transcript* ran a story entitled "Hot Revenge" in which a black woman ("with the masculine name of Samuel," said the paper, sending a message) poured the contents of a kettle of boiling water over the head of a white woman with whom she had argued in their Ann Street neighborhood. The religious press made the connection between the passionate temperament of blacks and their lack of morality, the *Christian Observatory* declaring that "the Africans, as a race, have been sinners exceedingly in the sight of the Lord, and have deserved all the pains and griefs, and toils, through which from generation to generation they have passed. They have been heathens of the most degraded and polluted kind. . . . and serve their own lusts." Their fears fueled by such rhetoric, angry and indignant whites took to the black neighborhood on Beacon Hill ostensibly to stamp out prostitution. (Such mob action against suspected prostitutes, as we have seen, was not unknown.) After one mob rousted "bad girls" from the hill, a broadside appeared that ridiculed the feelings of blacks whose property had been damaged in the sweep, and advertised the righteousness of white action to curtail instances of "uncontrolled passion" in Negroes. At the same time that such messages about passionate, impetuous Negroes circulated through the city, there appeared in various places representations of the feebleness of Negro emotionality. In the turmoil over the Anthony Burns fugitive slave incident in 1854, a story about the occasion of Burns's escape from slavery in Virginia became part of the standard recitation of the facts of the case. Burns, who became a cause celebre in anti-slavery circles, was quoted as saying that his leaving the South "was the result of an accident; that one day, while tired, he laid down on board a vessel to rest, got asleep, and that during his slumbers the vessel sailed!" Through such an appeal to stereotype, Burns's flight from his master was transformed into the story of a shiftless Negro, of a person whose escape was not the product of a strong feeling of hope or fear, but rather was the coincidental outcome of an emotionally inferior nature than made him lazy in just the right place at the right time. Reportage on the mob that attempted to rescue Burns from the State House, however, identified the culprits as mostly black men, all, like the whites who took part, "fanatics." And if anyone missed the meaning of the Burns story, there was the performance of minstrelsy in the city's theatres, a genre which, as one observer has suggested, "succeeded in fixing one stereotype deeply in the American consciousness: the shiftless, lazy, improvident, loud-mouthed Negro with kinky hair and large lips, over-addicted to the eating of watermelon . . ." In representing African Americans as both too emotional and not emotional enough, white Bostonians frustrated crossover from the black churches to white—and vice versa—during the revival; except in those rare instances where individual Negroes evidenced the proper emotional profile. One of those instances involved the well-publicized welcoming of a black man to a prayer meeting after church leaders ascertained that he was both sufficiently emotional and sufficiently in control of his emotions to participate profitably in the exercises. The report correlated emotional correctness with a certain view of the structuring of power: "At the Old South prayer meeting in Boston, on Thursday, a venerable colored man, called Father Hanson, was introduced as the original

Uncle Tom. He said that 47 years ago, he had learned *to love his master instead of hating him.*"[16]

ABOLITIONIST "FANATICS"

William Lloyd Garrison and his compatriots met in 1832 in the African Baptist Church off Belknap Street to organize the New England Anti-Slavery Society. The society grew large and influential in the decades before the Civil War, serving as a platform for a host of projects in Boston and New England. The local population frequently voiced the opinion that the members of the group were too emotional, too zealous in their opposition to slavery. Some Bostonians perceived the activities of the society, and the abolitionist cause in general, as fanaticism, as a crusade so saturated in emotion that it had lost its bearings in the everyday world of discussion, negotiation, and gradual solution. No matter that Garrison himself was mobbed in 1835 and again in 1850 by opponents of abolitionism. The press as a whole leaned to a view of abolitionists as dangerous fomenters of passion, and regularly ran stories reinforcing that image. Abolitionists appeared in the press in stereotypes much like those of the African Americans with whom they associated, and with whom they spoke, side by side, against slavery. White anti-slavery activists like Garrison, Wendell Phillips, Lydia Maria Child, Lucy Stone, Theodore Parker, James Freeman Clarke, and Abby Kelley frequently endured the epithet "fanatic" as they spoke and wrote against slavery, and especially if they advocated abolition. Their opponents during the 1830s regularly incited mobs against them, and what the *Independent* called the "mob law" of the "slave power" continued until the outbreak of the War (and even then remained in somewhat diminished form). Nonetheless, it was to the likes of Garrison and Kelley that the label "fanatic" stuck, in newspaper reports, in magazines, and, most telling of all, in diaries.[17]

Albert Barnes complained in 1857 that some people "usually represent the fact of being an abolitionist as being synonymous with being an infidel, a fanatic, a disorganizer, or an enemy of the Union." In an address on "The Life and Character of Charles Sumner" (the late senator from Massachusetts), a colleague from Oregon recalled the days when persons "denounced him as a fanatic, an abolitionist, an enemy of good order, of his country, and of mankind." Boston playwright John Townsend Trowbridge summarized the connection between abolitionism and the seemingly overly emotional zeal of its advocates at mid-century: "The followers of Garrison and Phillips were few; society looked upon them as dangerous fanatics, and the very name of abolitionist was covered with an opprobrium that clung to it long after the course of political events had justified their moral convictions." Trowbridge himself confessed that the passage of the Fugitive Slave Act in 1850 finally "made an 'antislavery fanatic' of me." James Freeman Clarke, on the other hand, admitted that while he was in Kentucky during the 1830s (he returned to Boston in 1841), "I knew nothing of Mr. Garrison and his movement, and supposed, as others did, that he was merely a violent fanatic." In 1860, Clarke was on the dais with Wendell Phillips and Francis Jackson at the Tremont Temple, delivering an address, when a mob opposed to the anti-slavery gathering upset the proceedings. Diarists such as Charles French and James Barnard Blake complained of abolitionists in the usual terms, the former observing the "ranting abolitionists at Faneuil Hall," and the latter condemning a speaker who "showed evidently that he was a fanatic, a dis-unionist and a vile abolitionist." The *Liberator*, responding to such criticism, tried to paint the earnestness of abolitionists in softer colors: "Excitement is as necessary to this kind of abolition, as air to life. It could not live one hour without it. . . . it would go out forthwith, if the vital element were not supplied, and leave a stench behind."[18]

Alongside such rhetoric another picture of the abolitionist crusade sometimes came to light in speeches and newspaper reports. It cast abolitionists as overly rational scientists, whose obedience to logic suppressed their exercise of emotion, especially sympathy. Their adversaries' characterizations of them came close to constructions of African American emotionality as both passionate and feeble. Abolitionists, like blacks, were made out to be both fanatics and emotionally deficient, unfeeling promoters of a grand scheme of social change. Accordingly, the *Independent* reporter covering a Christian Anti-Slavery Convention in 1851 felt obliged to explain that the gathering was not some forum for the cold-blooded drawing up of blueprints for social reform: "We are assured by a member of the committee that it is intended to be what the call purports, and not a packed committee to endorse some ultra-rational foregone conclusion, nor for the denunciation or destruction of anything but the sin of slaveholding." John Henry Hopkins, in a survey of the history of slavery (1864), had the same nagging doubt about abolitionists, wondering if their focus on eradicating slavery was not the product of an extreme rationality, a logic without flexibility. Condemning abolitionists' generalizing about the extent of cruelty to slaves, Hopkins argued: "Yet such is precisely the logic of the ultra-abolitionist when he makes the narrative of some hundred instances of cruelty a reason for the immediate emancipation, not of eighty thousand, but four million of Southern slaves." Southern writers elaborated on the point.

A discussion of slavery in New Orleans' *Debow's Review* began with a complaint about how "the abolitionist would discern, and prove conclusively according to his notions of logic" the most absurd propositions. The abolitionist thus was like Walter Scott, "to whose diseased vision, red and blue, and yellow and green, all look red, and in that color alone he had dipped his brush," in writing his "History of Napoleon." The result was a twisted story in which Napoleon appeared unlike what all knew him to be.[19]

A RITUAL OF REMEMBERING SOCIAL ORDER

The revival was an enactment of social order in Boston. White Protestant construction of the emotionality of Irish, African Americans, and abolitionists identified members of those three groups as outsiders, as emotionally unfit because of their excessive passion or unfeeling temperament, or both. Because temperament was linked to character, the character of persons in these three groups was assailed as well, as criticism translated perceived emotional flaws into character flaws (and vice versa). While Protestants believed that they could ascertain the temperament of a person and know that person's character through a consideration of temperament, they created no reliable instruments to measure emotionality or explicit calibrations of the appropriate and acceptable range of expression or concealment of feeling. In the absence of such measures, data such as language, skin color, surname, and ideological leanings served as a foundation on which to concoct estimations of emotionality. Anecdotal evidence about abolitionists or African Americans or Irish blended with a rich legacy of stereotypes to flesh out an image of persons in those groups as substantially different from, and inferior to, the middle-class Protestant population.

In spite of the gushing reports about the revival in the religious press and in books rushed to publication in the late 1850s, there is little evidence that the revival in Boston included persons from "all classes." Almost all Irish were Roman Catholics, and though magazines published a few stories about Roman Catholic converts in 1858, nothing suggests Catholic participation beyond a few well-publicized instances. Abolitionists tended to be theological liberals more concerned with social reform than the emotional performances of the prayer meeting. The *Liberator's* frequent condemnation of the "machinery" of the revival for its manufacture of flimsy piety indicates the position of liberal anti-slavery activists. The case of African American participation is more complicated,[20] although statistics collected by Kathryn Long show that in 1845, the Bromfield Street Church, a member of the growing New England Methodist Episcopal conference, included ninety-eight persons of color. One might assume that those persons participated alongside whites in any revival activities at the Bromfield Street Church. But we must remember that the older Protestant churches in Boston remained skeptical of Methodists, largely because of the reports of goings-on at Methodist camp meetings on Cape Cod and elsewhere in New England. (And some evidence indicates conversely that Methodists themselves had doubts about the revival.) Critics of those camp meetings thought that they were lacking in emotional control, too passionate, inimical to the spirit of sound and serious religious piety. So the question remains as to whether what might have happened in Methodist churches matched the activities at places such as Old South and Park Street, and, especially, whether there was any cordiality toward Methodist churches. Moreover, as George A. Levesque has shown, the four black churches in Boston at mid-century—two Baptist and two African Methodist—tended to keep their distance from the white churches, and were more inclined to schedule Theodore Parker, Frederic Douglass, William Lloyd Garrison, Wendell Phillips, and other reformers than Charles Finney. Such distance was reinforced by seating provisions in the white churches, which required blacks to sit in the "nigger pew." On one occasion in which a Negro obtained a pew at Park Street through a commercial transaction with a white person, the congregation was aghast on the Sunday that the man showed up with his family. One report explained: "His appearance and that of his family in that fashionable house of worship was accounted by all Boston as an outrage scarcely less flagrant than would have been the use of the pew as a pigpen." The trustees informed the man that he would have to relinquish rights to the pew and they immediately passed a rule forbidding any further such claim by a black family.[21]

The point here is not to estimate the participation of Irish, abolitionists, and blacks in the revival. Subsequent studies of social and religious life in Boston might uncover data that will clarify that participation, and perhaps amend it, beyond what is suggested here. Instead, this investigation considers the revival as the occasion for white Protestants to underscore differences between themselves and other groups by making a public display of their emotionality. As we have seen, promoters of the revival frequently made the point that there were no "excesses" or "religious fanaticism" in the revival. Prayer meetings were viewed as controlled expressions of religious piety. Men and women might pray fervently, but the kind of outbursts associated with camp meetings or previous revivals had no place in the Businessmen's Revival in Boston. By the same token, the prayer meetings were not dry, formal affairs. People made fervent appeals for divine help, wept openly, and "gave their hearts to God." In choosing to perform their emotional life in this way, revivalgoers signaled more than their investment in a certain quality of piety. The revival was, among other things, a demonstration of an emotional order, a public statement about the boundaries of emotional life, even a sanctification of those boundaries. The revival accordingly was not just a matter of "speaking boldly" one's prayer. It was also about speaking boldly about membership in a group (a membership cemented with "sympathy"). The process was especially important to those persons calling themselves "the young men," but it extended across a range of collectives from "maternal societies" and "sailors meetings" to "businessmen," "parents," "white Protestants," and even "clergy." At the most general level, it was the assertion of middle-class Protestant identity vis-à-vis other groups. The revival made emotion a primary marker of social difference, and that difference was dramatically represented for all Bostonians, regardless of background or class, in the mass performance of emotion in the revival. This aggressive blending of prayer, identity, assertiveness, and expectation of recognition (by both God and other persons) took on an increasingly clearer form in the decades after the revival, and remained a key element of American Protestantism down through the twentieth century.

The Meaning of the Revival and Its Legacy

THE MEANING OF THE REVIVAL

The Businessmen's Revival in Boston was the assertion of Protestant identity vis-à-vis other groups through the mass performance of emotion as a commodities transaction, regulated in specific ways, and carried out under the authority of contractual obligation. The revival manifested the profound linkage between group identity and that group's construction of emotion. For the purposes of a public demonstration, the display of emotion according to specific conventions was ideal, because it drew strong public notice by its show of excitement at the same time that it made a statement about the character of the group involved in the demonstration. Emotionality, the behaviors associated with a specific construction of emotion, served as a *primary* marker of group membership, as clearly as did skin color, language, dress, diet, or other such factors. Emotion was manifestly a category of collective identity. The remarkable attractiveness of the revival to Protestants stemmed from the fact that it made sense to participants as a personal spiritual exercise at the same time that it demonstrated group belonging and group boundaries. It was ideally suited to meet the collective anxiety of the city's Protestants about their predicament as Bostonians, their church problems, and their worries arising from financial catastrophe. It came about in concert with greater fluidity in gender roles, as part of the emergence of a class of "young men" who were poised to claim recognition for their cohort, and as an elaboration of the public pursuit of feeling in the urban culture more generally. Ultimately, it served as the foundation for ongoing Protestant reflection about emotion—and practice of emotion—that intersected in crucially important ways with cultural reconstructions of gender and the body in the latter nineteenth and twentieth centuries.

RELIGION AND EMOTION

Frances Merritt, looking over the events of the early spring of 1858, voiced her confidence that one day the meaning of those events would be known.

> Sunday March 14—What is now transpiring will become one day history. The facts of the present have a meaning and a purpose which are left for the future historian to discover. In many things we of the present are only fact-*gatherers* not fact-*unravellers*. We may catch glimpses, we may foretell; but it is left for the readers in the far-off future to note the succession of the present-means and study the adaptation of the present means to accomplish the Almighty purpose.[1]

Historian Kathryn Long, one of those fact-unravellers, recently has examined the grounds on which religious writers over the past century-and-a-half have debated the meaning of the Businessmen's Revival in New York City. Much of her insight applies as well to historical treatments of the revival in Boston, and at least one observation in her study would have pleased Frances Merritt. Long has shown that persons who have written about the revival frequently have approached their work with confidence that the revival was, indeed, part of an "Almighty purpose."[2]

Under the nineteenth-century canopy of the double self, Bostonians could conceive their emotional investment in the revival both as a mysterious process of divine intercession and as a more practical matter. The historical pathways leading to this moment include, first of all, the objectification of emotion and its construction as a commodity for exchange. This process took place as part of the emergence of the double self in New England, and, specifically, with reference to an emotional self constructed as both spiritual and physical, social and private, male and female. Defined with reference to the double self, emotion was pictured both as a commodity transacted in the business of the heart and a spiritualized subjective essence transcendent of conditioning social and cultural frameworks. Bostonians rarely undertook to be systematic in their thinking about emotion, and during the mid-century period of ferment they retained aspects of a discourse about feeling and passion that had informed the outlook of previous generations. New perspectives on emotion nevertheless emerged to reshape a broad range of middle-class thinking, and are perceptible in the organization of domestic relations as well as in the conceptualization of classroom dynamics, and, especially, in a Protestant construction of relationships between humans and God. The rhetoric of the revival represented relations with God as transactional. Encouraged to petition God in prayer, Protestants "gave the heart" in exchange for favors. Failure to ask forthrightly, to bring one's "desires" to God, was a breach of the terms of the transactional relationship. Prayer was a telegraph, in which humans wired emotion—called by poets electricity—to a God who responded with generous obligement.

The revival theology of prayer proceeded from the midst of the ongoing reconstitution of gender categories and from altered experiences of public and private. Prior notions of the feminine as pliancy, patient resignation, emotional virtuosity, and intuitive strength continued to dominate thinking about gender, in the same way that a notion of the masculine as bold, strong, active, and intellectual still exercised a determinative influence. However, Bostonians increasingly considered masculine and feminine as mutually constitutive categories, not blended in their entireties, but susceptible to some measure of complementary conjunction. At the same time, certain cultural incidents, such as the coalescence of women's subaltern publics and the intensification of male anxieties about public life, intrinsically questioned the legitimacy of customary distinctions between private and public, the counting-house and the home. The consequence of these transformative developments in the areas of gender and the social geography was a novel aggregation of components drawn from across the spectrum of these categories, instantiated as the business of the heart. Against a background of gradual objectification of emotion, Bostonians began to conceive family relations as exchanges, as transactions of emotion. At the same time, from within a maturing urban tradition of public exultation in spectacle, they more decisively envisioned the performance of emotion as a collective enterprise, but again, as a carefully regulated one. The differential between the masculinized public sphere and the feminized private sphere accordingly was diminished as each leaked into the other, informing and altering it.

The crash of 1857 brought to the fore latent anxieties about the relationship between social excitement and the means for its control. While embracing the notion that economic health was linked to an excited state of the market (just as the health of the body required "motion"), Bostonians, in the wake of the crash, wondered out loud about the adequacy of the regulatory mechanisms meant to channel and coordinate that excitement. Far from causing an outbreak of religious enthusiasm, the crash in fact influenced the nascent revival toward stricter controls of emotional expression in religious gatherings. Reinforced by rhetoric about the danger of squandering the commodity of emotion in literary and theatrical exercises, the language of the revival focused on highly scripted performances of emotion in which expression was constrained by specific regulations about the interval of public prayer (three to five minutes), the form of petitioning (make specific requests), and the duration of meetings (one hour, so businessmen could return to work and immediately take up their duties). The rationalization of petitionary prayer as a transaction likewise represented the tendency toward establishing disciplined management of emotion. Control of emotion overlapped with conservation of emotion, just as the regulation of financial investment coincided with the conservation of capital for subsequent investments.

Male participation in the revival was occasioned by the convergence of several trends. The revisions to theory about and the altered practice of gender and public/private life were fundamental (especially to middle-aged family men). So also was the influx of young men that made males a decisive majority in the city. Additionally, the revival provided a stage upon which the "young men," especially, could exhibit themselves as a body, as a population group with its own interests, solidarity, and agenda. Boston was a city with extreme population instability, where citizens questioned government authority, laity openly criticized clergy, businessmen often were reputed as scoundrels, mob action saved the lives of some African Americans as it ruined the lives of others, and young men and old men squared off against each other. Urban life was by no means anomic, but for males in their late teens or twenties—the bachelor apprentices, merchants-in-training, beginning schoolteachers, clerks, and shoe salesmen (and especially for young men who had just arrived in the city)—it was erratic, insecure, and unpredictable, and as such invited attempts to establish collective identities in various kinds of public performances. Young men expressed consciousness of their collective life and sought to reinforce it in forming associations, teams, gangs, and societies, in participation in YMCA activities, and by their unusually active involvement in the prayer meetings. The extent to which they succeeded in gaining recognition is reflected in the frequent references to their cohort in newspaper coverage of the revival, as well as in lectures and diaries.

The revival was heralded as a "union revival." In fact it was as much or more so a context for the announcement of difference. The major Protestant churches carved up the city into denomination-specific districts for the ministries of prayer teams and evangelizers. Women's prayer groups increased in number and in the frequency of their meetings. Regular meetings were held for special groups: policemen, firemen, mechanics, newsboys, sailors, and others. Northern writers commented that the revival had failed to catch on in the South. Irish and African Americans, their emotionality constructed as unsuitable to the character-enriching enterprise of revival, were, outside of a few notable instances, conspicuous nonparticipants. Laity took over from the clergy, heating up the simmering differences between the two groups. Ministers themselves quarreled over the nature and purpose of the revival. White middle-class critics—some were Protestant liberals such as Theodore Parker, who opposed the emotional "machinery" of the revival, while others thought the whole business plainly corrupt—asserted themselves in public and in so doing reinforced old differences and identified new ones. City fathers, innocent of tact, spent what was left of their authority on keeping preachers off the Common, an action that managed to deepen the rift between government and the citizenry.

The element of unity that remained after subtractions for difference was not the *Gemeinschaft* that many observers claimed for the revival. The religious commotions of 1858 indeed brought with them an elaboration of the bonds between persons, but those bonds were forged in a context tinctured with preference for rational-legal organization. Such a preference yielded associational rather than communal solidarity. In helping to establish a cultural beachhead for the commodification of emotion, the revival nurtured a unity characterized by regulated, transactional relations between individuals—the model of "companionate" marriage as the union of distinct individuals manifests such an arrangement—and advanced an understanding of a relationship with God as a matter of negotiated exchange. The dominant philosophy of business, the notion that firms (and regions, and nations) co-existed as distinct entities linked to each other in dynamic interdependencies based upon what one entity had and the other needed, imbued thinking about social and religious matters. Theological and social romanticism continued to inform language about the meaning of contacts with God, other persons, and other peoples (which in 1858 might include the South). And the "religious thrill" continued to animate the performance of revival. But in many ways factionalism had replaced patriarchy as the underlying principle of social cohesion (in Boston, Federalism was all but extinct), and investment in the notion of unity as the rational-legal transaction of differences had proceeded too far by 1858 to allow for any more than a token resurgence of romantic inventions of social and cosmic order. In fact, over the course of the next seven years, the complex rendering of a certain kind of unity as the product of differences (an idea found in James Madison's contributions to *The Federalist*) would be perverted and dramatized as tragedy, as the North more enthusiastically demonized the South, then went to war, in the interests of national unity. And after the war, the rhetoric of warfare would remain fundamental to the legacy of the Businessmen's Revival.

FROM REVIVAL TO MUSCULAR CHRISTIANITY AND PROMISE KEEPERS

Boundary-conscious Protestants worried keenly about the line between them and the "the world." It was of a course a futile worry, because Protestants lived in the world, and they knew that they lived in the world. To a certain extent they were forced to make their peace with the world, to accept their earthly predicament and to rely upon divine favor, available to them through petitionary prayer, as sustenance. Alongside that religious arrangement for their futures, however, they continued to embrace a notion of the world as their adversary, and of life as a war against it. In "Life and Death" (1854), a Boston poet called young and old alike to stand and fight:

> "What is life, father?" A battle, my child,
> Where the strongest lance may fail;
> Where the wariest eye may be beguiled,
> And the stoutest heart may quail;
> Where the foes are gathered on every hand,
> And rest not day or night,
> And the feeble little ones must stand
> In the thickest of the fight.

The *Massachusetts Teacher* accordingly urged parents and teachers to prepare their children for "the world's broad field of battle," something that Methodist minister Charles E. Harding kept in mind as he gave away his sixteen-year-old daughter to marriage across the state line in Nashua, New Hampshire: "How strange it seemed how sad we felt . . . could we shelter their heads no more from the storm, must they fight for themselves?"[3]

The battle with the world was the battle of the Christian against the forces of evil. When the *Christian Register* defined "A Christian" in 1850, it focused on the martial aspect of the upright life: "The Christian is a warrior, and must fight; but he is a conqueror, and must prevail." Fortunately, said the *Child's Friend*, warriors could outfit themselves for battle with the holy weapons available to them through divine benevolence: "Life is short . . . it is a warfare, a struggle; but God is your helper. The fight will be severe; but you have the Christian armor to put on." George E. Ellis, speaking to a congregation at Brattle Square in the closing months of the revival, reiterated the point with respect to the recent religious excitement.

A revival, he said, was "a new conflict, a new battle, . . . a new campaign against what is called the <u>world</u>." And a commentator for the *New Englander* also figured the revival as a momentous battle against the nation's sins, which swell like the tides of the sea and "which give a more or less periodical character to the action of the church upon the world, and concentrate at times, in one united effort, all its means of attack." The nation would soon have an opportunity to fight the battle for which it had been preparing, and in that great crisis, imagery of Christian warriors and causes would be freely deployed. And after the Civil War, the notion of a battle with evil would continue to shape the self-understanding of Christian men and women, finding an application in the fields of reform, missionary undertakings, and ongoing revivalistic religion.[4]

The metaphor of warfare played a central role in "muscular Christianity" as it emerged in the late 1850s in England and America, and especially in the writings of its leading English exponents, Charles Kingsley and Thomas Hughes. The *Christian Examiner*, quoting Kingsley on the nature of the Christian life, underscored the connection of masculinity with warfare: "I swore at my baptism to fight manfully under Christ's banner against the world, the flesh, and the devil." Although the term "muscular Christianity" first appeared in a review of Kingsley's *Two Years Ago* (1857), precursors to the themes explored by Kingsley, Hughes, and others were present in children's literature of the eighteenth century, Rousseau's *Émile*, and the religious idealism of English educationists. Muscular Christianity as it took shape in England at mid-century stressed moral courage, manly confrontation of evil, and steadfast dedication to Christian virtue. Such a complex of attributes coalesced in the image of the stalwart, active, athletic, and fully committed competitor on the playing field. Writers such as Kingsley and Hughes imagined sports as a testing ground for Christianity, as devotional activity in which a person's character was refined and improved. The process of rising to the challenge, asserting one's will, following through to victory—all within the context of sport as a confrontation—characterized the manly Christian and separated him from the casual, indifferent, or jelly-spined churchgoer. The popular image of such a Christian early on was drawn from Hughes's *Tom Brown's School Days* (1857), a novel about a boy's discovery of the meanings of strength and courage while boxing bullies at Rugby.[5]

Muscular Christianity was first articulated in America by Thomas Wentworth Higginson in his *Atlantic Monthly* article "Saints and Their Bodies" in 1858. Although he did not use the phrase "muscular Christianity" to identify the connection between physical prowess and Christian virtue, Higginson drew directly upon *Tom Brown's School Days* in outlining the relation between a strong body and a pure soul. Higginson, cast as one of the "Living Celebrities of New England" as early as 1864, was being described as a man "splendid in his lucubrations on 'Muscular Christianity'—a good writer and a good fighter." By the 1870s, American essays on Hughes and Kingsley employed the term "muscular Christianity" with ease, as if it were a well-established doctrine of Anglo-American life. *Appleton's Journal,* in surveying Kingsley's work, appraised "that doctrine of 'muscular Christianity' which has been constantly connected with his name. The doctrine has made its mark; it can be judged by its fruits." The journal called Kingsley "the very father of 'muscular Christianity.'" In viewing Hughes's *Tom Brown, Appleton's* likewise appeared to offer an anachronism, asserting that in the story, "Muscular Christianity was inculcated and the physical training of youth insisted upon." The term stuck easily in the American imagination and decorated all sorts of writing. Its rapid growth in popularity can be gauged by J. G. Holland's warning, in 1862—less than five years after the publication of Higginson's article—that "there is danger at first of overdoing our 'muscular Christianity'—danger of getting more muscle than Christianity," and by the *Ladies Repository* article in 1872 that observed how, in "spite of muscular Christianity and the prevalence of athletic sports, there still exists such a thing as a effeminate man." But an effeminate man, it turned out, was different from a man whose character included feminine elements.[6]

Much writing assumed that women were comprehended under the umbrella of muscular Christianity. Almost from the outset, the promoters and interpreters of muscular Christianity pictured women as participants alongside men. As we have seen, magazines such as the *Massachusetts Teacher* vigorously pushed for athletics for girls in the 1850s, and some of Boston's gymnasiums arranged their schedules to accommodate women who wished to exercise and to participate in sports. A biography of Boston socialite Fanny Fern in 1868 asserted that she "must have had from the first a rare amount of 'muscular Christianity'—must have been a conscientious self-care-taker . . . or she would have . . . stuck in some of the hurdles she has had to leap." And in the case of *Minor v. Board of Education of Cincinnati,* one argument against those who "have acquired a bad opinion of anything like muscular Christianity" was made by outlining the "perfect education": "Why, first the development of the life and vigor of the physical frame into the full proportions of manhood and womanhood; next the development and strengthening of the intellectual faculties; next, last, and not least, the improvement and culture of all the moral sentiments and affections." The argument was punctuated with a reference to an observation made "by a clergyman of the High Church that he knows a Presbyterian woman when she walks up the aisle, for she always walks upon her heels, whereas your High Church ladies have been taught to trip the light fantastic toe." Even the *Catholic World* wrote about "muscular Christianity," albeit somewhat non-commitally, beginning in the 1870s.[7]

Worries such as J. G. Holland's that there was too much sports and not enough Christianity in muscular Christianity were justified. In 1871, in an editorial defending inflation in the salaries of baseball players, one writer, after fervently recounting the manner in which a pitcher delivers the ball over the plate at a high rate of speed, asked the leading question: "Who will say that a person able to do this is not worthy of a salary greater than that of any university professor in our land! Is not the pitcher, too, a professor of muscular Christianity?" In fact, one Professor Knowlton, a.k.a. "A Christian Muscleman," already had made clear that "the church militant will become more rapidly the church triumphant, when her captains give more earnest heed to Muscular Christianity." Proposing the "'athletic virtue' of the gymnastic Greek as an essential aid in the acquisition of mental wealth and the exercise of spiritual power," Knowlton stated: "And we presume to introduce the oar, the bat, the foil, the gloves, the dumb-bell, and the Indian club as the most efficient helps to virtue and most potent means of grace." Such assertions led some persons to see muscular Christianity as mostly about muscles. In popular publications such as *Vanity Fair*, the term came to refer simply to acts of athletic grace and strength, or to heroism involving a physical struggle, with religion as a sideline if it was present at all. And descriptions of a person's physical profile—absent of any explicit reference to moral qualities—might be accomplished by invoking the term as one might invoke the word "strong" or "powerful." Appraising the physical stature of a certain man, one writer remarked simply: "tall, sunburnt, and powerfully built, he carried that solidity of gesture and firmness of tread sometimes so marked in muscular Christianity." Soon enough bowling was explicitly linked with muscular Christianity, and so was another indoor sport, "the billiard branch of muscular Christianity." But such interpretations of muscular Christianity were balanced by theological and moral understandings to which most publications paid heed. So, when *Appleton's* remarked that muscular Christianity "has become a creed not less approved by the godly than among the votaries of pure sportsmanship," it was reminding its readers that the movement was at least as much about religion as sports.[8]

When Henry T. Tuckerman surveyed popular fiction in New York in

1871, he paid particular notice to "that new form of liberal development, mental, bodily, and sympathetic, which is called muscular Christianity.'" Just as the *Minor* case argument claimed that a muscular approach to the education of Cincinnati schoolchildren involved the body, intellectual faculties, and "moral sentiments and affections," so Tuckerman recognized the key element of emotion alongside the physical. It was an accurate rendering of the complex of ideas known as muscular Christianity. For all of the discussion in print about muscular Christianity as athletic heroism, Protestants continued to embrace it as a combination of physical and emotional competencies. Such a blending was grounded in the assumption of the importance of masculine and feminine sides to Christian life. The caricaturing of muscular Christianity—which began in the 1860s and still turns up in contemporary histories—has obscured this fact. Anne Bloomfield, in a recent reappraisal of Kingsley, has observed that "the obsession, by numerous writers, with Kingsley's development of the physical exuberance and expression in this vein neither acknowledges the real significance of the spiritual or moral elements within the Muscular Christian movement nor the importance of the mind, body, and soul as believed by some other Victorian contemporaries as they sought to create a better world." In nineteenth-century America, many advocates of muscular Christianity stressed, like George M. Towle, the manner in which Kingsley and others were concerned above all with "saving the whole man, body, mind, and spirit." This meant that the whole person was to be involved in the salvific project, that emotions and ideas played a part alongside the muscles of the body. Feelings mattered as much as athletic endeavor. And, in fact, the earliest promoters of muscular Christianity constructed a picture of the muscular Christian as a balance of gendered attributes, including masculine boldness, competitive spirit, determination, action, and willingness to take risks, alongside feminine emotionality, submissiveness, patience, and restraint. So, as Malcolm Tozer points out, Kingsley's concept of manliness included many feminine characteristics, and, as Harry R. Harrington has argued, "Within Kingsley's private theodicy, the fallen athlete and the manly Christian are one in a fictional world redeemed by his faith in feminine virtue." Victorianist Claudia Nelson, in an analysis of Hughes's writing, in fact has stressed that the message of novels such as *Tom Brown* was that masculine and feminine qualities were blended in the Christian character. For Nelson, the novel is about "the androgyny of true manliness," and it specifically rejects the notion that masculinity is the opposite of femininity. Nelson cites instead Hughes's belief that "in their emotionalism and feeling for community. . . . manliness and womanliness are effectively synonymous." Accordingly, "Tom's growing willingness to express his deepest feelings is an important symptom of his maturation."[9]

An early review of Kingsley's *Two Years Ago* did not miss the point that masculine qualities should balance the feminine, not drive them out. In 1857, the *New Quarterly Review* observed that "the general tendency of this book, however, is . . . to make us value not only the more passive qualities which are supposed peculiarly to belong to religious man, but those which enable us to get on in the world—to conquer as well as yield—to struggle as well as to submit . . ." Unhappy with the way in which some critics had focused exclusively on the masculine in Tom Brown's character, Hughes delivered a series of lectures at the London's Workingman's College in 1876 in which he attempted to correct the misapprehensions of his thinking about religion and gender that had been caricatured as muscular Christianity. Collected and published as *The Manliness of Christ* (1879), they explored the notion of manliness in general, but primarily illustrated that notion with reference to an image of Jesus Christ. Hughes referred to "patience—a resolute waiting on God's mind" as "the noblest type of true manliness." Manliness was "tenderness, and thoughtfulness for others," as well as "sacrifice," "humiliation," and "self-restraint." As George Worth and others have suggested, given the nature of Victorian thinking about gender, such a notion of manliness was as easily applicable to women as to men. A review of *The Manliness of Christ* in the *Spectator* in 1880 confirmed the point, remarking that "on almost every page it is sufficiently evident that 'manliness' is not the old 'muscular Christianity,' only under a new name; but that it is humanity at its best:—in patience, in endurance, in courage, in sweetness, as in strength, in the self-forgetting laying-down of the whole life . . ."[10]

Within the context of a gender-blended muscular Christianity, men and women continued to express their feelings in prayer. Prayer as a telegraph for the transmission of feelings to God remained a live metaphor for the nineteenth century, and the twentieth as well, as Protestants exploited the rich possibilities for muscular Christianity as a combination of masculine and feminine attributes. The press kept track of the primary themes, reporting them in case-by-case accounts, and sometimes reading them back into antebellum history, as in an 1864 story about a tent meeting many years earlier, when a girl stood up to preach, "her clear, sweet tones, neither feminine nor masculine . . ." The "strong man, the spiritual hero," said one writer, was "keenly sensitive, with manly powers of indignation in him," and with "strong feelings and strong command over them." *Manliness for Young Men* (1864) taught that a man ought to live in a "world of gentle affections." Those affections, or "naturalness of feeling," Boston minister James Walker explained in 1877, were essential to the "efficacy of prayer." A stream of other writings continued to address the matter of efficacious prayer, often with reference to the role of feeling, and often armed with arguments for the claim that answers to prayer did not intrude upon God's plan for the world. William M. Taylor, writing in the *Princeton Review* in 1877, gave the typical response to nervous questions about the compatibility of petitionary prayer with the laws of the universe: "How do our men of science know that these laws have not been so adjusted as to admit God's answering prayer through their operation?" Protestants exercised their prayer-making in ongoing series of events ranging from weekday evening prayer meetings, to college gatherings for prayer, to large urban church meetings where individuals made specific requests in a concert of prayer with others. Popular understanding of the petitionary aspect of the prayer meeting—even among unbelievers—remained strong for decades, so that in 1886 Geraldine Bonner's fantastic "In Favila—A Phantasmagoria," could make easy reference to a "monster prayer-meeting" in Central Park, attended by a million people, in the days before a predicted impact of a comet on the earth. Protestant denominations continued to schedule a "week of prayer" each year as "a suitable expression of faith in the efficacy of prayer," and in the hands of skilled revivalists such as Dwight L. Moody, prayer meetings remained an occasion to make specific written requests—"the minuteness with which some of these requests entered into private family histories was almost startling"—a leading feature of public gatherings in England and America.[11]

Revivalists who built reputations in the latter part of the nineteenth and early twentieth centuries to one extent or another exploited the ideas about masculinity, femininity, emotion, and the bold petitioning of God in prayer that lay at the heart of muscular Christianity. Nineteenth- and twentieth-century analyses of revivalists' personae sometimes have suggested the connections between the emotionality of muscular Christianity and the development of revivalism since 1858. James F. Findlay Jr., for example, wrote of Moody that his "ambition, drive, and determination" was balanced by "a certain feline grace—a touch of femininity—that seemed to be a rudimentary part of his personality." William Jennings Bryan thought that southern evangelist Sam Jones had "a great mind, directed by a great heart." The *San Francisco Examiner* reported that Churches of God evangelist Maria B. Woodworth-Etter was "a woman of fine presence, much intelligence, some education, is on the easy side of middle age, and talks with thrilling force. Her gestures are few but forcible . . ." Woodworth-Etter's reputation during 1880–1920 rested on her capability to preach people literally into trances, while salvaging each "misguided wreck of a once noble manhood." Billy Sunday likewise was renowned for his preaching, but as Lyle W. Dorsett has written, Sunday was above all else the praying preacher, and his highly emotional muscular Christianity blended rhetoric about courage and bold action (and sports, Sunday being a retired professional baseball player) with an emotional, teary relationship with God through prayer. For Sunday, the crux of religion was the manly act of prayer, and prayer was a "manly duty." Aimee Semple McPherson, at the Angelus Temple in California and on the vaudeville stage in New York, projected the same image of assertive, prayerful action in asking God to heal and strengthen the body. And alongside the revivals associated with such figures, prayer meeting manuals continued to stress the understandings of prayer as they had emerged in the 1850s and had been refined in the following decades. John F. Cowan's *New Life in the Old Prayer-Meeting* (1906) listed the key aspects of prayer, including, "Petition. There is no prayer without asking, though all asking is not prayer." Cowan recommended that meeting leaders actively solicit requests, and sometimes write them on a blackboard in the front of the room, that ushers distribute slips of paper upon which participants could write requests, and that " a box . . . be fastened to the wall of the room" as yet another means of collecting them.[12]

Revivalism up through World War I by no means simply duplicated in its various occurrences the patterns of muscular Christianity. Urbanization, immigration, technological innovation, shifting ideas about gender and the changing experiences of men and women, and the increasing domination of everyday life by a capitalist industrial/financial order all contributed to the alteration of muscular Christianity. On the other hand, American success in the Spanish-American War and significant steps toward the realization of an American imperialist agenda, the professionalization of sport, the enduring appeal of emotional culture, the efflorescence of a consumer culture, and growing trust in the effectiveness of active negotiation in determining value of commodities all served to prop up important aspects of muscular Christianity. But, on balance, muscular Christianity in the form of revivalism—whether it be Billy Sunday's podium-pounding crusades or Aimee Semple McPherson's calls for the bold petitioning of God to heal disease—faded into a distinctly back-burner cultural artifact after the war. Its view of the world and of the relationship between Christians and their God remained tenable, but in the shadow of the Nineteenth Amendment, in an increasingly isolationist post-war atmosphere, and, especially, because of the vast rethinking of the nature of American life brought on by the Depression, muscular Christianity lost its power to persuade and to attract followers.

The Men and Religion Forward Movement of 1911–1912 should not be confused with muscular Christianity. Its masculinist emphases conformed in certain ways to aspects of muscular Christianity, but its purpose, as Gail Bederman has argued, was to "de-feminize" the Protestant churches. When Allyn K. Foster of Worcester summarized the course of the movement just as it came to a close in 1912, he boasted that "the word evangelism ought to be henceforth a term of wider significance. It can never again be limited to any type of emotional experience." Such rhetoric not only represented clerical fears about the preponderance of women in the churches (and hope that the disparity had been corrected), but also clearly distinguished the movement from the emotional revivalism of Billy Sunday, which was peaking at the time. Church politics (regrettably sometimes overlooked in cultural histories) thus combined with gender politics in Foster's understanding of the meaning of the movement as both masculinist and a challenge to muscular Christianity in the form of revivalism. Religion and Men Forward conformed to a certain surface profile of muscular Christianity but beyond that surface there was little congruity. Largely concerned with social reform, there was no exploration of the nature or meaning of religious experience in the movement, no interest in exploiting the notion of prayer redolent in muscular Christianity, and no attempt to attach to masculine character anything drawn from the pool of feminine attributes.[13]

Muscular Christianity did not disappear in the twentieth century, however. According to James A. Mathisen, "muscular Christianity was revived by American Protestant fundamentalists as they recovered from the religious depression of the 1920's-1930's." The re-emergence of muscular Christianity came about through the activities of organizations such as Youth for Christ, the Fellowship of Christian Athletes, Athletes in Action, Pro Athletes Outreach, and eventually, the International Sports Coalition. None of those organizations launched projects that simply reiterated the muscular Christianity of the nineteenth century. Rather, they resurrected aspects of muscular Christianity in an effort to make sports serve the purposes of evangelism. And to a certain extent they have institutionalized that linkage.[14]

The most dramatic rekindling of muscular Christianity has been the religious movement known as Promise Keepers. Founded by Bill McCartney, a former football coach at the University of Colorado, Promise Keepers was, as the movement's literature explains, "birthed in a time of prayer," the outcome of conversation between McCartney and a colleague in which they "were sharing their hearts during a three-hour drive to a Fellowship of Christian Athletes banquet." A transcript of the press conference announcing the Promise Keepers March on Washington in early 1997 began with the assertion by a movement leader that "Promise Keepers is really about prayer." Other official literature declares that "the power of prayer and prayer networks has been the vital link of sustaining the movement of Promise Keepers," that persons in the movement are essentially "men of prayer," and that the movement aims at "a revival in the hearts of men around the world."[15]

Promise Keepers maintains a "National Prayer Department" which publishes monthly "Prayer Lessons" online. Testimonies from members frequently mention prayer, as in "I have experienced a renewed prayer life that is almost constant." Small "prayer teams" fan out in urban neighborhoods to draw men into the community. Movement literature reiterates in manifold ways the belief that God answers prayers, sometimes in language quite similar to that utilized in the 1850s: "A person who prays must believe they are praying to someone who hears and answers." One online Prayer Lesson focused on "Prayer Issues to Pray for Men Specifically," listing thirty items, including "Nurture of children by fathers," "Christlike emotional expressions," and "Moral courage and integrity." In-house polls conclude that over 60 percent of members pray an hour or more a week, and leaders encourage men to keep a prayer journal which "helps you to turn inward and examine your thoughts and feelings," because "journaling is a journey of the heart." Public gatherings, which take place in sports stadiums and arenas, commonly feature highly emotional prayer, reported by individual members in their testimonies or through official channels. One official account reports the "sudden tide of emotions that overpowered 68,000 men" in Atlanta, while individuals frequently state that at such meetings they were "filled with so much emotion and tears," "broke into tears," "could not hold back the emotions," or report other observations such as "tears were rolling down his face."[16]

The leadership of the movement is keenly aware of the ways in which its advocacy of tearful prayer might not square with notions about masculinity held by men in its potential recruitment base. Leaders have addressed the matter directly in numerous ways, including publications, speeches, and small group meetings, in order to promote the view that highly emotional prayer is masculine. A Promise Keepers survey summary began with the assertion that "prayer is a spiritual discipline often relegated to women in our churches," but went on to report that 95 percent of its respondents had answered "Not true" when presented with the proposition, "Prayer seems un-masculine to me." Seventy-five percent of survey respondents answered "more" to the question, "Do you feel more or less confident in your sense of masculinity than you did five years ago?" and the vast majority of respondents think that the movement, for all of its emphasis on prayer and weeping "on our knees in humility," has enhanced their masculinity. The conceptual arrangement of the notion of prayer as feminine alongside the belief that male prayer requires the exercise of a feminized aspect of character (which in turn enhances masculinity) is evidenced in the fact that "prayer rooms" under the seating in Promise Keeper stadium events are staffed by women. Men leave their seats to pray with the women during the course of the meeting. According to Ken Abraham, "Most PK leaders attribute much of their success in the public rallies to the prayer of these women." Another indication of the manner in which gender categories become fluid in the context of prayer is the title given to women in the prayer rooms: "prayer warriors."[17]

There is no question, as Michael A. Messner has pointed out, that "the antifeminist and antigay backlash potential of Promise Keepers is obvious." Indeed, much analysis of the movement, perhaps the majority of commentators, has pictured it as regressive, an attempt to recapture certain aspects of male privilege at a time when gender roles, traditional notions of family, and ideas about sexual orientation are being challenged and changed. The movement also has been accused of being inhospitable to men of color. It is clear, however, that the movement represents the legacy of a view of masculinity and religious devotion that coalesced in the mid-nineteenth century. While not duplicating that view—the world after all has changed in the last 150 years—it embodies several key elements of the emotionology of the Businessmen's Revival. Americans have changed their thinking about gender in important ways since 1858. But even in the wake of the "sensitive man" movement in the 1960s and 1970s, and in spite of dramatic evidences of female accomplishment in "a man's world," white middle-class emotionology still leans toward a construction of men as intellectual, active, and independent, and women as emotional, quiescent, and dependent. Those constructions, wrapped up with a complex religious baggage, remain fundamental to the Promise Keepers movement. But at the heart of the movement there lies as well a belief in the necessity of men cultivating "feminine" behavior such as the performance of humility and weakness, crying alone or in groups with other men, a devotional life focused on frequent prayer, and participation in a discourse that values love, communication, and sacrifice. As was the case in 1858, the blending (probably an unequal blending but a blending nevertheless) of masculine and feminine elements is perceptible in the belief that when men offer their hearts to God in prayer, when they express themselves emotionally with tears, God will respond. Emotion, the heart, is a commodity offered to God in exchange for various things that a man requests. As the twenty-first century begins, men act the businessman as much as they did during the Businessmen's Revival.[18]

History, Religion, and Emotion: A Historiographical Survey

THE DEVELOPMENT
OF A HISTORIOGRAPHY OF EMOTIONS

A History of All Religions of the World, a cumbrous tome published in New York in 1884, announced in its opening paragraph that "mankind in common are endowed by nature with religious emotions, which form in man the natural basis of all religious development, and which in their influence over the character of individuals and nations are most powerful." At exactly the same time, William James was asking, "What is an emotion?" and preparing the pioneering *Principles of Psychology* that would challenge any such notion of an emotional endowment, proposing instead that emotion followed upon the heels of physiological changes. By the time that Alfred North Whitehead had linked the matter to metaphysics, asserting that a feeling cannot be abstracted from the feeler, much ink had been spilled at the desks of believers and non-believers alike over the issue of "religious emotion."[1]

Not all of that ink came from the pens of psychologists or philosophers, or from theologians. Nascent social science had begun to scrutinize emotion in connection with economy and society, and it undertook a series of explorations into the relation of emotion to religious life. Initial reconnaissance of that territory included writings of Karl Marx, Émile Durkheim, and Max Weber. In analyzing the social predicament of alienation and loss, Marx described a world that alternately was drenched with emotion (as anxiety, fear, and despair) and abstracted from emotion. In the latter case, he castigated the bourgeoisie, who had "drowned the most heavenly ecstasies of religious fervor, of chivalrous enthusiasm, of philistine sentimentalism, in the icy water of egotistical calculation."[2] Durkheim discovered in aboriginal society collective representations of social feelings and the emotional component of moral life. "In the midst of an assembly," wrote Durkheim, "animated by a common passion, we become susceptible of acts and sentiments of which we are incapable when reduced to our own forces." That passion or "sentiment" was represented through the "group incarnate and personified."[3] Max Weber's well-known distinction between this-worldly asceticism and other-worldly asceticism formed the basis for his linking the repression of emotion with capitalism, so that the descendants of Puritans were "specialists without spirit, sensualists without heart."[4]

The rich ferment of ideas among historians in France beginning in the 1920s produced a historiography steeped in the insights of such social science and capable of articulating a more clearly defined agenda of historical inquiry into emotion. Lucien Febvre outlined the direction of that project in an essay published in 1938 entitled "Histoire et psychologie": "The task is, for a given period, to establish a detailed inventory of the mental equipment of the men of the time, then by dint of great learning, but also of imagination, to reconstitute the whole physical, intellectual and moral universe of each preceding generation."[5] For Febvre this task translated to a test of the historian's ingenuity in developing investigative techniques that would make it possible "to reconstitute the emotional life of the past."[6]

The groundwork for Febvre's new kind of history had already been laid by Marc Bloch, whose study of popular belief in the cure of scrofula by the king's touch in medieval and early modern times was predicated on the notion that "the miracle of scrofula is incontestably bound up with a whole psychological system."[7] Bloch later detailed his thinking in the posthumous *The Historian's Craft*, wherein he argued that "historical facts are, in essence, psychological facts. Normally, therefore, they find their antecedents in other psychological facts." Taken together, these "psychological facts" and the circumstances of their existence made up for Bloch social reality understood "as a whole." The historian's task accordingly was to reconceive the whole in order to uncover the implicit meanings of collective behavior.[8]

Fundamental to the project of the history of emotion as represented in the work of Febvre and Bloch was a design of imaginative interrogation of historical artifacts that would, as Febvre wrote, "make mute things talk." Johan Huizinga's classic characterization of medieval emotionality, *The Waning of the Middle Ages*,[9] had broken fresh ground for such an undertaking a few years earlier. But the new endeavor made its most dramatic appearance in Fernand Braudel's study of the Mediterranean world in the age of Philip II, and eventually took shape as a species of social history characterized by its attention to everyday life, or what once was called "total history."[10] Braudel also articulated one of the cardinal verities of the Annales school: not only were events, or actions (*histoire événementielle*), to be distinguished from the historical structures that limited and controlled events (*histoire de la longue durée*), but actors themselves were considered to be imprisoned within those structures and thus determined in their possibilities. So for example in his study of capitalism and material life Braudel argued that "the hazards of harvest, the slowness or lack of transport, incomprehensible and contradictory demographic movements . . . , and the chronic deficiency of power resources" made people "unconscious prisoners," "locked in an economic condition" that determined their possibilities for action.[11] In line with Febvre's call for an inventory of the "mental equipment" of people, *annalistes* surmised that not only political, economic, and social activity, but also mental activity was constrained and compelled by historical structures. Thus *mentalités collectives,* or cast of mind, was ratified as an object of historical study.

But it was not the *annalistes* who initiated the study of *mentalités* per se. Sorbonne professor Lucien Levy-Bruhl had published *Primitive Mentality* a year before Bloch's book on the king's touch, and with numerous references to "collective representations," had theorized an evolution from pre-logical to logical social states.[12] Criticized by E. E. Evans-Pritchard, Levy-Bruhl's thinking was amended over time, and eventually led to a major body of theory in cultural interpretation among Anglo-American anthropologists. It is important that we recognize in the meantime that the ideas of Durkheim, as they were revised and dressed-out by Levy-Bruhl and by Claude Levi-Strauss (who largely rejected the judgment of "primitive mentality" but extended the notion of the universality of structure), exercised a more or less constant influence on the thinking of Annales historians. Durkheimian notions of collective life accordingly are apparent in Bloch's emphasis on the psychology of collective behavior, in Braudel's project of "total history," and in Le Roy Ladurie's study of peasant life in Languedoc.[13]

Concern for the psychology of the individual was not exclusively undertaken as probings of collective mentality, however. For all of his interest in group emotional activity Febvre repeatedly spotlighted the experience of individuals: Luther, Rabelais, and Margaret of Navarre.[14] While co-launching the Annales program for study of collective mentalities, Febvre held out the necessity for the historian to comprehend the relationship of the individual to the collective. The theoretical and practical aspects of that project were advanced steadily in the 1960s and 1970s in the work of his disciples Zevedei Barbu and Robert Mandrou, who mined the new field of "historical psychology."[15]

The term "historical psychology" was coined by Norbert Elias to describe the historical study of "the order underlying historical change." Elias was especially concerned with "the specific process of psychological 'growing up'" in Western societies. Drawing on psychoanalytic theory he accordingly described that process analogically as "nothing other than the individual civilizing process to which each young person, as a result of the social civilizing process over many centuries, is automatically subjected from early childhood." In a study of customs ranging from blowing one's nose to table manners and bedroom behavior, Elias, influenced by psychoanalysis, sought above all the relation of conscious to unconscious impulses, concluding that the "civilizing process" involved the progressive repression of emotion in favor of intellectual activity.[16]

The psychoanalytic tack in the historical study of emotion took shape in the United States as psychohistory. The original work of psychohistory was Freud's *Leonardo da Vinci and a Memory of His Childhood,* published in 1910.[17] In its American form, psychohistory was launched with aplomb in 1957, when William L. Langer, in his Presidential Address to the American Historical Association, proposed to the members of the profession that their "next assignment" involved the "urgently needed deepening of our historical understanding through exploitation of the concepts and findings of modern psychology."[18] The following year Erik Erikson published *Young Man Luther* and a year after that Norman O. Brown's *Life against Death* appeared. In fits and starts psychohistory framed a historical approach, nurtured by a core of academics that included by 1966 Erikson, Robert Jay Lifton, Kenneth Keniston, Leo Marx, Howard Zinn, Richard Sennett, and Rosabeth Kanter.[19] It was represented in Henry Lawton's definition of the field as "the interdisciplinary study of why man has acted as he has in history, prominently utilizing psychoanalytic materials,"[20] though a more ambitious psychohistory was advocated by Lloyd DeMause, who wrote that "psychohistory reduces all of its subject matter to 'psychological motives'" so that "narrative history describes sequences of historical events; psychohistory discovers laws of historical motivations."[21] In cases where histories have avoided doctrinaire Freudianisms and have developed a base of material more expansive than standard biography, they have proven not only serviceable but in several instances significant and widely influential. Philip Greven's investigation of the Protestant temperament, John Demos's portrait of family life in Plymouth colony, and valuable studies by Peter Gay and Christopher Lasch all rest on psychoanalytic principles.[22]

Historical investigation of emotion has been profoundly influenced by theory generated in the social and behavioral sciences. The emotions theme emerged in the American ethnography of Franz Boas and his followers, including Alexander Goldenweiser, whose definition of religion featured the emotional aspect, or what Goldenweiser called the "religious thrill," especially as it was intensified in ritual. For Robert Lowie, Paul Radin, and Ruth Benedict, emotion was a key element of religion as well. In the 1930s Talcott Parsons, the most influential American expositor of the thinking of Durkheim and Weber, in the course of attempting to frame a general theory that would provide a conceptual framework for all social research, articulated the notion of culture as a symbolic system. His students Robert Bellah and Clifford Geertz subsequently located emotion at the center of that system. For Bellah religion is a symbol system that evokes the "felt-whole." Geertz argued that religion was a system of symbols that established powerful "moods and motivations" in persons. Geertz later went on to identify emotions as cultural artifacts. That claim—enriched by subsequent explorations of the culturally constructed self—has been fundamental to the approach of many researchers in the last twenty-five years, and has led to the deployment of increasingly more sophisticated theories of emotions in writing about religion and culture. Michelle Rosaldo's groundbreaking study of the Ilongot, and Catherine Lutz's investigation of emotion among the Ifaluk in Micronesia both, to borrow Lutz's words, set out "to treat emotion as an ideological practice rather than as a thing to be discovered or an essence to be distilled." Fundamental to such an approach is what Judith Butler has called "performativity," that is, with regard to emotion, the interplay between collective identity, cultural standards for emotional display and concealment, and the imprisoning historical structures that constrain and determine possibilities for historical actors. Such a notion of performance has been effectively utilized in a broad range of studies of religion and emotion, historical and otherwise, including Timothy Mitchell's *Passional Culture: Emotion, Religion, and Society in Southern Spain,* Paul Bouissac's examination of the sacred in clown performances, Peter Iver Kaufman's *Prayer, Despair, and Drama: Elizabethan Introspection,* June McDaniel's *Madness of the Saints: Ecstatic Religion in Bengal,* and studies of religious weeping by William Christian, Eliot Wolfson, and Gary Ebersole.[23]

As historical scholarship has experimented with semiotic conceptualizations of culture,[24] it has invited collaboration with psychological researchers, and psychologists have responded, bringing to the conversation sets of questions that in turn have shaped historical inquiry. James R. Averill and Rom Harré, for example, have made cases for the social construction of emotion that are compatible with historical approaches, Averill arguing that *"emotions are social constructions.* That is, emotions are responses that have been institutionalized by society,"* and are manifest under an umbrella of "cognitive structures or 'rules' that govern emotional expression." In a recent essay psychologist Kenneth J. Gergen has called for an interdependency between psychological and historical study of emotion that would regard emotions as both "culturally situated performances" and as a discourse imbedded in history, in the undertakings of individual actors. At the same time, a style of cultural studies that values a synchronic perspective alongside the diachronic has opened opportunities for the integration of psychological and social scientific theory with historical narrative. Partly a reaction to perceived limitations in the history of mentalities, this kind of cultural history—instanced by Robert Darnton's analysis of a cat massacre in France, David Warren Sabean's interpretation of emotions and the Lord's Supper in sixteenth-century Germany, and Rhys Isaac's history of colonial Virginia—predicted several models for an interdisciplinary study of emotion in history. Recent work on the history of emotions accordingly embodies a variety of approaches, but virtually all of it exemplifies the possibilities inherent in a blend of theoretical and disciplinary standpoints in uncovering notions of self, and especially emotional life, in the past. Peter N. Stearns's history of jealousy in America, Kenneth Lockridge's study of gender and rage in the eighteenth century, and the essays in Barbara H. Rosenwein's *Anger's Past: The Social Uses of an Emotion in the Middle Ages,* in Joel Pfister and Nancy Schnog's *Inventing the Psychological: Toward a Cultural History of Emotional Life in America,* and in Peter N. Stearns and Jan Lewis's *An Emotional History of the United States* represent emerging historical approaches to the study of emotions as an admixture of literary and social history, sociological and psychological perspectives, and the utilization of "thick description" to disclose precisely contextualized "deep structures" alongside the traditional practice of historiography as the means of narrating historical change.[25]

Some recent historical investigation has utilized the research category of "emotionology" articulated by Peter N. Stearns and Carol Z. Stearns in 1985 as the "collective emotional standards of a society."[26] The Stearnses have argued that emotionology is detectable in a wide range of sources including manuals of military discipline, medical writings, formal essays about emotion, courtship behavior, division of labor in the family, treatments for mental illness, sermons on family life, and other indicators of thought and behavior. Alongside emotionology, however, and sometimes distinct from it, is the actual emotional experience of individual actors, traces of which are recoverable from diaries, autobiographies, illegitimacy rates, instances of fisticuffs, and so forth. For the Stearnses, the historian's task is to evaluate emotional experience against the backdrop of emotional standards in order to measure the extent to which emotional life was shaped by those standards, departed from them, or contributed to their transformation. Such an undertaking accordingly is geared to recognizing change: how and why culturally constructed contexts of collective meaning (specifically emotionology) were rendered outmoded or inadequate by changes in the emotional experience of groups of individuals,[27] and conversely how emotionologies themselves shape emotional experience. This historical quest unfolds within the larger context of attention to economics, demographics, and environment (in keeping with the model of "total history"), and with an eye to class, gender, race, ethnicity, and other particularizing factors. Moreover, in the Stearnses' view, historians should be willing to accept the likelihood that actors may be unaware of the full range of mental structures that affect both their cognition and emotions—or, in other words, that historians (like psychohistorians) are warranted in their search for unconscious influences and motives.[28]

The scholarly endeavor envisioned by the Stearnses is allied to previous approaches to emotions history in several ways. It is first of all an attempt to advance Febvre's vaunted program "to reconstitute the emotional life of the past." It is deployed largely as social history tilted toward the Durkheimian collective. In its regard for ingrained emotional standards, or emotionology, it adopts in principle the approach of the history of mentalities; that is, it incorporates the notion of determining mental frameworks such as are characteristic of the work of Bloch and Braudel. Though not inherently psychoanalytical in orientation, it assumes unconscious-ness in seeking to discover the ways in which collective emotional life may be determined and limited in ways relatively unknown to actors. As in some recent kinds of history, there is recognition of cultural differences and the expectation of encountering creative recombinations or new constructions of cultural meanings—in the Stearnses' case, in the dynamic relationship between emotionology and emotional experience. The Stearnses' project initially was not oriented to a performative view of emotion, however, and it was grounded in a preference for calculation of historical change over a period of a century or more. Progress in the study of the history of emotion will depend in part on the willingness of researchers to more intensely explore the element of performance—not only by historical actors but, as historian Greg Dening has argued, by historians themselves[29]—and innovate across disciplinary lines in crafting narratives perspectively more complex. It also will require historians to focus closely on emotional cultures within sharply delimited chronologies—ten years, or twenty years—in order to accurately track the numerous interlocking aspects of culture that shape emotion at any given historical moment. Such work, as it accumulates, will serve as a foundation for projects of a more ambitious historical sweep.

THE HISTORY OF EMOTIONS AND RELIGION

As is usually the case in the development of a field of historical inquiry, those approaches and interpretations that eventually are recognized as dominant emerge from the midst of many different types of historical scholarship, from studies scattered across many historical periods, geographical settings, and thematic foci. Historical approaches to the study of religion and emotion have taken interpretation in a wide variety of directions, in scholarship that is sometimes grounded in obvious perspectives (e.g., psychoanalysis), but just as often draws eclectically on a variety of perspectives in making a case for a certain understanding of emotion. Certain trends—some having to do with theme, others with certain religious traditions, others with specific emotions—are noticeable.

PROMINENT AREAS OF RESEARCH

Scholarly investigation of emotion in the religious past has been distributed across a broad range of topics and themes. However, several areas stand out in relief against this accumulated mass of research, largely because of the number of studies concentrated in those areas, and secondarily because of the depth and sophistication of the analysis characteristic of those studies. The four most prominent foci are Hindu *bhakti*, Christian revivalism, mysticism (especially Sufist and Christian), and women's experience.

The historical essence of the Hindu devotional movement of *bhakti* is emotion, especially the cultivation of emotion.[30] Forms or gradations of the devotees' feelings have been identified,[31] and a study of the historical meanings of the Sanskrit term emphasizes love of God.[32] Specifically, *bhakti* emerged and developed as the emotional involvement with a deity,[33] often as the relationship between lover and beloved.[34] The *bhakta* nevertheless has appeared historically in a variety of roles, including the guru, hero, and madman as well as the lover and beloved.[35] Some studies have emphasized the range of emotions involved in such devotionalism as it developed over the course of the eighth through the sixteenth centuries,[36] including, in the case of the sixteenth-century *bhakta* teacher Tukarama, love, guilt, sorrow, and ecstasy, among others.[37] The historical diversity of this strand of Hinduism was not without its limits, however, diversity occasionally giving rise to accusations of heterodoxy.[38] Historians have stressed the linkage between meditation and emotion in *bhakta*,[39] and the best historical studies address the manner in which this devotionalism is framed by sociological and political factors.[40] Some historians have argued that *bhakta* in privileging emotion over intellect embodied social revolt against Indian elites,[41] while one writer makes a comparison with the Christian gospel of love in its Johannine manifestation.[42]

Investigation of the role of emotion in revivalism has focused largely on British and American instances. Christian revivalism involves "ecstatic experiences" that are manifest in the physical exercises of the participants.[43] One American history depicted revivalism as a "recharging" of the "emotional power house" that moves the wheels of social life,[44] while another stressed emotion as a key element of a cultural revitalization through religious revival.[45] Theorizing about the importance of the public and collective display of emotion became a more common aspect of religion in America during the Enlightenment,[46] and though it has been argued that revivalism in England and America valued emotion over intellect,[47] it also has been shown that emotion was conceived as integrated with intellect, social experience, political thought, and other aspects of a coherent worldview.[48] The theory that revival was merely an emotional response to encounter of the American frontier has been challenged.[49] The claim that emotional outpourings that characterized eighteenth-century American revivalism represented innovative behavior has been rejected.[50] Historians have proposed that revival preaching was deliberately sentimental,[51] and revivals were judged by their capability to deliver excitement or heighten psychological tension.[52] Conversely it has been argued that nineteenth-century Methodists constructed meeting sites so as to deliberately limit emotion,[53] and that revival calmed passion by raising tranquil feelings.[54] In America, emotional revivalism is found in locations ranging from Appalachia, where it survives in its eighteenth- and nineteenth-century styles,[55] to back alleys of the nation's capital, where religion naturally took an emotional form.[56]

Emotion and mysticism were linked in ancient Mediterranean religions, such as the worship of Mithra in Rome[57] and later, most visibly in Christian and Sufi religious life, and in the devotions of the *bhakta*. Mystical ecstasy arises through preparation and the exercise of certain techniques.[58] While one observer suggests that mystics "feel a lot and know a little",[59] some historians have concluded that emotion and rationalist philosophy were joined, as in Sufi tradition through the influence of al-Ghazzali[60] and in Christianity as the union of emotionalism with an intellectualist strain of Augustinian devotionalism.[61] Mystical religion accordingly can generate theologies of feeling.[62] Not all mysticism stresses emotion: One historical study claims that St. John of the Cross thought reliance upon feeling a mistake.[63]

In the area of women and religion, historians have concentrated their attention on feminized constructions of religious emotion and the role of emotion in women's religious experience. The interpretation of historical instances of such phenomena has moved in several directions. One study concludes that the devotions of women in seventeenth- through nineteenth-century France were characterized more by fear than men's devotions,[64] while other studies argue that medieval women experienced status reversal vis-à-vis males in the course of their emotional religious exercises,[65] and that women in eighteenth-century England employed religion as a means to express anger against males who oppressed them.[66] Several studies propose that the religious ecstasies of medieval women issued from a profound awareness of the body and of pain, both physical and spiritual,[67] with St. Perpetua seeking through martyrdom escape from emotions that tied her to her father.[68] Much has been written about women and hysteria, again with varying conclusions. Early Christian female mystics were accused of being hysterics,[69] as were European women centuries later.[70] Ecstatic (and somnambulant) female preachers in early twentieth-century Finland likewise were called hysterics.[71] Although male fear of women led to witchcraft accusations,[72] Dr. Edward Jorden was among the first to defend a woman from charges of demonic possession and malfeasance by identifying her as suffering the medical condition of hysteria.[73] Women likewise escaped the charge of possession (and mysticism) in late nineteenth-century anti-clerical France through diagnoses of hysteria.[74] The emotionality of goddesses has been scrutinized by historians as well. While anger is a hallmark of some Indian and Sri Lankan goddesses,[75] the image of an affectionate bond between mother and child was exploited by medieval Franciscan preachers.[76] (At the same time, women who used love charms in sixteenth-century Modena were penalized by church authorities).[77] Franciscan and Carthusian preachers remade the figure of Mary as less emotional in the thirteenth through fifteenth centuries. She subsequently became a model for women to rein in their feelings,[78] and in Victorian England women rejected as a model a more emotional Mary.[79]

HISTORICAL STUDY OF SPECIFIC EMOTIONS

A substantial portion of historical scholarship has been concentrated on religion and expressions of the emotions of anger, fear, bliss, love, shame/guilt, hatred, mourning, and jealousy. Research also has addressed melancholy[80] and the emotional aspects of laughter[81] in some detail.

The nature of the anger of God in the Old Testament varies from text to text[82]—although one study explains it as the rationalization of the experience of exile[83]—and anger as it is depicted as a whole in the Old Testament suggests its complexity.[84] Anger was expressed in a variety of ways, such as in the ritual clapping of hands in ancient Mesopotamia and Israel.[85] The early Christian God also was angry,[86] like Indian and Sri Lankan goddesses,[87] and figures from Greek mythology (where anger was the proper response to the breaking of religious taboos).[88] A female saint's anger is made understandable through consideration of the seventh-century Frankish culture of emotion in which she was situated.[89] Cursing by medieval Celtic saints has only the appearance of anger,[90] and among Christian monks in the eleventh century cursing came to be associated with the absence of anger.[91] Similarly, swearing in anger was ruled not to be blasphemous in sixteenth-century Spain.[92] In Islam, representations of the prophet mark his greatness through reference to his anger.[93]

Historical surveys and overviews of fear address its nature and function across a spectrum ranging from "primitive religion" to monotheistic traditions and the Enlightenment.[94] Christian fears of divine judgment increased from the thirteenth through eighteenth centuries,[95] fears of hell were prevalent in early modern Europe,[96] the French feared sorcery in the nineteenth century,[97] and the African Igbo in the twentieth century lived a religion characterized by a "dread of the divine," which was a combination of the fear of death and the desire to escape divine wrath.[98] The fear of death underlay the popularity of miracle stories in fourteenth-century Christianity.[99] Christian tragedy historically has featured a blend of horror and guilt[100] and, by raising a "sacred terror" in their readers, various authors have illuminated and driven home the meanings of moral tales in nineteenth- and twentieth-century America.[101] In the twentieth century, fear has been linked to religious change in Ghana,[102] to the shamanic personality in the Congo,[103] and to visions of Mary in Spain.[104]

A large number of studies have addressed the experience of joy or bliss, which is depicted in the Upanishads as non-duality and wholeness.[105] Joy was associated with the movement from profane to sacred space in ritual in Israelite religion, and it was also connected to spontaneity in ancient Israel.[106] One study of bliss in India has likened it to the "oceanic feeling," while another study of Christianity in nineteenth-century Manchester casts joy as the feeling of submission to a higher power.[107] In Renaissance Christianity, joy was a key aspect of the cult of St. Cecelia.[108]

Love has been a key theological component of Sufism, Christianity, and Hinduism.[109] It was actualized in the Old Testament as the faithfulness of vassal to ruler, and in Tamil Shaiva sectarianism as servant-like devotion.[110] Courtly love traditions in the Christian West influenced the vision of St. Francis of Assisi as well as medieval women mystics,[111] although it has been argued that courtly love was transformed into Christian love by the fourteenth century.[112] The history of love in the West is marked by attempts to reconcile religious love with human love, and with love of nature,[113] with twelfth-century Cistercians defining *caritas* as both love of God and love of humans.[114] Mystical love has been studied utilizing insights from addiction research,[115] and eroticism and religious love frequently have been linked, as in Christian devotions to Mary.[116]

Guilt appears in historical studies of religion in a number of ways, from expected analyses of the relation of guilt to submission and expiatory sacrifice in Judaism and Christianity[117] to surprising discussions of guilt fantasies which were part of the piety of Afrikaaner women from the eighteenth through the twentieth century.[118] Christian family identity in the ancient Mediterranean was grounded in shame,[119] and the nineteenth-century French religious "culture of delirium" arose in response to feelings of guilt.[120] Historical research of hatred likewise has taken some anticipated directions, such as in discussion of the importance of hatred of a father in a saint's spiritual development,[121] and the hatred of religious groups that are not one's own.[122] Jealousy studies range from examinations of the "law of jealousy" in ancient Judaism, which prescribed the ritual handling of suspected adulteresses,[123] to analysis of Islamic contexts for friendship as generosity overcoming jealousy.[124]

Emotions associated with mourning are important in the history of religion, one study arguing that mourning and weeping have been a key part of Christian mysticism,[125] and another analyzing the ritual structuring of grief in fourteenth-century Christianity as an "extreme" form of cultural expression.[126] The public performance of tears in medieval Spain manifested an inner state of mourning for sin and contrition and was crucial to the ritual of collective repentance.[127] In sixteenth-century Judaism weeping also played a central role in spiritual development, not as mourning, but as a ritualized means by which a person ascended mystically to the heavens.[128]

THEMES AND PROSPECTS

Historical scholarship has explored the emotional component of religious life in a wide assortment of chronological and geographical settings, and with respect to several religious traditions. The majority of studies focus on the Christian West, but investigations of Hindu, Muslim, and Jewish emotional life have been steadily increasing. Currently there is only minimal historical interest in emotion in Japanese and Chinese religions outside of Buddhism, and although scholars interested in emotion have made a few historical forays into African, Oceanic, and native American religious life, for the most part those areas remain vastly underexplored as well.

The most important and currently the most promising topic among historians of religion and emotion is gender. Studies of women mystics have been particularly important, and especially those that interweave the themes of gender, body, domination, pain, and escape. Investigations of linkages and resistance to linkages between hysteria and women's religious experience likewise have opened important areas in the historical study of religion and emotion, particularly through reference to psychological and physiological aspects of religious life. Most of the scholarship that attends to gender has focused on fear and anger as specific emotional states, with some attention to the joy of mystical union. There has been comparatively little interest thus far in defining historical manifestations of shame and guilt, hatred, awe, jealousy, and the emotions associated with mourning in historical accounts of women's religious lives. Likewise, research on the ways in which women have practiced religious emotion in a public settings is only a fraction of what it could be given the potential richness of the topic. Some studies have taken the family as a primary context for understanding the historical meanings of emotions connected to worship, faith, and moral action.

Comparative histories of religion and emotion are needed. Only a handful of projects at this time address similarities and differences across religious traditions or historical periods. The ongoing integration of relevant anthropological, sociological, and psychological research into historical investigation should provide some possibilities for remedying that deficiency by fostering the invention of themes that are susceptible to comparative study. More badly needed are historical works that engage the very issue of the definition of emotion in religion. How is emotion as a category conceptualized by religious groups in various historical periods? How is it envalued or disparaged? How is it thought to intersect with intellectual life and action? To what extent is it objectified in religion? Should kinds of emotion (i.e., religious or non-religious) be distinguished?

The historical study of religion and emotion likely will continue to unfold as a project in three parts. First, there is the prospect that it will develop understandings of the historical contexts for the expression and concealment of emotion in various religious settings, with regard especially to specific emotional states of anger, fear, joy, and so forth. Second, indications are that concern with gender, and increasingly race and ethnicity, will play a major part in historical research of religion and emotion. Analysis of the role of class is desperately needed, but there is little evidence that beyond a handful of studies historians have engaged it seriously as a category alongside gender, and little reason to suppose that it will appear as prominently in the near future. Third, historians likely will broaden the nature of their cooperative enterprise with scholars whose primary interest is literature, whether that be religious scriptures and mythologies, poetry, fictional narratives, theological and philosophical treatises, or diaries, correspondence, and memoirs. The results of that cooperation might appear as more precise characterizations of the emotional lives of religious individuals and groups within a historical setting rendered as a system of feeling rules.

Emotion as Heart, Blood, and Body

The body has proven unusually attractive to historians during the last decade. The research that has been invested in studying its cultural construction and its service as a canvas upon which societies represent cultural forces and events has eventuated in a wide variety of contributions to cultural history, including the history of religion and emotion. The objectification of emotion in the nineteenth century was itself a cultural process closely linked to the manner in which persons thought about the body. One avenue into that thinking is through the engagement of medical theory about the body and emotion, and especially through consideration of the ways in which it grounded emotion in organic states and processes. The conception of emotion as a commodity grew directly out of its objectification as heart and blood.

MIND AND BODY

Nineteenth-century writers fiercely debated the constitution of the mind. Those debates evidence a broad range of opinion about not only whether any given theory was "scientific," but about the meaning of science as well, as they interwove myth with scientific claim, religious faith with mathematical truth, and wild speculation with disciplined method. Most importantly, debaters invoked the authority of science, of scientific method as they conceived it, to support a wide range of theories. Such invocation is modeled in the instance of a proposal regarding mythical creatures. In October 1831, no less an organ than the *American Journal of the Sciences* published "An Attempt to Prove the Existence of the Unicorn," Jacob Potter's translation of a treatise by J. F. Laterrade. Proposing that it was unscientific "to deny the existence of such a species as has not come under our observation," the essay argued that "this animal has in it nothing remote from the ordinary laws of nature." Claiming that no proof of the non-existence of the unicorn had ever been made, and taking into account certain skeletal remains uncovered in various parts of the world, the author argued that naturalists should remain on the lookout for living specimens of the creature, in the interest of science.[1]

Publications such as Potter's, which deployed "science" as an instrument for the recovery of myth, were not uncommon in the early nineteenth century, and they spurred debate about topics dear to the hearts of religionists and infidels alike. Typical was the ongoing animated discussion about about the nature of mind, which featured outspoken proponents of several different positions. John Smith, for example, speaking before the Western Medical Society in Pennsylvania in 1814, condemned the "pathless desert of conjecture" in medicine and urged his fellow doctors "to expel adulterated science from the medical department." Turning his attention to the mind, he noted its unity and simplicity, and then stressed that "the human mind is purely, and absolutely immaterial."[2] Medical theorist Athanasius Fenwick on the other hand flatly rejected the notion of an immaterial mind, proposing that the brain was the mind. He punctuated his opposition to the idea of an immaterial mind with a barb sure to reach its mark with religionists: "To call the human mind a ray of divinity appears to me to be absolute nonsense."[3] Thomas Middleton Stuart took another tack in his physician's dissertation in New York in 1819. Arguing that the brain and mind were closely connected but were not the same, he referred to a well-cited story from the history of dissections. Noting that one man's brain had been "almost entirely converted to pus," and yet the man until the moment of death appeared in full possession of his faculties, Stuart supposed that more than brain tissue was involved in thinking, feeling, and doing.[4] The overall dynamic, however, for him remained occult.

While Smith and Stuart and others clung to traditional notions of the immateriality of mind, or at least confessed uncomfortableness with the idea of a fully material mind, doctors and theorists such as Fenwick wrote imaginatively and systematically about linkages between mind and body, and especially about the physiological grounding of emotion. James Pendleton proposed that "the mind, heart, and body are reciprocally dependent, and controulled by the same natural law." Henry Rose likewise affirmed that "the mind and body although widely different in themselves, yet they are so formed, and wonderfully united in us, that the one may be affected by the other in reciprocal sympathy." Nonspecialists took the gist of such statements (which were common) to be a connection between mental activity and physical activity. Tracy Cheever's diary entry on the subject was typical: "These mere emotions which are placed on paper, and indulged for reverie in dreamland are worse than vain unless the 'deed' go with them." And Boston minister Orville Dewey, former president of the American Unitarian Association, on the eve of the Civil War recommended to his son Charles a book "that touches upon the mental work on a farm."[5]

For some persons, qualities of mind (especially thinking and feeling) were visible in a person's appearance. "We generally find men," wrote Benjamin Rush, "whose faces resemble each other, have the same manners and dispositions." *The Juvenile Lavater* accordingly explained how the facial muscles and veins, the qualities of the skin, bone structure, "eyeball symmetry," and other aspects of physiognomy revealed the moral quality of a person's "temperament." Developing language that was rich with racist implications, Americans asked: "Do we observe a certain size of the brain, and a peculiar cast of features, such as the prominent eye, and the aquiline nose, to be connected with extraordinary portions of genius?—We observe a similar connection between the figure and temperament of the body, and certain moral faculties.—Hence, we often ascribe good temper and benevolence to corpulency." Such ideas amounted to a sharpening of a perspective that had long been a part of the English-speaking world. Temperament had been cited to explain and debunk all sorts of things and had been especially useful in identifying distinguishing characteristics in non-English population groups. So, for example, in early New England, Harvard student Robert Hale entered the following "correct" answers to a question about nationality: "The English are melancholick, the French are rash and unsteady, the Germans are phlegmatic and martial, the Spaniards are jealous, proud, and lustful, and the Italians are grave and revengeful." By the early nineteenth century the art had blossomed into its characteristic form, phrenology, which yielded such offshoot treatises as *The Art of Kissing*, which defined a woman's emotional fitness and character by the shape of her lips and the slant of her chin, and, of course, the bumps on her head. And whether in search of enlightenment or just for an afternoon's amusement, many Americans sought out bump-readers in the early nineteenth century. Some, like Charles Dewey, who wrote excitedly to his mother in 1846 that a phrenologist had discovered that his sister Catherine "had a bump of conscientiousness very large," weighed the phrenologists' pronouncements heavily in their thinking about temperament and moral virtues. Most hoped for the discovery of physical evidence that their temperament was even, their portfolio of moral virtues diversified, and their feelings and thoughts in balance.[6]

The embodying of emotion was advanced through the progressive elaboration of the health benefits and risks of mental life. Thinking and feeling could vitalize and tune the body, but they could ruin it as well. Opinion about the salutary effects of thinking overflowed from the pens of teachers, ministers, government officials, and social commentators, and Americans invested much effort in researching the desirable practical consequences as well as the sheer pleasures of thinking. Thinking discovered truth, shaped character, aided digestion, improved circulation, strengthened the bones, gave the complexion a rosy glow, and developed the nervous system. And it was enjoyable to boot. The *Massachusetts Ploughman*, in language reminiscent of Jefferson's vision of a nation of gentleman farmers, preached the delights of a regular habit of thinking: "Let your relaxation be intellectual engagements and your amusements the entertaining developments of truth. Though perhaps wearisome at first, such a habit of study will find no refreshment like communion with graceful or exalted minds, and instead of a toil to be feared, you welcome release from other toil, that you may turn to the conversation of philosophy, a friend, ever ready and ever faithful." Thinking, thought Bostonians, brought with it an assortment of desirable ends, from physical health to better steam engines to better government. And thinking begat more thinking. The *Massachusetts Teacher* reported that "the Creator has so constituted the human intellect, that it can grow only by its own action, and by its own action it must certainly and necessarily grows." That growth eventuated in a multiplication of benefits of all sorts for the thinker.[7]

Too much thinking, however, was injurious to health. Theodoric Beck observed in 1811 that failure to discipline the intellect was a cause of insanity. By that he meant that overuse as well as underuse of the intellect led to harmful consequences, or, as George Scandlin wrote, the dangers of "the mind being exhausted by a close application of study." Joanne Harvey of suburban Boston expressed the problem more concisely in her diary in 1857, writing, simply, "I am stupified with *thinking, thinking*." Both Scandlin and Harvey were heirs to decades of theorizing about the danger of thinking too hard, and the multitude of instances cited in treatises, magazine articles, and home-cure remedy collections of death by thinking. In 1807, the *Monthly Anthology and Boston Review* had outlined the hazard with respect to the death of a man of scholarly reputation, reporting that "several days antecedent to the one of his death, the deceased had been so immersed in the depths of meditation, as not only to neglect the calls of his friends, but unable to take either sustenance or sleep." He was preoccupied with "*A dissertation on the Elements of our Tongue; in which it is ingeniously insisted, that the Alphabet has been reversed, in the order it now stands, and ought for the honor of letters to be restored to its native position.*" Deeply engrossed in the provocative thesis of the book, the man died from excessive exercise of the mind. Suffering from a similar malaise, the popular antebellum lecturer Mrs. Oakes Smith was said to have become disfigured by her exertions. According to the *Liberator,* "each of her features was good, yet she was by no means handsome; and she found the reason to be in her early culture and over-tasked brain, which had destroyed the health of the body, and had given her fine features the expression of pain." Religious magazines claimed that ministers were especially prone to the condition. Taking a more general tack, George S. Hilliard, addressing the Mercantile Library Association in 1850, voiced his alarm that "one quarter, at least, of the young men who are educated at our colleges leave them with impaired health." With such difficulties in mind, the new Unitarian prayerbook in 1857 proposed a special prayer for "Mental Rest." And popular magazines distilled the lesson into simple language: "So close is the immediate connection between mind and body, that the former cannot be over-exerted without the latter feeling the baneful effect of the undue excitement."[8]

Medical publications increasingly addressed the prevention and cure of overthinking. The first American edition of *The Book of Health: A Compendium of Domestic Medicine* (1830) advised that in order to avoid stroke "it will be of considerable advantage to avoid any strong or long-continued exertion of the mind." Writings specifically on mental illness were even more explicit, identifying "intense application of the mind," especially through "intense study," as a cause of insanity, and explaining in detail the physiological processes by which too much thinking led to insanity and death. Thomas Stuart and others, building upon the theories of Benjamin Rush, proposed that inordinate thinking produced an overabundance of blood in the brain, so that other parts of the body suffered shortages. "Excessive exertion of mind," Stuart argued, "long continued, or often repeated, soon affects the organs of digestion, and hence frequently originates that distressing mental complaint, well-denominated tristimania." And, Stuart pointed out, the condition was not confined to persons engaged in academic or scholarly investigation. Anyone could succumb to a disease of the mind as a result of excessive exercise of the mind, regardless of their background or the subject of their concern. Religious thinking, especially, could lead to outbreaks of insanity and severe physical debilitation. Stuart called such a condition "Amenomania." In the years after the Civil War, the West Virginia Hospital for the Insane was still admitting persons for "excessive thinking about religion." [9]

Of all the species of excessive thinking, the most dangerous occurred in children. *Gleason's Pictorial* featured an article on "Precocity of Intellect" in 1851 that described that condition as "often a mere manifestation of disease. The disease of a very fine but weak nervous organization." The *Massachusetts Teacher* observed that "early mental culture" that cultivated "precocity" was "unnatural." Young children were incapable of much mental exertion, and the magazine warned parents not to "force intellectual acquirements upon their tender minds, at the risk of exciting the nervous system, injuring the brain, and undermining the constitution." Elsewhere it stressed: "Children must not be taught too much too soon," claiming that early mental labor "destroys originality and substitutes an unreal and insipid taste, and unconscious hypocrisy." The proof of this, said the *Trumpet and Universalist*, was that "experience demonstrates that of any number of children of equal intellectual powers, those . . . who do not begin to learn to read and write until their constitution begins to be consolidated . . . very soon surpass in their studies those who commenced earlier, and read numerous books when very young." Americans who read the 1837 American edition of *The Economy of Health*, a book by an English physician, knew that "in infancy, the mind presides over, and furnishes energy to, every other organ and function in the body. If it were possible to bring intellectual operations into play in the mind of an infant, the brain could not provide the proper nervous power for digestion, assimilation, and nutrition; and the whole machine would languish or decay." This principle held true throughout the first fourteen years of life and explained "the havoc that is produced in youthful frames by premature exertion of the intellectual faculties!" The *Christian Observer* thought that the critical period was, on the other hand, "especially after the twelfth or fourteenth year," when "the process of education is driven forward with a rapidity that is dangerous both to the mental and physical health." Accordingly, said *Ballou's*, "it is imperative not to omit the importance of keeping their brains fallow as it were for several of the first years of their existence. The mischief perpetuated by a contrary course, in the shape of bad health, peevish temper, and developed vanity, is incurable." In an attempt to place the matter in a nutshell, the *Massachusetts Teacher* eventually concluded that a child's mind, like any mind, could simply become overstuffed.

Citing Joseph Priestley, the magazine declared that "the mind grows callous to new impressions continually; it being already occupied with ideas and selections which render it indisposed to receive others, especially of a heterogeneous nature." Parents and teachers nevertheless were obliged to cultivate the "mental culture" of children.[10]

Theorizing about catenations between emotion and the body proceeded in ways similar to that involving intellection. Emotion, after all, was interlocked with thinking and will in the Scottish philosophy that had become so influential, so it was only natural that the physical condition of the body be subject to the influence of feeling, and vice versa. Arguments representing that relationship often began with attempts to list or define emotions. While admitting that the terms "emotion," "passion," and "affection" were somewhat slippery (and imbricated), American writers nevertheless did not hesitate to expound upon them. Peter Townsend proposed that "a passion, in strict language, however, means sudden and violent commotion of the mind, accompanied and distinguished by certain preternatural phenomena of the voice, gesture, or expression," and he listed the passions as joy, anger, grief, and fear. But he acknowledged many different varieties of these passions, constructing a complicated table of their manifestations, as, in the case of anger, from disagreeable to furious to mad to outrageous, and so forth. And in the end, he argued that emotions were in fact feelings but positioned midway along a "chain unbroken between simple feeling and passion." Other writers simply referred to emotion, and did not attempt to map the differences between passion and emotion. Cooke's 1853 treatise on the mind and the emotions listed the latter as joy, grief, hope, fear, jealousy and envy, desire, anger, humility, pride, sympathy and pity, hatred, and love. Other writers, sometimes in the service of legitimating Anglo-Saxonism, went to considerable effort to stress ambition as well. No matter what theoretical distinctions might or might not be made between passions, emotions, feelings, and affections, the significance of these lists is in their simple, straightforward testimony to American willingness to consider feelings independently of the feeler, to walk along the path that would eventually arouse opposition in the form of Alfred North Whitehead's reactionary insistence, a century later, that a feeling cannot be abstracted from a feeler. The most dramatic expression of this antebellum American exercise of listing the passions was the publication and reception of Albert Brisbane's interpretation of Charles Fourier's ideas. The book contained a two-foot by two-foot beautifully engraved foldout diagram entitled: "Synoptical Table of the Functions of the Human Passions."[11]

The relative relaxation of judgment about the value or desirability of specific passions was integral to the process of their abstraction. Bostonians who came to a performance of *The Passions: A Poem Pronounced at the Odeon, December 28, 1835* heard that "the passions are our heritage." Such a viewpoint was indebted to Benjamin Rush and his disciples, who had made the case in earlier decades for a positive view of the passions. These earlier writers never denied the pain and suffering caused by passion. "Excessive grief," wrote Rush, echoing William Buchan's popular manual *Domestic Medicine,* "is the most destructive to health," and "melancholy, originating from religious terror, is truly deplorable." John Stearns, president of the Medical Society of the State of New York, told an audience in 1821 that "violent anger affects the liver with a spasm, and causes a regurgitation of bile into the stomach and immediate vomiting," which then could lead to depression, melancholy, and hypochondriasis. But a passion such as joy could also, as George Brewer wrote, give "health to the body," and Buchan counseled his physician readership not to "neglect to administer that greatest of all cordials, hope." [12]

In fact, many early nineteenth-century writers believed that the passions could be both good and bad for the body. Henry Rose explained that "the passions are necessary and natural parts of our constitution," and "as to the body, they preserve the health of that . . . as an agency and stimulus to the support of life." Rush himself, borrowing freely from the philosophical and medical vocabulary of Enlightenment in Edinburgh, set out the clearest statement of theory governing the usefulness of the passions. In *Three Lectures upon Animal Life* (1799), he wrote that motion was essential to life, and that "excitability denotes that property in the human body, by which motion is excited." Observing that "life is the effect of certain stimuli acting upon the . . . excitability," he concluded that "the passions pour a constant stream [of stimuli] upon the wheels of life," and, accordingly, are part of the "animal oeconomy." Rush theologized that "in the original constitution of our human nature, we were made to be stimulated by such passions and emotions only as have moral good for their objects," such as hope, love, and joy. However, "by the loss of his innocence, [man] . . . has subjected himself to the dominion of passions and emotions of a malignant nature; but they possess, in common with such as are good, a stimulus which renders them subservient to the purpose of promoting animal life." Accordingly, both good passions and bad passions were valuable, or, as Rush explained, "the effects of good passions and emotions, in promoting health and longevity, have been taken notice by many writers. . . . There are instances likewise of persons who have derived strength, and long life, from the influences of the evil passions and emotions." [13]

Alexander Anderson, Joseph Parrish, and Edward Cutbush reinforced Rush's conclusions about the positive role of both good passions and bad passions. They prescribed fear as a means of rousing a sick person from bed, and noted that terror in some instances raised the pulse sufficiently to pump blood to areas of the body—including the brain—suffering from a lack of it. They also explored the ways in which good passions could in fact lead to undesirable consequences. Drawing upon roughly the same body of anecdotal evidence, they repeated stories about persons who died from an overdose of joy after suddenly acquiring a great fortune, or hearing the news of a military victory. But all of this theorizing remained grounded in an understanding of the passions that had traded an essentialist notion of their existence—that they were either fundamentally good or bad—for one that rested on contingency and utility. Passions were means by which the body was excited into action, and therefore integral to the life of the human organism. "The passions," Buchan wrote, "have a great influence both in the cause and cure of diseases." Throughout life, including in old age, the body was stimulated through "the uncommon activity of certain passions. These are either good or evil." As James Pendleton summarized the matter, "Life, therefore, is excitement, and all the phaenomena in health, predisposition, and disorder, are entirely referable to the same cause."[14]

Philosophers and medical theorists were aware of their innovations in depicting the passions, but they were quick to credit the genius of the Creator for the extraordinary plan whereby "the <u>continuance</u> of human life, no less than its commencement" was made possible. Rush wrote that "some of the stimuli which produce animal life, are derived from the moral and physical evils of the world. From beholding these instruments of death thus converted by divine skill into the means of life, we are led to believe goodness to be the supreme attribute of the deity." This canopy of theology hung over thinking about the passions throughout the nineteenth century, and continued to shape understandings of passion in the popular imagination. Negative connotations to passion by no means disappeared: magazines such as the *Youth's Companion* ran stories such as "The Child Who Dies in a Passion," in which a three-year-old "flew into a rage," popped a blood vessel, and died. And the *Boston Evening Transcript* frequently connected tragedy with passion, as in a report headlined "Melancholy Occurrence," relating the suicide-by-razor of a man "under temporary insanity." But thinking about the passions sometimes merged more subtly with older theological traditions, yielding a positive outlook. The *American Baptist Magazine*, like other religious periodicals, presented pain and suffering as positive experiences, in which the moral benefits of suffering were blended with positive physical consequences of the "excitement." Typical was the story of a minister afflicted with acute back pain, who, at times, "under the <u>severe goadings</u> of these actual thorns in the flesh, <u>he should rise superior to pain</u>, and actually derive from it <u>an additional excitement</u> to his accustomed eloquence in preaching, and deliver on such occasions some of the most brilliant of his discourses."[15]

As various antebellum literatures reinforced linkages between physiology and thinking/emotion, they also eroded traditional notions of those activities as disembodied enterprises. Thinking and feeling increasingly were situated within a web of materialist assumptions, a positioning that progressively leached from them their subjectivist colorings and left them increasingly objectified, abstracted from a prior construction of self that had romanticized at least some of them as "a ray of divinity." Those materialist assumptions were to grow into a full-fledged religious and philosophical doctrine in the late nineteenth century, and would come to be understood in a precise rendering, "things are thoughts"/"thoughts are things," two sides of the same coin minted by Phineas Parkhurst Quimby, Mary Baker Eddy, and numerous other innovators in the nineteenth century, and by Emmet Fox, O. S. Marden, Dale Carnegie, and, in its most sophisticated form, by Norman Vincent Peale's program of "positive thinking" in the twentieth. Against such a background certain expressions took on more complex meanings, as in a report in Boston's *Ballou's Pictorial* in 1857: "ABSENCE OF MIND.—The latest case of absence of mind is that of a young lady, who, on returning from a walk with her lover, the other evening, rapped him on the face and bid goodbye to the door." A mind could be misplaced much like a pair of mittens. So could emotions, which, like thoughts, also were conceived as "things," as embodied phenomena abstractable from more ethereal notions of self.[16]

HEART AND BLOOD AND EMOTION

The practice of medicine in America was uneven in quality, poorly regulated or entirely unregulated depending on the community, and, in the eyes of at least one early-nineteenth-century critic, Dr. John Goodman, two centuries behind where it should have been. There are few clear indications of the extent of medical knowledge in the early nineteenth century, especially outside of academic and professional circles. In 1807, the *Monthly Anthology and Boston Review* published a long letter from an American visitor to Italy in which the author made fun of European artists for their paintings of saints holding their head or their heart in their hands. One indication of the popular understanding of medicine is imbedded in the fact that the author took the trouble to pronounce two such paintings, St. Dennis and Charles Borromeo, to be "absurd," because it was impossible to walk a mile holding one's severed head. American medicine itself sometimes worked like a charm, as in the case of young Israel Lombard, who in suburban Boston in 1848 had two teeth surgically removed while under the influence of chloroform, all the while "unconscious of pain" and suffering "nothing from after effects except a little nausea." Americans, following the examples of Europeans, also indulged in highly questionable medicine. Susan Heath of Brookline, like many other American women, frequently self-medicated with arsenic for an assortment of ailments. Questionable treatments for any number of health complaints were widely available in the cities, in a smorgasbord of therapies. Cleveland in 1851 boasted two medical colleges, one allopathic and one homeopathic, a wide range of traditional medical practices, and a water-cure establishment, among other options. In Boston, the Suffolk District Medical Society believed the range of medical practices to be far too broad, and proposed expelling from the society anyone describing their method as homeopathic, allopathic, antipathic, hydropathic, botanic, eclectic, analeptic," or any other sort of doctor" not part of the "communion of the Medical Church Catholic." Other complaints about treatment were more pointed. The *Liberator* in 1853 accused doctors of indecency with female patients, asserting that "God has decreed that every man shall have his wife, free from mercenary or other pollution, and no tampering of the medical faculty can for a moment be permitted. . . . The female shrinks from the corrupting touch of hireling corrupters." Mary Mudge of Boston wrote in her diary the following year about a relative who was raped by a doctor during a tooth extraction.[17]

The search for principles governing all disease dominated early-nineteenth-century medical theorizing. The most important of these principles set forth by investigators focused on connections between the mind and body. John Vaughan stated it as follows: "When a problem is traced to its connection between mind and body, it has arrived to the <u>ultimatum</u> or <u>ne plus ultra</u> of physiological investigation."[18] Therapy focused on the nature of that connection, and strove to expedite it, especially by promoting balance between body and mind, thinking and feeling, or specific organs such as the brain and the heart. "Curing," wrote John Bell in a book that influenced doctors and religionists throughout the nineteenth century, "consists in reestablishing the disturbed harmony . . . to reestablish the equilibrium which is lost in some part of the body." Medical practitioners often sought to raise, lower, or relocate "excitement" in the body as the pathway to harmony. Favored means of accomplishing this goal included cantharides, also known as Spanish fly, which, when rubbed upon the skin raised blisters, which, in turn, were lanced, giving up the toxins that upset organismic balance. John Parker Gough argued that "the good effects of the blisters" depended "upon the stimulus or impression which they excite." The appropriate number of cantharides excited the skin into blisters that would balance an excitement in the body elsewhere, or "counteract excitement existing in other parts of the system." Around the house, one might fall back on a mustard and cayenne poultice, but, as Charlotte Foster discovered, it sometimes "did not draw." Bell favored the use of magnets, especially arranged around the head in various configurations of polarities, because "bodies act and react upon each other. That from such an action and reaction, well-directed, results the harmony which prolongs their existence." The cure of insanity, in any of its various types—mania, melancholy, and so forth—rested largely upon disrupting the system with distractions, "to neutralize the attention of the mind," through stories, amusements, music, or if those proved unsuccessful, through more violent distraction brought on by the administration of purgatives. Such technique was designed to interrupt an inappropriate influence of the body on the mind.[19]

Bleeding was widely practiced in the early nineteenth century. Benjamin Rush vigorously promoted it, identifying circulation as the best marker of "excitement" in the system, and teaching that bleeding was required when vascular tension was too high. For Rush and his followers, an overabundance of blood in the system proved too much of an excitement, and could overwhelm the internal organs, including, as in the case of the child who died of stroke, the brain. In spite of Rush's well-publicized failures to stem the spread of infectious fevers during several urban outbreaks, American physicians treated patients by letting their blood. Jacob Porter of Plainfield, Massachusetts, like other doctors, recorded numerous cases of bleeding in his medical journal. One case involved an emotionally overwrought man "seized with a most violent fit," and "deprived of reason." Porter bled 24 ounces, and then later in the day, 12 ounces, then later 6 more ounces. Subsequently the patient appeared "deranged and comatose. I bled him again," and the next night "I was now obliged to have recourse to two moderate bleedings." Throughout the nineteenth century similar bleedings took place on an everyday basis, sometimes by a doctor in the home, sometimes in the barber shop or general store.[20]

In treating emotional disorders—and a great many persons were diagnosed with disorders such as hysteria and mania—doctors sometimes relied on bleeding, at other times on camphor, ammonium, garlic, cold water, angelica, cantharides, and other remedies. Sometimes, however, they prescribed a passion as a remedy, and provided instructions on how to raise that passion in the mind. A dose of fear or anger could raise a melancholy person from his bed, or cause a hysterical woman to cease trembling. For fear, Cutbush suggested throwing a person into cold water. For Anderson, "the judicious administration of hope and joy demands particular notice." When Benjamin Rush prescribed a dose of joy to a young man with symptoms of depression, he suggested that it be administered through rides in an open carriage filled with attractive young women. Cutbush agreed, but added, "they are known to have a greater power of animating the dejected; except, when they are the cause of the complaint." Over time, the perceived connection of emotional states to health was more pronounced, so that by mid-century, psychosomatic illness, understood as the product of an overly excited imagination, was thought by some to be the culprit in the majority of complaints. *Ballou's* captured the drift of this thinking in "The Will and the Health" in 1856: "Perhaps in eight cases of sickness out of ten, the disorder is brought on by the morbid and excited imagination of the victim. Intense fear of disease is sufficient to produce it, and in the sickly seasons of the year, we cannot too powerfully exert our will to banish apprehension."[21]

The coupling of emotion to the health of the body was articulated more precisely in discourse about the heart, the traditional seat of emotion. James Pendleton wrote that "when we reflect that the passions depend on a mechanical power, we may readily see why they are attached to the heart, where the greatest action exists." The experience of passion was correlated with an excessive amount of blood in the heart—and comparatively little in the head. "The passions depend on a mechanical force, " wrote Pendleton, "or a flux of blood to the heart, that stifles or weakens the intellectual power. . . . If a beautiful woman is presented to my view, the heart is instantly excited, and the mind remains inactive or is incapable of a correct examination into her merit and the propriety of the attachment." But as Rush pointed out, "the brain repays the heart for the blood that it sends it." That is, the brain, when properly nourished with blood, processes the stimuli that in turn excite the body into emotion or passion. The interconnection of blood, brain, and heart was described by Rush as a continuous series of actions and responses within the system: "This view of the reaction of the mind upon the body, accords with the simplicity of other operations of the animal oeconomy."[22]

Just as the brain could languish in the presence of a beautiful woman, so also could the heart become debilitated if too much blood was present in the head. Thinking too much, as we have seen, could be fatal. Bostonians read of the case of a man who thought so hard that his heart shriveled into a block of hard tissue. The dissection revealed that "the heart, it seems, was so contracted and indurated, as to make it next to impossible to perforate it with the instruments for the occasion. . . . The pillars, walls, and in fact all the parts of this organ were petrified and colourless, and when held up in sections for examination, reminded the spectators of some specimens of marble." Toward mid-century, as businessmen more commonly were accused of hard-heartedness, the explanation of the businessman's heart attack drew freely on the model of the marble heart. By 1859, when the *Boston Evening Transcript* story "Sudden Death of a Merchant" stressed the cause of death as "pericarditis," the paper's readership knew full well that merchants were more prone to such disease than others.[23]

The heart was the seat of character. The *Boston Medical Intelligencer* advised physicians to examine the heart in order to know the quality of a person's character. Affirming that "an accomplished physician is a most efficient auxiliar of morality and public order," the magazine stressed that doctors "should analyze the heart, ascertain the constituents of the moral agent, explore the secret springs of motion." And with confidence born of decades of collaboration between philosophy, theology, and medicine, it asserted that "medical cannot be separated from moral science, without reciprocal and essential mutilation." *Parlor Magazine* noted in 1846 that "a weak body is often found connected to an infirm will," and "a timid, desponding temperament with an irresolute, faltering, doubting heart." Accordingly it was important to strengthen the heart both by exercise—by sports, weightlifting, and gymnastics, the importance of which we already have seen—and by "educating" it. The *Massachusetts Teacher* stressed that "the first eight or ten years of life should be devoted to the education of the heart,—to the formation of principles rather than the requirement of what is usually termed knowledge." It observed that university learning faded, but not "the simple lessons of the home, enamelled upon the heart of childhood." Home, Bostonians knew, was the laboratory of the heart, where parents' love "flowed" to their children, where a child "enlarged the hearts" of the parents, where the "home-heart" was most effectively exercised, stretched, and tested, strengthened and improved, and where a man was truly human, for without a home "his heart, at least, the very fountain of life, is dead."[24]

The embodying of emotion in this way both refocused and reinforced traditional notions of the heart as the vessel of emotion. In nineteenth-century Boston, a person could have a "king's heart" or a "pope's heart," a woman ought to be able to "give her heart to the object of her choice," and Boston itself was "the stout heart of New England . . . sending out the life-blood of her religious faith and institutions to the rest of the nation." The exploitation of the metaphor "heart" in such images appears at a glance little different from language utilized for hundreds, even thousands of years, from the Peripatetics to Thomas Aquinas to the Puritans, who, as historian Norman Pettit pointed out, took the heart as "metonym" for the self. In the nineteenth century, however, traditional usage was overlapping with new conceptualizations of emotion, the excitability of the body, and the heart. Virginia Brereton, in a history of nineteenth-century conversion narratives, has written that in antebellum times the heart "moved into particular prominence and was especially closely connected with emotion and tears." By mid-century the heart was at once a representation of emotion imagined as a soulful, spiritual, mysterious, and romantic force, and a reference to the physical aspects of feeling, to emotion conceived as a matter of blood, vascular tension, organismic equilibrium, and pumping. Bostonians chose to overlook the potential contradictions in such an understanding, and, in fact, carried on as if a conjunction of the two (emotion as soul *and* emotion as body) was in fact a revelation, part of the progressive unfolding of the divine plan for mankind.[25]

In an attempt to make one theory from two, and visibly straining in so doing, the *New Englander* explained in 1853 that "the brain is admitted to be the seat of the mind—the ground of consciousness; and consequently the soul employs it, as the medium of its operations. Hence itself, and the ramifications of the nervous system, become the vehicle of thought and emotion." Accordingly, "the nervous system, constituting the link that united body and spirit, was made mainly for the purpose of being affected by the latter," and "is thus the vehicle of emotion." Such language figured an almost impossibly complex phenomenon—brain, consciousness, soul, nervous system, thought, and emotion all "seated," or "employed," serving as a "vehicle," or "linking," or being a "medium of operations" or a "ground." But for Protestants comfortable with a notion of Christian godhead as three-in-one—and for Unitarians as well, who embraced paradox even if they rejected Trinitarianism—such a characterization of emotion did not require a heroic leap of imagination. The construction of emotion as both soul and body, as both an airy spiritual essence and the raw physical business of organismic functioning, proved serviceable within the cultural contexts of white middle-class urban life. Like Jacob Potter, who put his trust in science and its laws of nature but also believed in unicorns, or John Smith, who waged a campaign to root out "adulterated science" from the practice of medicine but was certain that the mind was immaterial, middle-class Protestants in Boston approached emotion from two sides. And they exploited the frictive aspect in that construction of emotion as part of a performance of revival.[26]

Emotion and the Common Sense Philosophy

Philosophical discourse about emotion reinforced medical theorists' claims for embodied emotion by arguing for the inseparability of emotion, intellect, and will. By interlocking emotion with thinking and doing in the faculty triumvirate of the mind, and by describing mental activity as the product of sensory stimulation, they assured that emotion would not be set aside as ethereal spiritual essence, and they provided a conceptual platform for asserting the crucial relevance of emotion to judgment and choice. Most importantly, they linked feeling to thinking, which meant that, like thinking, the brain and nervous system somehow were involved in emotion. American disciples of Scottish philosophy aggressively pursued these issues in print and in the lecture hall, disseminating the "faculty psychology" widely across a middle-class audience, and profoundly influencing the curriculum at Protestant seminaries. Its importance for the Businessmen's Revival lies in its informing an understanding of emotion as a mental process subject to scientific investigation and analysis, an artifact of organic existence, phenomenon as much as noumenon.

VIBRATIONS AND LAWS

"After 1850," wrote H. M. Gardiner in his history of Western theories of emotion, "the hypothesis of a non-physiological mind or soul becomes extremely difficult to hold. . . . The central theories of feeling and emotion become *central psychophysiological theories.*" The Scottish Common Sense philosophy was an important step toward that reorientation of theory in the United States. Thinking, feeling, and doing, or, as such activities were spoken of at the time, intellect, emotion, and will, formed the centerpiece of American discussion about mind in the early nineteenth century. Such discussion was commonly said, in fact, to be about "the science of mind," as it had been established by Scottish philosophers late in the previous century. Most important were Thomas Reid, Dugald Stewart, and Thomas Brown, and their predecessor, David Hartley, whose *Observations on Man* (1749), with its emphasis on "vibratiuncles," or traces of sensory "vibration" in the brain, broke the ground for physiological interpretations of the activities of the mind. All physiological theories rested on the delineation of the pathways linking physical sensation to mental processes of thinking, feeling, and willing. For Common Sense philosophers, the "laws of association" authorized an assortment of mental operations that proceeded from stimulation of the senses to moral judgment and action. Emotion played a central role in the process. For the Scots, empirical philosophy, which held that perception arose through the receipt of impressions, lacked an explanation for the process of human judgment of value and therefore could not provide a motive to action. Rejecting John Locke's *tabula rasa,* they held that by principles of common sense, or "laws of association" that structured the workings of the mind, cognition was conformed to perception of objects. For them, moral distinctions were self-evident intuitions, or feelings. Those feelings, in turn, served as motives for moral action. Common Sense thinkers remained staunchly empiricist, frequently praising Baconian method and affirming their faith in the idea of a universe governed by scientifically detectable physical and moral laws. Invoking the laws of association, they sought to institute the science of observing consciousness. Scottish philosophers and their many disciples in France, England, and America consequently focused their attention on faculty psychology. In books such as Stewart's *Elements of the Philosophy of the Human Mind* and Brown's *Lectures on the Philosophy of the Human Mind,* and numerous other works, Scots divided the mind into three parts: (1) intellect, sometimes called reason or the understanding; (2) the will; and (3) the emotions, sometimes referred to as "susceptibilities" or "passions."[1]

Emotion lay at the very heart of the process of perception, intertwined with intellectual functions, yet adding to perception a quality that reason lacked. As Brown wrote: "But without the emotions which accompany them, of how little value would the mere intellectual functions had been? . . . By our other mental functions, we are mere spectators of the machinery of the universe, living and inanimate; by our *emotions* we are admirers of nature, lovers of man, adorers of God."[2] Reason pointed out the possible consequences of actions, and the will provided volition, but it was emotion that provided the motive for action. In the Scottish system, moral action was conjoined with feeling, and the emotions, true to their Latin root (*emovere:* "to move"), animated persons, moving them to moral action. The Scottish system found rich soil for its growth in America.[3] As the tradition was absorbed on this side of the Atlantic, it acquired a distinctly American cast as it came to terms with Edwardsian notions of the religious affections, but there is no mistaking the extent to which Common Sense infused American thought. And as it did so, it fostered a materialistic perspective on emotion, a view of emotion through the lens of physiology. Philadelphian Edward Cutbush, footnoting Hartley's *Observations on Man,* distilled Scottish thought into a simple formula and rested his medical dissertation upon it: "All our mental operations, all our thoughts, passions, sensations, and exertions are accompanied with corresponding motions and vibrations of which, although the nature is obscure, the existence cannot be doubted."[4]

In 1836, *Boston Monthly Magazine*, reviewing Dr. Daniel Oliver's inaugural address on his assuming a professorship at Dartmouth College, enthused that "the science of intellectual and moral philosophy"—terminology commonly employed at that time to identify the Scottish emphases—was nothing less than "the tree of knowledge in the garden of God, and all other sciences are its fruits; and in proportion to the vigor and life of the tree, is the abundance and richness of its bearings." All persons were drawn naturally to the study of mind almost from the moment of birth: "the principles, powers and capacities of the mind is a subject of reasoning to the infant as soon as he can compare and arrange his thoughts. . . . In every age, amongst the learned or unlearned, mental philosophy is a study to a greater or lesser extent." The magazine, perhaps in coy fashion seeking to excite interest in this style of philosophy, nevertheless complained that Americans had been slow to take up the study of mind in a systematic way, lamenting that "we have as yet crept pitifully along the pathway of the English and Scotch metaphysicians."[5] The complaint in any event would have been news to John Perkins, who like Oliver was a physician, and who thirty-five years earlier had arranged selections from Stewart in his notes under "Use. Knowledge Excerpts."[6] It also would have surprised many other writers, including Fenwick, Smith, Stuart, Peter Townsend, T. R. Beck, George Hayward, and their mentor, Benjamin Rush, as well as Rush's compatriot in the American Enlightenment, Thomas Jefferson, and a host of other Americans who regularly cited Scots in their writings.[7] It would have made no sense in later years to Theodore Parker, who before a large audience in the Boston Music Hall on the afternoon of February 14, 1858 outlined the Scottish faculty psychology with a practiced hand, emphasizing "an intellectual part . . . an emotional part . . . and . . . the practical part."[8] Parker's colleague James Freeman Clarke understood the Scottish "law of association," and did not hesitate to invoke it. His informed audience included boys from the Boston YMCA, whose library in 1855 included all the important works of Stewart, Brown, and Reid. Overseers and friends of the Boston school system stated their beliefs in distinctly Scottish terms: "The object of the school is to develop mind, to discipline the feelings, to give persistency to the will." The *Massachusetts Teacher* in the 1850s referred to the "science of mind" as a code for Scottish thought, and in case anyone did not understand, it published articles such as "The Scottish Training System" that spelled out the connections between the Common Sense philosophy and the education of children, and short features such as a prayer to be said every morning at school that implored, "strengthen the faculties of our minds." The preeminent message carried by such references involved the crucial role of emotion, and especially the mastery of "the principles which indicate the nature of emotion."[9]

PRIORITIZING FACULTIES

Some theological writers in America found a potential danger in the Scottish emphasis on three interrelated faculties of mind, and so attempted to explain the sequence of thought in a way that would identify the stages in chronological order. Such projects were not a significant part of the mainstream of theological and philosophical discussion until the late nineteenth century, when fresh language was invented to shape the issue. Nevertheless, concern about the priority of intellect over emotion, or vice versa, was unmistakable in religious-flavored magazines such as the orthodox *New Englander*, which published the following in 1859: "Man is made to be affected by truth, and, most of all, by religious truth. But he must apprehend a truth before he can feel in view of it. One can evidently have no emotion respecting that of which he knows nothing. And it is equally clear that a truth . . . will most powerfully tend to awaken emotion, when most clearly perceived."[10] More common, however, were statements asserting more complex connections between intellect and emotion, or, as Benjamin Waterhouse wrote in 1786, "the aptitude to understanding is a dead power in man, when not vivified by the passions." Over the years, commentators directed themselves with increasing vigor to working out the details of the relationship, but Waterhouse's phrase, expropriated from European writers, remained the coin of the realm, with relatively little adjustment, as in the remark of a writer in 1848 that "the fruit of the brain, unaided by the heart, will be a cold, lifeless philosophy that deserves not to prevail." Other writers offered theories on how the emotions themselves were awakened, including, as we shall see, by the feelings of other persons.[11]

When twenty-eight-year-old ex-sailor George Scandlin of Boston referred in his journal during the 1850s to his "feelings and thoughts which pervade the mind and heart," he was expressing the general sense of connection among the various faculties. So too was Tracy Patch Cheever, who noted in his diary in 1851 "the power of the will when directed by love." Both would have agreed with a magazine article proclaiming that "the mind is a unit, and however we may analyze and subdivide its powers, we cannot address and develop any one faculty independently. They are so interlaced that the right culture of any one in some measure quickens and develops others also."[12] Bostonians such as Scandlin and Cheever by the mid-nineteenth century increasingly were invested in the notion that emotion was the motive to action and was required for thinking, and that a person with limited affect, a person who did not experience a full range of emotion (however one might identify such a person) was incapable of coherent thought, or as the popular magazine *Ballou's Pictorial* opined: "Every man without passions has within him neither principle, action, nor motive to act." Elsewhere this creed was expressed as the centrality of "emotion or excitement to our feelings," which "influences our will in favor of a certain object." The conservative *New Englander*, however, added that "if this decision of the moral faculty is to be called an emotion, for the sake of distinguishing it from an act of the intellect, it is nevertheless of a character widely different from other emotions."[13]

Notes

The following abbreviations are used in the notes:

AAS   American Antiquarian Society
BPL   Boston Public Library
CL   Congregational Library
HL   Houghton Library
LC   Library of Congress
MHS   Massachusetts Historical Society
SL   Schlesinger Library

INTRODUCTION

1. Meta-emotion refers to emotion about emotion (e.g., laughter when afraid, shame when embarrassed). See John M. Gottman, Lynn Fainsilber Katz, and Carole Hooven, *Meta-emotion: How families communicate emotionally* (Mahwah, NJ, 1997), 6–8.

2. See Appendix 2.

3. Otniel E. Dror, "Creating the Emotional Body: Confusion, Possibilities, and Knowledge," in *An emotional history of the United States*, ed. Peter N. Stearns and Jan Lewis (New York, 1998), 173–78.

4. Peter N. Stearns, *American cool: Constructing a twentieth-century emotional style* (New York, 1994), 68; Richard Rabinowitz, *The spiritual self in everyday life: The transformation of personal religious experience in nineteenth-century New England* (Boston, 1989), 188, 217–18. Grounded in the Cartesian conception of the self-defining subject and reinforced, in New England, in the Cartesian-flavored curriculum at Harvard in the seventeenth and early eighteenth centuries, the claim for emotion as spiritual subjectivity was forcefully stated in the burgeoning Protestant pietistic theology. Rick Kennedy, ed., *Aristotelian and Cartesian logic at Harvard: Morton's "Logick Sys-*

tem" and *Brattle's* "*Compendium of Logick*" (Charlottesville, 1995); Norman Fiering, *Moral philosophy at seventeenth-century Harvard* (Chapel Hill, NC, 1981).

5. See Appendix 3.

6. Thandeka, *The embodied self: Friedrich Schleiermacher's solution to Kant's problem of the empirical self* (Albany, 1995), 87–89; Charles Taylor, *Hegel* (Cambridge, UK, 1975), 8. The religious tradition that shaped much Boston Protestantism not only is rich with references to "religious affections," "spiritual feeling," and "holy emotions," but includes centuries of religious practices explicitly geared to mortify the flesh in order to fully realize those affections. From Augustine to Calvin to the Puritans who came to Massachusetts Bay, a strong current of disembodied emotion—in the latter cases perceptible in one form as iconoclasm—informed theological reflection and religious life. Puritan disembodying of emotion was represented in what Charles Lloyd Cohen has called "holy despair" (*God's caress: The psychology of Puritan religious experience* [New York, 1986], 123) and is apparent in the thinking of colonists Cotton Mather and Jonathan Edwards. The former worried incessantly about the deleterious effects of the flesh on the cultivation of the religious affections, and the latter produced several treatises in which religious feeling, while visible in deeds, remained "spiritualized," a transcendent quality of feeling, a "sense of the heart" that was distinguished from everyday emotions and ordinary perception (see Terrence Erdt, *Jonathan Edwards: Art and the sense of the heart* [Amherst, 1980]). Ideas associated with Descartes, John Wesley, and Friedrich Schleiermacher ("the feeling of absolute dependence") reinforced the conceptual linkages between religious experience, bodily discipline, and transcendent emotion. See Gregory S. Clapper, *John Wesley on religious affections: His views on experience and emotion and their role in the Christian life and theology* (Metuchen, NJ, 1989), 42–97; 127–53; Eugene E. White, *Puritan rhetoric: The issue of emotion in religion* (Carbondale, IL, 1972), 3–64. For an example of the embodying of emotion in this context see John Corrigan, *The prism of piety: Catholick Congregational clergy at the beginning of the Enlightenment* (New York, 1991). Emotion at the same time has a long history of embodiment, as the four humours (melancholic, sanguine, phlegmatic, choleric) and in other ways. For a discussion of embodied love see John R. Gillis, "From Ritual to Romance: Toward an Alternative History of Love," in *Emotion and social change: Toward a new psychohistory,* ed. Carol Z. Stearns and Peter N. Stearns (New York, 1988), 87–121. See also the reference to embodied emotion in Stearns, *American cool,* 66–67.

7. Daniel Walker Howe, *Making the American self: Jonathan Edwards to Abraham Lincoln* (Cambridge, MA, 1997), 260; Charles Rzepka, *The self as mind: Vision and identity in Wadsworth, Coleridge, and Keats* (Cambridge, MA, 1986), 26.

8. Ralph Waldo Emerson, "The Transcendentalist," in *Ralph Waldo Emerson: Essays and lectures* (New York, 1983), 193, 205–6.

9. Samuel L. Mitchell, "A Double Consciousness, or a Duality of Person in the Same Individual," *Medical Repository* 3 (1817), 185–86; Hubbard Winslow, *Elements of intellectual philosophy* (Boston, 1853), 350; Edward Hitchcock, *The religion of geology and its connected sciences* (Boston, 1854), 435; Francis Wayland, *The elements of intellectual philosophy* (Boston, 1855), 115, 423–26; John Abercrombie, *Inquiries concerning the intellectual powers, and the investigation of truth* (New York, 1859), 221, 222; Lucy Towne, "The Imaginative and the Historical," *Ladies Repository* 12 (1852), 49; Henry Adams, *The education of Henry Adams* (New York, 1931), 8, 9.

10. John Herdman, *The double in nineteenth-century fiction* (New York, 1991), 89, 94; Karl Miller, *Doubles: Studies in literary history* (Oxford, 1985), 154–66, 449 n. 5; Oliver Wendell Holmes, *Elsie Venner* (Cambridge, MA, 1861), 445, 356; Dorothy C. Broaddus, *Genteel rhetoric: Writing high culture in nineteenth-century Boston* (Charleston, SC, 1998); William S. Plumer, "Mary Reynolds: A Case of Double Consciousness," *Harper's* 20 (May 1860), 807–12; William Pratt Breed, *Anthropos* (Philadelphia, 1865), 65; William James, *Principles of psychology*, vol. 1 (New York, 1890), 294; W. E. B. Du Bois, *The souls of black folk* (New York, 1989), 3. Jackson Lears discusses how models of the body were connected with subjectivity in advertising in the Victorian "merger of intimacy and publicity" in *Fables of abundance: A cultural history of advertising in America* (New York, 1994), 137–61. For background on the post-structuralist conceptualization of self and identity as fragmented and uncentered, see Edward E. Sampson, "The Deconstruction of the Self," in *Texts of identity*, ed. John Schlotter and Kenneth J. Green (London, 1989); Marcel Mauss, "A Category of the Human Mind: The Notion of the Person; the Notion of the Self" and Charles Taylor, "The Person," in *The category of the person: Anthropology, philosophy, history*, ed. Michael Carrithers, Steven Collins, and Steven Lukes (Cambridge, UK, 1985).

11. Georg Lukács, *History and class consciousness*, trans. Rodney Livingstone (Cambridge, MA, 1971), 124.

12. As subjective and spiritual, emotion was ambiguous and evanescent. But for nineteenth-century Bostonians it was enormously valuable for those very reasons. Conceived simultaneously and paradoxically as an object commodity and as fugitive subjectivity, emotion served centrally in a scheme of commercial exchange at the same time that it represented immeasurable value. Indeed, for Bostonians, its crucial relevance to revival was precisely its representation of immense value even as they treated it as a commodity, perhaps not quite like the trade of butter, shoes, linen, or nails, but nevertheless as a commercially viable artifact.

ONE. THE BUSINESSMEN'S REVIVAL

1. *Evangelist and Religious Review* (June 24, 1858). The variety of ways in which the revival was titled can be seen in some of the books that addressed it:

Samuel I. Prime, *The New York pulpit in the revival of 1858. A memorial volume of sermons* (New York, 1858), and *The power of prayer illustrated in the wonderful displays of divine grace* (New York, 1858); William C. Conant, *Narratives of remarkable conversions and revival incidents* (New York, 1858); Talbot W. Chambers, *The noon prayer meeting of the north Dutch Church, Fulton Street, New York* New York, 1858); Rev. James W. Alexander, D.D., *The revival and its lessons: A collection of fugitive papers, having reference to the Great Awakening, 1858* (New York, 1858); Rev. Harvey Newcomb, *The harvest and the reapers* (Boston, 1858); *Old South Chapel prayer meeting: Its origins and history* (Boston, 1859); Pauline Holmes, *One hundred years of Mount Vernon Church 1842–1942* (Boston, 1942); Frank Grenville Beardsley, *Religious progress through religious revivals* (New York, 1943); Edward Norris Kirk, D.D., *Lectures on revivals* (Boston, 1875); William G. McLoughlin, *Modern revivalism: Charles Grandison Finney to Billy Graham* (New York, 1959); H. Crosby Englizian, *Brimstone Corner: Park Street Church Boston* (Chicago, 1968); J. Edwin Orr, *The fervent prayer: Worldwide impact of the Great Awakening of 1858* (Chicago, 1974); John D. Hannah, "The Layman's Prayer Revival of 1858," *Bibliotheca Sacra* 134 (1977), 59–73; Timothy L. Smith, *Revivalism and social reform: American Protestantism on the eve of the Civil War* (New York, 1965); Leonard I. Sweet, "'A true nation born again': The Union Prayer Meeting Revival and Cultural Revitalization," in *In the great tradition, in honor of Winthrop S. Hudson,* ed. Joseph D. Ban and Paul R. Dekar (Valley Forge, PA, 1982), 193–221. The best review of the historiography of the revival (with an emphasis on New York) is by Kathryn Long, "The Power of Interpretation: The Revival of 1857–58 and the Historiography of Revivalism in America," *Journal of Religion and American Culture* 4 (1994), 77–105.

2. *The semi-centennial celebration of the Park Street Church and Society held on the Lord's Day, February 27, 1859 with the festival on the day following* (Boston, 1861), 144; *Christian Parlor Magazine* 2 (December 1845), 250; *Christian Observatory* 3 (February 1849), 96; *Boston Recorder* 34 (February 16, 1849); *Independent* (January 16, 1851, March 13, 1856); Eliphay Arnold Jr., Diary, January 22, 1851, MHS; *Youth's Companion* 25 (April 15, 1852), 203; Arthur Howard Nichols, Diary, February 15, 1852, MHS; *Watchman-Examiner* 35 (January 26, 1854) and 36 (September 20, 1855) and 37 (October 23, 1856, September 4, 1856); *Evangelist and Religious Review* (May 24, 3, 1855, June 5, 1856, February 26, 5, 12, 1857); *Christian Observer* 34 (February 17, 1855).

3. Theodore Parker, *Two sermons of the moral and spiritual condition of Boston* (Boston, 1849), 52[?]; *Boston Recorder* 34 (January 12, 1849); *Evangelist and Religious Review* (January 1, 1857); *Independent* February 2, 9, 1860); *Watchman-Examiner* 37 (March 6, January 10, 1856). Final quotation is from "The Revival and Its Results," *Independent* (April 29, 1858).

4. Richard Carwardine, *Transatlantic revivalism: Popular evangelicalism in Britain and America, 1790–1865* (Westport, CT, 1978), 159–97; *Evangelist and Religious Review* (November 3, 1859); Phoebe Palmer, *Promise of the fa-*

ther (New York, 1985; originally published in Boston, 1859), 229, 231, 234; Orr, *Fervent prayer*, 6. Orr thinks that the revival began with Palmer in Hamilton, Ontario (2). Charles E. White wrote that "her ministry helped to reintroduce the concept of lay ministry to the church and touch off the awakening of 1858" ("Palmer, Phoebe Worrall," in *Dictionary of Christianity in America*, ed. Robert D. Linder, Bruce L. Shelley, and Harry S. Stout (Downers Grove, IL, 1990), 861. See also White, *The beauty of holiness: Phoebe Palmer as theologian, revivalist, feminist, and humanitarian* (Grand Rapids, MI, 1986), 42–43, 44. The Tuesday Meetings originally were for women, but were opened to men in 1839 and became the core of the holiness movement in the Methodist Episcopal Church.

5. *Old South Chapel prayer meeting*, 9–25, 33, 35, 42, 43; *Evangelist and Religious Review* (November 17, 1859).

6. *Zion's Herald and Wesleyan Journal* 28 (January 28, 1857); Garth M. Rosell and Richard A. G. Depuis, eds., *The memoirs of Charles Finney: The complete restored text* (Grand Rapids, MI, 1989), 559–72, 560 n. 6, 561 n. 10, 563 n. 19; Englizian, *Brimstone Corner*, 147, 148, 149; *Evangelist and Religious Review* (March 5, April 2, March 26, 1857); Frances Merritt, Journal, 1856–58, June 13, 1858, SL.

7. *Evangelist and Religious Review* (July 2, 1857); *Watchman-Examiner* 38 (March 19, 1857); Beardsley, *Religious progress through religious revivals*, 42.

8. Prime, *The power of prayer*, 18–21, 44; Chambers, *The noon prayer meeting*, 40, 47, 48; Rosell and Depuis, *The memoirs of Charles Finney*, 562, 14.

9. See the article by D. P. Pike in *God moves in mysterious ways: The revival in Newburyport and other cities in New England, in 1857–'58* (Newburyport, CT, 1858); *Evangelist and Religious Review* (June 24, 1858); *Congregationalist* (March 12, 1858), quoted in Rosell and Depuis, *The memoirs of Charles Finney*, 560 n. 6.

10. Susan E. P. Brown, Diary, July 5, 1857, AAS; *Evangelist and Religious Review* (July 23, 1857, July 8, 1858); Jacob Merrill Manning, Diary, November 29, December 18, 1857; Rosell and Depuis, *The Memoirs of Charles Finney*, 563, 561, 563 n. 19. Kirk's letter is quoted in *Memoirs*, 561 n. 11. *Boston Evening Transcript* (August 3, 1857, January 27, March 15, 1858, July 11, 1859).

11. Taylor preached to a full house of sailors at the Seaman's Chapel and elsewhere on the docks during the revival, and participated in the goings-on at Eastham, on the Cape. His opposition to the revival was only partial, and appears to have arisen from a perception of the insufficiency of heartfelt feeling in the meetings.

12. *Evangelist and Religious Review* (April 29, 1858); Orville Dewey, Diary, March 25, 1858; Ezra Stiles Gannett, Diary, March 22, April 21, May 5, 1858; *The Liberator* 28 (April 30, 1858), 70 and (April 16, 1858), 64 and (April 30, 1858), 72; *Boston Evening Transcript* (February 20, 1858).

13. *Evangelist and Religious Review* (May 6, 1858); Rosell and Depuis, *The Memoirs of Charles Finney*, 567 n. 35.

14. Rosell and Depuis, *The memoirs of Charles Finney*, 566–67; *The Liberator* 28 (September 24, 1858), 156.

15. *Boston Evening Transcript* (March 27, 1858); Theodore Parker, *The revival of religion which we need. A sermon, delivered at the Music Hall, Boston, on Sunday, April 11, 1858* (Boston, 1858). The *Evangelist and Religious Review* made it clear that Parker's sermon was in part a response to "himself, as having been made the subject of special remark and prayer at some of the 'Revival' meetings" (29 [April 29, 1858]). Parker's image as a gadfly had been permanently established through a speech he gave in 1855 against the consequences of the Fugitive Slave Act. The account of his arrest and the legal investigation of his speech are in Theodore Parker, *The trial of Theodore Parker, for the "MISDEMEANOR" of a speech in Faneuil Hall against kidnapping* (Boston, 1855).

16. *Puritan Recorder* 35 (March 7, 1850); *Boston Evening Transcript* (August 12, 1831); *Gleason's Pictorial* 1 (September 13, 1851), 313; *Evangelist and Religious Review* (August 21, 1856).

17. *Congregationalist* (November 19, 1858); *Manual for the use of the members of the Church of Christ in Leyden Chapel*, 191; *The Liberator* 28 (May 21, 1858), 84; William Gray Brooks, Diary, March 23, 1858.

18. F. D. Huntington, *Permanent realities of religion, and the present religious interest* (Boston, 1858), 28, 29–30, 40, 41. Huntington was outspoken against slavery, sermonized in support of the social and economic advance of women, and ultimately decided he could not accept the Unitarian position at Harvard. He resigned his Harvard post over the objections of the faculty and the president in 1860, eventually taking orders in the Episcopal Church on his way to becoming "First Bishop of Central New York" (Arria S. Huntington, *Memoir and letters of Frederic Dan Huntington* [Boston and New York, 1906], 127–29, 141, 209). Theodore Tebbetts and Richard Pike published companion pieces defending the revival, Tebbetts urging Unitarian support for it (see Smith, *Revivalism and social reform*, 71).

19. *Congregationalist* (November 19, 1858); William Gray Brooks, Diary, April 3, 1858; Rosell and Depuis, *The Memoirs of Charles Finney*, 562; *New Englander* 16 (August 1858), 663; Prime, *The power of prayer*, 57; Newcomb, *The harvest and the reapers*, 231; *Old South Chapel prayer meeting*, 61.

20. *Old South Chapel prayer meeting*, 120, 121–22, 9; William Gray Brooks, Diary, April 30, 1858; *Evangelist and Religious Review* (October 21, 1858); Frances Merritt, Journal, March 14, 1858[?]; *Congregationalist* (November 19, 1858). Samuel I. Prime, in *The power of prayer*, used language similar to Merritt's: "Thousands and thousands of businessmen drop all employment at a given hour and go to the house of prayer" (366). Accounts of large-scale conversions of heads of households in surrounding areas appeared well before the fall of 1857. For events in Abington see the *Evangelist and Religious Review* (April 2, 1857).

21. William Gray Brooks, Diary, March 6, 1858; Rosell and Depuis, *The Memoirs of Charles Finney*, 563 n. 20; Wilberforce, Toplady, Jay, Jenks, and

Bickersteth [no first names given], *Parlor devotions: Consisting of morning and evening prayers* (Boston, 1842), 199; *Watchman-Examiner* 38 (April 9, 1857).

22. See the almost daily entries in John Henry Kenneally, Diary, 1857; *Evangelist and Religious Review* (November 25, 1858, June 23, 1859, September 8, March 10, 1859); *The Old South Chapel prayer meeting*, 75. For Samuel Prime, proof of the revival as a work of the Holy Spirit and not the machinery of the clergy were reports that "even ships at sea were overtaken in mid-ocean" (*The power of prayer*, 61).

23. *Evangelist and Religious Review* (March 10, 1859); Jacob Merrill Manning, Diary, April 5, 1858; *Old South Chapel prayer meeting*, 77–78, 146, 156; *Youth's Companion* 32 (April 29, 1858), 68.

24. Kathryn Long has pointed out that women participated in the revival in New York City as much as and sometimes even more than men. See also Long's discussion of the roles of several female leaders in New York, especially Phoebe Palmer and Harriet Olney ("The Revival of 1857–58," 69, 71, 76–81).

25. Rosell and Depuis, *The Memoirs of Charles Finney*, 565, 564, 564 n. 22, 564 n. 22; Holmes, *One hundred years of Mount Vernon Church*, 68, 70, 71; *Old South Chapel prayer meeting*, 65, 62; Arthur Howard Nichols, Diary, March 22, 1852; *Evangelist and Religious Review* (October 21, 1858, June 23, 1859); *Boston Daily Advertiser* (April 9, 1858). For Mary Mudge, see her diary entries for the summer and fall of 1854. For Susan E. P. Brown, see her diary entries for 1857–58. For Catherine Flint, see her diary entries for 1858–59. Susan Heath, Diary, December 26, 1858.

26. George E. Ellis, *The re-action of a revival upon religion* (Boston, 1858), 31, 33.

27. *Christian Observatory* 3 (April, 1849), 186; F. D. Huntington, *Permanent realities of religion*, 19, 45; Newcomb, *The harvest and the reapers*, 237, 248; *Puritan Recorder* 35 (February 7, 1850); *The Liberator* 28 (May 21, 1858), 84.

28. Newcomb, *The harvest and the reapers*, 249; *The Old South Chapel prayer meeting*, 63; Jacob Merrill Manning, Diary, December 30, 1858; White, *The beauty of holiness*, 48–49; *Christian Advocate and Journal* (March 18, 1858); Hannah, "The Laymen's Prayer revival of 1858," 67.

29. Newcomb, *The harvest and the reapers*, 249;

30. Rev. James Porter, *Revivals of religion; their theory, means, obstruction, uses and importance* (Boston, 1849), 121; *The Old South Chapel prayer meeting*, 60, 13, 116, 62–63; Rosell and Depuis, *The memoirs of Charles Finney*, 565, 570; William Gray Brooks, Diary, March 23, 1858; Sweet, "'A true nation born again ,'" 201, 202. Sweet observes: "The penetration of the revival into all classes was part of a predetermined strategy" (201). *Evangelist and Religious Review* (January 6, 1859); *Boston Journal* (March 26, 1858); Chambers, *The noon prayer meeting*, 294, 125.

31. Sweet, "'A true nation born again'" 201. Examples of meetings for individual professions are in the book of clippings, "Great Awakening, 1858," CL. *Evangelist and Religious Review* (November 4, 1858).

32. Seth Bliss, *Letters to members of the American Tract Society, on the tract controversy* (Boston, 1858), 5; Sweet, "'A true nation born again'" 194, 209; *New Englander* 16 (August 1858), 650; Parker, *The revival of religion which we need*, 11. Moody is quoted in McLoughlin, *Modern revivalism*, 192. *Congregationalist* (November 19, 1858).

33. Instances of reports of the revival west of the Mississippi are in the *Boston Evening Transcript* (April 5, 1858) and the *Evangelist and Religious Review* (May 27, 1858). The *New York Daily Tribune* (April 24, 1854) is cited in Rosell and Depuis, *The Memoirs of Charles Finney*, 565 n. 26. William M. Baker, *The life and labors of the Reverend Daniel Baker, D. D.* (Philadelphia, 1858); *Evangelist and Religious Review* (April 29, 1858); Joshua Bradley, A.M., *Accounts of religious revivals in many parts of the United States from 1815 to 1818* (Albany, NY, 1819). The (tenuous) case for ongoing and significant revival activity in the antebellum South is in Iain H. Murray, *Revival and revivalism: The making and marring of American Evangelicalism 1750–1858* Edinburgh, 1994), 415–24. Compare Murray's view with Donald G. Mathews's assertion that there has been a "common assumption that revivals were the means by which Evangelical expansion took place. This assumption has yet to be demonstrated empirically, although most Evangelical ministers in the Old South swore it was true. The evidence of church growth does not, however, verify their belief. Churches proliferated throughout the South without mass meetings and mass conversions, establishing through less dramatic means the structures upon which the subsequent, more stylized revivals could be based. Evangelicals throughout the South were notoriously imprecise when they reported revivals. Checking membership figures against such reports, one finds that frequently a revival was nothing more than an affirmation by outwardly pious people of their faith" (*Religion in the Old South* [Chicago, 1977], 243–44).

34. Orr, *Fervent prayer*, 11; *Puritan Recorder* (March 18, 1858); *Old South Chapel prayer meeting*, 81; Rev. Heman Humphrey, D.D., *Revival sketches and manual* (New York, 1859), 13, 281–82; *Evangelist and Religious Review* (December 9, 1858); *Zion's Herald and Wesleyan Journal* 28 (February 4, 1857).

35. *Boston Evening Transcript* (March 16, 26, 1858, May 7, April 12, 13, March 22, May 28, 1858); *Youth's Companion* 22 (April 29, 1858), 68; *Evangelist and Religious Review* (May 20, November 11, May 20, 1858, June 23, 1859); *Christian Watchman-Reflector* 36 (September 20, 1855); Rosell and Depuis, *The memoirs of Charles Finney*, 562, 565; Orr, *Fervent prayer*, 36–37.

36. *Evangelist and Religious Review* (May 20, July 22, April 29, July 15, 1858, January 6, 1859); *Puritan Recorder* (May 23, 1850). The *Boston Recorder* became the *Puritan Recorder* on May 17, 1849. Rev. Dr. Heman Humphrey, "Revivals," *Evangelist and Religious Review* (January 1, 1857); *Independent* (February 9, 1860).

37. Prime, *The power of prayer*, 366; William Gray Brooks, Diary, March 12, 1858; *The Liberator* 28 (April 16, 1858); *Old South Chapel prayer meeting*, 62–63, 121; *New York Tribune* (March 18, 1858); *Boston Journal* (March 19,

1858); Alexander, *The revival and its lessons,* 8; Beardsley, *Religious progress through religious revivals,* 47; Conant, *Narratives of remarkable conversions and revival incidents,* 363; *Boston Evening Transcript* (March 5, 1857). The story from the *Northern Christian Advocate* is reprinted in the *Evangelist and Religious Review* (May 5, March 17, 1859).

38. *Evangelist and Religious Review* (August 4, 1859).

TWO. THE ANXIETY OF BOSTON AT MID-CENTURY

1. J. T. S. Lidstone, ed., *The Bostoniad: Giving a full description of the principal establishments, together with the most honorable and substantial businessmen in the Athens of America* (Boston, 1853), 17.

2. The census figures are reprinted in the *Puritan Recorder* (June 27, 1850); Francis Bennett Jr., Diary, October 2, 1854, AAS; *Boston Evening Transcript* (August 21, 1857); Joseph G. Martin, *Twenty-one years in the Boston stock market* (Boston, 1856), 42–43, 52–53, 76–80, Appendix; *Boston Evening Transcript* (August 17, 1858); *The Liberator* 51 (December 18, 1857); *Independent* (May 8, 1851).

3. A story summarizing the valuation of the Fourth Ward is in the *Watchman-Examiner* 36 (September 27, 1855); Gamaliel Bradford, Diary, April 20, 1854, HL; *Watchman-Examiner* 37 (August 21, 1856).

4. *Boston Daily Advertiser* (November 2, 1858); *Boston Recorder* (January 19, 1849); *Boston Evening Transcript* (July 9, 1857); J. C. Warren, M.D., *The great tree on the Boston Common* (Boston, 1855), 10, 16; Charles E. French, Diary, June 21, 22, July 2, 1855, July 9, 1857, MHS; William Gray Brooks, Diary, May 1, 1858; John Henry Kenneally, Diary, July 4, 1857, BPL, July 4, 1857, MHS; James Barnard Blake, Diary, April 10, 1851, AAS. The state government typically advertised fast days, proclaimed by the governor as an occasion on which to "humiliate ourselves, without delaying until some national scourge shall be commissioned to sober our thoughtless impulses" (*Boston Evening Transcript* [April 15, 1857]).

5. *Boston Recorder* (January 19, 1849); *Boston Evening Transcript* (November 22, 1859, July 9, 1857, December 2, 1859); *Boston Daily Advertiser* (April 3, October 9, 1858); Ticket to admit "a gentleman and two ladies" to the "Ball at Faneuil Hall," in folder marked "Printed Matter," William W. Greenough Papers, LC; *Monthly Anthology and Boston Review* 4 (May 1807); *Evangelist and Religious Review* (February 22, 1855).

6. *Supplement to the Boston Evening Transcript* (May 28, 1858); *Watchman-Examiner* 37 (October 2, 1856); Charles Dickens, *American notes* (London, 1985), 23; *Watchman-Examiner* (January 12, 1854), 8 and (March 2, 1854), 35; *Massachusetts Teacher* 3 (June 1850), 161; *New Englander* 14 (November 1856), 509; *Christian Observatory* 2 (November 1848), 502.

7. *Puritan Recorder* (April 11, 1850); *Boston Daily Advertiser* (June 29, 1858); *Watchman-Examiner* 37 (February 21, 1856). The *Times* article is reprinted in the *Boston Evening Transcript* (July 12, 1858).

8. William Gray Brooks, Diary, September 17, 1857, MHS; Orville Dewey to his sister Jerusha, March 25, 1858; *Boston Evening Transcript* (January 15, 1857).

9. *Boston Daily Advertiser* (October 26, 1858); *Evangelist and Religious Review* (January 6, 1859). In 1740 the city had a population of approximately fifteen thousand and was divided into thirty districts for neighborhood meetings.

10. George Scandlin, Diary, August 13, 1856; *New York Times* (March 20, 1858) in book of clippings "Great Awakening, 1858," CL; *Evangelist and Religious Review* (June 17, 1856); *Boston Evening Transcript* (September 21, 1858, May 5, October 3, 1859).

11. Rev. Albert Barnes, "Revivals of Religion in Cities and Large Towns, *The American National Preacher* 15 (January 1841), 45; *Evangelist and Religious Review* (April 14, 1859); Daniel C. Eddy, *The Young man's friend: Containing admonitions for the erring; counsel for the tempted; encouragement for the desponding; hope for the fallen* (Lowell and Boston, 1850), 23; Elizur Wright to Brother Green, November 3, 1860, and to Brother, August 23, 1857, Elizur Wright papers, LC; Daniel C. Eddy, *The young woman's friend; or, the duties, trials, loves, and hopes of women* (Boston, 1858), 133; *Little Mabel: A new year's tract, for the children of the Warren Street Chapel, January 1, 1859* (Boston, 1859); *Boston Daily Advertiser* (June 23, July 30, 1858); *Boston Evening Transcript* (January 14, 1858, June 6, 1857); Samuel May to Richard Davis Webb, December 1, 1857, BPL; Mary Gardiner Davis, Commonplace Book, 1858, SL. Other children's fiction that addressed the theme includes stories in *The Well-Spring*, ed. Rev. Asa Bullard, which was produced every Friday by the Massachusetts Sabbath School Society (e.g., see the issues in vol. 16 [1858]).

12. *List of persons, copartnerships, and corporations, who were taxed of ten thousand dollars and upwards, in the city of Boston, in the year 1857* (Boston, 1858); "Character of the Population of Boston," *Boston Daily Advertiser* (June 29, 1858); Letter from Miriam Sears to Knyvet Winthrop Sears, February 21, 1860, MHS; *Evangelist and Religious Review* (September 2, 1858). An outstanding longitudinal statistical study of a sample of 2,808 persons in Boston during the 1860s is Peter R. Knights, *Yankee destinies: The lives of ordinary nineteenth-century Bostonians* (Chapel Hill, NC, 1991); see also Knights, *The plain people of Boston, 1830–1860: A study in city growth* (New York, 1971). In 1851 a police sweep of Ann Street netted 165 suspected prostitutes in thirty minutes (Edward H. Savage, *A chronological history of the Boston watch and police, from 1631–1865; together with the recollections of a police officer* (Boston, 1865), 257.

13. Charles E. French, Diary, February 6, 1857; Francis Bennett Jr., Diary, December 17, 1854; *Boston Evening Transcript* (April 3, 1857); Mary Mudge, Diary, June 15, 1854.

14. Knights, *The plain people of Boston,* 104.

15. *Evangelist and Religious Review* (February 12, January 29, 1857); Charles F. Low, Diary, January 20, 1857, BPL; Gamaliel Bradford, Diary, Feb-

ruary 10, 1856; *Watchman-Examiner* 38 (April 16, 1857); *Evangelist* (January 29, 1857); *Boston Evening Transcript* (August 28, 1858); Savage, *A chronological history*, 113. Roger Lane, *Policing the city: Boston, 1822–1885* (Cambridge, MA, 1967).

16. *Christian Observatory* 2 (April 1848), 162–63; Susan E. Brown, Diary, November 17, 20, 1857, Forbes Papers, AAS; Charles Henry Harvey, Diary, February 27, 1857, George Henry Harvey Papers, LC; *Ballou's Pictorial* 13 (September 22, 1858); Edward E. Hale, *A sermon delivered before his excellency Nathaniel P. Banks, Governor* (Boston, 1859), 24; *Boston Evening Transcript* (July 11, 1859).

17. Israel Lombard, Diary, March 30, 1849, AAS; Charles F. Low, Diary, February 12, January 20, 28, 1857; John Henry Kenneally, Diary, March 31, October 9, 18, 1857, March 22, 1858, BPL; *Boston Evening Transcript* (January 9, 1850); *Massachusetts Ploughman* 9 (April 13, 1850); Ball Fenner, *Raising the veil; or, scenes in the courts* (Boston, 1856). "Ratting" refers to boys' sport of hunting rats with firearms. Sometimes boys captured the rats and contributed them to "ratting" dens in the North End, where persons gambled on how many rats a dog could kill in a given time (Savage, *A chronological history*, 160–66).

18. Lane, *Policing the city*, 105–6, 238, 89, 112, 113, 231, 75–78; Savage, *A chronological history*, 198–201, 235–43, 99; Arthur Howard Nichols, Diary, "January, 1856," MHS; Michael Feldberg, *The turbulent era: Riot and disorder in Jacksonian America* (New York, 1980), 122; Charles E. French, Diary, May 8, 15, 17, 1855; Letter to Knyvet Winthrop Sears from his father, November 22, 1859, MHS; *The Liberator* 27 (December 18, 1857); *Evangelist and Religious Review* (February 12, 1857).

19. *Gleason's Drawing Room Companion* 1 (August 9, 1851), 240; *Boston Daily Advertiser* (April 3, 1858); James Barnard Blake, Diary, January 1, 1851; Mary Dewey to Charles Dewey, November 24, 1858, in Orville Dewey Correspondence, AAS; *The constitution and by-laws of the Boot and Shoe Makers Association* (John A. Green, printer, 1858); *The constitution and by-laws of the Boston infidel relief society* (Boston, 1858); "Rules and Regulations to Be Observed by Inmates of the Home for the Fallen," in "Boston Association of the Home for the Fallen," 1858, Pamphlet box "B," MHS; *The Evangelist* 28 (January 15, 1857); *Evangelist and Religious Review* (February 4, 1858); *Boston Evening Transcript* (March 23, 1859).

20. Henry Clark Wright, Journal, August 10, 1853, BPL; Francis Bennett Jr., Diary, August 29, 1854; Charles E. French, Diary, June 30, 1857; *Boston Daily Advertiser* (June 15, 1858); *Christian Advocate* 30 (September 13, 1855); *Congregationalist* (June 3, 1858); *Evangelist and Religious Review* (July 1, 1858).

21. *Boston Evening Transcript* (October 21, 1858); Miriam Sears to Knyvet Winthrop Sears, January 17, 1860, MHS; Newspaper clipping in George Scandlin Papers, AAS.

22. Susan E. P. Brown, Diary, February 22, 1857; Francis Bennett Jr., Diary,

March 27, 1854; *Evangelist and Religious Review* (February 19, 1857, April 19, 1855, May 5, 1857); *Massachusetts Teacher* 12 (July 1859), 270; *New Englander* 12 (May 1854), 274; *The Liberator* 22 (December 24, 1852); Theodore Parker, Scrapbook, 1856, p. 23, BPL.

23. *Boston Evening Transcript* (October 21, 1858); Francis Bennett Jr., Diary, November 22, 1854; Joanne Harvey, Diary, 1857–58; George Scandlin, Diary, January 1, 1852; Gamaliel Bradford, Diary, May 3, 1854; "A Western Woman," *Trumpet and Universalist* 23 (August 10, 1850), 36; "Folder," 1857, Franklin Scientific Institute, Papers, vol. 4, BPL; *Independent* (January 12, 1851, June 14, 7, 1860, March 6, 1856); *Evangelist and Religious Review* (December 18, 1856); William Gray Brooks, Diary, June 4, 1858.

24. *Evangelist* 28 (May 21, 1857) and 28 (June 18, 1857).

25. William Gray Brooks, Diary, February 2, March 23, 1858; *The Liberator* 24 (April 14, 1854); *Independent* (June 5, 1856); Elizur Wright, letter to his wife and children, December 2, 1857; Arthur Howard Nichols, Diary, block entry for January 1856; George H. Troup, Diary, May, 18, 1858; Theodore Parker, Scrapbook, 1856, BPL.

26. Gamaliel Bradford, Diary, May 26, 1854; *Massachusetts Teacher* 8 (December 1855), 363; Augustus C. Thompson, *The mercy-seat; or, thoughts on prayer* (Boston, 1863), 188; *Independent* (November 29, 1860) and (June 3, 1861), 3; *The Liberator* 30 (February 17, 1860), 26.

THREE. OVEREXCITEMENT, ECONOMIC COLLAPSE,
AND THE REGULATION OF BUSINESS

1. *Evangelist and Religious Review* (February 8, 1855); "Letter from Boston," *Evangelist and Religious Review* (February 12, 1857); *Watchman-Examiner* 36 (January 22, 1858).

2. *New Englander* 9 (February, 1851), 18; Gamaliel Bradford, Diary, July 17, 1854, November 23, 1, 1855; *Independent* (January 3, 1856) and (May 15, 1856), 157. The *Independent* recommended that "our California buyers should be required to pay 20 per cent. cash, and the balance on arrival, *before* delivery of the merchandise" (157). Martin, *Twenty-one years in the Boston stock market*, 42–33, 52–53, 76–80, Appendix A.

3. Israel Lombard, "Memoranda 1857–1859," 59–63, AAS; William Gray Brooks, Diary, "September, 1857"; Arthur Howard Nichols, Diary, "anno domini, 1857"; *Boston Evening Transcript* (February 26, 1858); John Robison, *Thirteenth annual report of the Rev. John P. Robison, missionary to seaman and rector of the free church of St. Mary, for sailors, Boston* (Boston, 1858), 6; Joanne Harvey, Diary, November 2, 5, 1857; *Atlantic Monthly* 1 (November 1857), 113; John Henry Kenneally, Diary, September 28, 1857; Martin, *Twenty-one years in the Boston stock market*, 77.

4. William Gray Brooks, Diary, September 11, May 5, 1857; John Henry Kenneally, Diary, September 21, 28, 1857; *Report of the investigating committee to the creditors of Pemberton Mills* (Boston, 1858); Joanne Harvey, Di-

ary, November 2, 1857; Joanne Harvey to Charles Harvey, October 17, 1857; *Watchman-Examiner* (January 22, 1858); Martin, *Twenty-one years in the Boston stock market*, 77; E. P. Bigelow, *Remarks on the depressed condition of manufactures in Massachusetts, with suggestions as to its cause and its remedy* (Boston, 1858), 14.

5. William Gray Brooks, Diary, June 3, 1857; Joanne Harvey, Diary, October 30, November 17, 1857; *Boston Evening Transcript* (May 19, 1858, June 2, October 12, February 20, 1858).

6. *Boston Daily Advertiser* (February 10, January 14, October 10, 1858; *Boston Evening Transcript* (April 10, 3, 1858); *Evangelist and Religious Review* 30 (March 17, 1859); Joanne Harvey to Charles Harvey, October 17, 1857; William Gray Brooks, Diary, December 26, 1857; Joanne Harvey, Diary, December 22, 1857.

7. Henry W. Haynes, Diary, November 28, 1851; Gamaliel Bradford, Diary, July 10, 1854, November 23, 1855; *Evangelist and Religious Review* (June 21, 1855); William Gray Brooks, Diary, December 31, 1857; George H. Troup, Diary, January 9, 1858; Henry Larcom Abbott, Diary, April 11, 1858; *Boston Daily Advertiser* (April 12, 1858); *Boston Evening Transcript* (June 4, 11, 1858); Charles E. French, Diary, March 27, 1855. Newspapers had reported suicides and Bostonians had talked about them throughout the 1850s. The reasons most commonly given for suicides were financial catastrophe, insanity, and religion. Sometimes these reasons overlapped. Henry Haynes, looking over the records of his literary club in 1851, lamented the death of his friend, Bob Paine, who was the comic of the group: "He to commit suicide! But he must have been insane, a religious monomaniacal; a singular instance, but not unparalleled" (Henry W. Haynes, Diary, October 23, 1851).

8. *Evangelist and Religious Review* (April 21, June 23, 1859).

9. *Boston Evening Transcript* (June 7, 12, 1858); *Watchman and Reflector* 37 (January 10, 1856); *Independent* (February 11, 1858), 5; *New Englander* 15 (August 1857), 706, 705.

10. William Gray Brooks, Diary, November 30, 1857; Joanne Harvey, Diary, September 30, 1857; *Evangelist and Religious Review* (May 13, 1858); *Boston Evening Transcript* (October 14, 1857); *Boston Daily Advertiser* (May 28, 1858); *Currency explosions, their cause and cure* (New York, 1858), 16; George Opdyke, Wilson G. Hunt, James Gallatin, and John Eadie, *A report of the currency* (New York, 1858), 31.

11. "Meeting of the Boston Board of Trade," *Boston Evening Transcript* (April 7, 1858).

12. Notes for debate of December 11, 1857, Franklin Scientific Association Papers.

13. Samuel Hurd Walley, *The Financial revulsion of 1857* (Boston, 1858), 18, 25, 16–18; *Independent* (January 7, 1856), 21; Bigelow, *Remarks on the depressed condition of manufactures*, 25. The report of the Boston Board of Trade is excerpted in the *Boston Evening Transcript* (April 7, 1858).

14. *New Englander* 12 (February 1854), 11; *Boston Evening Transcript*

(September 30, 1859); George H. Troup, Diary, March 9, 1858; John Henry Kenneally, Diary, November 11, 1857; Charles E. French, Diary, March 13, 1855; William Gray Brooks, Diary, February 28, 1858.

15. See Appendix 2.

16. William Gray Brooks, Diary, February 2, 1858; *Ballou's Pictorial* 14 (April 24, 1858), 271 and (January 16, 1858), 45; *Boston Evening Transcript* (March 31, August 2, November 12, 1859, April 17, 1858); *Boston Daily Advertiser* (October 8, May 4, 1858).

17. *New Englander* 16 (August 1858), 662; *Boston Evening Transcript* (May 9, 1858); *The Liberator* 28 (April 30, 1858), 72; *Evangelist and Religious Review* (April 29, 1858).

18. *Evangelist and Religious Review* (February 8, 1855).

19. *Evangelist and Religious Review* (December 18, 1856, November 18, 1858, February 22, 1855); *Independent* (January 9, 1851); Gamaliel Bradford, Diary, April 18, May 22, April 29, 1854; Francis Bennett Jr., Diary, July 5, 1854; Joanne Harvey to Charles Harvey, March 2, 1856; John Townsend Trowbridge, *My own story with recollections of noted persons* (Boston, 1903), 173; "Printed Matter" folder, William W. Greenough Papers; *Ballou's Pictorial* 11 (August 2, 1856), 68.

20. Leman Thomas Ride, *The art of money-getting; showing the means by which an individual may obtain and retain health, wealth, and happiness* (Boston, 1832), 28; Anson D. F. Randolph, *The man of business* (New York, 1856); *Evangelist and Religious Review* (February 19, 1857, November 11, 1858, February 10, 1859).

21. *Christian Parlor Magazine* (January 1847), 274 and (February 1847), 19–20; *Trumpet and Universalist* 23 (June 12, 1850), 12; A. B. Muzzey, *The young man's friend* (Boston, 1836), 60, 61–65, 74–78; *Youth's Companion* 33 (September 15, 1859), 147 and 28 (July 20, 1854), 54; *Independent* (February 7, 1856); *Massachusetts Teacher* 6 (April 1853), 101; *Christian Observatory* 1 (September 1847), 395; *Watchman-Examiner* (March 2, 1854), 35.

22. Henry W. Haynes, Diary, October 12, 1858; Obituary clipping, October 30, 1868, Alfred Mason Badger Papers; *New Englander* 10 (May 1852), 191; Muzzey, *The young man's friend,* 130. On Emerson's notion of self-reliance and sincerity see Mary Kupiec Cayton, *Emerson's emergence: Self and society in the transformation of New England, 1800–1845* (Chapel Hill, 1989), 221–32.

23. "Picture of Boston," *Boston Anthology and Monthly Review* (June 1807), 289.

24. *The Liberator* 28 (May 28, 1858), 88.

25. "Promiscuous Leaves from my diary. by a convict . . . Charlestown, Massachusetts, 1864," ms., AAS; Charles E. French, Diary, August 8, May 24, 1857; Gamaliel Bradford, Diary, November 19, 1855; *Massachusetts Teacher* 7 (June 1854), 163 and 9 (February 1858), 42; *Christian Observatory* 1 (1847), 44; *How to do business. a pocket manual of practical affairs, and Guide to success in Life* (New York, 1857); "What Is the Unconscious Influence of Your

Daily Life?" *Evangelist and Religious Review* (January 29, 1857); *Manual for use of the members of the Church of Christ in Leyden Chapel, Boston*, 9.

26. "Commerce and Wealth," *Christian Watchman and Reflector* 35 (March 30, 1854); Ezra Stiles Gannett, *The state of the country, delivered in the Federal Street meetinghouse Boston, June 8, 1856* (Boston, 1856), 10; Muzzey, *The Young man's friend*, 102; Barnes, "Revivals of Religion," 23; James Barnard Blake, Diary, March 30, 1851; *Independent* (January 16, 1851); Rev. James T. Coolidge, *An address delivered before the Boston YMCU* (Boston, 1853), 9; *Evangelist and Religious Review* (February 10, 1859); Trowbridge, *My own story*, 150.

27. H. G. Atwell, *Jimmy, a Christian*, 2d ed. (Boston, 1859), 59; Tracy Patch Cheever, Diary, February 15, March 20, 1854; *Massachusetts Ploughman* 9 (February 9, 1850).

28. *Independent* (February 6, 1851) and "From our Boston Correspondent," *Independent* (January 16, 1851); *Massachusetts Teacher* 9 (March 1856), 106 and 8 (May 1855), 143 and 13 (September 8, 1860), 322 and 10 (April 1857), 186; Gamaliel Bradford, Diary, April 23, 1854; *Gleason's Pictorial Drawing-Room Companion* 1 (May 3, 1851), 38 and 4 (January 15, 1853), 45; *Evangelist and Religious Review* (January 20, 1859, February 12, 1857); *The Liberator* 22 (March 12, 1852), 32 and 10 (March 11, 1859), 40; Anne Wales Abbott, ed., "Ellie Claire and Nellie Brown," *Child's Friend and Family Magazine* 30 (1858), 222.

29. *Evangelist and Religious Review* (February 3, 1859, October 21, 1858); *New Englander* 9 (February 1851), 12–13; *Independent* (May 8, 1851), 5; *Zion's Herald and Wesleyan Journal* 28 (January 28, 1857).

30. *Evangelist and Religious Review* (December 18, 1856). Commerce "unites distant branches of the human family, cultivates the relation between them, encourages an interest in each other, and promotes that brotherly feeling which is the strongest guarantee of a permanent friendship" (*Ballou's Pictorial* 11 [August 2, 1856], 68).

31. *Puritan Recorder* (March 7, 1850).

FOUR. EMOTION, COLLECTIVE
PERFORMANCE, AND VALUE

1. Scholarly literature on the cultural construction of emotion is growing rapidly, but useful overviews are Richard A. Shweder and Robert A. LeVine, eds., *Culture theory: Essays on mind, self, and emotion* (New York, 1984); Shinobu Kitayama and Hazel Rose Markus, *Emotion and culture: Empirical studies of mutual influence* (Washington, DC, 1994); James R. Averill, "The Social Construction of Emotion: With Special Reference to Love," in *The social construction of the person*, ed. Kenneth J. Gergen and Keith E. Davis (New York, 1985), 89–109; Rom Harré, ed., *The social construction of emotions* (Oxford, 1986); Gene A. Fisher and Kyum Koo Chon, "Durkheim and the Social Con-

struction of Emotions," *Social Psychology Quarterly* 52 (1989), 1–9; Pnina Werbner and Helen Basu, eds., *Embodying charisma: Modernity, locality and the performance of emotion in Sufi cults* (London, 1998); Catherine Lutz, *Unnatural emotions: Everyday sentiments on a Micronesian Atoll and their challenge to Western theory* (Chicago, 1988); Barbara H. Rosenwein, ed., *Anger's past: The social uses of an emotion in the middle ages* (Ithaca, 1998).

2. Charles E. French, Diary, July 10, 1857; *Gleason's Drawing Room Companion* 1 (July 19, 1851), 192; William Gray Brooks, Diary, February 3, 1858; Israel Lombard, Diary, September 13, 1858; Edward A. Teulon, Diary, August 22, 1854, AAS; Arthur Howard Nichols, Diary, March 6, 1852; Rev. Peter Randolph, *From slave cabin to the pulpit* (Boston, 1893), 28; Francis Bennett Jr., Diary, June 16, December 16, 1854; R. M. Field et al., "Souvenir Program, Boston Museum," June 1, 1903, AAS; *Boston Evening Transcript* (July 9, 1857); *Boston Daily Advertiser* (April 17, 1858); Savage, *A chronological history*, 110.

3. Edward Everett Hale, *A New England boyhood* (New York, 1927), 133–36; Charles E. French, Diary, April 17, 1855, May 2, June 15, 1857; George H. Troup, Diary, January 1, 24, 1858; Arthur Howard Nichols, Diary, May 22, June 2, 3, July 10, 1852; Alfred Mason Badger, Diary, October 17, 20, 27, November 5, 21, December 18, March 16, May 4, 1835.

4. Joanne Harvey to Charles Henry Harvey, October 17, 1857 and April 18, 1856; Henry W. Haynes, Diary, October 29, 1851; Susan Heath, Diary, March 14, 1858; *Youth's Companion* 32 (April 1, 1858), 52; Mary Gardiner Davis, Notebook (see "Finder's Guide" to Gardiner Family Papers, SL); Mary Mudge, Diary, July 3, 1854.

5. George H. Troup, Diary, May 14, 1858; Francis Bennett Jr., Diary, October 4, 30, 31, November 1, 14, 15, 1854; see also Eliphay Arnold Jr., Diary, March 8, 1850, MHS; Tracy Patch Cheever, Diary, February 15, 1854; William W. Greenough to his father May 31, 1849; Joanne Harvey, Diary, March 7, 1857, Charles Henry Harvey Papers, LC; William Gray Brooks, Diary, February 14, 22, 1858. Discussion of the issues of display of identity and the affirmation of ideology can be found in Sallie A. Marston, "Public Rituals and Community Power: St. Patrick's Day Parades in Lowell, Massachusetts, 1841–1874," *Political Geography Quarterly* 8 (July 1989), 257–69 and in David Scobey, "Anatomy of the Promenade: The Politics of Bourgeois Sociability in Nineteenth-Century New York," *Social History* 17 (May 1992), 203–27.

6. Francis Bennett Jr., Diary, November 20, 1854; Eliphay Arnold Jr., Diary, September 18, 19, 1851; Trowbridge, *My own story*, 159–61; "The Queen's Message," *Boston Daily Advertiser* (April 19, 1858); *Boston Evening Transcript* (August 16, 1858); Charles E. French, Diary, August 8, 1858; William Gray Brooks, Diary, August 5, 1858; see also Jacob Merrill Manning, Diary, September 6, 1858, MHS.

7. Arthur Howard Nichols, Diary, January 1, 1858; Frederic Cunningham, Diary, January 1, 1858, MHS; William Gray Brooks, Diary, January 1, 1858;

Ceremonies on the occasion of the dedication of the Public Library Building (Boston, 1858).

8. *The Charlestown Convent; its destruction by a mob on the night of August 11, 1834* (Boston, 1870); Joan D. Hedrick, *Harriet Beecher Stowe: A life* (New York, 1994), 67–69. The contents of Mayhew's sermon on civil rights are available in notes in the Jonathan Mayhew MSS, Boston University. *Monthly Anthology and Boston Review* 4 (1807), 429; *Ballou's Pictorial* 15 (July 3, 1858); *Evangelist and Religious Review* (July 26, 1855).

9. "Order of Services at the Installation of Rev. Arthur B. Fuller, as the pastor of the New North Religious Society, Boston, Wednesday, June 1, 1853," Broadside, BPL. The broadside collection at the Boston Public Library contains many examples of the order of service, for many different occasions. My conclusions are based on a selection of broadsides from 1825 to 1861. Iterations of order of services were not the exclusive province of the churches. Broadsides listing the order of exercises for visitation and exhibitions at the Boston Public Latin School from 1825 to 1855 list as many as eighteen separate exercises. Comparatively, some meetings were organized with a light touch, perhaps because of confidence in the focus of the congregation, or because a group simply would not submit to a detailed order of exercises. The latter is suggested in a broadside for a YMCA meeting listing only six exercises ("Boston Young Men's Christian Association. Tremont Temple, Sunday Evening, February 18, 1855. Order of Services," MHS). *Evangelist and Religious Review* (May 6, 1858).

10. *The theatres and public halls of Boston* (Philadelphia, 1879), Booklet, AAS; J. Smith Homans, *History of Boston, from 1630–1856* (Boston, 1856), 151; H. Earle Johnson, "Longfellow and Music," *American Music Research Center Journal* 7 (1997), 14; Arthur Howard Nichols, Diary, January 1, 1858; Charles E. French, Diary, March 21, 1855; Susan E. Brown, Diary, April 25–31, 1857, September 9, December 19, 1857; Eliphay Arnold Jr., Diary, August 18, 21, 22, 1851; Susan Heath, Diary, April 17, 1858; Charles F. Low, Diary, February 12, 1857; Israel Lombard, Diary, January 3, 1856; Edward A. Teulon, Diary, June 26, 1849; Alfred Mason Badger, December 7, 1835; Frederic Cunningham, Diary, January 7, 1858; Henry W. Haynes, Diary, December 5, 1851; John Henry Kenneally, Diary, June 5, 1857; Francis Bennett Jr., Diary, December 25, 1854; *Boston Evening Transcript* (April 6, 1858).

11. R. M. Field et al., "Souvenir Program, Boston Museum" (June 1, 1903), 9, 17, 21, 31, AAS; *The theatres and public halls of Boston*; Homans, *History of Boston*, 151; Tracy Patch Cheever, Diary, September 13, 1854; Dickens, *American notes*, 54; William Henry Smith, Diary, March 31, June 9, October 2, November 20, 1852; Oral Sumner Coad and Edwin Mims Jr., *The American stage* (New Haven, CT, 1929), 120; Charles E. French, Diary, March 5, 1855; Susan E. Brown, Diary, January 1, 1858. Not just white men appeared in blackface. "When Negroes were admitted to the professional stage they took over bodily the entire minstrel convention, even to the use of burnt cork and

the thickened lips" (Edith J. R. Isaacs, *The Negro in the American theatre* [New York, 1947], 25, 21 23).

12. William Gray Brooks, Diary, March 29, 1858; Gamaliel Bradford, Diary, April 19, 1854; *Boston Evening Transcript* (March 5, 1857); Karen Haltunnen, *Confidence men and painted women: A study of middle-class culture in America, 1830–1870* (New Haven, CT, 1982), 178–79, 185–86; *Godey's Lady's Book* 49 (December 1854), 516, quoted in Haltunnen, 178; Mary Gardiner Davis, Commonplace Book, 1854.

13. Francis Bennett Jr., Diary, October 4, 1854; Edward A. Teulon, Diary, June 26, 1849; William Henry Hoyt, Journal, April 4, 1851; Henry Larcom Abbott, Diary, November 2, 1855; Longfellow quoted in H. Earle Johnson, "Longfellow and Music," 15; Gamaliel Bradford, Diary, May 11, 1854; H. Pease and Jane H. Pease, *The web of progress: Private values and public styles in Boston and Charleston, 1828–1843* (New York, 1985), 141; Mary Dewey to Julia Dewey, December 8, 1859, and Orville Dewey to Charles Dewey, January 16, 1860, in Orville Dewey Correspondence, AAS; Ezra Stiles Gannett, Diary, February 20, 1857; Tracy Patch Cheever, Diary, May 23, 1854.

14. Dickens, *American notes*, 51; Barnes, "Revivals of Religion," *New Englander* 13 (February 1855), 98; Robert Turnbull, *The theatre, in its influence upon literature, morals and religion*, 2d ed. (Boston, 1839), v, 12, 16, 22, 37–40, 50, 70, 71, 81.

15. Turnbull quotes Wayland's *Elements of moral science*, 3d ed., 305 (*The theatre*, 95–96); Barnes, "Revivals of Religion," 67; *Youth's Cabinet* 2 (May 30, 1839), 85; William Henry Smith, Diary, January 29, 1852; *The young woman's friend*, 58; William Henry Hoyt, Journal, February 24, 1851.

16. *Manual for the use of the members of the church of Christ in Leyden Chapel, Boston, Mass.* (Boston, 1846), 151; R. W. G. Vail, "Random Notes on the History of the Early American Circus," *Proceedings of the AAS* 43 (1933), 116–85; Benjamin Rush, *Medical inquiries and observations*, vol. 2 (Philadelphia, 1793), 34; Elizur Wright to Harriet, March 5, 1858; Franklin Scientific Association Papers, vol. 4, January 12, 1857; Susan E. P. Brown, Diary, June 12, 1857. Rush's theories are mentioned in Appendix 2.

17. Charles E. French, Diary, December 11, 1858; Gamaliel Bradford, Diary, May 20, 1854; William Henry Hoyt, Journal, May 24, 1851; William W. Greenough to his father, July 4, 1858; *Boston Evening Transcript* (September 26, 1859); "Boston Theatre . . . Ronzani Ballet Troupe," Broadside, BPL; Trowbridge, *My Own Story*, 161–62; Gamaliel Bradford, Diary, May 20, 1854; William Collins, "The Passions," in *The Beauties of Poetry* (Baltimore, 1804); William Buchan, *Domestic medicine* (Philadelphia, 1772), 306–307; Alexander Anderson, *An inaugural dissertation on chronic mania* (New York, 1796), 29; Daniel C. Eddy, *The Young Man's friend: Containing admonitions for the erring; counsel for the tempted [sic] encouragement for the desponding; hope for the fallen* (Lowell and Boston, 1850), 96; Frederic Cunningham, Diary, January 16, 1858.

18. Scholarly literature on the subject is vast. Two studies fundamental to

any consideration of nineteenth-century Protestant religious performance are Chris R. Vanden Bossche, "Preaching and Performance," in *Lectures on Carlyle and his era,* by Carlisle Moore, Rodger Tarr, and Chris Vanden Bossche (Santa Cruz, CA, 1982) and Victor Turner, *From ritual to theatre: The human seriousness of play* (New York, 1982). Other relevant studies include Sam D. Gill, *Native American religious action: A performance approach to religion* (Columbia, SC, 1987); Margaret Thompson Drewal, *Yoruba ritual: Performers, play, agency* (Bloomington, IN, 1992); Richard Schechner, *The future of ritual: Writings on culture and performance* (New York, 1993); and *By means of performance: Intercultural studies of theatre and ritual,* ed. Richard Schechner and Willa Appel (Cambridge, UK, 1991), especially Schechner, "Magnitudes of Performance," 19–49. An approach that emphasizes preaching is R. Laurence Moore, *Selling God: American religion in the marketplace of culture* (New York, 1994), 43–52. Though preaching was a key component of nineteenth-century American Protestantism, it was only one aspect of a complex of interwoven actions.

19. *Boston Evening Transcript* (January 18, 1857, February 14, 1859); *Evangelist and Religious Review* (May 5, 1859); Edward Cutbush, *An inaugural dissertation on insanity* (Philadelphia, 1794), preface.

20. *Massachusetts Teacher* 6 (October, 1853), 306; *New Englander* 10 (May 1852), 237. R. Laurence Moore stresses the "moral sensationalism" of reading in antebellum America (Moore, *Selling God,* 13–39). Though there was a moral element in some sensationalistic reading, it sometimes lacked the moral element and was engaged in purely for its ability to stimulate emotion.

21. David S. Reynolds, *Beneath the American renaissance: The subversive imagination in the age of Emerson and Melville* (New York, 1988), 7, 169–210. Ronald J. Zboray and Mary Saracino Zboray suggest that Reynolds places too much emphasis on books, newspapers, and other writings as the source of social meaning for antebellum Americans, arguing that the literary text "is only one source of many possible social meanings" ("Books, Reading and the World of Goods in Antebellum America," *American Quarterly* 48 [December 1996], 621 n. 91).

22. Trowbridge, *My own story,* 136; Sally Ripley, Journal, November 24, 1799; *Christian Observatory* 3 (February, 1849), 93 and (April, 1849), 171; *Child's Friend and Youth's Magazine* 18 (1852), 229; *Massachusetts Ploughman* 29 (April 20, 1850); *Massachusetts Teacher* 9 (December 1856), 563; Mary Gardiner Davis, Commonplace Book, April 16, 1858.

23. Mary Josephine Faxon Forbush, Diary, December 30, 1852, Boston Athenaeum; Henry W. Haynes, Diary, October 6, November 3, October 16, November 15, 23, 1851; Arthur Howard Nichols, Diary, May 15, 1852; Tracy Patch Cheever, Diary, June 15, June 15, 1854; George H. Troup, Diary, December 31, 1862.

24. *Massachusetts Teacher* 6 (July 1853), 209; E. H. Derby, *Boston: Commercial metropolis in 1850. Her growth, population, wealth, and prospects* (Boston, 1850); Domingo F. Sarmiento, *Sarmiento's travels in the United States*

in 1847, trans. Michael Aaron Rockland (Princeton, 1970), 244; Charles E. French, Diary, March 5, 1855; *Ballou's Pictorial* 12 (February 7, 1857), 87 and 17 (November 19, 1859), 327; *Boston Journal of Philosophy and the Arts* 1 (May 1823), 179–84; Joanne Harvey, Diary, January 20, 1857.

25. *Christian Register* 27 (November 25, 1848); *Gleason's Pictorial Drawing Room Companion* 1 (August 23, 1851), 267; *Monthly Law Reporter* 14 (March 1852) 641; *Youth's Companion* 30 (October 18, 1860), 166; Joanne Harvey, Diary, September 28, 1857; see also William Gray Brooks, Diary, September, 18, 19, 1857; Edward A. Teulon, Diary, September 27, 1854.

26. Knights, *Yankee destinies*, 105; *Christian Observatory* 1 (February 1847), 54 and 2 (January 1848), 43; "Sensation Newspapers," *Evangelist and Religious Review* (March 17, 1859); *New Englander* 13 (February 1855), 2; Anon., *A letter of the celebrated John Foster to a young minister, on the duration of future punishment* (Boston, 1849); *Massachusetts Quarterly Review* 7 (June 1849), 394–95.

FIVE. EMOTIONAL RELIGION AND THE MINISTERIAL "BALANCE-WHEEL"

1. *Boston Daily Advertiser* (December 3, June 10, 1858); *Boston Evening Transcript* (February 10, 1857, August 9, 1859, February 13, 1858, February 13, 1858); *Congregationalist* (June 3, 1858); Catherine Flint, Diary, July 4, 1858; Charles E. French, Diary, April 29, 1855; *Evangelist and Religious Review* (January 1, 1857); William A. Stearns, "Charge to the Pastor," in *Sermon and addresses at the installation of the Rev. Jacob M. Manning* (Boston, 1857); Susan E. P. Brown, Diary, September 2, 1855; *Evangelist* (September 23, 1858); *Independent* (June 28, 1860); Arthur A. Christy, *The Orient in American Transcendentalism. A study of Emerson, Thoreau, and Alcott* (New York, 1972), 201. I am indebted to William Gilmore for sharing his work-in-progress on reading in New England, and especially his analysis of circulation patterns at the Worcester Atheneum Library, which indicate that Bush's book was one of the most sought-after volumes in the library's collection in the years after it was published. The Harper's Family Library edition was published as: George Bush, *The life of Mohammed: Founder of the religion of Islam, and of the empire Saracens* (New York, 1836). Henry Ward Beecher broke with public opinion about Parker, but not in a way that could be construed as support for Parker: "If I were asked who is doing most to spread infidelity, you think I would say Theodore Parker. No; he is harmless because he is open" (*Boston Evening Transcript* [May 13, 1859]).

2. Derby, *Boston: Commercial Metropolis in 1850*, 16; J. D. B. DeBow, *The seventh census of the United States: 1850* (Washington, 1854), 61–63, 1016; *Evangelist and Religious Review* (January 29, February 26, 1857, September 23, 1858); *Watchman-Examiner* 38 (February 5, 1857, February 28, 1856).

3. *Boston Evening Transcript* (September 20, January 27, 1859, August 2, 1858); "Plan and Valuation of the Pews in the Mount Vernon Congregational

Church," May 15, 1845, Broadside, BPL; *Boston Daily Advertiser* (April 20, 30, February 10, April 19, 1858); Homans, *History of Boston*, 76–107; *Independent* (November 29, 1860), 3. *Gleason's* ran a series of profiles of twenty-one Boston churches in the summer and fall of 1853, and *Ballou's* occasionally published special features on Boston churches (e.g., *Gleason's* 5 [July 2, 1853], 12; *Ballou's* 8 [February 17, 1854], 109); Tracy Patch Cheever, Diary, May 31, 1854.

4. *Watchman-Examiner* 36 (March 6, 1856) and 37 (March 20, January 3, 1856); *The Theatres and Public Halls of Boston* (Philadelphia, 1879); *Boston Daily Advertiser* (August 16, October 4, 25, May 12, April 22, June 18, October 22, 1858); *Evangelist and Religious Review* (July 29, 1858, January 6, 1859, October 9, 1856); *Boston Evening Transcript* (July 14, October 5, 1859, September 14, 1857); *Christian Inquirer* 13 (October 2, 1858); *Evangelist and Religious Review* (January 6, 20, 1859, January 9, July 9, 1857); *Independent* (November 15, 1860); *The semi-centennial celebration of the Park Street Church and Society*, 162, 166; *Chronicles of the Old South Church* (Boston, 1863), 10.

5. George Scandlin, Diary, September 20, 1854; *Boston Daily Advertiser* (October 15, 1858); *Watchman-Examiner* (October 2, 1856, September 20, 1855); *Evangelist and Religious Review* (October 21, 1858, July 30, 1857, August 14, 1856); *Boston Evening Transcript* (September 5, July 2, 1859, September 6, 1858); Rev. Seth Sweetser, *Ministerial education* (Boston, 1858), 6.

6. Joseph Ballard, *Reasons for the appointment of a committee to investigate the prudential affairs of the Old South Church in Boston* (Boston, 1859), 3–4; Steven H. Phillips, *Attorney general, &c., at the request of Joseph Ballard, informant vs. "The Old South Society in Boston," and "The Ministers and Deacons of the Old South Church in Boston"* (Boston, 1860); *Chronicles of the Old South Church*, 8; *Boston Daily Advertiser* (November 22, 1858); *Evangelist and Religious Review* (January 20, 6, 1859, January 11, 1855).

7. *Boston Evening Transcript* (August 24, 1858, August 31, 1859); letter to the *Baptist Standard*, quoted in the *Independent* (July 26, 1860); *Independent* (June 14, 1860); "A Covenant of the Church in Federal Street," in Mary Gardiner Davis, Commonplace Book, Gardiner Family Papers, 1858[?], SL; *The Confession of faith and form of covenant of the Old South Church* (Boston, 1855); *Articles of faith and covenant of the Park Street Church with a list of members* (Boston, 1859)

8. *Boston Evening Transcript* (February 14, 1859); *New Englander* 12 (August 1854), 421; *Boston Daily Advertiser* (October 26, 1858).

9. Ezra Stiles Gannett, Diary, May 25, 1857; *Evangelist and Religious Review* (February 10, 1859). See the *Christian Observatory* 2, 3 (July 1848–May 1849), 1 (July 1847); George Scandlin, Diary, July 31, 1854.

10. *Watchman-Examiner* 27 (August 21, 1856); *Evangelist* (April 30, 1857); Theodore Parker to Dr. Bowman, July 11, 1858, MHS; Lucy Larcom to Esther S. Humiston, August 2, 1858, in *Lucy Larcom: Life, letters, and diary*, ed. Daniel Dulany Addison (New York, 1895); Jacob Merrill Manning, Diary, December 18, 1857, January 16, 17, 1858; *Gleason's Pictorial* 5 (July 2, 1853), 12 and (September 24, 1853), 204; *The Liberator* 23 (November 18, 1853), 181;

Evangelist and Religious Review (January 6, 1859, March 19, 1857); Henry W. Haynes, Diary, October 14, 1858.

11. *Sermons and Addresses at the Installation of the Rev. Jacob M. Manning* (Boston, 1857), 64; James Barnard Blake, Diary, February 2, 9, March 2, 1851; Susan E. Brown, Diary, December 28, 1857; *Boston Evening Transcript* (May 2, 1857); *Evangelist and Religious Review* (May 4, 1857, May 6, 1858); George Scandlin, Diary, July 14, October 6, 1854; *Gleason's Pictorial* 5 (September 17, 1853), 188; William Gray Brooks, Diary, April 30, 1858; Stephen Salisbury Jr. to his family, June 6, 1858, AAS; Francis Bennett Jr., Diary, September 17, December 7, 1854; Susan E. P. Brown, Diary, April 30, 1857; Arthur Howard Nichols, Diary, March 22, 31, June 27, July 18, 1852.

12. William Gray Brooks, Diary, January 3, February 28, 1858; *Evangelist and Religious Review* (October 30, 1856, May 6, 1858, March 5, 1857, May 13, 1858); *Watchman-Examiner* 37 (February 22, November 6, 1856).

13. *New Englander* 14 (August 1856), 417; *Watchman-Examiner* 37 (November 6, 1856).

14. *Gleason's Pictorial* 5 (September 17, 1853), 188; Trowbridge, *My own story*, 137–39; Dickens, *American notes*, 52; *New Englander* 10 (May 1852), 245; Mary Mudge, Diary, December 13, 1854; *Ballou's Pictorial* 13 (December 19, 1857), 398; *Boston Daily Advertiser* (September 4, June 24, 1858); *Evangelist and Religious Review* (July 1, 1858); George Scandlin, Diary, October 6, 1854 to March 3, 1858.

15. *Evangelist and Religious Review* (December 30, 1858, February 22, 1855, September 4, 1866); *Ballou's Pictorial* 14 (June 19, 1858); *New Englander* 14 (August 1856), 427.

16. *New Englander* 14 (August 1856), 354–56; *Sermons and addresses at the installation of the Rev. Jacob M. Manning,"* 30–31; Susan E. P. Brown, Diary, January 13, 1858; William Henry Hoyt, Diary, May 6, 1851; Gamaliel Bradford, Diary, October 28, 1855; Charles E. French, Diary, April 8, 1855; *Zion's Herald and Wesleyan Journal* 28 (January 28, 1857); *The Liberator* 28 (November 5, 1858), 180.

17. *The Liberator* 27 (August 21, 1857), 134 and 26 (May 16, 1856), 80 and 22 (December 21, 1852), 208 and 29 (June 24, 1859), 97.

18. *The Liberator* 28 (April 9, 1858), 64; *Boston Recorder* (February 2, 1849); *Evangelist and Religious Review* 30 (May 5, 1859); *New Englander* 11 (November 1853), 526–27.

19. Bret E. Carroll offers a useful overview that stresses Spiritualism's ideological aspects and its seriousness as a religion *(Spiritualism in antebellum America* [Bloomington, IN, 1997]). Spiritualism—as an umbrella term for an assortment of phenomena—was more sensationalistic in Boston than Carroll suggests (13–14). Ann Braude focuses on ways in which it was hospitable to women (*Radical spirits: Spiritualism and women's rights in nineteenth-century America* [Boston, 1989]).

20. William Gray Brooks, Diary, June 30, 1857; *New Englander* 15 (November 1857), 567; Ezra Stiles Gannett, Diary, March 20, 1857; *The journal of*

Charlotte Forten: A free Negro in the slave era, ed. Ray Allen Billington (New York, 1981), 57, 93; M. S. Perry, M.D., "Principles and Objects of the Massachusetts Medical Society," *Medical Communications* 9 (1960), 219; George H. Troup, Diary, May 6, 1858; Mary Mudge, Diary, April 25, 1854; *Boston Evening Transcript* (August 17, 1858).

21. *Evangelist and Religious Review* (August 16, July 9, 1857); *Boston Evening Transcript* (August 22, 1857, August 6, 1859); *Boston Daily Advertiser* (April 26, 1858); George Scandlin, Diary, January 22, 1852; *The Liberator* 23 (May 13, 1853) and 22 (July 23, 1852), 120.

22. Carroll, *Spiritualism in antebellum America,* 46; Braude, *Radical Spirits,* 174–82. Observing Spiritualism as a national phenomenon, Braude proposes that the sensational aspects of Spiritualism did not become pronounced until the 1870s. In Boston in the late 1850s, those sensational aspects already were evident.

23. *Boston Medical Intelligencer* 1 (1823), 14; *Massachusetts Teacher* 5 (September 1852), 260; *Christian Observatory* 3 (February 1849), 72.

24. *The Young Woman's Friend,* 148–167; Susan E. P. Brown, Diary, December 30, 1858; *The Liberator* 24 (January 13, 1854), 8 and 23 (June 10, 1853), 92; Henry Clark Wright, Journal, August 23, 1853.

25. Dr. John Perkins, Papers ca. 1750–1780, 38, AAS; Rush, *Medical inquiries and observations,* 70–71; Athanasius Fenwick, *An essay on volition and pleasure* (Philadelphia, 1818), 36; Gamaliel Bradford, Diary, May 30, 1854; *Puritan Recorder* (March 25, 1858[?]), in "Great Awakening, 1858," Clippings box, CL; George H. Troup, Diary, January 19–24, 1858; Arthur Howard Nichols, Diary, January 1857 (block entry); William Henry Smith, Diary, March 30, 1853, October 21, 1852; Henry W. Haynes, Diary, October 17, 1858. Protestantism had identified virtue with temperance well before the activism of Anthony and Stanton, thoroughly and actively adopting it as a plank in the overseas mission platform. Missionaries carried the gospel of temperance to distant shores, and reported back in despair that native peoples would rather burn in hell than give up their traditional beverages (*Baptist Missionary Magazine* 18 [October 1838], 253).

26. Henry W. Haynes, Diary, November 24, 1851; "To the inhabitants of Boston . . . February 6, 1833," Broadside, BPL; *Boston Recorder* 34 (September 13, 1849); *Boston Daily Advertiser* (October 22, 1858); *Young America,* no. 5 (May 1858), 60; Arthur Howard Nichols, Diary, January 5, 23, February 13, April 14, 1852; *Atlantic Monthly* 1 (November 1857), 78; *Christian Watchman and Reflector* 36 (June 21, 1855). On belief in the efficacy of prayer in converting people to temperance see *Youth's Companion* 28 (May 11, 1854), 9 and (June 1, 1854), 28; *Evangelist and Religious Review* (January 6, 1859); *Child's Friend and Family Magazine* 27 (1856), 14; *Christian Observer* 32 (November 5, 1853), 177.

27. See Martin Moore, *Boston revival, 1842. A brief history of the evangelical, churches of Boston, together with a more particular account of the revival of 1842* (Boston, 1842).

28. Alexander Goldenweiser, *History, psychology, and culture* (Gloucester, MA, 1968), 377–84.

SIX. MEN, WOMEN, AND EMOTION

1. *The Art of kissing*, preface, 38, 41, 43, 48; *The Liberator* 27 (December 4, 1857), 195. *The Liberator* said of Vermyle, "Shame on him!" (195); *Ballou's Pictorial* 12 (May 23, 1857), 335.

2. Mary Josephine Faxon Forbush, Diary, December 12, 1852; *Gleason's Pictorial* 4 (April 16, 1853), 246; Catherine Flint, Diary, July 27, August 5, October 4, 1858; Susan Heath, Diary, June 19, 11, 1858; Joanne Harvey to Charles Harvey, May 1, 1853, LC.

3. William Henry Hoyt, Journal, February 1, 4, 8, 12, 13, 18, 22–24, 1851; Henry W. Haynes, Diary, October 10, 1858.

4. William Henry Hoyt, Diary, February 10, 1851; Henry W. Haynes, Diary, November 1, October 15, 1851; Charles E. French, Diary, June 26, August 23, June 6, 1857, March 12, 1858; Susan Forbes, Diary, February 10, 1858, September 13, 1857, November 16, 2, 1858.

5 Charles E. French, Diary, February 6, March 30, 1858; William Gray Brooks, Diary, July 31, 1857; Catherine Flint, Diary, January 26, February 16, 1859; Waldo Flint to Catherine Flint, July 16, 1856, AAS.

6. *The Liberator* 26 (March 28, 1856), 52; *Gleason's Pictorial* 1 (November 22, 1851), 475; *Massachusetts Ploughman* 9 (September 21, 1850); *Ballou's Pictorial* 13 (September 26, 1857), 203; *Evangelist and Religious Review* (December 30, 1858). Bostonians linked clothes, class, and reputation. Following her attendance at a funeral in Dorchester, Susan Heath wrote that "everybody looked so rich & respectable!" (Diary, May 3, 1858).

7. *New Englander* 10 (May 1852), 259, 268; *American Baptist Magazine* 12 (18[??]), 238; Eddy, *The young woman's friend*, 20; *Massachusetts Teacher* 7 (November 1854), 354; *Ballou's Pictorial* 12 (April 11, 1857), 238; *Christian Observer* 32 (September 3, 1853), 44; Frances Merritt, Journal, May 30, 1858; Susan Heath, Diary, May 11, June 5, 1858.

8. *Youth's Companion* 34 (September 20, 1860), 162; *Massachusetts Teacher* 4 (March 1851), 77 and 1 (September 1, 1848), 257 and 2 (June 1849), 192; *Monthly Anthology and Boston Review* 4 (May 1807), 253.

9. *New Englander* 10 (May 1852), 262 and 13 (February 1855), 51; *The Liberator* 26 (September 12, 1856), 152; *Child's Friend and Family Magazine* 29 (Cambridge, 1857), 178; *Gleason's Pictorial* 2 (February 14, 1852), 104; *Massachusetts Teacher* 7 (June 1854), 184; Elizabeth Palmer Peabody, "Journal of Margaret Fuller's conversation classes," Booklet 1, ms., AAS.

10. Joanne Harvey to Charles Harvey, November 30, 1858; Mary J. Walker, Journal, October 31, 1848, in Walker School Journals, vol. 1, SL; Elizabeth Palmer Peabody, Journal, "18th conversation"; *New Englander* 10 (May 1852), 259.

11. *Gleason's Pictorial* 1 (May 3, 1851), 46; *The Liberator* 25 (September 28,

1855), 156; T. Cogan, *A philosophical treatise on the passions* (New York, 1821), 160; Eddy, *The young woman's friend*, 42; *Boston Monthly* 1 (May 1826), 622; *Massachusetts Teacher* 1 (May 15, 1848), 157 and 2 (June 1849), 192 and 9 (December 1856), 556; *Christian Observer* 30 (May 3, 1851), 72.

12. *Youth's Companion* 29 (February 21, 1856), 176. See chap. 2, "Education of the Body," in Harvey Newcomb, *How to be a lady: A book for girls, containing useful hints on the formation of character*, 15th ed. (Boston, 1855); *The Well-Spring* 15 (July 2, 1858), 106; *Child's Friend and Youth's Magazine* 18 (1852), 269 and 23 (1854), 174; Henry W. Haynes, Diary, November 3, 1851.

13. Gamaliel Bradford worried over his relationship with a Miss Skelton because "no exercise & no emotion can call a drop of blood to her cheeks, & one misses the blush that great index of the feelings" (Diary, March 30, 1856). Tracy Patch Cheever wrote of how his Uncle Giddings "would almost at the same breath indulge in a most pious homily, and tell a story to cover with mortification and blushes the cheek of a woman" (Diary, September 2, 1854); *Christian Register* 28 (October 27, 1849), 170.

14. Sally Ripley, Journal, May 8, 1801; *Ballou's Pictorial* 17 (November 5, 1859), 295. Ripley's sketch likely was drawn from Hannah Webster Foster, *The coquette; or the history of Eliza Wharton*. It was originally published in England in 1797. J. Horatio Nichols adapted it as a play entitled *The New England coquette: From the history of the celebrated Eliza Wharton: A tragic drama in three acts* (Salem, MA, 1802).

15. *Massachusetts Teacher* 9 (December 1856), 559; Susan Heath, Diary, June 6, 1858; Lucy Larcom, letter to Esther Huniston, November 18, 1857, MHS; Gamaliel Bradford, Diary, November 29, 1855.

16. Joanne Harvey, Diary, December 11, 1857. Collingwood is quoted in the *Massachusetts Teacher* 7 (June 1854), 176 and 9 (July 1856), 295. *Gleason's Pictorial* 2 (September 14, 1852), 104. *Gleason's* reported the rule and then criticized it. *Boston Weekly Magazine* 2 (October 20, 1804), 202; Fenner, *Raising the veil*, 243; Susan E. P. Brown, Diary, January 1, 1855. The peculiar dynamics of diary writing as both a private and a public exercise complicated it for anyone who took pen to paper. Brown's protestations did not stop her from producing a rich record of her activities and thoughts.

17. *Boston Monthly Magazine* 1 (June 1825), 110. The extent of that industriousness was profiled by the *Massachusetts Ploughman* in an article entitled "Smart Woman": "A lady in Albany last week did the whole week's washing for a large family, and got breakfast for them, before seven o'clock in the morning, made new dresses for two of her children, cleaned up the house, and got dinner before one o'clock; baked half a dozen loaves of bread and two mince pies, before four o'clock in the afternoon, and promenaded Broadway till six o'clock; got supper for the family at seven, and in the evening white washed three rooms. A smart woman" (9 [September 14, 1850], no pagination).

18. Sewing above all other domestic activities came to represent the mixing of industrious labor with affectionate companionship before the hearth. It also symbolized willingness to work for the good of others, as many sewing

projects were undertaken to produce shirts, socks, dresses, and coats for family members and friends. The children's story "My Thimbles" featured the struggle of a young girl, Lucy Jarvis Pemberton, to make a shirt for her father in time for his birthday. Her success in making the deadline is rewarded with praise from him for being "patient, industrious, and willing to work for others" (*Child's Friend and Youth's Magazine* 13 [1852], 231). Young Boston women such as Charlotte Foster and Mary Russell Curson sewed all day, alone or with friends (Foster, Diary, February 24, 1858; Curson, Diary, "June," 1850). One man petitioned a Boston oculist, John Williams, to treat his wife for free, writing about his concern that she "has been affected with sore eyes these seven years. during said time she could not darn a whole in a stocking" (Letter to John Williams [sender illeg.], March 18, 1836, John Williams Papers, 1836, LC). Women met regularly in sewing circles. Men and boys sometimes attended the women's meetings but gathered in their own meetings as well (Arthur Howard Nichols, Diary, May 12, February 18, 1852; Jacob Merrill Manning, Diary, December 9, 1857, January 14, 1858).

19. *The Liberator* 27 (December 4, 1857), 196. *The Liberator* criticized the standard argument of anti-suffragists that women would be "contaminated" by participation in the polls (28 [October 1, 1858], 160). *New Englander* 10 (May 1852), 262; *Christian Observer* 33 (April 22, 1854), 64; Mary Ryan, *Women in public: Between banners and ballots, 1825–1880* (Baltimore, 1990) and *Civil wars: Democracy and public life in the American city during the nineteenth century* (Berkeley, 1997); Nancy Fraser, "Rethinking the Public Sphere: A Contribution to the Critique of Actually Existing Democracy," in *Postmodernism and the re-reading of modernity,* ed. Francis Parker, Peter Hulme, and Margaret Iversen (New York, 1992), 197–231. Fraser coins the phrase "subaltern counterpublics" on p. 210. The groundbreaking work on "woman's sphere" in New England is Nancy F. Cott, *The bonds of womanhood: Woman's sphere in New England, 1780–1835* (New Haven, 1977). A good survey of some of the literature is Linda Kerber, "Separate Spheres, Female Worlds, Woman's Place: The Rhetoric of Women's History," *Journal of American History* 75 (June 1988), 3–39. She writes: "Little is left of Tocqueville except what he left to implication: that political systems and systems of gender relations are reciprocal constructions" (39). Some of the scholarship which has demonstrated the need for rethinking the construct of "woman's sphere" is Cott, *The grounding of modern feminism* (New Haven, 1987); Rosalind Rosenberg, *Beyond separate spheres: Intellectual roots of modern feminism* (New Haven, CT, 1982); John Mack Faragher, *Women and men on the overland trail* (New Haven, CT, 1979); Jean Fagan Yellin, *Women and sisters: The antislavery feminists in American culture* (New Haven, CT, 1989); Nancy Grey Osterud, *Bonds of community: The lives of farm women in nineteenth-century New York* (Ithaca, NY, 1991); Susan M. Reverby and Dorothy O. Helly, "Introduction: Converging on History," in *Gendered domains: Rethinking public and private in women's history,* ed. Reverby and Helly (Ithaca, NY, 1992). Michelle Rosaldo called for a rejection of a model of analyses based upon two opposing

spheres, proposing instead that research focus on the ways in which men and women alike cooperate with social constructs and institutional structures that separate them or unite them ("The Use and Abuse of Anthropology: Reflections on Feminism and Cross-Cultural Understanding," *Signs* 5 [1980], 417).

20. "Elegy, occasioned by the loss of several valued friends," *Boston Monthly Anthology* 5 (1808), 154; Joanne Harvey, Diary, February 5, 4, 1857; *Child's Friend and Youth's Companion Magazine* 19 (1852), 201–2 and 26 (1856), 37; Gamaliel Bradford, Diary, May 25, 1854.

21. *The Liberator* 24 (March 31, 1854), 52; *Boston Daily Advertiser* (April 21, 23, 1858); *Christian Observer* 32 (December 24, 1853), 208. Chauncy Hall became coeducational in 1858. Ladd was hired shortly afterward (Edward H. Cole, *The Chauncy Hall story* (Boston, 1963). *Independent* (January 12, 1854); *Evangelist and Religious Review* (December 30, May 13, 1858); *Massachusetts Ploughman* 9 (March 9, 1850); Stephen Salisbury Jr. to his family, October 21, 1858, AAS; Mary Josephine Faxon Forbush, Diary, January 23, 1850. Even among women who managed to find a place in an occupational area normally reserved for men, the notion of "woman's sphere" sometimes remained to influence their thinking about other women. The Unitarian Eunice Hale Cobb, who was married to Rev. Sylvanus Cobb, editor of the *Freeman*, made her debut as a preacher on July 31, 1863. She believed that it was a great success. A few days earlier, however, she had witnessed another woman preach and had remarked negatively upon it: "Have heard Miss Brown deliver two very good sermons. . . . Her performances were all good and acceptable, but I cannot yet see, that, as a 'settled pastor;' '*the* minister,' she is in her right sphere, and I doubt not, that time, and experience will prove it. It is not natural and, the better minister she is, the less a woman she must be . . ." (Journal, July 24, 1863, BPL). On Lucy Stone see Andrea Moore Kerr, *Lucy Stone: Speaking out for equality* (New Brunswick, NJ, 1992).

22. Stanton's opposition to Smith is referred to in Dorothy Sterling, *Abby Kelley and the politics of antislavery* (New York, 1991), 267 n. Caroline Dall, *Alongside* (Boston, 1900); Paulina W. Davis, *A history of the national woman's rights movement* (New York, 1871); Sylvia D. Hoffert, *When hens crow: The woman's rights movement in antebellum America* (Bloomington, IN, 1995); *Boston Daily Advertiser* (April 7, November 17, 1858); *The Liberator* 29 (October 7, 1859), 159 and 23 (April 29, 1853), 68 and 20 (February 15, 1850), 28, 32 and 20 (March 15, 1850), 44; *Monthly Law Reporter* 15 (April 1852), 680.

23. *The Budget* 1 (March 19, 1849[?]), in William W. Greenough Papers, LC; Eddy, *The young woman's friend*, 22; *The Liberator* 27 (January 15, 1858), 12; *Christian Observer* 34 (July 7, 1855), 108 and on the "Chronicles of England" 34 (March 3, 1855); *Christian Observatory* 1 (1847), 91; *Youth's Companion* (December 25, 1856), 143; *Young America* 1 (January 1858), 12; Henry W. Haynes, Diary, October 15, 1851, Tracy Patch Cheever, Diary, July 27, 1855.

24. Susan L. Porter, "Victorian Values in the Marketplace: Single Women and Work in Boston, 1800–1850," *Social Science History* 17 (1993), 128. Sarah

Deutsch sees the later nineteenth century as a time when women "posed the cooperative, nurturing values of home as an alternative to the competitive, individualist values of the marketplace and formal politics" ("Learning to Talk More Like a Man: Boston Women's Class-Bridging Organizations, 1870–1940," *American Historical Review* 97 [1992], 379–404).

25. *Massachusetts Teacher* 3 (February 1850), 40; Charles E. French, Diary, September 5, 1858; Henry W. Haynes, Diary, October 16, 1851; Gamaliel Bradford, Diary, April 26, 1854; Hale, *A New England boyhood*, 208; "Promiscuous leaves from my diary, by a convict" (Charlestown, MA, 1864); *Child's Friend and Family Magazine* 31 (Cambridge, 1858), 242. Literature that bears upon domesticity, emotionality, and Victorian masculinities in England and America includes David G. Pugh, *Sons of liberty: The masculine mind in nineteenth-century America* (Westport, CT, 1983); John Tosh, "Domesticity and Manliness in the Victorian Middle Class," in *Manful assertions: Masculinities in Britain since 1800* (London and New York, 1991); Steven M. Gelber, "Do-It-Yourself: Constructing, Repairing and Maintaining Domestic Masculinity," *American Quarterly* 49 (March 1997), 66–112. E. Anthony Rotundo suggests that mothers taught boys emotion and fathers taught them achievement ("Learning about Manhood: Gender Ideals and the Middle-Class Family in Nineteenth-Century America," in *Manliness and morality: Middle-class masculinity in Britain and America 1800–1940*, ed. J. A. Mangan and James Walvin [Manchester, 1987], 35–51). See also Rotundo, "Body and Soul: Changing Ideals of American Middle-Class Manhood, 1770–1920," *Journal of Social History* 16 (1983), 23–38. Rotundo's *American Manhood: Transformations in masculinity from the revolution to the modern era* (New York, 1993) accepts the argument that men and women lived in separate spheres and stresses "manly self-assertion" as the distinguishing feature of nineteenth-century masculinity (14–17, 24, 322 n. 6). In *Manhood in America: A cultural history* (New York, 1996), Michael Kimmel takes a similar tack in arguing that "men's reliance on women to meet all their emotional needs is a sad product of the separation of spheres" (56). Mark C. Carnes and Clyde Griffen, *Meanings for manhood: Constructions of masculinity in Victorian America* (Chicago, 1990); Glenn Hendler, "Pandering the Public Sphere: Masculinity and the Market in Horatio Alger," *American Quarterly* 48 (1996), 415–38.

26. Eddy, *The Young Man's friend*, 13, 15, 17, 18, 19, 22, 26, 31, 34; William Winter, *The Emotion of sympathy: A metrical essay* (Boston, 1856), 15–16; Samuel May to Richard Davis Webb, December 1, 1857; Tracy Patch Cheever, Diary, March 28, 1854; *Massachusetts Teacher* 3 (December 1850), 378; *Christian Parlor Magazine* 4 (1847 [no month given]), 332; George W. Prescott, Notebook ca. 1860, AAS.

27. *Massachusetts Ploughman* 9 (March 9, 1850); *New Englander* 8 (August 1850), 444; Tracy Patch Cheever, Diary, January 9, 1854); Frances Merritt, Journal, May 30, 1858; Charles E. French, Diary, July 5, 1855; Stephen Salisbury Jr. to his father, August 31, 1858, AAS; James Barnard Blake, Diary, Feb-

ruary 25, 1851; Joanne Harvey, Diary, August 1, 1857; George Scandlin, Diary, May 1854 [no date]; Hanford Wright to Elizur Wright, June 23, 1858, LC; *Gleason's Pictorial* 6 (May 27, 1854), 327; Tracy Patch Cheever, Diary, May 2, 1854; Eliphay Arnold Jr., Diary, April 11, 1850, January 19, February 10, 1851; J. D. Pratt to Eliphay Arnold Jr., March 19, 1849 (ms. with diary), MHS.

28. Gamaliel Bradford, Diary, August 20, 1856; Henry William Tisdale, Diary, March 9, 10, 1856, BPL.

29. Reid Mitchell, *The vacant chair: The northern soldier leaves home* (New York, 1993). Cited material from pp. 10, 12.

30. Mitchell, *The vacant chair*, 18; Samuel J. Watson, "Flexible Gender Roles during the Market Revolution: Family, Friendship, Marriage, and Masculinity among U.S. Army Officers, 1815–1846," *Journal of Social History* 29 (fall 1995), 82; Stephen M. Frank, "'Rendering Aid and Comfort': Images of Fatherhood in the Letters of Civil War Soldiers from Massachusetts and Michigan," *Journal of Social History* 26 (fall 1992), 23; *Boston Recorder* 34 (May 11, 1849); Ephraim Peabody, account of his death in Peabody Papers, MHS.

31. *New Englander* 9 (November 1851), 585; *Christian Parlor Magazine* (June 1844), 82; Henry W. Haynes, Diary, October 16, 1851; Gamaliel Bradford, Diary, May 7, 18, 1854; *Massachusetts Teacher* 1 (1848), 28 and 6 (September 1853), 257; Joanne Harvey to Charles Harvey, April 18, 1856, Charles Henry Harvey Papers, LC; Samuel A. Eliot to William W. Greenough, April 31, 1851, William W. Greenough Papers, LC; William Plumer Jr., *Manhood, or scenes from the past* (Boston, 1843), 12; *Boston Masonic Mirror* (January 1, 1825).

32. "Birthplace of Franklin, in Milk St. Jan. 6 1706," BPL; Francis Bennett Jr., Diary, August 28, 1854; William Henry Hoyt, Diary, February 12, 1851; Muzzey, *The young man's friend*, 68; *Christian Observatory* 1 (October 1847), 465.

33. *The Liberator* 25 (December 14, 1855), 200 and (September 28, 1855), 156 and 23 (August 12, 1853); *Youth's Companion* 32 (March 25, 1858), 46; James Barnard Blake, Diary, January 15, 1851; *Gleason's Pictorial* 1 (May 3, 1851), 46; *Evangelist and Religious Review* (August 26, 1858); *Watchman-Examiner* (October 30, 1856).

34. *New Englander* 10 (February 1852), 115; James Barnard Blake, Diary, February 16, 1851. Henry William Tisdale expressed a concern similar to Blake's: "I need to learn to be intense and at the same time not excited in debates and conversation" (Diary, September 24, 1863, BPL). *Child's Friend and Family Magazine* 27 (1856), 33; *Christian Observer* 30 (June 21, 1851), 100; *Independent* (January 17, 1856); *The Liberator* 27 (April 17, 1857), 64.

35. *Monthly Religious Magazine* 28 (September 1862), 137–42; *The Liberator* 22 (February 20, 1852), 32 and 26 (November 28, 1856), 190; *New Englander* 16 (November 1858), 781 and 30 (May 1850), 293–94; *Evangelist and Religious Review* (August 11, 1859); *Independent* (June 8, 1860).

36. William Henry Smith, Diary, February 16, 1853; *Boston Evening Tran-*

script (November 11, 1858); Theodore Parker, *Theodore Parker to a young man* (Boston, 1851), 2 (this is a pamphlet that reprints his article, originally published in the *Christian Register* [July 9, 1851]). Tracy Patch Cheever, Diary, March 20, 1854.

37. David Leverenz, *Manhood and the American Renaissance* (Ithaca, NY, 1989), 72; *Christian Observer* 33 (March 4, 1854), 36; *Child's Friend and Family Magazine* 29 (Cambridge, 1857), 65; *Monthly Anthology and Boston Review* 4 (1808), 366; *Massachusetts Teacher* 8 (August 1854), 238; Jacob Porter, Diary, January 4, 1807; Henry W. Haynes, Diary, November 3, 1851; Charlotte Foster, Composition Book, April 19, 1851, MHS. The reference to Shakespeare is *Othello*, act 1, scene 1 (vol. 7 of the Collier collection [1843]).

38. *Evangelist and Religious Review* (July 15, 1858); *Ballou's Pictorial* 8 (March 31, 1855), 195; "Berenger," in *Child's Friend and Family Magazine* 28 (Cambridge, 1857), 125; Mary J. Walker, Diary, October 13, 1848; *Christian Observer* (April 22, 1855), 64; *Gleason's Pictorial* 2 (April 10, 1852), 235; Eddy, *The young woman's friend,* 23; Plumer, *Manhood, or scenes from the past,* 24; *Christian Parlor Magazine* (June 1844), 36.

39. *The Liberator* 28 (October 29, 1858), 174 and "The Female Pests," 23 (September 16, 1853), 148; Henry W. Haynes, Diary, November 5, 1851; *Constitution and by-laws of the Boston Fencing Club* (Boston, 1850), art. 6.

40. *Gleason's Pictorial* 5 (October 15, 1853), 241 and 1 (June 14, 1851), 104 and 4 (April 23, 1853), 268; *Boston Evening Transcript* (January 8, 1859); *Ballou's Pictorial* 14 (April 3, 1858), 221; *The Liberator* 23 (November 18, 1853), 181; Francis Bennett Jr., Diary, May 26, 1852, November 24, 1854; Charles F. Low, Diary, June 3, 1860; Henry W. Haynes, Diary, October 28, November 2, 1851; Charles E. French, Diary, August 8, 1857. Carroll Smith-Rosenberg provides useful context for cross-dressing and other practices which represented fluidity in gender categories in *Disorderly conduct: Visions of gender in Victorian America* (New York, 1985). See also Marjorie Garber, *Vested interests: Cross-dressing and cultural anxiety* (New York, 1992) and Richard Elkins, *Male femaling: A grounded theory approach to cross-dressing and sex-changing* (London, 1997).

41. An example of this is given by Bret E. Carroll in "Breasted and Bearded Manhood in Victorian America: Cultural Androgyny and the Mediumship of John Shoebridge Williams," *Journal of Religion and American Culture* 7 (1997), 27–60.

42. *Ballou's Pictorial* 8 (April 21, 1855), 247; *Massachusetts Teacher* 7 (November 1854), 352 and 11 (October 1858), 394; *Monthly Law Reporter* 14 (August 1851), 227; Charles E. French, Diary, March 27, 1855; *The Liberator* 37 (September 18, 1857), 152; *New Englander* 12 (November 1854), 491.

43. *New York Times* (March 22, 1858); *The Liberator* 23 (April 15, 1853), 57; "Robertson's Sermons," *New Englander* 17 (November 1859), 863; Eddy, *The young man's friend,* 31; *New Englander* (May 1857), 320.

44. Karen Lystra, *Searching the heart: Women, men, and romantic love in nineteenth-century America* (New York, 1989), 156.

SEVEN. DOMESTIC CONTRACTS

1. Jane Donahue Eberwein, *Dickinson: Strategies of limitation* (Amherst, MA, 1985), 103; Mary Loeffelholz, *Dickinson and the boundaries of feminist theory* (Urbana, IL, 1991), 37. Ruth Miller saw the "him" as God (*The poetry of Emily Dickinson* [Middletown, CT, 1968], 81).

2. Emily Dickinson, "The Contract," (#580) in *Poems*, ed. T. W. Higginson and Mabel Loomis Todd (Boston, 1890).

3. I. R. Butts, *Businessman's companion* (Boston, 1858), 10; see also Butts, *The United States business man's law cabinet* (Boston, 1857); *Boston Daily Advertiser* (April 20, 1858); *Monthly Law Reporter* 21 (May 1858), 301 and 20 (October 1857), 346 and 4 (August 1851), 203 and 21 (July 1858), 165; Francis Wayland, *The elements of moral science* (Boston, 1856), 307; *Massachusetts Teacher* 11 (February 1858), 67. Glenda Riley observes that prenuptial contracts in the nineteenth century are found in all classes, but especially among wealthy southerners (*Divorce: An American tradition* [New York, 1991], 43).

4. *Christian Parlor Magazine* 2 (May 1845), 9; *Ballou's Pictorial* 15 (September 11, 1858), 167 and 16 (January 15, 1859), 47 and 15 (August 21, 1858), 127; *The Liberator* 26 (January 11, 1856), 5.

5. Young men frequently found the likelihood of emotional trauma in proposing marriage more than they could bear, and this may have been the case with Bradford, who had made a detailed entry in his diary about the suicide of a young woman over the breakup of an engagement (Diary, July 14, 1854). John Townsend Trowbridge was crushed by a woman's rejection of him as a prospect for marriage, so that "I wet my pillow with tears. Is it all illusion?" (Diary, August 24, 26, 31, 1854). Stephen Salisbury Jr. wrote to his family on news of a friend's engagement: "What astonishes me is that one can make his mind [*sic*] to propose! All this no doubt requires great effort on the part of the party" (Stephen Salisbury Jr. to his family, July 21, 1858, AAS).

6. *Youth's Companion* 27 (January 12, 1854), 151; *Ballou's Pictorial* 17 (July 16, 1859), 42 and 14 (January 16, 1858), 45 and 13 (December 26, 1857), 413 and 15 (August 14, 1858), 107 and 14 (February 13, 1858), 103; Gamaliel Bradford, Diary, November 10, October 29, December 19, 1855, January 5, 25, 1856.

7. *The new complete letter writer; or, the art of correspondence* (Boston, 1798), 18–19; *Young America* 1 (April 1858), 43; *Gleason's Pictorial* 1 (September 13, 1851), 318.

8. *Gleason's Pictorial* 1 (May 10, 1851), 29; *Youth's Companion* 29 (August 30, 1855), 75; *New Englander* 11 (May 1853), 305; *Ballou's Pictorial* 8 (May 26, 1855), 333 and 13 (October 17, 1857), 253; Eddy, *The young woman's friend*, 52; *The Liberator* 21 (April 11, 1851), 60. The prostitution theme was common. *The Liberator* cited Mrs. Mary F. Davis's remark to the Woman's Rights Convention in New York in December 1856 that "the marriage institution" was "a system of legalized prostitution" (26 [December 5, 1856], 196).

9. Karen Lystra, *Searching the heart: Women, men, and romantic love in*

nineteenth-century America (New York, 1989), 236; Jacqueline S. Reinier, *From virtue to character: American childhood, 1775–1850* (New York, 1996), 6; Chris Dixon, *Perfecting the family: Antislavery marriages in nineteenth-century America* (Amherst, MA, 1997), 202; Robert H. Chused, *Private acts in public places: A social history of divorce in the formative era of American family law* (Philadelphia, 1994), 5.

10. Mary Josephine Faxon Forbush, Diary, December 4, 1858; *The Liberator* 20 (February 15, 1850), 32 and 22 (June 18, 1852), 100 and 25 (March 9, 1855), 40 and 30 (June 1, 1860), 88 and 29 (February 11, 1854), 24.

11. *The Liberator* 21 (September 12, 1851), 146 and 23 (February 25, 1853), 32 and 23 (November 25, 1853), 187 and 25 (May 4, 1855), 71; *Monthly Law Reporter* 14 (July 1851), 153–54 and 14 (August 1851), 206–7.

12. *Monthly Law Reporter* 19 (February 1857), 581 and 21 (January 21, 1859); *The Liberator* 27 (March 5, 1858), 40 and 30 (March 2, 1860), 36. Some debate before the Ohio Senate included the assertion that "instead of making a union such as is contemplated by marriage, it [married woman's right to contract as an individual] was but a mere partnership contract" (*The Liberator* 30 [March 2, 1860], 36). Commentary on the proposed 1859 statute to define more broadly the right of married women to property and independent contract suggested that the title of the statute should be changed from "'Of certain rights,'" to "'Of the uncertain rights and liabilities of husband and wife'" (*Monthly Law Reporter* 21 [January 1859], 530). The English background for understanding ideas about women as free individuals in contract marriages is in Susan Staves, *Married women and property in England, 1660–1823* (Cambridge, MA, 1990).

13. Reinier, *From virtue to character,* ix; Steven Mintz, *A prison of expectations: The family in Victorian culture* (New York, 1983), 199; *Ballou's Pictorial* 15 (August 21, 1858), 116; Henry Clark Wright, Diary, August 27, 1853.

14. *Ballou's Pictorial* 11 (August 30, 1856), 132; Mintz, *A prison of expectations,* 104, 134; *New Englander* 11 (February 1853), 54 and 16 (August 1858), 633; *Christian Parlor Magazine* 2 (May 1845), 9; Theodore Parker, *Prayers* (Boston, 1862), 133.

15. *Ballou's Pictorial* 17 (November 5, 1959), 295. Steven Mintz has suggested that in Victorian thinking about marriage "two distinct themes are intertwined: a contractual and a sacramental view of the marriage relationship." Those two ideals were represented in evangelical imagery applied to marriage as Christian love and Christian freedom (*A prison of expectations,* 133–34). Mintz proposes that the significance of that representation was as a means "of exorcising worries and insecurities that Victorians brought to marriage." I see the significance as a means of addressing the porousness of categories of masculine/feminine and public/private by mutually stressing the contractual nature of the relationship and its emotional component.

16. Anne C. Rose, *Victorian America and the Civil War* (Cambridge, 1992), 147; James Barnard Blake, Diary, January 5, 1851; Charles E. French, Di-

ary, March 6, 7, April 1, 1858, June 26, 1857; Joanne Harvey, Diary, March 27, April 17, 1857.

17. Riley, *Divorce*, 61, 60, 84.

18. For discussion of the manner in which mutual and relative dependencies shape the nature of exchange see Linda D. Molm, *Coercive power in social exchange* (Cambridge, UK, 1997). See also "Affect and Social Exchange: Satisfaction in Power-Dependence Relations," *American Sociological Review* 56 (August 1991), 475–93. On the exchange of emotion see Margaret S. Clark and Carolyn Taraban, "Reactions to and Willingness to Express Emotion in Communal and Exchange Relationships," *Journal of Experimental Social Psychology* 27 (1991), 324–36. A seminal study on exchange in marriage is G. W. McDonald, "Structural Exchange and Marital Interaction," *Journal of Marriage and the Family* 43 (1981), 825–39. See also Gary L. Hansen, "Moral Reasoning and the Marital Exchange Relationship," *Journal of Social Psychology* 131 (1991), 71–81. The broader framework of my approach is constructed from fetish and reification theory drawn in part from the following: Karl Marx, *Capital*, part 1 ("Commodities & Money" and especially sec. 4, "The Fetishism of Commodities") and part 2 ("The Transformation of Money into Capital"); Marcel Mauss, *The Gift*, trans. Ian Cunnison (New York, 1967); Georg Lukács, "Reification and the Consciousness of the Proletariat," in *History and class consciousness*, trans. Rodney Livingstone (London, 1971), 83–222; Sigmund Freud, "Fetishism," in *The standard edition of the complete psychological works of Sigmund Freud*, trans. James Strachey, vol. 21 (London, 1955–74), 149–58; Walter Benjamin, "Theses on the Philosophy of History," in *Illuminations*, edited by and with an introduction by Hannah Arendt, trans. Harry Zohn (New York, 1968), 253–64; Luce Irigaray, "Commodities among Themselves" and "Women on the Market," in *This sex which is not one*, trans. Catherine Porter (Ithaca, NY, 1985), 192–97, 170–91.

19. *Ballou's Pictorial* 13 (August 1, 1857), 68. Images of the commodification of character and identity in English Romantic literature are analyzed by Andrea K. Henderson, *Romantic identities: Varieties of subjectivity, 1774–1830* (Cambridge, UK, 1996), 38–58.

20. *Ballou's Pictorial* 12 (May 9, 1857), 297; *Christian Observatory* 3 (March 1849), 136; "The Birthplace of Washington," *Child's Friend and Family Magazine* 6 (Cambridge, 1857), 50 and 2 (Boston, 1855), 61 and 1 (Boston, 1855), 83; *Christian Parlor Magazine* (June 1844), 35; *New Englander* 35 (August 1851), 372.

21. Harvey J. Graff, *Conflicting paths: Growing up in America* (Cambridge, MA, 1995); Mary P. Ryan, *Cradle of the middle class: The family in Oneida, New York, 1790–1865* (Cambridge, UK, 1981), 159; see also Reinier, *From virtue to character*, ix; Horace Bushnell, *Views of Christian nurture* (Hartford, CT, 1847). Bostonians could read reviews of Bushnell's book in numerous religious publications and some anthologies and literary magazines. The *Massachusetts Quarterly Review* summarized the argument of the book: "This vol-

ume contains two discourses on human nurture, designed to show, that if you educate the religious nature of a child the child will commonly turn out a religious man, without needing to go through the process of transformation in a 'revival'" (1 [December 1847], 127). Scholarship outlining various aspects of the intensification of emotional relationships within the family includes John Demos, "The American Family in Past Time," *American Scholar* 43 (1974), 422–46 and Stephen Kern, "Explosive Intimacy: Psychodynamics of the Victorian Family," *History of Childhood Quarterly* 1 (1974), 437–62; Bernard Wishy, *The child and the republic: The dawn of modern American child nurture* (Philadelphia, 1968). Peter N. Stearns emphasizes the separation of males and females according to gender roles in the nineteenth century in the course of outlining a Victorian emotional ideal ("Girls, Boys, and Emotions: Redefinitions and Historical Change," *Journal of American History* 80 [1993], 36–74). I have focused on the manner in which gender roles became sufficiently fluid to allow for limited blending of "public" and "domestic" aspects of adult life, and for contractual relationships between emotionally involved parties.

22. *Ballou's Pictorial* 10 (June 28, 1856), 410 and 15 (October 23, 1858), 272 and 10 (March 1, 1856), 141; *Gleason's Pictorial* 7 (December 9, 1854), 363; *Christian Parlor Magazine* 2 (September 1845), 146; Theodore Parker, *A sermon on the dangerous classes in society* (Boston, 1847), 14; *Massachusetts Teacher* 10 (April 1857), 186 and 10 (December 1857), 550.

23. *The Liberator* 23 (September 23, 1853), 152; *Christian Observatory* 4 (February 1850), 89; *American Baptist Magazine and Missionary Intelligencer* 9 (May 1818) 189; *The Well-Spring* 15 (November 19, 1858), 188 and 15 (August 6, 1858), 126.

24. Sisterly affection for brothers was the second-most commented-on family relationship. "None of the little vanities, heart-burnings and jealousies that, alas for poor human nature! Are but too apt to spring up in female hearts can . . . arise between brother and sister" (*Gleason's Pictorial* 2 [June 12, 1852], 379).

25. *Gleason's Pictorial* 2 (April 24, 1852), 379; *Boston Monthly Magazine* 1 (May 1826), 622; *Youth's Companion* 29 (July 12, 1855), 48; Gamaliel Bradford, Diary, April 20, 1854; *Ballou's Pictorial* 13 (August 29, 1857), 138; *Child's Friend and Youth's Magazine* 20 (1852) 71; Joanne Harvey to Charles Harvey, May 1, 1853, LC; Charles Harvey to family, July 24, 1854, LC; *Massachusetts Ploughman* 9 (March 23, 1850). See Jan Lewis, "Mother's Love: The Construction of Emotion in Nineteenth-Century America," in *Social history and issues of human consciousness: Some interdisciplinary connections*, ed. A. E. Barnes and Peter N. Stearns (New York, 1989), 209–29.

26. Muzzey, *The young man's friend*, 85; *Christian Parlor Magazine* 1 (June 1844), 37 and 3 (November 1846), 205; William Henry Hoyt, Diary, February 13, 1851; Linda D. Molm, "Structure, Action, and Outcomes: The Dynamics of Power in Social Exchange," *American Sociological Review* 55 (June 1990), 429.

27. James Barnard Blake, Diary, January 1, 1851; *Massachusetts Teacher* 1 (March 1848), 70 and 7 (November 1854), 352; *Christian Observatory* 2 (July 1848), 313; *Gleason's Pictorial* 1 (May 17, 1851), 38; *Youth's Cabinet* 2 (May 54, 1838), 2.

28. *Massachusetts Teacher* 11 (February 1858), 67 and 9 (September 1856), 415 and 2 (August 1849), 254 and 4 (November 1851), 334. See also "Love of Teaching," *Massachusetts Teacher* 1 (April 1, 1848). *The Well-Spring* 15 (August 13, 1858), 131.

29. *Massachusetts Teacher* 6 (June 1852), 173 and 5 (February 1852), 41 and 10 (February 1857), 57 and 7 (February 1854), 45.

30. Robert Hale, "Arithmetick," 370, 327, 389, 383, 370, Papers, AAS; Peter S. Townsend, *A dissertation on the influence of the passions in the production and modification of disease* (New York, 1816), 69–70.

31. Frances Merritt, Journal, May 30, 1858; Hon. Emory Washburn, *Anniversary address delivered before the Young Men's Christian Union, November 26, 1855* (Boston, 1856), 17; Rev. James I. T. Coolidge, *An address delivered before the Boston YMCU* (Boston, 1853), 11; Catherine Beecher, *The Elements of Mental and Moral Philosophy* (Hartford, CT, 1831), 427, 82, 274, 276–77; Muzzey, *The young man's friend*, 14; *Evangelist and Religious Review* 26 (April 19, 1855); *New Englander* 9 (May 1851), 188, 189; see also John Corrigan, "'Habits from the Heart': The American Enlightenment and Religious Ideas about Emotion and Habit," *Journal of Religion* 73 (April 1993), 183–99. Emotion was a key force in the dynamics of "association"—that is, the Scottish understanding of the integrated action of intellect, emotion, and will. Without emotion, or, as Scots sometimes termed it, "susceptibility," the mind would be unable to make associations. Joseph John Gurney stressed the importance of the "Law of association" to habit. "Association may safely be regarded as the strength and main-spring of habit" (*Thoughts on habit and discipline* [Philadelphia, 1845], 57).

32. "From Our Boston Correspondent," *Independent* (January 16, 9, 1851); *Christian Parlor Magazine* 3 (February 1847), 292.

33. Peter N. Stearns and Carol Z. Stearns, "Emotionology: Clarifying the History of Emotions and Emotional Standards," *American Historical Review* 90 (1985), 813; Niklas Luhman, *Love as passion: The codification of intimacy* (Cambridge, MA, 1986), 14. On emotion as a "communicative act" involving exchange see Brian Parkinson, *Ideas and realities of emotion* (London, 1995), 264–304.

EIGHT. CLERKS, APPRENTICES, AND BOYCULTURE

1. Francis Bennett Jr., Diary, December 31, 1854; *Boston Evening Transcript* (September 27, 1847, quoted in Knights, *Yankee destinies*, 28 (and see also 26–31 on migration from the countryside); Trowbridge, *My own story*, 173; Washburn, *Anniversary address delivered before the Young Men's Chris-*

tian Union, 5; *Christian Observatory* 2 (September 1848), 429; William Henry Hoyt, Journal, February 23, 1851; *Evangelist and Religious Review* (December 23, 1858); *Youth's Companion* 34 (August 2, 1860), 122; *Child's Friend and Family Magazine* 8 (Cambridge, 1858), 126; W. E. Boardman, *The higher Christian life* (Boston, 1920), 28; Knights, *The plain people of Boston*, 27–28. The male/female ratio of the city's African American population in 1840 was about seven to five (George A. Levesque, *Black Boston: African American life and culture in urban America, 1750–1860* [New York, 1994], Table I-21, p. 99).

2. Elizur Wright to daughter Jane [?], September 20, 1860, Elizur Wright Papers, LC; *Child's Friend and Family Magazine* 6 (Cambridge, 1857), 239; *Boston Evening Transcript* (October 30, 1858).

3. Joseph Kett, *Rites of passage: Adolescence in America 1790 to the present* (New York, 1977); Arthur Howard Nichols, Diary, April 5, 1852; Charles E. French, Diary, March 5, 1855; Joanne Harvey to Charles Harvey, June 17, 1855, Charles Henry Harvey Papers, LC; Francis Bennett Jr., Diary, August 3, September 14, 15, August 28, September 5, 1854; Coolidge, *An address delivered before the Boston YMCU*, 7; Mary Dewey to Charles Dewey, May 23, 1857, in Orville Dewey, Correspondence, AAS.

4. Francis Bennett Jr., Diary, June 30, 1854; George H. Troup, Diary, May 27, 29, 1858; *A brief history of the Somerset Club of Boston* (Boston, 1913), 8; *Youth's Companion* 30 (November 15, 1860), 182; "The Five Points Illustrated," in *Boston Masonic Mirror; and Mechanics Intelligencer* 1 (November 27, 1824); Charles E. French, Diary, March 5, 1855; George S. Hilliard, *The dangers and duties of the mercantile profession. An address delivered before the Mercantile Library Association . . . November 13, 1850* (Boston, 1850), 18–19; Franklin Scientific Association, Manuscripts, vol. 4, BPL; Marion L. Bell, *Crusade in the city: Revivalism in nineteenth-century Philadelphia* (Lewisburg, PA, 1977).

5. Patricia Cline Cohen, "Unregulated Youth: Masculinity and Murder in the 1850's City," *Radical History Review* 52 (1992), 46.

6. Holmes, *One hundred years of Mount Vernon Church*, 44; *Young Men's Christian Union Charter and Bylaws* (Boston, 1852), 4; Washburn, *Anniversary address delivered before the Young Men's Christian Union*, 6; *Catalogue of the library of the Boston Young Men's Christian Union* (Boston, 1855); "Circular from the Boston Young Men's Christian Union," October 20, 1859, BPL.

7. Francis Bennett Jr., Diary, October 8, 9, 11, 12, 13, 16, 18, 20, 26, 27, 28, 29, 30, 1854; George H. Troup, Diary, March 25, 31, 1858, April 1, 5, 7, 9, 10, 11, 13, 1858. Quotation from Bennett's diary, October 18, 1854.

8. *Young Men's Christian Union Charter and Bylaws*, 1–4; "Report of the Executive Committee of the Young Men's Christian Association of the United States and British Provinces, September 25, 1869," "YMCA, Boston" collection, Box L (1912), MHS; Jacob Merrill Manning, Diary, November 29, December 3, 1857; Ezra Stiles Gannett, Diary, May 17, 1857, February 14, 1858; *Boston Evening Transcript* (January 17, 1859); *Youth's Companion* 32 (April 29, 1858), 68; "Constitution of the Waltham Young Men's Christian As-

sociation" (Waltham, MA, 1854), "Section 8"; "Constitution of the Young Men's Parochial Association of Christ Church, Boston" (Boston, 1858). Besides the Christ Church group, there was the Young People's Society founded by Kirk at Mount Vernon, which included a young Dwight L. Moody on its membership list, and which numbered three hundred members by 1860 (Holmes, *One hundred years of Mount Vernon Church*, 73).

9. Graff, *Conflicting paths: Growing up in America*, 185; H. W. Beecher, "A Chapter on Boys," *The Liberator* 27 (November 13, 1857), 184; Theodore Parker, *A sermon on the dangerous classes in society* (Boston, 1847), 4; Henry W. Haynes, Diary, October 16, 1851; Washburn, *Anniversary address delivered before the Young Men's Christian Union*, 6; *Gleason's Pictorial* 4 (April 23, 1853), 407; *New Englander* 9 (November 1851), 588.

10. Patrick Collins, in *Old South Chapel prayer meeting*, 77–78, 146, 156. George Scandlin, Diary, October 26, 1855; Orville Dewey to Charles Dewey, January 16, 1860, AAS; "Riot at Faneuil Hall. Mr. Quincy's Letter" (to editor of *Boston Post*, November 17, 1850), Broadside, BPL; Joanne Harvey to Charles Harvey, April 18, 1856, LC; Franklin Scientific Association, Papers; *Massachusetts Teacher* 1 (February 1848), 52 and 13 (November 1860), 404; *Gleason's Pictorial* 5 (September 17, 1853), 189; *Christian Observatory* 2 (January 1848), 18; *Ballou's Pictorial* 8 (May 5, 1855), 283 and 10 (April 5, 1856), 221; *Evangelist and Religious Review* (February 1, 1855). The *Christian Parlor Magazine* opined that, in fact, the young felt more deeply, more profoundly, than older persons (2 [May 1845], 9).

11. Joanne Harvey, Diary, July 21, 1857; Joanne Harvey to Charles Harvey, June 17, 1855; *The wonderful adventures of the little man and his little gun* (Boston, 1859[?]), 9, 5, 10; Charles F. Low, Diary, February 7, 18, 20, 21, 23, 28, March 19, April 11, 1857, August 10, 1859, June 22, 1860; *Massachusetts Teacher* 7 (March 1854), 90; Sarah Swan Weld Blake, *Diary and Letters of Francis Minot Weld, M.D.* (Boston, 1925), April 3, July 14, 1855; Charles Dewey to family, December 20, 1846.

12. *Puritan Recorder* (March 1858), clipping in "Great Awakening, 1858" collection, CL; George H. Troup, Diary, April 2, 11, 15, 1858; Gamaliel Bradford, December 18, 1855; Henry W. Haynes, October 12, 17, 1851; Dickens, *American notes*, 54; James Barnard Blake, Diary, January 6, 9, February 19, 1851; Riess, *City games*, 17; George H. Troup, Diary, February 23, March 9, 1858; Gamaliel Bradford, Diary, January 1, 1856; March 13, 1855; Tracy Patch Cheever, Diary, October 13, 1854. The first American national billiards championship was held in Detroit in 1859. Steven A. Riess writes: "Few sports were as accessible to working-class urbanites as billiards." Usually "billiard halls were situated mainly in and around the downtown area in close proximity to the city's saloons and brothels. Many unattached, transient males resided in that neighborhood . . ." (*City games: The evolution of American urban society and the rise of sports* [Urbana, 1989], 17). Trowbridge, *My own story*, 238; Charlotte Foster, Diary, March 16, 1858; Susan E. P. Brown, Diary, March 24, 1857; Coolidge, *An address delivered before the Boston YMCU*, 10–11; *Youth's*

Companion 24 (October 17, 1850), 100 and 25 (April 8, 1852), 200; *Ballou's Pictorial* 15 (September 22, 1858), 205; Mary Mudge, Diary, July 3, 1854; Miriam Sears to Knyvet Winthrop Sears, January 17, 1860, MHS. Mischief took a variety of forms, but much was directed toward teachers and school. Fifteen boys at Arthur Howard Nichols's school were caught breaking schoolhouse windows, and his classmates succeeded in causing the resignation of their teacher after one month by stamping their feet, slamming desktops, making noises, and so forth (Diary, June 8, 1852, and "January, 1856"). As the precursor to "Contract Bridge," Whist required a keen sense of contractual obligations and exchange. Playing Whist practiced persons in the mentality of regulated transaction. Henry G. Bohm's *The handbook of games* (London, 1850) included the following in the section on the rules of Whist: "Since all right of communication between parties is founded on their individual and mutual responsibility, it is, consequently, necessary to adopt some means of punishment in which a player may be involved by the ignorance or inattention of their partner" (sec. 9, art. 109, p. 135). For a sketch of Whist as played in America in the nineteenth century see Richard Rankin, "'The Seat of Smiling Mirth': The Ninepenny Whist Club of Wilmington, North Carolina, 1801–ca. 1807," *North Carolina Historical Review* 68 (January 1991), 38–57.

13. Like young women, young men went to church to look for candidates for romantic encounters. Gamaliel Bradford captured the thoughts of other men when he wrote: "Miss O[tis] being out of town it was no use to go to church so I read the papers until dinner time" (Diary, December 30, 1856).

14. "The Sporting World," *Massachusetts Teacher* 12 (September 1859), 336, 338, 337, 340.

15. *Massachusetts Teacher* 2 (November 1849), 346; Gamaliel Bradford, Diary, May 3, April 18, 1854; *Ballou's Pictorial* 10 (March 29, 1856), 205 and 12 (February 28, 1857), 141; *Gleason's Pictorial* 1 (August 2, 1851), 209; Charles F. Low, Diary, January 24, 28, February 5, 1857; Charles E. French, Diary, June 9, 1855; Francis Bennett Jr., Diary, September 1, 1854; Mary Dewey to Charles Dewey, May 23, 1857, in Orville Dewey, Correspondence, AAS; Eliphay Arnold Jr., Diary, March 9, 12, 22, 1850; Arthur Howard Nichols, Diary, "Remembrances for the Year 1855"; George H. Troup, Diary, April 21, 1855; Blake, *Diaries and letters of Francis Minot Weld, M.D.*, 76; Christian K. Messenger, *Sport and the spirit of play in American fiction: Hawthorne to Faulkner* (New York, 1981), 133; Thomas Wentworth Higginson, "Saints and Their Bodies," *Atlantic Monthly* 1 (May 1858), 588.

16. On the "new, physical ideal of manliness" in Victorian America see Rotundo, "Body and Soul," 26–29. See also Rotundo, "Learning about Manhood," 3, 43–48.

17. Arthur Howard Nichols, Diary, June 22, 1852, January 1, 1858; Joanne Harvey to Charles Harvey, May 18, 1857, LC; G. B. Windship, M.D., "Physical Culture," *Massachusetts Teacher* 13 (March 1860), 128, 129–31, 132.

18. Rush, *Medical Inquiries and Observations*, 19; Higginson, "Saints and Their Bodies," 582–95; Oliver Wendell Holmes, "The Autocrat of the Break-

fast Table," *Atlantic Monthly* 1 (May 1858), 881. See Riess, *City games*, 26–30; Stephen Hardy, *How Boston Played: Sport, recreation, and community, 1865–1915* (Boston, 1982); John A. Lucas, "Thomas Wentworth Higginson: Early Apostle of Health and Fitness," *Journal of Physical Education, Health Education, and Recreation* 42 (1971), 30–33.

19. *Christian Parlor Magazine* 3 (August 1846), 120; George Scandlin, Diary, January 2, 1852; *Massachusetts Teacher* 10 (June 1857), 313; Horace Mann, "Abuse of Health and Wealth," *Trumpet and Universalist* 23 (October 26, 1850).

20. "Description of Our Savior," *Christian Observer* 31 (June 19, 1852), 100. William Ramsey previously had written in the *Observer:* "This much, then, we do know; that the Christian will be like Christ, not only in his moral character, but also in his bodily appearance" (30 [September 27, 1851], 253). Higginson, "Saints and Their Bodies"; *Boston Daily Advertiser* (October 20, April 30, 1858); Andrew L. Stone, *Service, the end of living* (Boston, 1858), 32, 33; *The Liberator* 28 (December 24, 1858), 208 and 21 (May 16, 1851), 80; "The Christian Race," *Christian Observer* 30 (October 18, 1851), 165; James Barnard Blake, Diary, January 5, 6, 9, 1851; *Christian Register* 29 (August 24, 1850), 133 and 29 (September 28, 1850), 153 and 28 (December 15, 1849), 194; George H. Troup, Diary, April 21, 1858; Eliphay Arnold Jr., Diary, March 22, 1850; *Christian Parlor Magazine* 3 (August 1846), 120. Haynes conjured an image of powerful physical presence mixed with compassion in his description of Armstrong as a "noble specimen of a whole-souled, hearty, old sailor; moreover he is a fine looking man very, [*sic*] tall, & with such a breadth of shoulders. He looks like a man for the quarterdeck. He was very kind and polite and made a present of a beautiful stick of some california wood" (Diary, October 15, 1851).

21. By the same token, "highest refinement of the mind, without improvement of body presents but half a human being" (*Boston Medical Intelligencer* 1 [June 10, 1823]).

22. *Massachusetts Teacher* 2 (October 1849), 297 and 10 (February 1857), 75 and 12 (March 1859), 94 and 3 (August 1850), 247; *Gleason's Pictorial* 7 (September 30, 1854), 206; *Christian Register* 27 (March 4, 1848), 37; *Christian Observer* 32 (September 10, 1853), 148.

23. Stephen Hardy, commenting on sporting clubs in Boston after the Civil War, argued that they "helped to define and strengthen interest communities" while at the same time reinforcing perception of social differences between members of one club and another (*How Boston played*, 189).

24. Riess, *City games*, 33–35; John Allen Krout, *Annals of American sport* (New Haven, CT, 1929), 114–99; *Ballou's Pictorial* 16 (June 4, 1859), 360; *Massachusetts Teacher* 7 (December 1854), 380; *Gleason's Pictorial* 1 (August 2, 1851), 209. In late nineteenth-century Canada cricket was promoted as an essential part of a program "fostering a 'cult of manliness'" in boys (Paul L. Bennett, "In Defense of Cricket," *History and Social Science Teacher* 24 [1989], 164); Arthur Howard Nichols, Diary, April 29, 31, 1852; Tracy Patch Cheever,

Diary, April 7, 1854; Charles E. French, Diary, May 30, 1857; Walt Whitman, "Song of Myself," song 33, line 751, *Leaves of grass* (Philadelphia, 1856).

25. Riess, *City games*, 19–20; *Christian Register*, reprinted in *The Liberator* 28 (December 24, 1858), 208; George H. Troup, Diary, February 5, 1858; *Gleason's Pictorial* 8 (February 24, 1855), 124; *Child's Friend and Youth's Magazine* 19 (1852), 223; *Ballou's Pictorial* 13 (March 28, 1857), 204. On occasion even walking was pictured as a manly exercise (*Ballou's Pictorial*, 12 [June 6, 1857]), 364.

26. This does not mean that women did not evidence initiative and daring in their sports or in other aspects of their lives.

27. Catherine E. Beecher, "Letters to the People on Health and Happiness," in *Massachusetts Teacher* 8 (December 1855), 343; *Massachusetts Teacher* 9 (December 1856), 557 and 13 (February 1860), 72; *Ballou's Pictorial* 13 (July 25, 1857), 79 and 12 (February 28, 1857), 141 and 9 (March 29, 1856), 205; *Gleason's Pictorial* 1 (August 2, 1851), 209 and 1 (December 20, 1851), 542.

NINE. PRAYERFUL TRANSACTIONS

1. *Christian Observer* 33 (October 7, 1854), 157; *The Liberator* 28 (April 9, 1858), 60. Like much coverage of the revival, the reference to "men" here is specifically to males, and especially to the business men ("counting-house") for whom the revival was named.

2. John Brazer, *The efficacy of prayer* (Boston, 1832), 2, 16–31; *Christian Observatory* 1 (April 1847), 159, 160; *Child's Friend and Family Magazine* 26 (Boston, 1856), 44, 45; *Christian Observer* 32 (November 5, 1853), 177.

3. *Christian Observer* 33 (July 1, 1854), 104 and 33 (July 15, 1854), 112 and 34 (January 6, 1855), 1 and 34 (August 18, 1854), 129–30; *Christian Observatory* 3 (October 1849), 492; *Youth's Companion* 32 (June 17, 1858), 95; *New York Tribune* report reprinted in *The Liberator* 30 (September 14, 1860), 148; "Temples Not Made with Hands," *The Liberator* 21 (October 17, 1851), 168; *New Englander* 11 (February 1853), 22; Mary Gardiner Davis, Notebook, "Thoughts for Life" (1850–1856[?]), Gardiner Family Papers, SL.

4. John Calvin, *Tracts relating to the Reformation* (Edinburgh, 1844), 158; William Perkins, *An exposition of the Lord's Prayer* (London, 1595), 2; Hannah More, *The spirit of prayer* (London, 1825), 24, 25; Eliphay Arnold Jr., Diary, March 17, 31, 1850.

5. Nathaniel Vincent, *The spirit of prayer* (Boston, 1832), xxxii, viii, 52. Vincent's discussion of prayer included the claim that "in prayer, things must be asked for according to the will of God" (52); Gardiner Spring, D.D., *The mercy seat; thoughts suggested by the Lord's Prayer* (New York, 1854), 178, 358, 359. Edward Everett Hale, ed., *James Freeman Clarke: Autobiography, diary and correspondence* (New York, 1891), 256; James Freeman Clarke, *The Christian doctrine of prayer* (Boston, 1856), xi–xii, 14, 15. Clarke stressed that to ask for something in prayer was not to attempt to subvert the divine plan, but to act in accord with divine law: "Just as, when a man plows the ground and

plants his seed, he cooperates with divine laws, the natural result of which is a harvest; so when a man prays for anything he really wants, and while he prays endeavors to abide in the spirit of Christ and pray out of that, he cooperates with other divine laws, the natural result of which is the receiving of what he asks" (xi–xii). Clarke's argument was structured along the same lines as the traditional explanation for the manner in which God acts on the hearts of men. Thomas W. Jenkyn, D.D., explaining how God "honors the laws of his free agency," compared God's operation on the heart with altering the direction of a stream of water, concluding that "whatever agency is ascribed to a river, it is, in either direction, in full and free activity. Now, God influences the streams of the human heart with the same nice and accurate attention to their laws; and one operation is quite as intelligible as the other" (*The union of the Holy Spirit and the church in the conversion of the world* [Boston, 1846], 289).

6. Thompson, *The mercy-seat*, 22–23; 322, 323–31.

7. *Child's Friend and Family Magazine* 26 (Boston, 1856), 150, 45; *Youth's Companion* 34 (October 25, 1860), 171; "Prayer," *Ballou's Pictorial* 13 (July 4, 1857), 10.

8. *Christian Advocate* 30 (January 18, 1855); Henry Adolphus Miles, *The altar at home: Prayers for the family and the closet* (Boston, 1857); *New Englander* 13 (August 1855), 458, 469; "A Temperance Prayer-Meeting," *Christian Observer* 32 (November 5, 1853), 177; "A Prayer for the Nation," *The Liberator* 24 (April 14, 1854), 60; *New York Tribune* (March 22, 1858); *Evangelist and Religious Review* (September 2, July 15, 1858); *Old South Chapel prayer meeting*, 91; Rev. Norris Day, *Day's revival sermons* (Boston, 1860), 166. Publications aimed at youths repeatedly stressed the importance of "having something to say" in prayer (*The Well-Spring* 15 [October 8, 1858], 163; *Youth's Companion* 33 [February 17, 1859], 26).

9. Rev. Caleb Stetson, *Domestic worship* (Boston, 1842), 3–4; *Child's Friend and Youth's Magazine* 18 (Boston, 1852), 216; "God Answers Prayer," *Christian Observer* 34 (August 18, 1855), 129; *Youth's Companion* 29 (May 24, 1855), 20; Frances Merritt, Journal, April 18, March 14, 1858.

10. See Chapter 6, note 43 and the referent text.

11. S. D. Burchard, D.D., "Religious Insensibility," in *The New York pulpit in the revival of 1858*, ed. Samuel I. Prime (New York, 1858), 321; Newcomb, *The harvest and the reapers*, 161; Edward A. Park, D.D., "Sermon on the Revelation of God in His Works," in *Sermons and addresses on the installation of the Rev. Jacob M. Manning*, 30–31; Jenkyn, *The union of the Holy Spirit and the church*, 293; *Boston Journal* (March 25, 1858); "What Prayer Is," *Ballou's Pictorial* 14 (May 1, 1858), 282 and 13 (December 5, 1857), 364; *Massachusetts Teacher* 12 (September 1859), 350; *Youth's Companion* 34 (May 3, 1860), 71; More, *The spirit of prayer*, 16; Pond, in Vincent, *The spirit of prayer*, xii, xviii; Stetson, *Domestic worship*, 3; Thompson, *The mercy-seat*, 14. Of Henry Ware Jr. the *New Englander* wrote that "earnestness was characteristic of him" and led to "manliness of thinking" (8 [May, 1850]), 258.

12. *Evangelist and Religious Review* 29 (May 13, 1858); Austin Phelps, *The*

still hour; or, communion with God (Boston, 1867), 29, 20; Clarke, *The Christian doctrine of prayer*, 23.

13. Rabinowitz, *The spiritual self in everyday life*, 188, 217.

14. A "virtuous woman will have an equal right with men to give her heart to the object of her choice" (*The Liberator* 21 [April 11, 1851], 60). "What a curious thing the heart is— . . . How proud a man ought to be, to have it placed in his keeping—to have a pretty girl love him so well that she will give it to him . . . (*Ballou's Pictorial* 17 [November 1859], 295). Julian Cramer published a poem that proposed: "Oh, there are offerings that the wealthy bring, / . . . But, sister, I have no such valued thing: / A *brother's heart* is all that I can bring" (*Christian Parlor Magazine* 2 [August 1845], 103).

15. Humphrey, *Revival sketches and manual*, 435, 455, 462; *Union prayer meeting hymns* (Philadelphia, 1858), 197; James Caughey, *Helps to a life of holiness* (Boston, 1854), 106; Lyman H. Atwater, *The revivals of the century* (New York, 1876), 706; Joshua Huntington, *Gropings after truth: A life journey from New England Congregationalism to the one true catholic and apostolic church* (New York, 1868), 18. Edward A. Lawrence, "Faith and Trust," *Princeton Review* 6 (1877), 702.

16. Stetson, *Domestic worship*, 6. Michael T. Taussig wrote: "People relate to one another not directly but through the mediation of the market guiding the circulation and relations of commodities. Their livelihoods depend on the relations established by commodities, and the market becomes the guarantee of their spiritual coherence. The market established basis of livelihood becomes in effect a constantly lived out daily ritual, which, like all rites, joins otherwise unconnected links of meaning into a coherent and apparently natural network of associations" (*The devil and commodity fetishism in South America* [Chapel Hill, 1980], 26).

17. Phelps, *The still hour*, 42–43, 43–44.

18. Hilliard, *The dangers and duties of the mercantile profession*, 16.

19. The notion of a heart as money already was in circulation through articles such as the one in the *Christian Parlor Magazine*, which had criticized factory owners with reference to their coldness: "Men seem to harden themselves against their fellows, as if they would coin their own hearts, and put them in their coffers" (9 [March 1845], 1).

20. *New Englander* 16 (November 1858), 792; *Evangelist and Religious Review* (January 6, 1859); Tracy Patch Cheever, Diary, August 27, 1854.

21 *Puritan Recorder* 35 (February 7, 1850); Huntington, *Permanent realities of religion*, 48; *Youth's Companion* 28 (February 1, 1855), 163; *The Liberator* 28 (April 16, 1858), 63.

22. *Atlantic Monthly* 1 (November 1857), 2; *The Liberator* 28 (April 30, 1858), 72.

23. *Youth's Companion* 24 (August 8, 1850), 59; Newcomb, *The harvest and the reapers*, 249, 237; Vincent, *The spirit of prayer*, xiv, 112; Thompson, *The mercy-seat*, 227–30, 26; Henry Rose, *An inaugural dissertation of the effects of the passions upon the body* (Philadelphia, 1794), 13–14; *Child's Friend*

and Family Magazine 26 (Boston, 1856), 238; Gamaliel Bradford, Diary, May 19, 1854; Eliphay Arnold Jr., Diary, March 24, 1851, April 11, 1850; H. G. Atwell, *Jimmy, a Christian,* 34, 35, 37, 56, 59, 71, 75, 76, 95, 96, 99, 101, 106, 107; *Little Mabel,* 2; *Gleason's Pictorial* 1 (August 9, 1851), 229 and 1 (August 4, 1851), 241; John Eliot, *Tears of repentance: A further narrative of the progress of the gospel amongst the Indians of New England* (London, 1853); *Christian Parlor Magazine* 3 (April 1, 1847), 373; *New Englander* 13 (1855), 458, 463; *Boston Recorder* (February 16, 1849); *Christian Observatory* 1 (April 1847), 159; *Christian Observatory* 3 (April 1849), 186.

24. "Industrial Museum: Exhibition of New Inventions, Domestic Manufactures, and American Fine Arts," Broadside, June 1858, BPL; *Boston Recorder* (January 26, 1849); Charles E. French, Diary, March 5, 1855; George H. Troup, Diary, February 9, 1858; "Practical Men," *Gleason's Pictorial* 4 (April 16, 1853), 252; *Puritan Recorder* 35 (April 11, 1850); Henry Clark Wright, Journal, September 11, 1853; *Independent* (January 16, 1851); Carl Siragusa, *A mechanical people: Perceptions of the industrial order in Massachusetts, 1815–1880* (Middletown, CT, 1979), 2.

25. Boel Berner, "Introduction: Doing Feminist Research on Technology and Society," in *Gendered practices: Feminist studies of technology and society,* ed. Boel Berner (Linkoping, Sweden, 1997), 15; Laurie Smith Keller, "Discovering and Doing: Science and Technology, an Introduction," in *Inventing women: Science, technology, and gender,* ed. Gill Kirkup and Laurie Smith Keller (Cambridge, UK, 1992), 31; Rosalind Gill and Keith Grint, "The Gender-Technology Relation: Contemporary Theory and Research," in Gill and Grint, *The gender-technology relation: Contemporary theory and research* (London, 1995), 8–11; Margaret Lowe Bentson, "Women's Voices/Men's Voices: Technology as Language, in Kirkup and Keller, *Inventing women,* 38–39. Judy Wajcman writes, "Technology fundamentally embodies a culture or a set of social relations made up of certain beliefs, desires and practices. Treating technology as a culture has enabled us to see the way in which technology is expressive of masculinity, and how, in turn, men characteristically view themselves in relation to those machines" (*Feminism confronts technology* [Cambridge, UK, 1991], 149). Ira Mayhew, *Popular education: For the use of parents and teachers, and for young persons of both sexes* (New York, 1850), 126; Charles Sumner, *Recent speeches and addresses* (Boston, 1856), 255; Maurice A. Richter, *Internal relations of the cities, towns, villages, counties, and states of the Union; or, the municipalist: a highly useful book for voters, tax-payers, statesmen, politicians and families* (New York, 1859), 138; Freeman Hunt, *Worth and wealth: A collection of maxims, morals, and miscellanies for merchants and men of business* (New York, 1856), 238; Orville Dewey, "On Patriotism," in *Sermons on slavery & the civil war* (Boston, 1865), e26 [*sic*]; Mark Hopkins, *Lectures on the evidences of Christianity, before the Lowell Institute* (Boston, 1856), 168; Sylvester Judd, *Philo; an evangeliad* (Boston, 1850), 133.

26. Daniel Webster, "Second Speech on the Sub-Treasury," quoted in Siragusa, *A mechanical people,* 69–70; Stephen Colwell, *New themes for the*

Protestant clergy (Philadelphia, 1853), 241; Francis Wharton, *A treatise on theism* (Philadelphia, 1859), 172; *New Englander* 9 (August 1851), 386.

27. Francis Wayland, *Letters on the ministry of the gospel* (Boston, 1863), 124.

28. Theophilus Gale, *Brief Instructions for Administering Animal Electricity* (Hartford, CT, 1805), iv, 15; John Vaughan, *Observations on animal electricity* (Wilmington, Delaware, 1797), vi, passim; Cutbush, *An inaugural dissertation on insanity*, 41; Fenwick, *An essay on volition and pleasure*, 2–3; Walt Whitman, "O you whom I so often and silently come where you are, that I may be with you," in "Calamus," *Leaves of grass* (Boston, 1860–61), line 3; James Gates Percival, "Prometheus," book "CI," *The poetical works* (Boston, 1859), lines 901–2; Julia Ward Howe, "Rome," in *Passion flowers* (Boston, 1854), 417–22; Thompson, *The mercy-seat*, 294–95. Thomas Green Fessenden, under the pseudonym Christopher Caustic, M.D., wrote a poem about the misuse of electricity by doctors, "Canto II. Conjurations!" in *Terrible Tractoration, with other poems*, 3d ed. (Boston, 1836). *Boston Monthly* 1 (1825), 153; *New Englander* 15 (May 1857), 180–81; Hitchcock, *The religion of geology and its connected sciences*, 436; Eliphay Arnold Jr., Diary, January 14, 1851. The *Puritan Recorder* reported that some persons thought the cholera outbreak of 1849 a product of "the absence of electricity" in the city (34 [August 30, 1849]).

29. "Religious Excitements," *Evangelist and Religious Review* (April 19, 1855); *New Englander* 16 (February 1858), 44; Francis Bennett Jr., Diary, November 14, 1854; *Boston Evening Transcript* (December 2, 1859); T. Hall, *Book of the telegraph*, 2d ed. (Boston, 1858), 3; *Young America*, no. 10 (October 1858), 116; Charles E. French, Diary, August 8, 1858; William Gray Brooks, Diary, August 5, 1858; Jacob Merrill Manning, Diary, September 6, 1858; William B. Sprague, *A sermon on the completion of the Atlantic telegraph* (New York, 1858); Ezra Stiles Gannett, *The Atlantic telegraph: A discourse* (Boston, 1858), 17–18. Manning celebrated the event in New York. The cable put into service in 1858 soon failed, and permanent service was not restored until 1866.

30. *Massachusetts Teacher* 11 (October 1858), 394; *Boston Evening Transcript* (September 6, 1858); Thompson, *The mercy-seat*, 32–33.

31. Thompson, *The mercy-seat*, 33, 35, 36, 234–36.

TEN. EMOTION, CHARACTER, AND ETHNICITY

1. Jane Tompkins, *Sensational designs: The cultural work of American fiction, 1790–1860* (New York, 1985), xviii, 133, 218 n. 15; Townsend, *A dissertation on the influence of the passions*, 22; William Cooke, *A commentary of medical and moral life; or, mind and the emotions* (Philadelphia, 1853), 135; *Youth's Companion* 33 (April 28, 1859), 67; *Christian Observatory* 1 (December 1847), 534 and 1 (September 1847), 394; George Lakoff, "The Contemporary Theory of Metaphor," in *Metaphor and thought*, ed. Andrew Ortony

(New York, 1993), 202–51; *Child's Friend and Youth's Magazine* 22 (Cambridge, 1854), 69 and 29 (Cambridge, 1857), 250; Charlotte Foster, Composition book, May 8, 1852.

2. *Evangelist and Religious Review* (April 19, February 8, 1855); *The Liberator* 24 (April 7, 1854), 54; Fenwick, *An essay on volition and pleasure*, 28; William Winter, *The emotion of sympathy: A metrical essay* (Boston, 1856).

3. *Monthly Anthology and Boston Review* 5 (1808), 88; James Barnard Blake, Diary, January 3, 1851; *Evangelist and Religious Review* (April 19, 1855); *Sermons and addresses at the installation of the Rev. Jacob M. Manning*, 73; *New Englander* 15 (May 1857), 239.

4. Benjamin Rush, *Sixteen introductory lectures* (Philadelphia, 1811), 444, and *Medical inquiries and observations*, 191; *Massachusetts Ploughman* 10 (December 28, 1850); *Massachusetts Teacher* 6 (October 1853), 306 and 9 (March 1856), 106; Henry Clarke Wright, Journal, September 3, 1853; *New Englander* 17 (August 1859), 647.

5. Susan Heath, Diary, May 6, 1858; *Baptist Missionary Magazine* 4 (1824), 237, 345; *Massachusetts Teacher* 1 (May 1848), 137; "Promiscuous Leaves from my diary by a convict," ms., AAS; *New Englander* 10 (August 1852), 443; *Evangelist and Religious Review* (April 29, 1858); *Child's Friend and Family Magazine* 30 (Cambridge, 1858), 46.

6. Gamaliel Bradford, Diary, May 18, 1854.

7. One wonders about the larger goals of the recently proposed notions of "emotional intelligence." See Daniel Goleman, *Emotional intelligence* (New York, 1995); Elaine De Beauport, *The three faces of mind: Developing your mental, emotional, and behavioral intelligences* (Wheaton, IL, 1996); Peter Salovey and Daniel J. Sluyter, eds., *Emotional development and emotional intelligence: Educational implications* (New York, 1997).

8. *Gleason's Pictorial* 4 (April 16, 1853), 252.

9. *Watchman-Examiner* 37 (August 21, 1856); Laurens P. Hickok, *Empirical psychology; or, The human mind as given in consciousness. For the use of colleges and academies* (Schenectady, NY, 1855), 47; George Douglas Brewerton, *The war in Kansas. A rough trip to the border, among new homes and a strange people* (New York, 1856), 167; Richard Francis Burton, *The city of the saints, and across the Rocky mountains to California* (New York, 1862), 88; James W. Redfield, *Comparative physiognomy; or, Resemblances between men and animals* (New York, 1852), 281.

10. Michael Hogan, *The Irish soldiers of Mexico* (New Orleans, 1997); *Evangelist and Religious Review* (June 16, 1859); *Gleason's Pictorial* 1 (September 13, 1851); John Francis Maquire, *The Irish in America* (New York, 1868), 281; J. E. S. W., "An English Dinner-Party," *Appleton's Journal* 11 (1874), 403; Junius Henry Browne, *The great metropolis: A mirror of New York* (Hartford, CT, 1869), 623.

11. James Barnard Blake, Diary, January 26, 1851; "Trouble in the Boston Schools," *Evangelist and Religious Review* (March 31, 1859); *Youth's Companion* 34 (June 1860), 48; Lane, *Policing the city*, 76; *Christian Watchman* 35

(April 20, 1854); Theodore Parker, *A sermon on false and true theology* (Boston, 1858), 4.

12. Fredrika Bremer, *The homes of the New world; impressions of America* (New York, 1853), 316; E. A. Pollard, "Regathering of Black Diamonds in the Old Dominion," *Southern Literary Messenger* 29 (1859), 296; J. Milton Mackie, *From Cape Cod to Dixie and the tropics* (New York, 1864), 345; Ephraim Langdon Frothingham, *Philosophy as absolute science, founded in the universal laws of being, and including ontology, theology, and psychology made one, as spirit, soul, and body* (Boston, 1864), 200, 201; L. S. M., "Negro-Mania," *Debow's Review* 12 (1852), 518.

13. Samuel Stanhope Smith, *An essay on the causes of variety of complexion* (Philadelphia, 1787), 81–82; Thomas Roderick Dew, "Professor Dew on Slavery," in *The proslavery argument; as maintained by the most distinguished writers of the southern states* (Charleston, 1852), 424; William Henry Holcombe, "Characteristics and Capabilities of the Negro Race," *Southern Literary Messenger* 33 (1861), 403, 404; Chancellor Harper, "Memoir on Slavery, Part I," *Debow's Review* 8 (1850), 235; Moncure Daniel Conway, *The rejected stone; or, Insurrection vs. resurrection in America* (Boston, 1862), 126. Benjamin Rush noted the peculiarity of the slave emotional constitution in the instances of slaves laughing when whipped (*Sixteen introductory lectures*, 434).

14. George A. Levesque concludes that the separate school system had been requested by blacks for many years, and finally was approved after much debate by the various city boards (*Black Boston: African American life and culture in urban America, 1750–1860* [New York, 1994], 165–229).

15. Knights, *The plain people of Boston*, 28–32; Levesque, *Black Boston*, 265, 266–313; Adelaide M. Cromwell, *The other Brahmins: Boston's black upper class 1750–1950* (Fayetteville, AR, 1994), 35–44; *Evangelist and Religious Review* (April 5, 1855).

16. *Boston Daily Transcript* (January 9, 1850); *Christian Observatory* 3 (October 1849), 461; "Riot on Negro Hill," Broadside, MHS; *The Boston slave riot and the trial of Anthony Burns* (Boston, 1854), 5; Ossie Davis, "Foreword," in Loften Mitchell, *Voices of the black theatre* (Clifton, NJ, 1975), 19; *Boston Journal* (March 26, 1858). The Burns case, as Edward A. Teulon wrote, caused "great excitement on slavery in & about Boston" (Diary, May 26, 29, June 2, 4, 1854). It was not the first time that whites and blacks had attempted to rescue a fugitive slave from the authorities. As in the case of Burns, however, the "mob" label was fitted more securely on the black participants. Of an incident in 1854 William Barnard Blake wrote: "The Negroes I understand had quite an altercation at the courthouse today, having rushed in & seized a fugitive slave from the hands of the officers in the Court room" (Diary, February 16, 1851). William Henry Hoyt reported on the same incident, stressing that a "group of negroes" rescued the fugitive slave from the courthouse (Diary, February 15, 1851).

17. *Independent* (December 6, 1860).

18. Albert Barnes, *The church and slavery* (Philadelphia, 1857), 25; United

States 43d Congress, 1st session, *Memorial addresses on the life and character of Charles Sumner* (Washington, 1874), 95; Trowbridge, *My own story*, 215; Clarke, *Autobiography, diary and correspondence*, 221, 239; Charles E. French, Diary, March 5, 1858; James Barnard Blake, Diary, February 9, 1851; *The Liberator* 20 (August 16, 1850), 130.

19. *Independent* (June 19, 1851); John Henry Hopkins, *A scriptural, ecclesiastical, and historical view of slavery* (New York, 1864), 329; "Life of Julius Caesar," *Debow's Review* 1 (1866), 562.

20. Statistics collected by Kathryn Long show that membership and annual growth rates among African American members of the Methodist Episcopal church in the South were less in 1858–59 than in 1853–54 ("The Revival of 1857–58," 145, Appendix B, Table 2).

21. Levesque, *Black Boston*, 263–313; Oliver Johnson, *William Lloyd Garrison and his times* (London, 1882), 100; Englizian, *Brimstone Corner*, 132–33.

EPILOGUE

1. Frances Merritt, Journal, March 14, 1858.

2. Long, "The Revival of 1857–58," 11–25.

3. *Child's Friend and Youth's Magazine* 23 (Boston, 1854), 161; *Massachusetts Teacher* 3 (March, 1850), 77; Charles E. Harding, "Autobiography," chap, 30, p. 22, ms., AAS. The Harding reference is not clearly dated but appears to be in the late 1850s/early 1860s.

4. *Christian Register* 29 (August 24, 1850), 133; *Child's Friend and Youth's Magazine* 25 (Boston, 1855), 119; George E. Ellis, *The re-action of a revival upon religion* (Boston, 1858), 9, 11; "The Religious Awakening of 1858," *New Englander* 16 (August 1858), 659.

5. *Christian Examiner* 75 (November 1863); Thomas Collett Sanders, "Review of *Two years ago*," *Saturday Review* 3 (February 21, 1858), 176–77; Charles Kingsley, *Two years ago* (Cambridge, 1857); Thomas Hughes, *Tom Brown's school days* (Cambridge, 1857); James A. Mathiesen, "Reviving 'Muscular Christianity': Gil Dodds and the Institutionalization of Sport Evangelism," *Sociological Focus* 23 (1990), 234–35; David Rosen, "The Volcano and the Cathedral: Muscular Christianity and the Origins of Primal Manliness," in *Muscular Christianity: Embodying the Victorian age*, ed. Donald E. Hall (Cambridge, 1994), 17–44.

6. Thomas Wentworth Higginson, "Saints and Their Bodies," *Atlantic Monthly* 1 (1858), 582–95; G. M. Steele, "Living Celebrities of New England, Part III," *Ladies Repository* 24 (1864), 395; E. L. Burlingame, "Charles Kingsley," *Appleton's Journal* 13 (1875), 204; "Editor's Table," *Appleton's Journal* 13 (1875), 180; George M. Towle, "Thomas Hughes," *Appleton's Journal* 9 (1873), 145; J. G. Holland, *Lessons in life* (New York, 1862), 169; "Effeminate Men and Masculine Women," *Ladies Repository* 9 (1872), 300.

7. *Eminent women of the age being narratives of the lives and deeds of the most prominent women of the present generation* (Hartford, 1868), 78; John D.

Minor, *The Bible in the public schools* (Cincinnati, 1870), 238; "Laughing Dick Cranstone," *Catholic World* 17 (1873), 395.

8. Myron B. Benton, "A Midwinter Day," *Appleton's Journal* 5 (1871), 226; Prof. E. Knowlton, "Muscular Christianity," *Overland Monthly and Out West Magazine* 2 (1869), 533; "The 'Old Sport' of the 'Herald,'" *Vanity Fair* 5 (1862), 115; "The Telegraph Tour," *Vanity Fair* 2 (1860), 124; *Catholic World* 26 (1878), 752; Marvin Richardson Vincent, *Amusement; a force in Christian training* (Troy, NY, 1867), 35; "The Romance and Religion of Billiards," *Vanity Fair* 2 (1860), 194; "Editor's Table," *Appleton's Journal* 5 (1878), 89.

9. Henry T. Tuckerman, "Literature of Fiction, Part I," *Appleton's Journal* 6 (1871), 321; Anne Bloomfield, "Muscular Christian or Mystic? Charles Kingsley Reappraised," *International Journal of the History of Sports* (1994), 175; George M. Towle, "Charles Kingsley, Parson, Poet and Politician," *Penn Monthly* (1875), 200; Malcolm Tozer, "Charles Kingsley and the 'Muscular Christian' Ideal of Manliness," *Physical Education Review* 8 (1975), 35–40; Henry R. Harrington, "Charles Kingsley's Fallen Athlete," *Victorian Studies* 21 (1977), 73–86; Claudia Nelson, "Sex and the Single Boy: Ideals of Manliness and Sexuality in Victorian Literature for Boys," *Victorian Studies* 33 (1989), 538, 536 n. 22. See also Norman Vance, *The sinews of the spirit: The ideal of Christian manliness in Victorian literature and religious thought* (Cambridge, 1985).

10. "New Novels," *New Quarterly Review* 6 (1857), 233; Thomas Hughes, *The manliness of Christ* (London, 1879), 85, 21, 130; George Worth, "Of muscles and manliness; some reflections on Thomas Hughes," in *Victorian literature and society: Essays presented to Richard D. Altick*, ed. James R. Kincaid and Albert J. Kuhn (Columbus, OH, 1984), 310; Claudia Nelson suggests that, in fact, "true manliness may come more easily to the woman than to the man" ("Sex and the Single Boy," 531). "Mr. Hughes on the Manliness of Christ," *Spectator* 53 (1880), 436–538.

11. Rev. L. B. Gurley, "Rev. Adam Poe," *Ladies Repository* 24 (1864), 707; "Stray Thoughts," *Ladies Repository* 2 (1868), 312; Beriah B. Hotchkiss, *Manliness for young men and their well-wishers* (Philadelphia, 1864), 22, 23; James Walker, *Reason, faith and duty* (Boston, 1877), 75; Andrew P. Peabody, *Christianity and science* (New York, 1875), 221–22; John William Dawson, *Nature and the Bible* (New York, 1875), 62–63; Rev. William M. Taylor, "Some Phases of Modern Thought," *Princeton Review* 6 (1877), 617; "Book Reviews," *Overland Monthly and Out West Magazine* 15 (1890), 560; J. B. Johnston, *The prayer-meeting, and its history* (Pittsburgh, 1870), 187, 188; Geraldine M. Bonner, "In Favila—A Phantasmagoria," *Overland Monthly and Out West Magazine* 7 (1886), 515; *The doctrines and discipline of the Methodist Episcopal Church* (New York, 1876), 371; William Haven Daniels, *D. L. Moody and his work* (Hartford, CT, 1876), 363.

12. James F. Findlay Jr., *Dwight L. Moody: American Evangelist 1837–1899* (Chicago, 1969), 37; Bryan quoted in Kathleen Minnix, *Laughter in the Amen corner: The life of evangelist Sam Jones* (Athens, GA, 1993), 241; *San*

Francisco Examiner quoted in Wayne E. Warner, *The woman evangelist: The life and times and charismatic evangelist Maria B. Woodworth-Etter* (Methuen, NJ, 1986), 77; Lyle W. Dorsett, *Billy Sunday and the redemption of urban America* (Grand Rapids, MI, 1991), 31, 42, 57, 106, 125; Roger A. Bruns, *Preacher: Billy Sunday and big-time American evangelism* (New York, 1992), 15; Edith L. Blumhofer, *Aimee Semple McPherson: Everybody's sister* (Grand Rapids, MI, 1993); Daniel Mark Epstein, *Sister Aimee: The life of Aimee Semple McPherson* (New York, 1993); John F. Cowan, D.D., *New life in the old prayer-meeting* (New York, 1906), 88, 90; Jonathan M. Butler, *Softly and tenderly Jesus is calling: Heaven and hell in American revivalism, 1870–1920* (Brooklyn, 1991); George M. Thomas, *Revivalism and cultural change: Christianity, nation-building, and the market in the nineteenth-century United States* (Chicago, 1989), 12–65. Kathryn Long has suggested likewise that Moody was able to "bring together masculine and feminine evangelicalism" ("The Revival of 1857–58," 91).

13. Gail Bederman's analysis of the movement in the context of social change articulates its objective to "de-feminize" the churches ("The Women Have Had Charge of the Church Work Long Enough": The Men and Religion Forward Movement of 1911–1912 and the Masculinization of Middle-Class Protestantism," *American Quarterly* 41 [1989], 432–65). This is true not only if one considers the movement largely as a matter of gender politics within the institutional framework of the various Christian denominations that participated, but also—and Bederman does not extend her analysis in this direction—if one considers the theological underpinnings of the movement. Men and Religion Forward was not an instance of muscular Christianity as it had been practiced in the nineteenth century or even in the early twentieth century. (Billy Sunday, that most muscular of the period's revivalists, was not actively involved in the movement.) It rejected complexly gendered notions of character and the activity of prayer, embracing instead a uniformly masculinist notion of social action, leadership, and strength. Allyn K. Foster, "The Dream Come True," in *Making religion efficient*, ed. Clarence A. Barbour (New York, 1912), 18. Michael Kimmel likewise sees Religion and Men Forward as an "imitation" of Sunday's revivalism, which it was not (*Manhood in America*, 180).

14. James A. Mathisen, "Reviving 'Muscular Christianity': Gil Dodds and the Institutionalization of Sports Evangelism," *Sociological Focus* 23 (1990), 233.

15. All citations are from literature online at the official movement website, http://www.promisekeepers.org. "Guidelines toward the Establishment of a Promise Keepers Movement in any Country," http://www.promisekeepers.org/international/guidelines.htm; "The Ministry of Promise Keepers: The History of Promise Keepers," http://www.promisekeepers.ord/2aoe.htm; "Press Conference Transcript Announcing 'Stand in the Gap: A Sacred Assembly of Men,'" http://www.promisekeepers.org/2cde.htm; "PK Vision Statement," http://www.promisekkepers.org/prayernetworks.htm; "October

Prayer Lesson," http://www.promisekeepers.org/29oa.htm; "How do I start a men's small group?" *http://www.promisekeepers.org/2aae.htm.*

16. "February Prayer Lesson," http://www.promisekeepers.org/2c2e.htm; "Testimony of the Week: Anonymous," http://www.promisekeepers.org/testimny/testimony01098.htm; "September Prayer Lesson," http://www.promisekeepers.org/29be.htm; "June Prayer Lesson," http://www.promisekeepers.org/2d46.htm; "Meet Jesus," http://www.promisekeepers.org/gospel.htm; "Report from Serve the City—Detroit," http://www.promisekeepers.org/28ce.htm; "February '97 Survey Results," http://promisekeepers.org/2c82.htm; "November Prayer Lesson," http://www.promisekeepers.org/29de.htm; "For the Love of My Father," http://promisekeepers.org/28ae.htm; "Testimony of the Week: Randy Conrad," http://www.promisekeepers.org/testimny/21ba_15a.htm; "Testimony of the Week: Brian Mowers," http://www.promisekepers.org/testimny/testimony103097.htm; "Testimony of the Week: Paul Austin," http://www.promisekeepers.org/testimny/21f2_15a.htm; "Testimony of the Week: Kent Graham," http://www.promisekeepers.org/testimny/21c6_15a.htm.

17. "February '97 Survey Results," http://www.promisekeepers.org/2c7e.htm; "May '97 Survey Results," http://www.promisekeepers.org/2d62.htm and *htttp://www.promisekeepers.org/2d5e.htm;* "PK Calendar Letter, October 7, 1996," *http://www.promisekeepers.org/2972.htm;* Ken Abraham, *Who are the Promise Keepers? Understanding the Christian men's movement* (New York, 1997), 116.

18. Michael A. Messner, *Politics of masculinities: Men and movements* (Thousand Oaks, CA, 1997), 32.

APPENDIX 1. HISTORY, RELIGION, AND EMOTION:
A HISTORIOGRAPHICAL SURVEY

1. William Burder et al., *A history of all religions of the world, doctrinal, statistical, and biographical. From the earliest records to the present time* (New York, 1884); William James, "What Is an Emotion?" *Mind* 9 (1884), 188–205; James, *Principles of psychology,* vols. 1 and 2 (New York, 1890); Alfred North Whitehead, *Process and reality: An essay in cosmology* (New York, 1929), 338 (III. I. 3). James's theory of emotion was refined the following year by Danish physiologist Carl J. Lange (James-Lange theory). Until recently American study of emotion in religion has been dominated by a nexus formed from the work of Friedrich Schleiermacher and Rudolf Otto, with some accommodation of James, a fact that suggests the manner in which Protestantism has controlled the categories for the academic study of religion for much of the twentieth century. When Paul Ricouer observed that "something is missing, not only in my own work, but in philosophy at large, that is, an investigation of the field of feelings," he was voicing dissatisfaction with the narrow view of religion and emotion that had limited research (Interview with Charles E. Reagan, in *Paul*

Ricouer: His life and work [Chicago, 1996], 120). Philosophy in fact has vigorously researched emotion in recent decades (see Robert Solomon, *The passions* [New York, 1966] and the investigations collected by Amélie Oksenberg Rorty in *Explaining emotions* [Berkeley, 1980]). Signs of a new approach by theological writers are visible in Paul Lauritzen's *Religious belief and emotional transformation: A light in the heart* (Lewisburg, PA, 1992).

2. Karl Marx and Frederick Engels, "Manifesto of the Communist Party," in *The Marx-Engels reader,* ed. Robert Tucker (New York, 1972), 337–38.

3. Émile Durkheim, *The elementary forms of the religious life,* trans. Joseph Ward Swain (Glencoe, IL, 1947), 209–10. See also Marcel Mauss, *A general theory of magic,* trans. Robert Brain (New York, 1972): "The individual feels constantly subordinate to forces which are outside his power—forces which incite him to action. If we are able to demonstrate that within the field of magic there are similar powers to those existing in religion, we shall have shown that magic has the same collective character as religion" (90).

4. Max Weber, *The Protestant ethic and the spirit of capitalism,* trans. Talcott Parsons (New York, 1958), 26–27.

5. Lucien Febvre, "History and Psychology," in *A new kind of history and other essays,* ed. Peter Burke, trans. K. Folca (New York, 1973), 9. The essay was originally published in 1938. For discussion of the role of the Annales school in the emergence of the study of popular culture (with valuable references to the issue of emotion) see Stewart Clark, "French Historians and Early Modern Popular Culture," *Past and Present* 10 (1983), 62–99.

6. Lucien Febvre, "Sensibility and History: How to Reconstitute the Emotional Life of the Past," in *A new kind of history,* 12–26.

7. Marc Bloch, *The royal touch,* trans. J. E. Andersen (New York, 1961), 29. Originally published 1923.

8. Marc Bloch, *The historian's craft,* trans. Peter Putnam (New York, 1973), 194.

9. Febvre, "A New Kind of History," in *A new kind of history,* 34; Johan Huizinga, *The waning of the Middle Ages* (London, 1924).

10. Fernand Braudel, *The Mediterranean and the Mediterranean world in the age of Philip II,* 2 vols., trans. Sian Reynolds (New York, 1972; originally published 1949). See also Braudel's *Capitalism and material life, 1400–1800,* trans. Miriam Kochan (New York, 1973; originally published 1967). Braudel claimed that he was "starting at the bottom level with material life, the ground floor (as it were) of history" (ix).

11. Braudel, *Capitalism and material life,* xiv, ix. Braudel proposed to explore "the foundations of the house" before he analyzed the activity of agents within it (445). Braudel wrote that "little or nothing existed before 1949 in the immense domain of 'structural history'" (*The Mediterranean and the Mediterranean world in the age of Philip II,* 1274). He traced his brand of *histoire événementielle* to the influence of French economic historian and Durkheimian François Simiand: "My definition of 'event' is closer to that of

Paul Lacombe and François Simiand: the pieces of flotsam I have combed from the historical ocean and chosen to call 'events' are those essentially *ephemeral* yet moving occurrences, the 'headlines' of the past" (1243).

12. Lucien Levy-Bruhl, *Primitive mentality*, trans. Lilian A. Clare (New York, 1978). "Primitive mentality immediately passes from the event that has affected it to a mystic cause which appears imaginary to us, but which actually forms a part of his experience, made up as it is from the sum-total of the collective representations of the social group" (261). See also *The notebooks on primitive mentality*, trans. Peter Riviere (New York, 1975), 25–28, 155–59; "The conclusion at which we arrive at concerning participations between objects or individuals and their appurtenances is as follows: they are not based on perceived relationships, be they as evident as those of the part of the whole, but rather on the *feeling* of the true presence of the individual or object, directly suggested by the presence or appurtenance. And this feeling has no need of legitimation other than the very fact that it is felt" (157).

13. Le Roy Ladurie, *The peasants of Languedoc*, trans. John Day (Urbana, IL, 1974). Originally published 1966. Andre Burguiere distinguishes Bloch's focus on collective mentality (as influenced by Durkheim) from Febvre's continuing concern for the individual and her milieu ("The fate of the History of *Mentalités* in the *Annales*," *Comparative Studies in Society and History* 24 [1982], 424–37). Michael A. Gismondi analyzes criticism from British Marxists of problems of context, class, and the nature of historical change in Annales history ("'The Gift of Theory': A Critique of the *histoire des mentalités*," *Social History* 10 [1985], 211–30). See also Peter Burke, "Strengths and Weaknesses of the History of Mentalities," *History of European Ideas* 7 (1986), 439–51; G. E. R. Lloyd, *Demystifying mentalities* (Cambridge, 1990), especially 1–13.

14. Lucien Febvre, *The problem of unbelief in the sixteenth century, the religion of Rabelais*, trans. Beatrice Gottlieb (Cambridge, MA, 1982).

15. Zevedei Barbu, in a book dedicated to Febvre, argued that historical psychology differed from anthropology in that the former studied "the variations of the human mind on a vertical line, or the changes that have occurred in the mental structure of groups of individuals as a result of the development in time of their culture as a whole" (*Problems of historical psychology* [New York, 1960], 5). Robert Mandrou, *Introduction to modern France: An essay in historical psychology*, trans. R. E. Hallmark (New York, 1975). Mandrou replaced Le Roy Ladurie at the *Sixième* section.

16. Norbert Elias, *The civilizing process: The history of manners*, trans. Edmund Jephcott (New York, 1978), xiii. Originally published 1939.

17. Frank E. Manuel proposes that Herder, Hegel, and Dilthey preceded Freud in utilizing psychological approaches to history ("The Use and Abuse of Psychology in History," in *Varieties of psychohistory*, ed. George M. Kren and Leon H. Rappoport [New York, 1976], 38–62). Freud's method, which subsequently was adopted by historians, was the "psychoanalytical" approach.

18. William L. Langer, "The Next Assignment," *American Historical Review* 63 (1958), 284–85.

19. The group met regularly on Cape Cod. See Robert Jay Lifton, ed., *Explorations in psychohistory: The Wellfleet papers* (New York, 1974).

20. Although *vide* the recent lament of Henry Lawton that "there is still no uniformly accepted definition for psychohistory" ("The Field of Psychohistory," *Journal of Psychohistory* 7 [1990], 353). The Group for the Use of Psychology in History (GULPH) was formed in 1972 and has taken a less doctrinaire view of the project of applying psychoanalytic principles to historical interpretation than the membership of the International Psychohistorical Association, which was founded by DeMause (Lawton, 353). "Psychohistorians believe that a new field, independent of the traditional disciplines, is needed to successfully make the jump to the fuller understanding of emotion that we seek to achieve" (354). For a less confident endorsement of the centrality of psychoanalytical theory to the project of psychohistory see William Gilmore, *Psychohistorical inquiry* (New York, 1984).

21. Lloyd DeMause, *Foundations of psychohistory* (New York, 1982), iv. According to DeMause psychohistory "strives to be a science of patterns of historical motivations" (149). Whether in fact psychohistorical investigation of motive is new remains open to discussion. Thucydides knew something of the relation between motive and historical action and so did Vico. See David Bidney, "Vico's New Science of Myth," in *Giambattista Vico: An international symposium*, ed. Giorgio Tagliacozzo and Hayden V. White (Baltimore, 1969), 259–77; R. G. Collingwood, *The idea of history* (New York, 1972), 63–71. Psychohistory's partiality to biography follows both from its criticism of historical writing for its supposed preoccupation with the collective and from research constraints intrinsic to its method (i.e., psychoanalysis is best suited to study of an individual). Psychohistorians have searched for ways to grow more encompassing narratives about the past from the seeds of individual life stories. But even Rudolph Binion—a leading practitioner and advocate of psychohistory who in fact believes that psychohistory can unlock the secrets of "collective motives"—cautions that "the individual psyche remains the basis of our conceptualizations until further notice" and advises novice psychohistorians to "pick a biographic subject" ("Doing Psychohistory," in *Psychohistory: Readings in the method of psychology, psychoanalysis and history*, ed. Geoffrey Cocks and Travis L. Crosby [New Haven, 1987], 76, 69). For an elaboration of psychohistory's inability to effectively address the history of groups see Richard L. Schoenwald, review of Robert J. Brugger, ed., *Our selves/our past: Psychological approaches to American history*, in *Social Science History* 7 (1983), 345–47. For a wide-ranging discussion of ego psychology, history, and literary theory that treats the problem of individual and collective history see Cushing R. Strout, *The veracious imagination: Essays on American history, literature, and biography* (Middletown, CT, 1981), especially 223–44. R. G. Collingwood (*The idea of history* [New York, 1956]) cast a skeptical eye on both psycho-

analysis and biography. David Brion Davis has suggested that biography, "by showing how cultural tensions and contradictions may be internalized, struggled with, and resolved within actual individuals," holds a "promising key to the synthesis of culture and history" ("Some Recent Directions in American Cultural History," *American Historical Review* 73 [1968], 705). Peter N. Stearns and Carol Z. Stearns have pointed out the "key weakness of psychohistory—the failure to deal effectively with groups in the past" ("Emotionology: Clarifying the History of Emotions and Emotional Standards," *American Historical Review* 90 [1985], 815).

In interpreting a life, psychohistorians have focused most sharply on parent-child relations. Whether writing about Charles Darwin, Theodore Herzl, Adolf Hitler, Jimmy Carter, or William L. Langer himself, psychohistorians have attended, frequently in great detail, to childhood events ranging from the generation of anal-retentive personality characteristics, to trauma involving separation from a parent or to retarded autonomy and shame. DeMause asserts that "the evolution of childhood is the historical source for all new historical personalities, and the genes of historical change lie wholly in adult-child interactions" ("The Independence of Psychohistory," in *The new psychohistory*, ed. Lloyd DeMause [New York, 1975], 12). See also Glenn Davis, *Childhood and history in America* (New York, 1976). For a concise discussion of some of the problems and possibilities of "character" psychology and collective emotional history see Bruce Mazlish, "Group Psychology and Problems of Contemporary History," in *Psycho/History: Readings in the method of psychology, psychoanalysis, and history*, ed. Geoffrey Cocks and Travis L. Crosby (New Haven, CT, 1987), 225–36.

22. Philip Greven, *The Protestant temperament: Religious experience and the self in early America* (New York, 1977); John Demos, *A little commonwealth: Family life in Plymouth colony* (New York, 1970) and *Entertaining Satan: Witchcraft and the culture of early New England* (New York, 1982); Peter Gay, *The bourgeois experience: Victoria to Freud* (New York, 1984); Christopher Lasch, *Haven in a heartless world: The family besieged* (New York, 1977).

23. See Alexander Goldenweiser's overlooked essay, "Spirit, *Mana*, and the Religious Thrill," collected with other of his writings in *History, psychology, and culture* (Gloucester, MA, 1968), 377–84; Paul Radin, *Primitive religion: Its nature and origin* (New York, 1937) and *The trickster: A study in American Indian mythology*, with commentaries by Karl Kerényi and C. G. Jung (New York, 1956); Robert Lowie, *Primitive religion* (New York, 1924); Ruth Benedict, "Psychological Types in the Culture of the Southwest," *Proceedings of the twenty-third international congress of Americanists, 1928* (New York, 1928), 527–81 and *Patterns of culture* (New York, 1934). Clifford Geertz, "Religion as a Cultural System," in *Anthropological approaches to the study of religion*, ed. Michael Banton (London, 1969), 8–12. Elsewhere Geertz writes: "What the cockfight says it says in a vocabulary of sentiment—the thrill of risk, the despair of loss, the pleasure of triumph. Yet what it says is not merely that risk is exciting, loss depressing, or triumph gratifying, banal tautologies of affect, but

that it is of these emotions, thus exampled, that society is built and individuals put together" ("Deep Play: Notes on the Balinese Cockfight," *Myth, symbol, and culture,* ed. Clifford Geertz [New York, 1971], 27); Clifford Geertz, *Local knowledge* (New York, 1983). "The Western conception of the person as a bounded, unique, more or less integrated motivational and cognitive universe, a dynamic center of awareness, emotion and judgment and action organized into a distinctive whole and set contrastively both against other such wholes and against its social and natural background is, however incorrigible it may seem to us, a rather peculiar idea within the context of the world's cultures. Rather than attempting to place the experience of others within the framework of such a conception, which is what the extolled 'empathy' actually comes down to, understanding them demands setting that conception aside and seeing their experiences within the framework of their own idea of what selfhood is" (59); Robert Bellah, *Beyond belief: Essays on religion in a post-traditional world* (Berkeley, 1991; originally published 1970). An excellent introduction to emotional life as culturally constructed is Michelle Z. Rosaldo, *Knowledge and passion: Ilongot notions of self and social life* (Cambridge, 1980). Lutz, *Unnatural emotions,* 4. See also the essays by Geertz, Rosaldo, Robert Levy, Robert Solomon, and Melford Spiro in *Culture theory: Essays on mind, self and emotion,* ed. Richard A. Schweder and Robert A. LaVine (Cambridge, 1984). Judith Butler, "Performative Acts and Gender Constitution: An Essay in Phenomenology and Feminist Theory," in *Performing feminisms: Feminist critical theory and theatre,* ed. Sue-Ellen Case (Baltimore, 1990), 210–82; Timothy Mitchell, *Passional culture: Emotion, religion, and society in southern Spain* (Philadelphia, 1990); Paul Bouissac, "The Profanation of the Sacred in Circus Clown Performances," in *By means of performance: Intercultural studies of theatre and ritual,* ed. Richard Schechner and Willa Appel (New York, 1991), 194–207; R. Marie Griffith, "'Joy Unspeakable and Full of Glory': The Vocabulary of Pious Emotion in the Narratives of American Pentecostal Women, 1910–1945," in *An emotional history of the United States,* ed. Peter N. Stearns and Jan Lewis (New York, 1998), 218–40; Peter Iver Kaufman, *Prayer despair, and drama: Elizabethan introspection* (Urbana, 1996); June McDaniel, *Madness of the saints: Ecstatic religion in Bengal* (Chicago, 1989); William A. Christian Jr., "Provoked Religious Weeping in Early Modern Spain," *Religious organization and religious experience,* ed. J. Davis (London, 1982), 97–114; Eliot R. Wolfson, "Weeping, Death, and Spiritual Ascent in Sixteenth-Century Jewish Mysticism," in *Death, ecstasy and other worldly journeys,* ed. John J. Collins and Michael Fishbane (Albany, 1995), 209–47; Gary L. Ebersole, "The Function of Ritual Weeping Revisited: Affective Expression and Moral Discourse," *History of Religions* 39 (2000), 211–46. See also Owen M. Lynch, ed., *Divine passions: The social construction of emotion in India* (Berkeley, 1990); Wazir Jahan Karim, ed., *Emotions of culture: A Malay perspective* (New York, 1990).

24. Of the sort associated with Clifford Geertz and Michel Foucault.

25. James R. Averill, "Emotion and Anxiety: Sociocultural, Biological, and

Psychological Determinants," in *Explaining emotions*, ed. Amélie Oksenberg Rorty (Berkeley, 1980), 37 and *Anger and aggression: An essay on emotion* (New York, 1982); Rom Harré, ed., *The social construction of emotions* (Oxford, 1986) and Rom Harre and W. Gerrod Parrott, eds., *The emotions: Social, cultural, and biological dimensions* (London, 1996); Kenneth J. Gergen, "History and Psychology: Three Weddings and a Future," in Peter N. Stearns and Jan Lewis, eds., *An emotional history of the United States* (New York, 1998), 27; Robert Darnton, "Workers Revolt: The Great Cat Massacre of the Rue Saint-Severin," "A Bourgeois Puts His World in Order: The City as a Text," and "A Police Inspector Sorts His Files: The Anatomy of the Republic of Letters," in *The Great Cat Massacre and other episodes in French cultural history* (New York, 1984), 75–189; David Warren Sabean, "A Prophet in the Thirty Years' War: Penance as a Social Metaphor," "The Sacred Bond of Unity: Community through the Eyes of a Thirteen-Year-Old Witch (1683)," in *Power in the blood: Popular culture and village discourse in early modern Germany* (Cambridge, 1984), 61–112; Rhys Isaac, *The transformation of Virginia, 1740–1790* (Chapel Hill, NC, 1982). See also Natalie Zemon Davis, *Society and culture in early modern France* (Stanford, 1975), especially chaps. 3 and 5 on women in French society. See also Peter N. Stearns, *Jealousy: The evolution of an emotion in American history* (New York, 1989) and the study of class, gender, sexuality, authority, and emotional control by Steven M. Stowe, *Intimacy and power in the Old South: Ritual in the lives of the planters* (Baltimore, 1987). This style of cultural history has been criticized by some social historians—and most trenchantly by French and British Marxist historians—for its flirtation with ahistoricity. See E. P. Thompson, "Folklore, Anthropology, and Social History," *Indian Historical Review* 3 (1978), 3–16; Michel Vovelle, *Ideologies and mentalities*, trans. Eamon O'Flaherty (Cambridge, 1990), especially 13–23, 81–113, 126–76, 232–45. See also Dominick LaCapra, "Culture and Ideology: From Geertz to Marx," in *Soundings in critical theory* (Ithaca, 1989), 133–54. Kenneth A. Lockridge, *On the sources of patriarchal rage: The commonplace books of William Byrd and Thomas Jefferson and the gendering of power in the eighteenth century* (New York, 1992); Rosenwein, *Anger's past*; Joel Pfister and Nancy Schnog, eds., *Inventing the psychological: Toward a cultural history of emotional life in America* (New Haven, CT, 1997). Jan Lewis's attention to the gendering of emotion is manifest in her analysis of the nineteenth-century construction of "maternal love" as a dialectic between theologically derived rules for female emotional suppression and the social demand for moral exemplars necessary to idealized democracy ("Mother's Love: The Construction of an Emotion in Nineteenth-Century America," in *Social history and issues in human consciousness: Some interdisciplinary connections*, ed. Andrew E. Barnes and Peter N. Stearns [New York, 1989], 209–29). Two recent volumes have gathered methodologically diverse essays on American emotions history: Peter N. Stearns and Jan Lewis, eds., *An emotional history of the United States* and Joel Pfister and Nancy Schnog, eds., *Inventing the psychological: Toward a cultural history of emo-

tional life in America (New Haven, CT, 1997); Stearns and Lewis, *An emotional history of the United States.*

26. "The concept of emotionology is necessary, quite simply, to distinguish between professed values and emotional experience" (Stearns and Stearns, "Emotionology," 824). Criticism of the Stearnses' approach is in John E. Toews, "Cultural History, the Construction of Subjectivity, and Freudian Theory: A Critique of Carol and Peter Stearns' Proposal for a New History of Emotions," *Psychohistory Review* 18 (1990), 303–18. See also Peter N. Stearns, "Historical Analysis in the Study of Emotion," *Motivation and Emotion* 10 (1986), 185–93. Charles Lloyd Cohen in his study of Puritanism, John Gillis in his history of British marriages since 1600, and Michael MacDonald in writing about family life, anxiety, and medicine in seventeenth-century England all propose that historians refrain from describing early modern emotional states in any language other than that used by the actors themselves (Michael MacDonald, *Mystical Bedlam: Madness, anxiety, and healing in seventeenth-century England* [Cambridge, 1981], xii–xiii, chap. 4; John R. Gillis, *For better, for worse: British marriages, 1600 to the present* [New York, 1985] and "From Romance to Ritual"; Charles Lloyd Cohen, *God's caress: The psychology of Puritan religious experience* [New York, 1986], 20 ff.).

27. The Stearnses are especially interested in collective emotional life (see "Emotionology," 814 and passim).

28. See Carol Z. Stearns, "'Lord Help Me Walk Humbly': Anger and Sadness in England and America, 1570–1750," in *Emotion and social change: Towards a new psychohistory,* ed. Carol Z. Stearns and Peter N. Stearns (New York, 1988), 68 n. 89. The Stearnses' proposal leaves open the possibility of "biopsychological continuities" in emotions history ("Emotionology," 828–29).

29. Greg Dening, *Performances* (Chicago, 1996).

30. For a comprehensive overview and bibliography of works on religion and emotion see John Corrigan, Eric Crump, and John Kloos, *Emotion and religion: A critical assessment and annotated bibliography* (Westport, CT, 2000). Bhagabat Kumar Goswami, *The Bhakti cult in ancient India.* Chowkhamba Sanskrit Series, vol. 52 (Varanasi, India, 1965; originally published 1924).

31. Krishna Sharma, *Bhakti and the Bhakti movement: A study in the history of ideas* (New Delhi, 1987); Chinmayi Chatterjee, *Studies in the evolution of Bhakti cult: With special reference to Vallabha School,* part 2. Jadavpur University Sanskrit Series, no. 9 (Calcutta, 1981).

32. Mariasusai Dhavamony, *Love of God according to Saiva Siddhanta: A study in the mysticism and theology of Saivism* (Oxford, 1971).

33. Karel Werner, "Love and Devotion in Buddhism," *Love divine: Studies in Bhakti and devotional mysticism,* ed. Karel Werner. Durham Indological Series, no. 3 (Richmond, Surrey, UK, 1993), 37–52.

34. Manjula Bhattacharyya, "Medieval Bhakti Movements in Gujarat," *Medieval Bhakti movements in India: Sri Caitanya quincentenary commemoration volume,* ed. N. N. Bhattacharyya (New Delhi, 1989), 97–105.

35. June McDaniel, *The madness of the saints: Ecstatic religion in Bengal* (Chicago, 1989).

36. Bhattacharyya, *Medieval Bhakti movements in India.*

37. Ajit Lokhande, *Tukarama: His person and his religion: A religio-historical, phenomenological and typological inquiry* (Frankfurt, 1976).

38. Susmita Pande, *Medieval Bhakti movement (its history and philosophy)* (Meerut, India, 1989).

39. Andrew Rawlinson, "Love and Meditation in the Bhakti Tradition," *The saints: Studies in a devotional tradition of India,* ed. Karine Schomer and W. H. McLeod (Berkeley, CA, Berkeley and Delhi, 1987, 53–58); Vasudha Narayanan, *The way and the goal: Expressions of devotion in the early Sri Vaisnava tradition* (Washington, DC, 1987).

40. Friedhelm Ernst Hardy, *Viraha-Bhakti: The early history of KRSNA devotion in South India* (Oxford, 1983).

41. Klaus Konrad Klostermaier, "Will India's Past Be America's Future? Reflections on the Caitanya Movement and Its Potentials," in *Tradition and modernity in Bhakti movements,* ed. Jayant Lele (Leiden, 1981), 94–103.

42. A. J. Appasamy, *Christianity as Bhakti Marga: A study of the Johannine doctrine of love* (Madras, 1930).

43. Paul K. Conkin, *Cane Ridge: America's pentecost* (Madison, 1989).

44. J. H. Denison, *Emotional currents in American history* (New York, 1932).

45. William G. McLoughlin, *Revivals, awakenings, and reform: An essay on religion and social change in America, 1607–1977* (Chicago, 1978).

46. John Corrigan, *The prism of piety: Catholick Congregational clergy at the beginning of the Enlightenment* (New York, 1991).

47. Michael J. Crawford, *Seasons of grace: Colonial New England's revival tradition in its British context* (New York, 1991).

48. John Corrigan, *The hidden balance: Religion and the social theories of Charles Chauncy and Jonathan Mayhew* (Cambridge, UK, 1987).

49. John C. Boles, *The Great Revival, 1787–1805* (Lexington, KY, 1972).

50. Marilyn Westerkamp, *Triumph of the laity: Scots-Irish piety and the Great Awakening, 1625–1860* (New York, 1988).

51. Jonathan M. Butler, *Softly and tenderly Jesus is calling: Heaven and hell in American revivalism, 1870–1920* (Brooklyn, NY, 1991).

52. Whitney R. Cross, *The burnt-over district: The social and intellectual history of enthusiastic religion in western New York, 1800–1850* (Ithaca, NY, 1950); John Kent, *Holding the fort: Studies in Victorian revivalism* (London, 1978).

53. Roger Robins, "Vernacular American Landscape; Methodists, Camp Meetings and Social Responsibility," *Religion and American Culture* 4 (1994), 165–91.

54. Sandra S. Sizer, *Gospel hymns and social religion: The rhetoric of nineteenth-century revivalism,* ed. Allen F. Davis (Philadelphia, 1978).

55. Deborah Vansau McCanley, *Appalachian mountain religion: A history* (Urbana, IL, 1995).

56. James Borchert, *Alley life in Washington: Family, community, religion, and folk life in the city, 1850–1970* (Urbana, IL, 1980).

57. Cyril Bailey, *Phases in the religion of ancient Rome* (London, 1932).

58. Bankey Behari, "The Way to Ecstasy," in *Sufi Studies: East and West: A symposium in honor of Idries Shah's services to Sufi studies by twenty-four contributors marking the 700th anniversary of the death of Jalahuddin Rumi (A.D. 1207–127)*, 3 (Tonbridge, Kent, 1974), 183–205.

59. Agehananda Bharati, *The light at the center: Context and pretext of modern mysticism* (Santa Barbara, CA, 1976).

60. S. Ameer Ali, "The Mystical and Idealistic Spirit in the Islamic Expression," in *The Sufi mystery*, ed. Nathaniel P. Archer (London, 1980), 192–213.

61. David Knowles, *The English mystical tradition* (London, 1961).

62. R. A. Knox, *Enthusiasm: A chapter in the history of religion, with special reference to the XVII and XVIII centuries* (Oxford, 1950).

63. Robert Michael Garrity, "Bernard of Clairvaux and John of the Cross: Divergent Views of Human Affectivity in Christian Spirituality." Ph.D. diss., Catholic University of America, 1990.

64. Raymond Sala, "La Mort dans le Haut-Vallespir: XVIIe, XVIIIe, et 1ere moitié du XIXe siècle: Approche des sensibilités et des mentalités religieuses," *Histoire, Économie et Société* 8 (1989), 613–17.

65. Elizabeth Alvilda Petroff, "The Rhetoric of Transgression in the Lives of Italian Women Saints," in *Body and soul: Essays on medieval women and mysticism*, ed. Elizabeth Alvilda Petroff (Oxford, 1994), 161–81.

66. Anna Clark, "The Sexual Crisis and Popular Religion in London, 1770–1820," *International Labor and Working-Class History* 34 (1998), 56–69.

67. Mariateresa Fumagalli Beonio-Broccheri, "The Feminine Mind in Medieval Mysticism," in *Creative women in medieval and early modern Italy: A religious and artistic renaissance*, ed. E. Ann Matter and John Coakley (Philadelphia, 1994); Cheryl Riggs, "Julian of Norwich and the Ecstatic Experience," in *Tradition and ecstasy: The agony of the fourteenth century* (Ottawa, 1997). 109–22.

68. Mary R. Lefkowitz, "The Motivations for St. Perpetua's Martyrdom," *Journal of the American Academy of Religion* 44 (1976), 417–21.

69. Margaret Y. MacDonald, *Early Christian women and pagan opinion: The power of the hysterical woman* (Cambridge, 1996).

70. Christina Mazzaroni, *Saint hysteria: Neurosis, mysticism and gender in European culture* (Ithaca, NY, 1996).

71. Aarni Voipio, *Sleeping preachers: A study in ecstatic religiosity.* Suomalaisen Tiedeakatemian Toimituksia Annales Academiae Scientiarum Fennicae, vol. 75 (Helsinki, 1951).

72. G. R. Quaife, *Godly zeal and furious rage: The witch in early modern Europe* (London, 1987).

73. *Witchcraft and hysteria in Elizabethan London: Edward Jorden and the Mary Glover case*, edited and with an introduction by Michael MacDonald (London, 1991).

74. Jan Goldstein, "The Hysteria Diagnosis and the Politics of Anti-Clericalism in Late Nineteenth-Century France," *Journal of Modern History* 54 (1982), 209–39.

75. Pauline Kolenda, "Pox and the Terror of Childlessness: Images and Ideas of the Smallpox Goddess in a North Indian Village," in *Mother worship: Themes and variations*, ed. James J. Preston (Chapel Hill, NC, 1982), 225–50; A. J. Weeramunda, "The Milk Overflowing Ceremony in Sri Lanka," in *Mother worship: Themes and variations*, ed. James J. Preston (Chapel Hill, NC, 1982), 251–62.

76. Daniel R. Lesnick, *Preaching in medieval Florence: The social world of Franciscan and Dominican spirituality* (Athens, GA and London, 1989).

77. Mary O'Neil, "Magical Healing, Love Magic and the Inquisition in Late Sixteenth-Century Modena," *in Inquisition and society in early modern Europe*, ed. Stephen Haliczer (Sydney, 1987).

78. Rebecca Ann Hinton, "The Humanization of Mary in the English Religious Lyrics of the Thirteenth, Fourteenth, and Fifteenth centuries." Ph.D. diss., Miami University, 1990.

79. Carol Marie Englehardt, "Victorians and the Virgin Mary: Religion, National Identity, and the Woman Question in England, 1830–1880." Ph.D. diss., Indiana University, 1997.

80. Michael Heydt, "Robert Burton's Sources on Enthusiasm and Melancholy: From Medical Tradition to Religious Controversy," *History of European Ideas* 1 (1984), 17–44; Peter Iver Kaufman, *Prayer, despair, drama: Elizabethan introspection* (Urbana and Chicago, 1996); Michael Heyd, "Richard Burton's Sources on Enthusiasm and Melancholy: From a Medical Tradition to Religious Controversy," *History of European Ideas* 5 (1984), 17–44; Rivka Schatz Uffenheimer, *Hasidism as mysticism: Quietistic elements in eighteenth-century Hasidic thought*, trans. Jonathan Chipman (Princeton, 1993).

81. M. Conrad Hyers, *Zen and the comic spirit* (London, 1974); Athalya Brenner, *On feminism, anger, and humour in biblical studies* (Nijmegen, 1994); and Brenner, "On the Semantic Field of Humour, Laughter and Comic in the Old Testament," in *On humour and the comic in the Hebrew Bible*, ed. Yehuda T. Radday and Athalya Brenner. Bible and Literature series, no. 23 (Sheffield, 1990), 39–58; Flemming Friis Huidberg, *Weeping and laughter in the Old Testament: A study of Canaanite-Israelite religion* (Leiden, 1962); Yehuda T. Radday and Athalya Brenner, eds., *On humour and the comic in the Hebrew bible*. Bible and Literature series, no. 23 (Sheffield, 1990); Gábor Klaniczay, *The uses of supernatural power: The transformation of popular religion in medieval and early-modern Europe* (Cambridge, UK, 1990); Robert M. Polhemus, *Comic faith: The great tradition from Austen to Joyce* (Chicago, 1980).

82. B. E. Baloian, *Anger in the Old Testament.* American University Studies, Theology and Religion, no. 99 (New York, 1992).

83. Kari Latvus, *God, anger, and ideology: The anger of God in Joshua and Judges in relation to Deuteronomy and the priestly writings.* Journal for the Study of the Old Testament Supplement Series, no. 279 (Sheffield, 1998).

84. Eugene W. Brice, "A Study of Hatred and Anger in Old Testament Man." Ph.D. diss., Yale University, 1997.

85. Nili S. Fox, "Clapping Hands as a Gesture of Anguish and Anger in Mesopotamia and Israel," *Journal of the Ancient Near Eastern Society* 23 (1995), 49–60.

86. Hyam Maccoby, *The sacred executioner: Human sacrifice and the legacy of guilt* (Bath, 1982).

87. Kolenda, "Pox and the Terror of Childlessness," 225–50; Weeramunda, "The Milk Overflowing Ceremony in Sri Lanka," 251–62.

88. Leonard Muellner, *The anger of Achilles* (Ithaca, NY, 1996).

89. Catherine Peyroux, "Gertrude's Furor: Reading Anger in an Early Medieval Saint's Life, in *Anger's past: The social uses of an emotion in the Middle Ages,* ed. Barbara H. Rosenwein (Ithaca, NY, 1998), 36–55.

90. Wendy Davies, "Anger and Celtic Saints," in *Anger's past: The social uses of an emotion in the middle ages,* ed. Barbara H. Rosenwein (Ithaca, NY, 1998), 191–202.

91. Lester K. Little, "Anger in Monastic Curses," in *Anger's past: The social uses of an emotion in the Middle Ages,* ed. Barbara H. Rosenwein (Ithaca, NY, 1998).

92. Maureen Flynn, "Blasphemy and the Play of Anger in Sixteenth-Century Spain," *Past and Present* 149 (1995), 29–56.

93. Zouhair Ghazzal, "From Anger on Behalf of God to 'Forbearance' in Islamic Medieval Literature," in *Anger's past: The social uses of an emotion in the Middle Ages,* ed. Barbara H. Rosenwein (Ithaca, NY, 1998), 203–30.

94. Oscar Pfister, *Christianity and fear: A study in history and in the psychology and hygiene of religion* (London, 1949); Aloysius Roche, *Fear and religion* (London, 1938); Edwin W. Smith, *The religion of the lower races. As illustrated by the African Bantu* (New York, 1923); Geoffrey H. Woolley, *Fear and religion* (London, 1930).

95. Jean Delumeau, *Sin and fear: The emergence of a Western guilt culture thirteenth–eighteenth centuries,* trans. Eric Nicholson (New York, 1990; originally published 1983).

96. Piero Camporesi, *The fear of hell: Images of damnation and salvation in early modern Europe,* trans. Lucina Byatt (Cambridge, UK, 1900; originally published 1987).

97. Judith Devlin, *The superstitious mind: French peasants and the supernatural in the nineteenth century* (New Haven, CT, 1987).

98. Cyril C. Okorocha, *The meaning of religious conversion in Africa: The case of the Igbo of Nigeria* (Aldershot and Sydney, 1987).

99. Michael E. Goddrich, *Violence and miracle in the fourteenth century: Private grief and public salvation* (Chicago, 1995).

100. Ulrich Simon, *Piety and terror: Christianity and tragedy* (London, Macmillan, 1989).

101. Edward J. Ingebretsen, *Maps of heaven, maps of hell: Religious terror as memory from the Puritans to Steven King* (London, 1996).

102. J. C. Steemers, "Cultural Embarrassment and Religious Fear," *Religion in a pluralistic society,* ed. J. S. Pobee (Leiden, 1976), 97–109.

103. Wyatt McGaffey, *Modern Kongo prophets: Religion in a plural society* (Bloomington, IN, 1983).

104. William A.Christian Jr., *Visionaries: The Spanish Republic and the reign of Christ* (Berkeley, CA, 1994).

105. G. Gispert-Sauch, *Bliss in the Upanishads: An analytical study of the origin and growth of the Vedic concept of Ananda* (New Delhi, 1977).

106. Gary A. Anderson, *A time to mourn, a time to dance: The expression of grief and joy in Israelite religion* (University Park, PA, 1991); Yochanan Muffs, *Love and joy: Law, language and religion in ancient Israel* (New York and Jerusalem, 1992).

107. J. Moussaieff Masson, *The oceanic feeling: The origins of religious sentiment in ancient India* (Dordrecht and Boston, 1980); Howard M. Wach, "A 'Still, Small Voice' from the Pulpit: Religion and the Creation of Social Morality in Manchester, 1820–1850," *Journal of Modern History* 59 (1991), 317–30.

108. Thomas Connolly, *Mourning into joy: Music, Raphael and Saint Cecilia* (New Haven, CT, 1994).

109. Bimanbehari Majumdar, "Religion of Love: The Early Medieval Phase (c. AD 700–1486)," in *Mediveal Bhakti movements in India: Sri Caitanya quincentenary commemoration volume,* ed. N. N. Bhattacharyya (New Delhi, 1989), 1–16.

110. W. L. Moran, "The Ancient Near Eastern Background of the Love of God in Deuteronomy," *Catholic Biblical Quarterly* 25 (1963), 77–87; Margaret Trawick, "The Ideology of Love in a Tamil Family," in *Divine passions: The social construction of emotion in India,* ed. Owen M. Lynch (Berkeley, CA, 1990), 37–63.

111. Anthony Mockler, *Francis of Assisi: The wandering years* (Oxford and New York, 1976); Elizabeth Alvilda Petroff, "Gender, Knowledge, and Power in Hadewich's *Strophische Gedichten,*" in *Body and soul: Essays on medieval women and mysticism,* ed. Elizabeth Alvilda Petroff (Oxford, 1994), 182–203.

112. Sir Maurice Bowra, *Medieval love-song.* The John Coffin Memorial Lecture (London, 1961).

113. Irving Singer, *The nature of love. Volume I: Plato to Luther,* 2d ed. (Chicago, 1984) and *The nature of love. Volume II: Courtly and romantic* (Chicago, 1984).

114. Martha G. Newman, *The boundaries of charity: Cistercian culture and ecclesiastical reform, 1098–1180* (Stanford, CA, 1996).

115. Garrity, "Bernard of Clairvaux."

116. Jean LeClerc, *Monks and love in twelfth-century France: Psycho-historical essay* (Oxford, 1979).

117. Jacob Milgrom, *Cult and conscience: The Asham and the priestly doctrine of repentance* (Leiden, 1976); Maccoby, *The sacred executioner.*

118. Christina Landman, *The piety of Afrikaans women: Diaries of guilt* (Praetoria, South Africa, 1994).

119. Philip F. Esler, "Family Imagery and Christian Identity in Gal 5:13 to 6:10," in *Constructing early Christian families: Family as social reality and metaphor,* ed. Halvor Moxmes (London, 1997).

120. Devlin, *The superstitious mind.*

121. Mockler, *Francis of Assisi.*

122. Leonard J. Moore, *Citizen klansmen: The Ku Klux Klan in Indiana, 1921–1928* (Chapel Hill, NC, 1991).

123. Adriana Destro, *The law of jealousy: Anthropology of Sotah.* Brown Judaic Studies, no. 181 (Atlanta, 1989).

124. Charles Lindholm, *Generosity and jealousy: The Swat Pukhtun of Northern Pakistan* (New York, 1982).

125. Sandra McIntire, "The Doctrine of Compunction from Bede to Margery Kempe," in *The medieval mystical tradition in England,* ed. Marion Glasscoe (Cambridge, UK, 1987), 77–90.

126. Goddrich, *Violence and miracle in the fourteenth century.*

127. William A. Christian, "Provoked Religious Weeping in Early Modern Spain," 97–114.

128. Wolfson, "Weeping, Death, and Spiritual Ascent in Sixteenth-Century Jewish Mysticism," 209–47.

APPENDIX 2. EMOTION AS HEART, BLOOD, AND BODY

1. J. F. Laterrade, "An Attempt to Prove the Existence of the Unicorn," trans. Jacob Potter, *American Journal of the Sciences* 21 (October 1831). Copy in the AAS.

2. John Augustine Smith, "An Oration delivered before the Western Medical Society: On the philosophy of the human mind and the agency of the human mind on the organized body," delivered 1814 (Washington, PA, 1815), 3, 4, 15.

3. Fenwick, *An essay on volition and pleasure,* 41.

4. Thomas Middleton Stuart, *An inaugural essay on genius and its diseases* (New York, 1819), 11.

5. James Pendleton, *Materials for an alphabet to the science of medicine embracing an inquiry into the nature of the mind and passions* (Philadelphia, 1805), 32; Rose, *An inaugural dissertation of the effects of the passions upon the body;* 9; Tracy Patch Cheever, Diary, March 28, 1854; Orville Dewey to Chareles Dewey, January 1, 1850, Orville Dewey correspondence, MHS; Benjamin Rush and Benjamin Waterhouse were among the most influential writ-

ers who argued for the connections between body and mind. See Philip Cash, "The Well-Placed and Misplaced Philosophes, Benjamin Rush of Philadelphia and Benjamin Rush of Boston," *Transactions and studies of the College of Physicians of Philadelphia,* 5th series, vol. 9, no. 1 (Philadelphia, 1988), 24–44.

6. Rush, *Medical inquiries and observations,* 40; George Brewer, *The juvenile Lavater* (New York, 1815), 1–43 and passim; Robert Hale, Commonplace book, Harvard University Archives; *The Art of kissing, anatomically and physiologically explained,* by "an amateur" (New York, 1841); Charles Dewey to his mother, June 28, 1846, in Orville Dewey Correspondence, AAS.

7. *Massachusetts Ploughman* 9 (February 1850) and 10 (October 1850); *Massachusetts Teacher* 6 (December 1853), 371 and 9 (April 1856), 152. See also "On the Government of the Passions," *Boston Weekly Magazine* 32 (October 20, 1804), 203; Rose, *An inaugural dissertation,* 10.

8. Theodoric Romeyn Beck, *An inaugural dissertation on insanity* (New York, 1811), 22–23; George Scandlin, Diary, January 2, 1852; Joanne Harvey, Diary, March 2, 1857, in Charles Henry Harvey Papers, 345, LC; *Monthly Anthology and Boston Review* 4 (February 1807), 82; *The Liberator* 25 (March 1855), 44; *New Englander* 11 (November 1853), 527; George S. Hilliard, *The dangers and duties of the mercantile profession* (Boston, 1850), 32; *The altar at home,* 215–17; *Massachusetts Teacher* 8 (November 1855).

9. *The book of health: A compendium of domestic medicine* (Boston, 1830), 59; see especially Cutbush, *An inaugural dissertation on insanity,* 23; Stuart, *An inaugural essay on genius and its diseases,* 32–42; Log book, October 22, 1864–December 12, 1889, West Virginia Hospital for the Insane, Weston, WV.

10. *Gleason's Pictorial Drawing Room Companion* 1 (November 15, 1851), 452; *Massachusetts Teacher* 8 (November 1855), 345 and 7 (December 1854), 383 and see also 2 (August 1849), 282; "Premature Education," *Trumpet and Universalist* 23 (September 1850), 60; James Johnson, M.D., *The economy of health; or the stream of human life, from the cradle to the grave* (New York, 1837), 27, 58–59; *Christian Observer* 30 (September 1851), 256; "Premature Education," *Ballou's Pictorial* 15 (December 11, 1858), 379; *Massachusetts Teacher* 11 (September 1858), 354; *Youth's Companion* 32 (October 1858), 162.

11. Townsend, *A dissertation on the influence of the passions,* 12, 22, 28; Cooke, *A commentary of medical and moral life,* 135. On ambition see for example Johnson, *The economy of health,* 108 and George Scandlin, Diary, November 14, 1856; Alfred North Whitehead, *Process and reality: An essay in cosmology* (New York, 1929), 338 (II. I.3); Charles Fourier, *The social destiny of man . . . with a treatise on the function of the human passions . . . by Albert Brisbane,* vol. 1, trans. Henry Clapp Jr. (New York, 1840), 15 (AAS copy).

12. *The passions: A poem pronounced at the Odeon, December 28, 1835* (Boston, 1836), 14, 17; Rush, *Sixteen introductory lectures* 38, 41. Buchan, 69; John Stearns, "On the Functions and Diseases of the Liver," *Transactions of the medical society of the state of New York* (Albany, 1821), 27–28; Brewer, *The juvenile Lavater,* 95; Buchan, *Domestic medicine,* 69.

13. Rose, *An inaugural dissertation,* 11; Benjamin Rush, *Three lectures upon animal life* (Philadelphia, 1799), 4, 5, 6, 21–22.

14. Anderson, *An inaugural dissertation,* 18–20; Joseph Parrish, *An inaugural dissertation on the influence of the passions on the body* (Philadelphia, 1805), 9–28; Cutbush, *An inaugural dissertation on insanity;* Buchan, *Domestic medicine,* 66; Rush, *Three lectures upon animal life,* 41; Pendleton, *Materials for an alphabet,* 8.

15. Rush, *Three lectures upon animal life,* 81–82; *Youth's Companion* 29 (October 11, 1855), 100; *Boston Evening Transcript* (June 11, 1858); *American Baptist Magazine* 12 (18[??]), 7.

16. *Ballou's Pictorial* 13 (December 1857), 398–99. See also *Child's Friend and Youth's Magazine* 22 (Boston, 1854), 86 and 25 (1855), 63; Samuel Ireneus Prine, "Thoughts upon Thought," *Christian Parlor Magazine* (1845), 29. As some New Englanders on the Oregon trail and other places in the West discovered, when one "lost one's mind," it was now possible to employ a shaman to enter the invisible world and bring it back. Doctors nevertheless sought to explain Indians' success in terms of standard Euro-American medical theory. Doctor William Cooke wrote that "it will not be questioned that the Native doctor among the North American Indians, in his frightful costume, and by his performance of most ridiculous ceremonies, do sometimes remove disease by the excitement of the mind and of some of the moral feelings, acting upon the nervous system," by a power akin to "animal magnetism" (*A commentary of medical and moral life,* 302).

17. Dr. John D. Goodman, *Contributions to physiology and pathologic anatomy* (Philadelphia, 1825), 10; *Monthly Anthology and Boston Review* 4 (April 1807), 180; Israel Lombard, Diary, August 5, 1848, AAS; Susan Heath, Diary, June 5, 1858, MIIS; "Domestic Correspondence," *Independent* 3 (February 20, 1851); *Medical Communications* 9 (1860), 298; *The Liberator* 23 (September 9, 1853), 144; Mary Mudge, Diary, December 13, 1854, SL.

18. Vaughan, *Observations on animal electricity,* 22.

19. John Bell, *Animal electricity and magnetism* (Lancaster, 1792), 36, 41, 29; John Parker Gough, *An essay on cantharides* (Philadelphia, 1800), 26, 24; 44–45; Charlotte F. Foster, Diary March 1, 1858, MHS; Buchan, *Domestic medicine,* 306–7.

20. Rush outlines his theory of excitement in *Three lectures upon animal life;* Jacob Porter, Medical journal, January 10, 1810, AAS. See also Richard Harrison Shryock, *Medicine and society in America, 1660–1860* (New York, 1960), 111.

21. On cures for illnesses see the Samuel Stearns Papers, and especially Folder 2, "The North Americans Dispensatory," AAS; Cutbush, *An inaugural dissertation on insanity,* 44–45; Anderson, *An inaugural dissertation,* 26; *Ballou's Pictorial* 11 (September 6, 1856), 173.

22. Pendleton, *Materials for an alphabet,* 31–32; Rush, *Three lectures upon animal life,* 20.

23. *Monthly Anthology and Boston Review* 4 (February 1807), 81; *Boston Evening Transcript* (May 5, 1859).

24. *Boston Medical Intelligencer* 1 (1823), 15; *Parlor Magazine* 3 (August 1846), 20; *Massachusetts Teacher* 1 (October 1848), 303 and 9 (May 1856), 248; *Christian Observatory* 2 (September 1848), 396; *Ballou's Pictorial* 11 (August 2, 1856), 68; *New Englander* 11 (November 1853), 520.

25. Norman Pettit, *The heart prepared: Grace and conversion in Puritan spiritual life* (New Haven, CT, 1966); Virginia Brereton, *From sin to salvation: Stories of women's conversions, 1800 to the present* (Bloomington, IN, 1991), 24–25.

26. *New Englander* 11 (November 1853), 525 and 17 (November 1859), 10; J. Worth Estes, "Therapeutic Practice in Colonial New England," in *Medicine in colonial Massachusetts, 1620–1820* (Boston, 1980), 346. One wonders what New England dissectionists thought about a holding a human heart in their hands.

APPENDIX 3. EMOTION AND
THE COMMON SENSE PHILOSOPHY

1. H. M. Gardiner, Ruth Clark Metcalf, and John G. Beebe-Center, *Feeling and emotion: A history of theories* (Westport, CT, 1970), 276; David Hartley, *Observations on man, his frame, his duties, and his expectations* (London, 1749), part 1, chap. 1, sec. 2, proposition 9.

2. Thomas Brown, *Lectures on the philosophy of the human mind*, vol. 2 (Philadelphia, 1824), 253.

3. For recent emphases on the role of Common Sense philosophy in America, see Howe, *Making the American self* and Joseph Alcana, *The social self: Hawthorne, Howells, William James, and nineteenth-century psychology* (Lexington, KY, 1997). Herbert Schneider wrote that "the Scottish Enlightenment was probably the most potent single tradition in the American Enlightenment" (*A history of American philosophy* [New York, 1946], 246); Mark A. Noll referred to the "triumph of Common Sense in American intellectual life" ("Common Sense Traditions and American Evangelical Thought," *American Quarterly* 37 [1985], 218); George M. Marsden wrote of its domination in mid-nineteenth-century America *(Fundamentalism and American culture* [New York, 1980], 7). American Protestants already were immersed in debates about the will, and to some extent as well the affections, in the decades following Jonathan Edwards's groundbreaking treatises on those subjects (e.g., *Distinguishing marks* [1741], *Treatise on religious affections* [1746], *Freedom of the will* [1754]). The Scottish emphasis on emotion and experience also dovetailed with the conversionist religion that traditionally had occupied a prominent place in American Protestantism.

4. Cutbush, *An inaugural dissertation on insanity*, 22. The transmission of Scottish philosophy to America was not systematic or even, however. The *Boston Journal of Philosophy and the Arts* rightly complained that "the scientific

labours of European philosophers are made known to the world from so many different quarters, their productions are spread over so wide a surface, are scattered amongst so great a number of journals and volumes, and the valuable are so connected and mingled with the worthless, that it is very difficult for the individuals in America . . . to get a complete view of the progress of Science and the Arts" ([May, 1823], preface).

5. Review of "An address delivered in the chapel of Dartmouth College, May 19, 1825 by Daniel D. Oliver, M.D.," *Boston Monthly Magazine* 4 (1825), 191–92.

6. Dr. John Perkins papers, AAS.

7. E.g., Fenwick, *An essay on volition and pleasure,* 11, 69; Smith, *Revivalism and social reform,* 5; Stuart, *An inaugural essay on genius and its diseases,* 9–13; Townsend, *A dissertation on the influence of the passions,* 16, 31; Beck, *An inaugural dissertation on insanity,* 10–11; George Hayward, *Some observations on Dr. Rush's work* (Boston, 1818), 2; Rush, *Sixteen introductory lectures.* On Jefferson see the excellent dialogue between head and heart that he wrote when he was in turmoil over his relationship with Maria Cosway in *The writings of Thomas Jefferson,* vol. 4, ed. Paul L. Ford (New York, 1894), 318–20. For an example of the manner in which Scottish thought was popularized in America see the American publication of the Englishman T. Cogan's *A philosophical treatise on the passions,* especially 234–40.

8. Parker, *A sermon on false and true theology,* 3.

9. James Freeman Clarke, *The Christian doctrine of prayer* (Boston, 1856), 16; Catalogue of the library of the Young Men's Christian Union (Boston, 1855); *Massachusetts Teacher* 9 (August 1856), 405 and (April 1856), 154 and (October 1856), 466 and 1 (October 1848), 320 and 6 (September 1853), 261.

10. *New Englander* 17 (August 1859), 641; see also (August 1854), 348–50.

11. Benjamin Waterhouse, *A synopsis of a course of lectures* (Boston, 1786), 1;

Massachusetts Teacher 1 (November 1848), 331 and 8 (July 1855), 206.

12. William George Scandlin, Diary, November 14, 1856, AAS; Tracy Patch Cheever, Diary, MHS, January 9, 1851.

13. *Ballou's Pictorial* 3 (October 1857), 287; *Massachusetts Teacher* 3 (March 1857), 97; *New Englander* 14 (May 1856), 246, 244–50.

Selected Manuscript Diaries, Journals, Correspondences, and Papers

For abbreviations used below, see first page of notes (p. 299).

Abbot, Henry Larcom. Diary, 1855(?)–1858 (HL).
Andrew, John A. Letters, 1853–1867 (AAS).
Arnold, Eliphay, Jr. Diary, 1850–1851 (MHS).
Babcock, James F. Papers, 1857–1895 (AAS).
Badger, Alfred Mason. Alfred Mason Badger Papers, 1835–1868 (LC).
Banks, Nathan P. Correspondence, c.1852–1885 (AAS).
Barker, Eben. Diary, 1852–1853 (MHS).
Bartlett, Enoch. Papers, 1809–1862 (AAS).
Bascom, Ruth Henshaw. Diary, 1845–1846 (AAS).
Bennett, Francis, Jr. Diary, 1852–1857 (AAS).
Bigelow, Andrew. Papers, 1806–1889 (AAS).
Blake, James Barnard. Diary, 1851 (AAS).
Bradford, Gamaliel. Diary, 1854–1856 (HL).
Brooks, William Gray. Diary, 1857–1858 (MHS).
Brown, Susan E. P. *See* Forbes, Susan E. Parsons Brown.
Chase, Charles Augustus. Diary, 1854, Chase Family Papers (AAS).
Chauncy Hall School. Papers, 1842–1852 (AAS).
Cheever, Tracy Patch. Diary, 1851–1855 (MHS).
Chickering Club. Records, 1865–1876 (AAS).
Child, Lydia Maria. Letters, 1845–1880 (AAS).
Cobb, Eunice Hale. Journal, 1863 (BPL).
Cole, Elijah Lyman. Notebooks, 1842–1862 (AAS).
Cullis, Charles. Papers and Correspondence, 1853–1890 (AAS).
Cunningham, Frederic. Diary, 1858 (MHS).
Cunningham, James Henry. Journal, 1849 (AAS).
Curson, Mary Russell. Diary, 1850–1852 (HL).
Davis, Mary Gardiner. Notebook, 1850–1856 (SL).
———. Commonplace Book, 1854–1858 (SL).

Dewey, Orville. Orville Dewey Correspondence, 1837–1885 (AAS).

Drake, Sam G. Historical Notes, in Boston, Massachusetts, Papers, folder 5 (AAS).

Drake, Samuel Gardner. Papers (AAS).

Edes, Sarah Louise Lincoln. Diaries, 1852–1853 (AAS).

Fiske, James Ferdinand. Diaries, 1857–1860 (AAS).

Flint, Catherine Dean. Diary, 1858–1859 (AAS).

———. Cookbook, Cookbooks Collection (AAS).

Flint, Waldo. Letter, 1856 (AAS).

———. Diaries, 1872–1878 (AAS).

Flint Family Papers, 1818–1879 (AAS).

Forbes, Susan E. Parsons Brown. Diaries, 1841–1908 (AAS).

Forbes Papers, 1857–1858 (AAS).

Forbush, Edward. Diary, 1856 (Boston Athenaeum).

Forbush, Mary Josephine Faxon. Diary, 1854–1869 (BA).

Foster, Abigail Kelley. Papers, 1837–1893 (AAS).

Foster, Charlotte F. Composition Book, 1851–1852 (MHS).

———. Diary, 1858 (MHS).

Franklin Scientific Association. Manuscripts (BPL).

Franklin Scientific Association Papers (BPL).

Franklin Scientific Institute Papers, 1857 (BPL).

French, Charles E. Diary, 1855–1858 (MHS).

Gannett, Ezra Stiles. Diary, 1857–1858 (MHS).

Gardiner Family Papers (SL).

Greenough, William W. William Greenough Papers, 1849 (LC).

Hale, Edward Everett. Papers, 1855–1906 (AAS).

Hale, Robert. Commonplace Book (Harvard University Archives).

———. Papers (AAS).

Harding, Charles E. "Autobiography," 1807–1869 (AAS).

Harrington, Henry Francis. Papers, 1836–1887 (AAS).

Harvey, Charles Henry. Charles Henry Harvey Papers, 1853–1858 (LC).

Haynes, Henry W. Diaries, 1851–1858 (MHS).

Heath, Susan. Diary, 1858 (MHS).

Hoyt, William Henry. Journal, 1851 (BPL).

Johnston, David Claypoole. Family Papers, 1824–1940 (AAS).

Kellogg, Ralph. Account Books, 1840–1850 (AAS).

Kenneally, John Henry. Diary, 1857–1858 (BPL).

Kilburn, Samuel Smith. Sketchbooks, 1855–1860 (AAS).

Larcom, Lucy. Letters, 1857–1859 (MHS).

Lee, Sarah. Diaries, 1834–1848 (AAS).

Lombard, Israel. Diaries, 1848–1862 (AAS).

———. Memoranda, 1857–1859 (AAS).

Low, Charles F. Diary, 1857–1860 (BPL).

Manning, Jacob Merrill. Diary, 1857–1858 (MHS).

May, Samuel. Letter, 1857 (BPL).

Merritt, Frances. Journal, 1856–1858 (SL).

Mifflin, Mary. Journal, 1857 (BPL).

Mudge, Mary. Diary, 1854 (SL).

Newton Family Papers (AAS).

Nichols, Arthur Howard. Diary, 1852–1858 (MHS).

Norcross, Grenville Howland, Diaries (AAS).

Osgood Family Correspondence, 1842–1861 (AAS).

Park Family Papers, 1800–1890 (AAS).

Parker, Theodore. Papers, 1832–1904 (AAS).

———. Scrapbook, 1856 (BPL).

———. Correspondence, 1858 (MHS).

Perkins, John. Papers, 1750–1780 (AAS).

Peabody, Elizabeth Palmer. Papers, 1843–c.1867 (AAS).

Peabody Family Papers (MHS).

Plummer, Farnham. Papers 1776–1879 (AAS).

Porter, Jacob. Diary, 1802–1839 (AAS).

———. Medical Journal, 1810 (AAS).

Pratt, J. D. Correspondence, 1849 (MHS).

Prescott, George W. Notebook, 1860 (AAS).

"Promiscuous Leaves from my diary. by a convict…" 1864 (AAS).

Ripley, Sally. Journal, 1799–1807 (AAS).

Salisbury, Stephen, Jr. Letters and Diary, Salisbury Family Papers (AAS).

Sanborn, Franklin Benjamin. Papers, 1847–1915 (AAS).

Scandlin, William George. Diaries, 1849–1864 (AAS).

Sears, Miriam, Letters, 1859–1860 (MHS).

Smith, William Henry. Diary, 1852–1853 (BPL).

Stearns, Samuel. Samuel Stearns Papers (AAS).

Teulon, Edward A. Diary Extracts, 1846–1861 (AAS).

Tisdale, Henry William. Diary, 1863 (BPL).

Troup, George H. Diary, 1855–1862 (MHS).

Trowbridge, John Townsend. Diary, 1853–1854 (BPL).

Walker, Mary J. Diary, 1848 (SL).

White, Caroline Barrett. Papers, 1844–1915 (AAS).

Williams, John. John Williams Papers, 1836 (LC).

Winchester Family Papers, 1800–1872 (AAS).

Wright, Elizur. Elizur Wright Papers 1817–1910 (LC).

Wright, Henry Clark. Journal, 1853 (BPL).

Index

Compositor: G&S Typesetters, Inc.
Text: 10/13 Aldus
Display: Aldus
Printer and Binder: Haddon Craftsmen